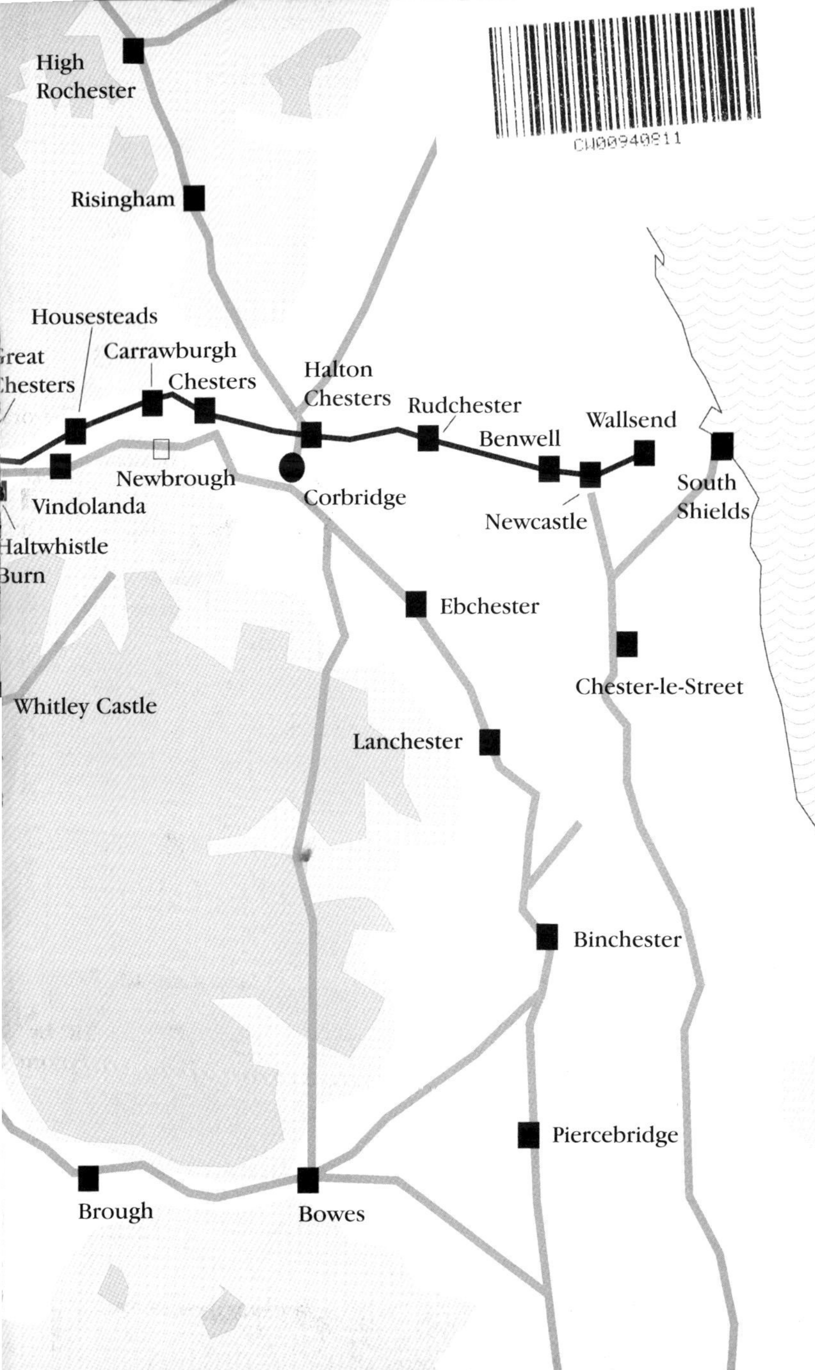
High Rochester
Risingham
Housesteads
Carrawburgh
Chesters
Halton Chesters
Rudchester
Benwell
Wallsend
South Shields
Newbrough
Vindolanda
Corbridge
Newcastle
Ebchester
Chester-le-Street
Whitley Castle
Lanchester
Binchester
Piercebridge
Brough
Bowes

HANDBOOK TO

THE ROMAN WALL

John Collingwood Bruce

HANDBOOK TO
THE ROMAN WALL

J. Collingwood Bruce
LLD, DCL, FSA

Fourteenth Edition
by

David. J. Breeze
BA, PhD, FSA, Hon FSA Scot, FRSE

Maps and plans by
Sandra Rowntree

Book design and layout by
Linda Kay

Published by the Society of Antiquaries
of Newcastle upon Tyne

2006

First Published 1863 (J. Collingwood Bruce)
Second Edition 1884 (J. Collingwood Bruce)
Third Edition 1885 (J. Collingwood Bruce)
Fourth Edition 1895 (R. Blair)
Fifth Edition1907 (R. Blair)
Sixth Edition 1909 (R. Blair)
Seventh Edition 1914 (R. Blair)
Eighth Edition 1921; Reprinted 1925 and 1927 (R. Blair)
Ninth Edition 1933: Reprinted 1937 (R. G. Collingwood)
Tenth Edition 1947: Reprinted 1951 (I. A. Richmond)
Eleventh Edition1957 (I. A. Richmond)
Twelfth Edition 1966 (I. A. Richmond)
Thirteenth Edition 1978 (C. M. Daniels)
Fourteenth Edition 2006 (D. J. Breeze)

The suggested bibliographical reference for this book is:
David J. Breeze, *J. Collingwood Bruce's Handbook to the Roman Wall*
14th edition (Newcastle upon Tyne 2006)

Society of Antiquaries of Newcastle upon Tyne
The Black Gate
Castle Garth
Newcastle upon Tyne
NE1 1RQ
admin@newcastle-antiquaries.org.uk
www.newcastle-antiquaries.org.uk

ISBN 0 901082 65 1

Design and layout by Linda K. Graphic Design Studio

Printed by Bath Press Limited

Front cover: Hadrian's Wall looking east towards Housesteads
Back cover: The Ilam Pan

CONTENTS

CHAPTER 3

CHAPTER 4

CHAPTER 5

PREFACE
TO THE FOURTEENTH EDITION

Hadrian's Wall is, with Stonehenge, the most famous monument in Britain to have come down to us from antiquity. It is the best preserved frontier of the Roman empire, one of the greatest empires which the world has known. The main purpose of this *Handbook* is to provide an account of both the visible and invisible remains of this great frontier complex. The first edition of the *Handbook* was written by John Collingwood Bruce and published in 1863. Bruce was the great interpreter of Hadrian's Wall in the second half of the nineteenth century. He was born in 1805 and, after graduating from Glasgow University, became a schoolmaster and Presbyterian Minister in Newcastle upon Tyne. In 1848 he began his study of Hadrian's Wall, the following year leading the first Pilgrimage along it and two years later publishing *The Roman Wall*. Two editions followed, and in 1863 he produced the *Wallet-book of the Roman Wall, a guide to pilgrims journeying along the barrier of the lower isthmus*. He changed its name to the *Handbook* at the time of the second edition. For 40 years Bruce was the foremost authority on Hadrian's Wall. Since his death in 1892 four editors have kept the *Handbook* up-to-date, Robert Blair, R. G. Collingwood, Sir Ian Richmond and Charles Daniels; this is the fourteenth edition.

The *Handbook* is an unusual publication, not merely in its antiquity, but also in its intent. It is not strictly a guide-book, but a guide to the surviving remains as well as an academic study providing information on the invisible features, bringing to a wider audience the fruits of excavation and research on Hadrian's Wall. It is in connection with the latter purpose that a detailed bibliography of the Wall and its works is included. The *Handbook* concentrates on the military (and associated civilian) remains and does not attempt to provide a rounded view of life on the northern frontier nor of the post-Roman history of Hadrian's Wall: such descriptions may be found elsewhere and are referred to in the bibliography. In short, the *Handbook* is essentially an attempt to understand and interpret a monument. As such, this is a book to be taken into the field, to become, as R. G. Collingwood remarked, honourably scarred and stained in the service of pilgrims to the Wall.

Since 1863 the number of guide-books to the Wall and the area has multiplied. Accordingly, there has been no attempt to move from the traditional formula of the *Handbook* and provide information which is easily available elsewhere. So far as is possible, the style of the earlier editions has been retained though pruned of extraneous material. Yet, while the style has been maintained, together with the idiosyncratic arrangement of the contents and many of the woodcuts, the text has been completely re-written, with all statements checked both against excavation reports and descriptions and observation in the field. The opportunity has been taken to extend Chapter II, in which the archaeological evidence is presented and analysed; attention is also drawn to contradictions in that evidence.

I was invited to edit the *Handbook* by the Society of Antiquaries of Newcastle upon Tyne. In my task I have been ably supported by an editorial committee consisting of Miss Barbara Harbottle, President of the Society, succeeded by Mrs Beryl Charlton, and then Mrs Grace McCombie, Dr Brian Dobson (Chairman), Dr Nick Hodgson and Miss Lindsay Allason-Jones. I am also grateful to a wide range of friends and colleagues for their help and advice and for commenting on the text: Mr Paul Austen, Mr Richard Bellhouse, Mr Paul Bidwell, Mr Alan Biggins, Professor A. R. Birley, Dr R. E. Birley, the late Mr John Charlton, Dr Walter Cockle, Mr Roger Fern, Dr Brenda Heywood, Dr Peter Hill, Mr Nick Holmes, Dr Sonja Jilek, Ms Rebecca Jones, Miss Cherry Lavell, Professor Valerie Maxfield, Mr John Poulter, Mr David Sherlock, Mrs Margaret Snape, Dr Vivien Swan, Dr David Taylor, Mr Humphrey Welfare, Professor J. J. Wilkes, Mr Tony

Wilmott, Mrs Charmian Woodfield, Mr Paul Woodfield and Dr David Woolliscroft. The text has been copy edited by Ms Jackie Henrie, Dr Anna Ritchie and the late Dr J. N. G. Ritchie. The maps and plans have been prepared by Ms Sandra Rowntree and the book designed by Ms Linda M. Kay.

To quote John Collingwood Bruce: "with these acknowledgments which the author gratefully makes, he once more commits 'The Roman Wall' into the hands of the reader. Whatever defects may be found in his work he is conscious that he has done his best to make it as full and accurate as possible".

I am grateful to the following for kind permission to reproduce illustrations: the Administrators of the Haverfield Bequest for the drawings from the *Roman Inscriptions of Britain* volume 1; Stuart Laidlaw and the Portable Antiquities Scheme for the Ilam Pan; Dr Grace Simpson for the drawings by her father, F. Gerald Simpson; Timescape Surveys for the geophysical surveys; the Vindolanda Trust for the drawings of objects found at Vindolanda; and Dr D. J. Woolliscroft for the aerial photographs. The Society is grateful to the Roman Research Trust and the Marc Fitch Fund for grants towards the preparation of the *Handbook*.

In preparing this edition, I have walked the whole length of the Wall. I am grateful to my fellow walkers, my wife Pamela, and my brother-in-law and sister-in-law, Graham and Anne Silvester, for their companionship, support and discussion: this book is dedicated to them. We all hope that this *Handbook* will encourage others to take a similar pilgrimage along Hadrian's Wall, following in the steps of many eminent travellers including William Camden who, so carried away by what he saw over 400 years ago, wrote, "verily I have seene the tract of it over the high pitches and steep descents of hills, wonderfully rising and falling".

David J. Breeze

ACCESS

Although considerable portions of the Wall system are accessible to the general public, some of the sites described remain in private ownership and inaccessible. Inclusion below, therefore, is no indication of public right of way. However, the creation of the National Trail along Hadrian's Wall will aid walkers, though readers should be warned that this book is not a guide to the Trail which sometimes diverges from the Wall (for the Trail see: A. Burton, *Hadrian's Wall Path*, London 2003).

MEASUREMENTS, NUMBERS, CONVENTIONS AND TERMINOLOGY

Bold type has been used to denote individual sites – for example, forts and the buildings within them, milecastles and turrets – as well as visible structures. Where measurements are provided, for example for milecastles and forts, the north-south dimensions are always given first. Dimensions of forts are always over the ramparts. Every visible site is normally illustrated together with important other sites.

One Roman mile (*mille passuum*, that is a thousand paces, one pace being two steps totalling five Roman feet) = 1,618 yards = 1,479 m.

One Roman foot = 11.64 imperial inches = 296 mm

Roman dimensions are given where appropriate, but normally measurements are provided in metric, with imperial dimensions in brackets. A straight translation can sometimes be misleading as the original measurements were often not as precise as a detailed metric figure can imply. Some latitude has therefore been allowed, for example when 'yards' have been used to indicate an approximate distance. Metric measurements are given to the second decimal point, except where this detail has not been provided in the original excavation report.

A numbering system for the structures on the Wall was created in 1930, and for those on the Cumbrian Coast in 1961.

The milecastles (MC) are numbered 0-80 from Wallsend to Bowness with the two turrets (T) between each pair of milecastles designated a and b. The milefortlets (MF) and towers (T) on the Cumbrian Coast are numbered separately, starting at Bowness, and to avoid confusion could be rendered T 16a CC. Each has a name as well as a number, and both are normally cited, e.g. MC 37 (Housesteads) and T 48a (Willowford East). TW refers to the Turf Wall and SW the Stone Wall.

The majority of known Wall-miles, that is the distance between a pair of milecastles, are about 1479 m (1618 yards) long while the average space between each pair of turrets is 495 m (540 yards).

In this volume the plans have been reproduced at uniform scales, 1:400 for turrets, towers, milecastles, milefortlets and some other structures; 1:800 for small forts; 1:2500 for forts.

Generally, modern place names are used, rather than Roman names, though these are usually also given. The exception is Chesterholm, now generally known by its Roman name Vindolanda. The Romans called the Wall *vallum* on inscriptions and in the *Notitia Dignitatum*, and *murus* in literature. Bede, writing in the early eighth century, continued to refer to the Wall as a *murus*, but he considered that the earthwork behind the Wall was an early turf frontier and therefore called it a *vallum*, as we still do. The Roman road along the frontier is known as the Military Way, while the late-eighteenth-century road is called the Military Road (the modern B6318 still follows this road).

MUSEUMS

Finds from the Wall and the Cumbrian Coast are housed and displayed in the Museum of Antiquities in Newcastle and Tullie House Museum in Carlisle, and in the site museums at South Shields, Wallsend/Segedunum, Corbridge, Chesters, Housesteads, Vindolanda, the Roman Army Museum at Carvoran, Birdoswald and Maryport (the Senhouse Roman Museum). The Northumberland National Park visitor centre is at Once Brewed, 5 km (3 miles) west of Housesteads.

KEY TO MAPS

These symbols have been used on the maps of Hadrian's Wall and the Cumbrian Coast.

Wall visible	fort visible
Wall not visible	fort not visible
Wall inferred	milecastle/milefortlet/fortlet visible
Vallum visible	milecastle/milefortlet/fortlet not visible
Vallum not visible	turret/tower visible
ditch visible	turret/tower not visible
ditch not visible	camp
modern roads	

KEY TO PLANS

These symbols have been used on the plans of turrets, towers, milecastles, milefortlets and some other structures.

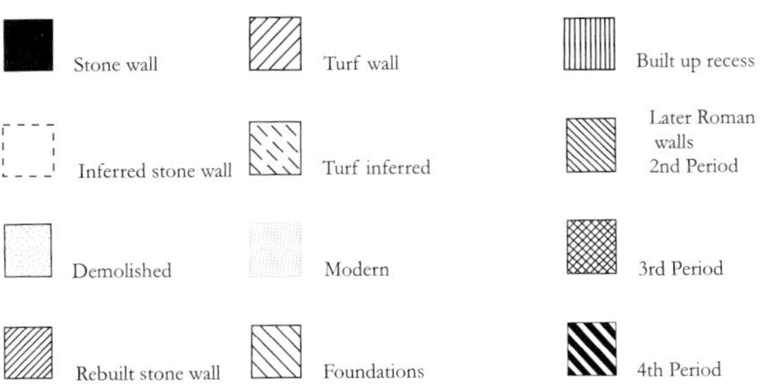

Housesteads from the air looking south. The full circuit of the defences is visible, including all four gates and some of the towers along the walls. Hadrian's Wall approaches the fort at the north-west corner, to the right, and the north-east corner, centre left: along this stretch of the Wall is the Knag Burn Gate. The headquarters building in the centre is flanked this side by the granaries and on the far side by the commanding officer's house; behind it sits the hospital. In the foreground are two barrack-blocks. Some buildings of the civil settlement are visible beyond the fort.

CHAPTER 1

INTRODUCTORY

Hadrian's Wall has been studied by visitors, historians and archaeologists for over four centuries. Eric Birley's *Research on Hadrian's Wall* conveniently described, analysed and referenced such work up to its publication in 1961. A brief overview of the early research on the Wall follows.

EARLIER ACCOUNTS

Knowledge of the date of the construction of Hadrian's Wall was soon lost within Britain. In the sixth century Gildas stated that it was built by the islanders on the advice of the Roman army returning to Britain after its abandonment about 410 in order to protect the former provincials from the depredations of the Picts and the Scots. Bede, writing in the monastery of Monkwearmouth/Jarrow in the early eighth century, was able to use the ancient historians, Gildas and his own local knowledge of the physical remains of the Wall. He differentiated between the Vallum (the great earthwork which accompanies the Wall to the south) and the Wall itself. He considered the former to be a frontier built of turf, hence his name for it, and dated it to the time of the Emperor Septimius Severus about 200. He retained Gildas' date for the construction of the Stone Wall, which, he added, still survived eight feet thick and twelve feet high. So knowledge and understanding of the Wall remained until the sixteenth century.

John Leland and others wrote about the Wall in the sixteenth century, but the first important account is by William Camden, the great Elizabethan antiquary, written in 1599 and printed in the fifth edition (1600) of his *Britannia*. Camden himself visited the Wall but not its central part, because of the danger of robbers. He advanced a complete explanation of the Wall and its works which held the field for 250 years.

The *Britannia*, written in Latin, was translated into English in 1610 by Philemon Holland, in consultation with Camden; Henry Holland, his son, produced a new edition in 1637. The Holland translations long remained standard works on the archaeology of Britain, and passed through many revisions, notably those by Bishop Gibson (1695, 1722, 1753, 1772) and Richard Gough (1789, 1806). Gibson's later editions contain the results of a fresh examination of the Wall in 1708-9 and, for the first time, an account of the whole line. Gough's editions are based upon the work of John Horsley, Presbyterian minister and schoolmaster at Morpeth. Horsley's *Britannia Romana*, published in 1732 shortly after his death, is still a primary treatise on the Roman antiquities of Britain while his description of the Wall remains worthy of study for his penetrating analysis of the monument. His material was used, without acknowledgement, by Alexander Gordon, whose *Itinerarium Septentrionale* was published in 1726; and a plagiarised version of his description of the Wall was published by Warburton in 1753 under the title of *Vallum Romanum*.

William Stukeley's *Iter Boreale*, published in 1776, includes memoranda of a journey made along Hadrian's Wall in 1725 with Roger Gale. It contained a new theory for the relation between Wall and Vallum, and a number of drawings most useful in showing the state of the remains in his time. Another short, first-hand account of the Wall came from John Brand, in an appendix to the first volume of his *History of Newcastle* (1789).

William Hutton of Birmingham, at the age of 78, walked the Wall from end to end in 1801 and recorded his enthusiastic observations in *The History of the Roman Wall*. In the same year the Rev. John Skinner of Camerton in Somerset took 15 days to travel from South Shields to Bowness: his journal was not to be published for nearly 200 years. In 1807, the Rev. Dr. John Lingard walked from Wallsend to Gilsland, making manuscript notes entitled *Mural Tourification*. The fourth volume of *Magna Britannia* (1816) by Daniel and Samuel Lyons contained an article on the Wall and a good account of Roman inscriptions in Cumberland.

Meanwhile, the Rev. John Hodgson, incumbent of Jarrow and Heworth, had written *The Picture of Newcastle upon Tyne* (1812) with a comprehensive and useful account of the Wall. In 1840 he devoted a large part of the last volume of his *History of Northumberland* to the Walls of Hadrian and Antoninus. Everyone since Camden had viewed the Vallum as Hadrian's frontier-work with the Wall built nearly 100 years later by the Emperor Septimius Severus. Hodgson saw that the evidence of inscriptions made this untenable: he assigned the Wall to the reign of Hadrian, and he regarded Wall and Vallum as contemporary, the latter being a rearward defence, an idea partly anticipated by Stukeley.

Hodgson also excavated on the Wall, as did his contemporaries John Clayton and Anthony Hedley. Clayton inherited the Chesters estate in 1843 and during the course of a long life – he died in 1890 – bought up large sections of the Wall and several forts. He had his workmen replace fallen facing stones on the Wall and excavate many structures including MCs 37 (Housesteads), 39 (Castle Nick) and 42 (Cawfields), Chesters fort, and the bath-house and Coventina's Well at Carrawburgh. Successive owners of Birdoswald examined that fort from the early 1830s into the 1850s, while Algernon, fourth Duke of Northumberland, financed excavations at High Rochester in 1852.

In 1848 John Collingwood Bruce commenced his study of Hadrian's Wall. The following year he led his formal tour along Hadrian's Wall: this was later recognised as the first 'Pilgrimage', an event now held every ten years and organised by the Society of Antiquaries of Newcastle upon Tyne and the Cumberland and Westmorland Antiquarian and Archaeological Society. Two years later came the publication of *The Roman Wall*. Two further editions were published in 1853 and 1867. The last is a detailed description of the remains, excellent in the east and centre, less good in the west, with accounts of Roman sites near the Wall, inscriptions and other objects. Bruce's work summarised the results of John Clayton's excavations in the central sector, and publicised Hodgson's theory of the Hadrianic date of the Wall. In 1863 Bruce produced his distilled version, the *Wallet-book*, later *Handbook, to the Roman Wall*. This offered the first, modern, statement of the function of Hadrian's Wall: "The Roman Wall…is a great fortification intended to act not only as a fence against a northern enemy, but to be used as the basis of military operations against a foe on either side of it". Bruce did much to raise public interest in Hadrian's Wall, as was rightly recognised during his lifetime.

A Survey of the Roman Wall, the first accurate survey of the Wall, was prepared by Henry MacLauchlan in the years 1852-4 for the Duke of Northumberland, and was published in 1858 with an explanatory *Memoir*, which records his acute observations of the frontier works. MacLauchlan's survey was the basis of the map which appeared in all editions of the *Handbook* from the second to the tenth. It is now succeeded by the Ordnance Survey maps, the first edition of which (1964) remains a valuable depiction of the state of survival of the Wall and its ancillary works: there remains a need for a detailed map of the Wall plotting the current state of knowledge.

Although 'disengagement' of the remains was undertaken earlier, the era of scientific excavation on the Wall can be said to have begun in the 1890s. Francis Haverfield began his examination of the Vallum in 1894 on behalf of the Cumberland Excavation Committee and in 1898 R. C. Bosanquet excavated Housesteads fort. Perhaps more significant was the investigation of T 44b (Mucklebank) by J. P. Gibson in 1892 for this led on to a series of partnerships and the start of a long programme of research with the aim of determining the building history of the Wall and its chronology. Gibson was joined by F. G. Simpson in 1907. Simpson was to work on

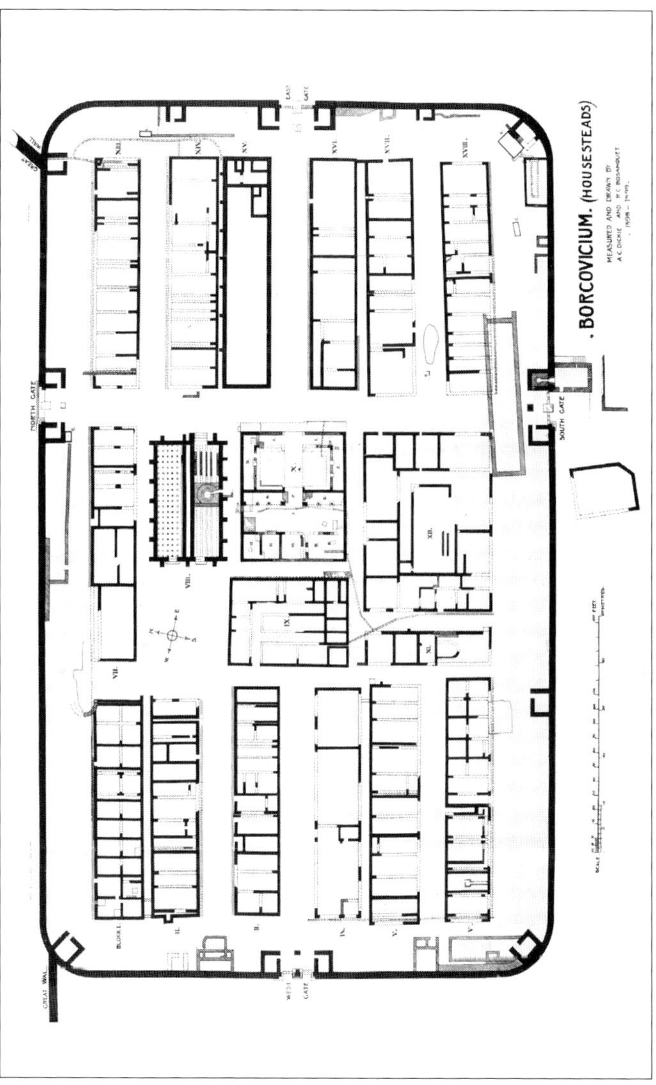

R. C. Bosanquet's plan of his 1898 excavation of Housesteads.

Hadrian's Wall for 40 years and much of our knowledge of the building of the Wall rests upon his investigations. Gibson died in 1912 and I. A. Richmond joined Simpson in 1928. R. G. Collingwood was also an important member of the group, seeking to place the discoveries in a wider context, and writing

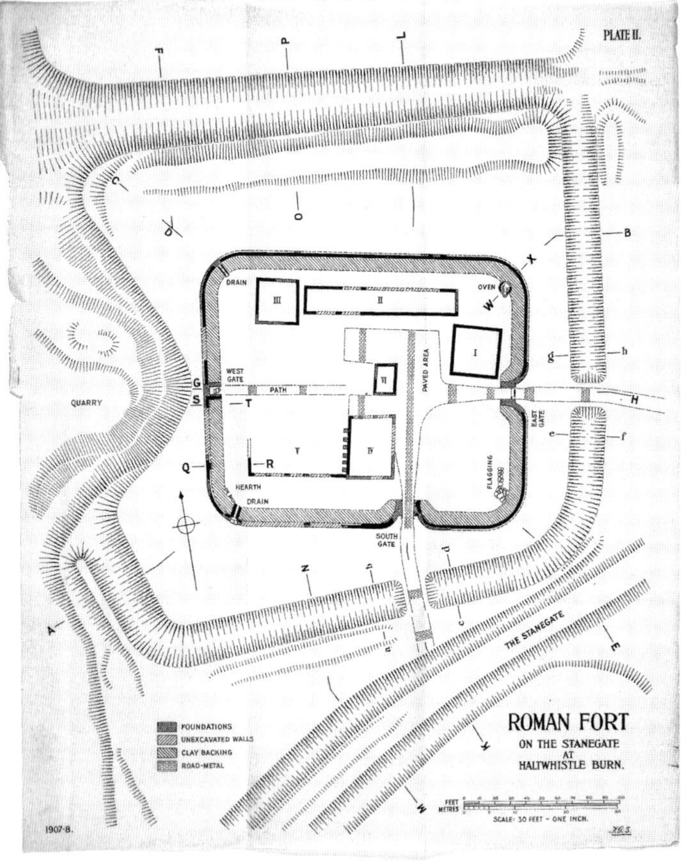

Haltwhistle Burn fortlet, drawn by F. G. Simpson. Simpson brought new standards of excavation and draughtsmanship to Hadrian's Wall.

influential discussion papers. He also established the system of numbering the structures on the Wall which we still use today. Eric Birley joined the team at Birdoswald in 1929, an excavation which led to the formation of a revised framework for the history of the Wall.

Gibson had recognised three periods in T 44b (Mucklebank) in 1892; the need for repair, he suggested, resulted from repeated attacks on the Wall, thus repeating the view held since at least 1856 when Bruce assigned damage at Housesteads to the invasion of about 180. The Gibson-Simpson investigation of MC 48 (Poltross Burn) in 1909 led to a chronology for the Wall being postulated, based on the coin evidence. The first period started in 122 and was divided into two phases. At the close of the first phase (IA) many milecastles had the pivot stones at their north gates broken or removed. The second phase (IB) ended with the invasion of about 180. The second main period also ended in destruction, some time after 270. The third period began before 300 and ended about 330, though at the time it was believed that this third period continued in the forts until 364-69, when they were destroyed, to be subsequently re-built, surviving down to 383.

There was a significant distinction between the contents of the various layers in milecastles and turrets. There was little debris between phases IA and IB, but later layers contained much masonry debris. It was argued that the first phase (IA) ended when Hadrian's Wall was abandoned in favour of the newly-constructed Antonine Wall, the pivot stones then being broken when gates were removed to allow free access through the Wall. Later periods, however, ended with violent destruction caused by invaders from the north, hence the masonry debris.

In 1929 this chronology was refined as a result of the excavation at Birdoswald. Four main periods were now defined. Period I commenced with the building of the Wall and, broken by the occupation of the Antonine Wall, continued until about

195 (rather than 180) when, it was argued, the northern tribes took advantage of the absence of the army on the Continent to invade the province. Period II commenced with the repair of that damage in 200/205 and lasted until about 295, when again the absence of the army defending the island from attack was seen as an invitation to invasion from the north. Period III ran from 297/300 until 368 and Period IV covered the final years of occupation down to about 383. This, together with the elucidation of the history of the Turf Wall over the decade 1925-1935, led to the premature assertion that all the problems of Hadrian's Wall had been solved.

Table 1: The changing chronology of Hadrian's Wall

Period	1909	1929
I	c.120-180	c.120/5-c.195
II	-270+	c.200/5-c.295
III	before 300-364/9	c.297/300-368
IV	-383	c.370-c.383

It is now accepted that not all sites on the Wall fit into such a straitjacket, though it remains a useful broad framework, at least within the second century. Today, there is more emphasis on the invasion of about 180 as the cause of damage on Hadrian's Wall at the end of the first period, most of the evidence being restricted to the forts in the vicinity of Dere Street: Rudchester, Halton Chesters and Corbridge. The problem with the reasons advanced in 1929 for the destruction of the Wall in the 190s and 290s is that no invasion is recorded at either time. Hadrian's Wall is not mentioned in the account of the invasion of Britain in 367, but archaeologists have tried to link the treachery of the *areani* (frontier scouts) at that time to destruction of the Wall. Finally, re-analysis of the coin evidence has demonstrated that Hadrian's Wall continued in occupation until at least the end of the fourth century.

The late 1920s and early 1930s were years of intense activity on Hadrian's Wall. The re-established Cumberland Excavation

Committee under F. G. Simpson and I. A. Richmond investigated the nature of the Turf Wall while the North of England Excavation Committee was founded by the Society of Antiquaries of Newcastle in 1924 to encourage "under proper supervision the excavation of sites in the North". It tended to concentrate on the eastern end of the Wall. Also in the east, the improvement of the Military Road resulted in a series of rescue excavations. The importance of this work was recognised by Durham University, which appointed Simpson as its director of excavation in 1924, a post he relinquished in 1931 to allow Eric Birley to be appointed as a lecturer. Birley was to stay at Durham for 40 years, directing his students to research on a wide range of aspects of the Wall and the Roman army

Throughout these years, excavations took place at Corbridge. Wide-ranging exploration from 1906 to 1914 provided a basic plan of the town. In 1933, the core of the site was placed in state care and the following year a new campaign of excavation commenced, focussed on the Roman fort under the town, which continued, with a break for the Second World War, until 1973.

Research on Hadrian's Wall through the nineteenth century and well into the twentieth was mainly undertaken by private individuals, the local societies and, latterly, by Durham and Newcastle Universities. In 1928 the Government took into care its first sections of the Wall. Since 1945 English Heritage and its predecessors have funded or sponsored much excavation on the Wall including clearing and consolidating many miles of the Wall and undertaking a major operation to examine and expose the buildings within the fort at Housesteads. Much has been discovered as a result of rescue excavations in advance of developments.

This work has been complemented by the activities of the National Trust in the central sector, which included investigation of MC 39 (Castle Nick) as well as the discovery of an additional tower at Peel Gap. Excavations in advance of developments have also taken place, for example at Wallsend, and in Carlisle, which have revolutionised our knowledge of the history of that city. Cumbria County Council has sponsored excavations at Birdoswald, and Tyne and Wear Museums at South Shields and Wallsend which have provided valuable evidence relating to the later history of the Wall, as well as leading to the public display of the remains. At the same time, our knowledge of the Cumbrian Coast owes much to the single-handed endeavours of Richard Bellhouse, while the long-running research excavations at Vindolanda have led to the display of additional buildings in the fort and extensive areas of the civil settlement.

Three significant developments have considerably extended our knowledge over recent years. Of major international importance has been the discovery at Vindolanda of some 2000 writing tablets dating to the years around 100. The writing tablets not only shed a fascinating light on life on the northern frontier during the years immediately before the construction of the Wall - military intelligence, building, supply, and the minutiae of daily life - but, as so many of the documents are broadly similar to those found on the Roman empire's eastern frontier, they allow these other documents to be used with confidence to illuminate life on the northern frontiers as well. Tree-ring dating has been an important factor in determining the chronology of sites where conditions have permitted the preservation of timbers, in particular Carlisle and Vindolanda. It has also demonstrated that building work was not confined to one season for timbers dating to 9 out of the 12 years that the first fort at Carlisle was occupied have been recovered during excavations. Finally, geophysical surveys have led to considerably more evidence, in particular for the extent and planning of civil settlements, amplifying, and indeed superseding, the earlier evidence of ground survey and aerial photography. Meanwhile, excavations, accompanied by work in the study, have continued to extend our knowledge of

Hadrian's Wall, challenging past assumptions and offering . interpretations. One such discovery is of pits on the berm - ι space between the Wall and the ditch - in several different locations in the eastern sector of the Wall.

HISTORICAL SUMMARY

The following account of the history of Hadrian's Wall is based upon the literary sources, inscriptions and coins, with the archaeological material mainly brought into play in the more detailed general account which forms the second chapter of this book.

Britain was known to both Greeks and Romans by the fourth century BC, but first came into contact with Roman military power when Julius Caesar invaded in 55 and 54 BC. Conquest was, however, reserved for the Emperor Claudius in AD 43. His army rapidly overran southern and eastern England. The Brigantes, who occupied most of northern England under their queen Cartimandua, became allied to Rome. In 69, however, she was overthrown by her former consort and rescued by Rome, who then invaded and occupied the kingdom. The new governor, Petillius Cerialis, reached the Solway: tree-ring analysis has demonstrated that the timbers used to build a fort at Carlisle were felled in the winter of 72/3. Yet the ambitions of the emperor, Vespasian, who had served in Claudius' army of invasion, were wider: he ordered the conquest of the Welsh and then the north British tribes. Julius Agricola, governor from 77 to 84, brought Roman arms to the fringe of the Highlands of Scotland, winning a victory over the Caledonians at the Battle of Mons Graupius, which has yet to be located. The people thus conquered were controlled by forts linked by roads which provided for ready movement within the province as well as northwards if defence against invasion from that quarter was required.

There is little literary evidence for events in Britain during the 35 years following Agricola's campaigns. Military disasters on the Danube frontier led to the withdrawal of one of the four legions from Britain, the Second Adiutrix, probably with some auxiliary units, perhaps as early as the winter of 85/6. Coins suggest the abandonment of all forts down to the northerly fringes of the Cheviots in or shortly after 86. Subsequently, it would appear, all forts north of the Tyne-Solway isthmus were abandoned. Various factors indicate that this occurred in or shortly after 103.

Coin of Hadrian recording on the reverse the visit of the emperor to Britain.
(actual size)

Hadrian succeeded his cousin Trajan as emperor in 117. At that time, it was recorded that "the Britons could not be kept under Roman control". This is but one of several references to warfare in Britain during Hadrian's reign. The first is usually presumed to refer to the northern frontier, but an uprising within the province cannot be ruled out. A coin issued in 119 has been taken to imply victory in Britain. At Vindolanda the fragmentary memorial of a centurion of the regiment in residence in the late first and early second century records his death in a war. There are two inscriptions recording an *expeditio Britannica*, which ought to be a military expedition and not just the visit of the emperor in 122. T. Pontius Sabinus served in a British expedition, commanding a 3000-strong detachment drawn from the three legions of the provinces of Upper Germany and Spain: his career suggests that this was in the second half of the 120s. M. Maenius Agrippa was chosen by the emperor and sent on the British expedition: here he commanded the First Cohort of Spaniards stationed at Maryport where he is attested dedicating four of the annual altars to Jupiter. Finally, in 162 Cornelius Fronto wrote of the large number of soldiers killed under Hadrian by the Britons and the Jews: the Jewish war dated to the early 130s, but the British war was not necessarily the same date. There is still debate as to whether there was but one war in Britain, in 117-9, or, in addition, a second some years later; accumulating evidence points to there having been a second war, perhaps in the mid-120s.

The visit of Hadrian to Britain was recorded by his fourth-century biographer, who described his decision to build a Wall thus: "Hadrian was the first to build a wall, 80 miles long, to separate the Romans from the barbarians". This is the Wall of which the present volume gives some account.

Hadrian came to Britain from Lower Germany and the date can be calculated as 122. A military diploma (a certificate of privileges issued to retiring soldiers) issued on 17 July 122 records the arrival of the new governor of Britain, Aulus Platorius Nepos, shortly before. Nepos also came from Lower Germany, where he had been governor, and we may presume emperor and governor travelled together. At about the same time, the Sixth Legion was also moved from Germany to Britain and, it may be presumed, came over with the emperor and the new governor. A certain M. Pontius Laelianus, it was later recorded, was "military tribune of legion VI Victrix, with which he crossed from Germany to Britain". The emperor appears to have been accompanied by his wife, Sabina, the commander and a detachment of the Praetorian Guard, and other government officials, including Suetonius, his secretary for correspondence, who is better known for his biographies of the early emperors.

Independent corroboration of Hadrian's visit to Britain is provided by the contemporary poet Florus, who wrote: "I would not like to be Caesar, to walk through Britain…". Later coins commemorate the visit, the *adventus Aug(usti) Britanniae*, as well as Hadrian addressing the army of the province.

We cannot be certain that the emperor visited the site of the Wall. Its very size and impressiveness have been taken as an indication of the involvement of the emperor, who, we may note, fancied his architectural skills, while the rigidity of its planning points to some decisions being taken without local knowledge.

The emperor did not remain in the province to see the completion of the Wall. He left Britain in 122 for Gaul *en route* to Spain. Nepos carried forward the plans and began to modify them; he stayed in Britain, probably until 126, but work continued, it would appear, up to the very end of Hadrian's reign.

Hadrian died in July 138 to be succeeded by Antoninus Pius. In the next year, preparations began, under the governor Quintus Lollius Urbicus, for a fresh advance into Scotland, consolidated by the construction of a new Wall, of turf, between Forth and Clyde, the Antonine Wall. This has been linked to a comment by the Greek author Pausanias who stated that "Antoninus never willingly made war, but ... in Britain, he appropriated most of the territory of the Brigantes, because they too had begun a war, invading *Genunia*, which is subject to the Romans". The invasion of Scotland in 139/42 was the only time that Antoninus Pius took the title '*Imperator*' (Conqueror) as a result of warfare and is the most appropriate occasion for Pausanias' statement.

Excavation has demonstrated that Hadrian's Wall was largely abandoned at this time, and rendered open to free passage, though some of the forts were retained. The Antonine Wall was only held for a generation and in 158 an inscription recording work on Hadrian's Wall indicates that this was to become the northern frontier again. At the same time, another inscription records that the fort at Birrens, one of the original outpost forts of Hadrian's Wall, was rebuilt: excavation has indicated that this followed destruction but whether at the hands of an enemy or preparatory to a change of garrison is not clear. There are hints at military activity a few years earlier. A coin issued in 155 depicts *Britannia*, supposedly subdued, which may reflect fighting shortly before.

The reason for the abandonment of the Antonine Wall is not known. Its occupation may have stretched the resources of the army of the Britain. Troops appear to have been sent from Britain for service elsewhere. An inscription found in the River Tyne apparently records a detachment setting out for the armies of the two Germanies; others may have served in the Mauretanian War in north Africa.

Antoninus Pius died in 161, when, it was recorded, "war was threatening in Britain" and the new Emperor, Marcus Aurelius, sent Calpurnius Agricola against the Britons; again this is taken to be a reference to trouble on the northern frontier. Agricola was one of a succession of senior generals who governed the province, presumably reflecting military necessities. Several inscriptions record building work in Wall forts under Agricola and his immediate successors.

War, again, we are informed, was about to break out in the early 170s. Shortly after, in 175, the army in Britain was strengthened by the addition of 5,500 Sarmatians from the Lower Danube region enrolled in the army as a result of a treaty obligation.

Medallion of Commodus recording victory in Britain. (actual size)

The reign of the Emperor Commodus (180-92) saw a most serious event which was recorded by the contemporary historian Cassius Dio: "the tribes in the island crossed the wall that separated them from the Roman forts, doing much damage and killing a general and the troops he had with him; so Commodus in alarm sent Ulpius Marcellus against them. … Marcellus inflicted a major defeat on the barbarians". It is regrettable that our source does not mention which Wall was crossed, but it was presumably Hadrian's Wall. Victory was commemorated by a coin issue in 184. A military diploma records that Marcellus was already in Britain on 23 March 178. Did the invasion occur during his governorship, or was he sent back to the province to deal with it as the language of Cassius Dio suggests? Ulpius Marcellus is recorded on Hadrian's Wall, on an altar at Benwell and on building stones at Chesters, one of which names the Second Cavalry Regiment of Asturians, still at the fort over 200 years later.

Commodus was assassinated at the end of 192, and there followed a struggle for the empire in which Septimius Severus, governor of Upper Pannonia (modern Austria), was ultimately triumphant. One of the contenders, and perhaps the most experienced, was Clodius Albinus, governor of Britain, who in 197 led the army of Britain to the continent to fight his rival, but was defeated at Lyons.

Virius Lupus, the first governor sent by Severus to Britain in 197, arrived to find that "the Caledonians instead of honouring their promises had prepared to defend the Maeatae and since at that time Severus was devoting himself to the Parthian war, Lupus had no choice but to buy peace from the Maeatae for a considerable sum of money, recovering a few captives". It would appear that the northern frontier was in a disturbed state with the main culprits being the Maeatae, who, the evidence of place names indicates, lived around the head of the Forth in the area of modern Stirling. Possibly the withdrawal of troops to fight Severus had presented too inviting an opportunity to Rome's northern neighbours. A number of coin hoards of the early third century found in Scotland may have had their origins in this action of Lupus.

Ten or more inscriptions record the building work of Severus' governors in forts on the Wall, the hinterland and to the north, while stone was quarried in the valley of the River Gelt, 6 km (4 miles) south of Castlesteads, in 207. Later literary sources went further and assigned the construction of the Wall itself to the emperor, and this, as we have seen, was the generally accepted view into the nineteenth century.

Dio mentioned warfare in Britain in 207, which the Romans were winning, but in 208 the Emperor Septimius Severus came to Britain with his sons, Caracalla and Geta, to campaign against the Caledonians and the Maeatae, staying here for three years.

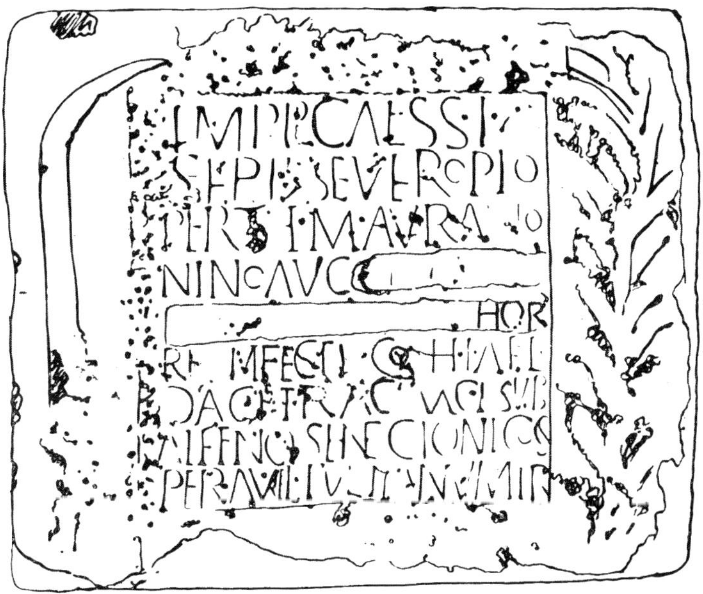

Inscription found at Birdoswald in 1929 recording building work under the Emperor Septimius Severus. (762 x 940 mm).

Coin of Septimius Severus recording his victory in Britain.
(actual size)

His intention according to Dio was to complete the conquest of the island. The death of Severus at York on 4 February 211 brought an end to fighting. Caracalla and Geta arranged peace with the northern tribes, abandoned forts and returned to Rome. One of the forts built under Severus but abandoned by his sons was Carpow on the River Tay, its northern location substantiating the extent of Severus' conquests.

Our literary sources are silent on events in Britain for almost a hundred years. Inscriptions go some way to filling the gap for they record much building work at forts on Hadrian's Wall and in its hinterland in the early third century: the last dates to 262-6. Formerly regarded as the result of destruction, it is now argued that this work reflects the repairs consequent upon old age, as some inscriptions specifically state, and the introduction of new facilities. The *Notitia Dignitatum*, a list of officers in the Roman army dating to about 400 (see pages 36-38), records that to the south of Hadrian's Wall many forts had different units based there, and indeed different types of units, than are attested at the forts in the third century. The inference drawn from this is that the earlier units had been withdrawn in the third century - this in turn implying a period of peace - to be replaced by new-style units as a reaction to the disturbed conditions of the fourth century. This is in contrast with the Wall, where the units listed in the *Notitia* are those first recorded there in the late second or early third centuries, thereby indicating continuity of occupation.

It was events played out on the imperial stage at the end of the third century which drew attention to Britain again. Carausius, who had charge of a fleet to repress piracy in the English Channel, in 287 assumed the sovereignty of Britain. He retained power until 293, when he was assassinated and his position usurped by his finance minister, Allectus. In 296, the Caesar Constantius Chlorus reconquered Britain and restored it to Rome. History now records for the first time the Picts, who, later evidence records, lived beyond the Forth. Under Constantius repairs are recorded at Birdoswald and possibly Housesteads and other work on the Wall has been assigned to these years. Constantius himself was back in Britain in 305, campaigning against the Picts. He was at York when he died in 306. His son, Constantine, known to history as 'the Great', was proclaimed emperor there on 25 July 306.

Constantine took the title *Britannicus Maximus* in 315, which may indicate warfare, and the presence of the emperor, in Britain: a coin issue of 314 lends some support to the latter possibility. His son, Constans, came over in the winter of 342/3 to help the Britons; it is usually assumed that this refers to a disturbance on the northern frontier. Trouble is recorded in 360 when "the Scots and Picts were carrying out raids in Britain, having disrupted the agreed peace, and laying waste places [*loca*] near the frontier", and in 367 when "a conspiracy of barbarians [Picts, Attacotti and Scots, the latter both from Ireland] brought Britain to her knees. Count Nectaridus, the officer responsible for coastal defences, was killed and the duke [of the Britains], Fullofaudes, circumvented by the enemy". The situation was retrieved by Count Theodosius, who was sent to Britain by the emperor Valentinian I with a powerful force, cleared out the invaders, and restored fortifications, "protecting the frontier with sentries and forts". He also abolished the *areani*: "their official duty was to range backwards and forwards over long distances with information for our generals about disturbances among neighbouring nations" - an appropriate description of frontier scouts - but "it was clearly proved against them that they had been bribed with quantities of plunder, or promises of it, to reveal to the enemy what was happening on our side".

In 382, Magnus Maximus campaigned against the Picts and Scots after they had invaded the empire. Thereafter watch over the frontier continued, at least if the poet Claudian's panegyrics to Stilicho (virtual ruler of the western empire for his son-in-law, Honorius, from 395 to 408) are to be believed. It would appear to have been Stilicho who further strengthened the army of Britain by the establishment in the island of a small field army at the very end of the fourth century: the location of its base(s) is not known. Although in 401 troops were withdrawn in order to aid the defence of Italy, there was no 'withdrawal of the legions' in 410, rather a loosening of ties over the years 407-411 and recognition by central government that it could no longer defend the island. When Roman rule in Britain ended, Hadrian's Wall was still maintaining its purpose.

What happened thereafter is still a matter of conjecture. Birdoswald appears to have continued in use, though perhaps as the base of a local warlord; other forts may have been abandoned. Anglo-Saxon objects have been found at some sites, but there is no evidence for the occupation of any military installation on the Wall by such incomers.

ANCIENT SOURCES FOR PLACE NAMES AND MILITARY UNITS

The Rudge Cup, the Amiens Skillet and the Ilam Pan

A small enamelled cup found at Rudge in Wiltshire in 1725 is now at Alnwick Castle. Its decoration is a frieze crowned by the inscription A MAIS ABALLAVA UXELODUM CAMBOGLANS BANNA. These are the names of the forts at the west end of the Wall, starting from Bowness-on-Solway and running eastwards: Burgh-by-Sands, Stanwix, Castlesteads and Birdoswald. A comparable vessel, found in 1949 at Amiens, carries the words MAIS ABALLAVA UXELODUNUM CAMBOGLA[LANI]S BANNA

The Rudge Cup: the names MAIS (Bowness) and ABALLAVA (Burgh-by-Sands) are visible. (450 mm high)

ESICA. These forts would appear to be Bowness, Burgh-by-Sands, Stanwix, Castlesteads, Birdoswald and Great Chesters.

The Ilam pan (illustrated on page 358), also known as the Staffordshire Moors pan, found in 2003, bears the following inscription: RIGORE VALI AELI DRACONIS MAIS COGGABATA VXELODVNVM CAMMOGLANNA. It is not known where the inscription starts, but the above would read either: "On the line of the Wall, (the product *or* property) of Aelius Draco…", or "On the line of the Aelian Wall, (the product *or* property) of Draco…". Then follow the names of four forts at the western end of Hadrian's Wall: Bowness, Drumburgh, Stanwix, Castlesteads. The fort name *Aballava* is omitted, presumably either in error or because the fort was not occupied when the bowl was made. The pan may indicate that the original name for Hadrian's Wall was *vallum Aelii*, the Wall of Aelius, Aelius being Hadrian's family name.

These vessels, which form part of a larger group, all appear to have been made in Britain. They date to the second century and are high-quality objects, not souvenirs produced for a mass market. It has been suggested that the decoration on the Rudge Cup is a depiction of Hadrian's Wall. This is uncertain and, in view of its use, upside down, on the Bath Pan which is not related to Hadrian's Wall, unlikely.

The *Notitia Dignitatum*

This early fifth-century document, entitled *Notitia Dignitatum et Administrationum, tam civilium quam militarium, in partibus Orientis et Occidentis*, records the distribution of imperial officials, civil and military, throughout the Roman world. The section headed item *per lineam Valli* (also along the line of the Wall), which appears to run on along the Cumbrian Coast, is here translated, and the modern names are added in brackets.

Tribune of the Fourth Cohort of Lingones, *Segedunum* (Wallsend)
Tribune of the First Cohort of Cornovii, *Pons Aelii* (Newcastle)
Prefect of the First Ala of Asturians, *Condercum* (Benwell)
Tribune of the First Cohort of Frisiavones, *Vindobala* (Rudchester)
Prefect of the Ala Sabiniana, *Hunnum* (Halton Chesters)
Prefect of the Second Ala of Asturians, *Cilurnum* (Chesters)
Tribune of the First Cohort of Batavians, *Brocolitia* (Carrawburgh)
Tribune of the First Cohort of Tungrians, *Borcovicium* (Housesteads)
Tribune of the Fourth Cohort of Gauls, *Vindolanda* (Chesterholm)
Tribune of the Second Cohort of Asturians, *Aesica* (Great Chesters)
Tribune of the Second Cohort of Dalmatians, *Magna* (Carvoran)
Tribune of the First Cohort of Hadrian's Own Dacians … *Camboglanna*
Prefect of the Ala Petriana, *Petriana* (Stanwix)
Prefect of Aurelius's Own Moors, *Aballava* (Burgh-by-Sands)

Tribune of the Second Cohort of Lingones, *Congavata* (Drumburgh)
Tribune of the First Cohort of Spaniards, *Axelodunum*
Tribune of the Second Cohort of Thracians, *Gabrosentum* (Moresby)
Tribune of the First Cohort of Hadrian's Own Marines, *Tunnocelum* (Ravenglass?)

The great value of the list is that it supplies the ancient names of nearly all the Wall forts. The list does not coincide with the names on the Rudge Cup and Amiens Skillet. *Maia* (Bowness) does not appear nor does *Banna*, whose omission may best be put down to a copying error, a scribe omitting parts of two lines, '*Banna*' after the First Cohort of Dacians, which inscriptions place at Birdoswald, and 'Tribune, Second Cohort of Tungrians' at the beginning of the next line before *Camboglanna*, again inscriptions demonstrating that this unit was stationed at Castlesteads. These two lines might be restored:

Tribune of the First Cohort of Hadrian's Own Dacians, *Banna* (Birdoswald)
Tribune of the Second Cohort of Tungrians, *Camboglanna* (Castlesteads).

The name of Stanwix according to the two vessels and the *Ravenna Cosmography* was *Uxelodunum*. It seems likely that Petriana was erroneously repeated, the fort's name perhaps later appearing in the list misspelt as *Axelodunum*. In which case the First Cohort of Spaniards may have been based at Bowness, this line being restored as:

Tribune of the First Cohort of Spaniards, *Maia* (Bowness).

A diploma of 158 issued to a soldier in the First Cohort of Hadrian's Own Marines has been found at Ravenglass. The straightforward conclusion is to identify *Tunnocelum* as

Ravenglass, an attribution supported by the *Ravenna Cosmography*. If correct, this would be a unique case in Britain of a regiment remaining in the same fort from the mid-second to the late fourth century.

The Antonine Itinerary

The *Antonine Itinerary* is a list of routes within the empire, providing names and distances. It does not appear to be of one date but could contain material collected at various times during the second and third centuries. Two roads start on the frontier (called both *limes* and *vallum*), that on the east at *Bremenium* (the outpost fort of High Rochester), whence the road (now termed Dere Street) leads south to *Corstopitum* (probably more correctly known as *Coria* = Corbridge) and beyond, while on the west the route starts at the outpost fort of *Blatobulgium* (Birrens) and runs first to *Castra Exploratorum* (Netherby) before crossing the Wall at *Luguvalium* (Carlisle) and thence running on south.

The Ravenna Cosmography

The Ravenna List is an early eighth-century copy of a collection of geographical information from both within and without the empire. Twelve forts are listed from east to west along the Wall, all names rather garbled in relation to other sources but nevertheless recognisable: *Serduno, Condecor, Vindovala, Onno, Celuno, Brocoliti, Velurtion, Esica, Banna, Uxelludamo, Avalana* and *Maia*. Missing from this list are Newcastle, Carvoran, Castlesteads and Drumburgh. Two of these (Carvoran (*Magnis*) and Castlesteads (*Gabaglanda*)) appear elsewhere, together with Chesterholm (*Vindolanda*) and Carlisle (*Lagubalumi*).

The Cumbrian Coast forts also appear in the document. From south to north are listed: *Iuliocenon* (= *Tunnocelo*), *Gabrocentio, Alauna* and *Bribra*, followed by *Maio*, which, it is presumed, is a repetition of *Maia* (= Bowness). These forts would appear to be Ravenglass, Moresby, Maryport and Beckfoot. Elsewhere in the document *Fanocodi* is clearly *Fanum Cocidi* (Bewcastle).

Inscriptions

Inscriptions provide the names of some forts. One at Birdoswald refers to the *venatores Bannienses*, the hunters of Banna, presumably the name of the fort, while the *vicani Vindolandesses* are the people of the civil settlement at *Vindolanda*: an altar found close by records the Textoverdi, perhaps the local people of the neighbourhood. *VER* at Housesteads is presumably an abbreviation for *Vercovicium*. Inscriptions are also a great source of information on the regiments stationed on the Wall, the soldiers who commanded and served in those regiments, and their dependants. Building inscriptions record the construction of military installations and their repair. In addition, inscriptions provide evidence of civil organisation, for example, not only the self-governing communities at *Vindolanda* and at Housesteads, but also the larger body known as the *civitas Carvetiorum* centred on the Eden Valley.

Occasionally an inscription refers to events of wider significance. For example, an altar dedicated by a legionary legate at Kirksteads between Stanwix and Burgh-by-Sands refers to successful operations beyond the Wall (*vallum*). At Carlisle the prefect of a cavalry unit recorded the killing of a band of barbarians, while at Corbridge another cavalry prefect erected an altar "after slaughtering a band of Corionototae", who are otherwise unknown. A fourth-century tombstone at Ambleside, well behind the Wall, records a soldier "killed in the fort by the enemy".

THE ARMY AND ITS OFFICERS

The Roman provincial army was divided into two main groups: the legions, composed of Roman citizens, and their support troops (literally auxiliaries) originally drawn from their allies. At the time of the construction of the Wall, there were three legions in Britain: the Second Augusta based at Caerleon-on-Usk, the Twentieth Valeria Victrix at Chester, and the Sixth Victrix later to take up residence at York, all some distance behind the frontier. The last is still recorded at York in the *Notitia Dignitatum*, that is about 400. By this date, the Second Augusta had moved to Richborough in Kent, while the Twentieth had disappeared from the military record.

Under Hadrian, the legions, each about 5,000 strong, were highly-trained and heavily-armed infantry, with a small cavalry detachment. They wore a distinctive armour formed of metal strips to aid flexibility and were equipped with a sword, dagger, two spears and a rectangular shield; the cavalry wore mail shirts and fought with a longer sword. Legions were organised into ten cohorts, each 480 strong, with the exception of the first which was formed of 800 men arranged in five double-strength centuries. Their length of service was 25/26 years. The commander was the *legatus legionis*, the legate of the legion, a senator, a member of the nobility holding his commission directly from the emperor. The second-in-command was the *tribunus laticlavius*, the tribune with a broad stripe, a man destined for the senate. There were five other tribunes, all from the lower nobility. Each of these officers held their post for

Building stone of the Second Legion showing its two symbols, a capricorn and a pegasus found at Benwell. (254 x 380 mm)

about three years during a career in the emperor's service which alternated military and civil positions. The third-in-command was the *praefectus castrorum*, the prefect of the camp; he was a professional soldier, having previously served as a centurion. The centurions, 59 in total, had normally risen from the ranks and formed the backbone of the legion. Each commanded a century (*centuria*), nominally 80 strong. Upon them fell the day-to-day maintenance of discipline and efficiency. Each centurion had under him a second-in-command (the *optio*), a standard-bearer (*signifer*), and other junior officers. There was an elaborate system of junior officers and 'tradesmen' forming a highly-specialised administrative, clerical, surveying, engineering and building staff.

The legions formed the main building force on Hadrian's Wall, though some work was undertaken by auxiliary units and even the British fleet. It was the auxiliary units which occupied the forts on the Wall, though legionaries are also attested on the frontier, apparently on garrison duty.

The auxiliaries differed from the legionaries in many ways. They were not recruited from Roman citizens, but from among the peoples of frontier provinces. The regiments on the Wall had originally been raised in provinces stretching from Spain to Syria, but once in Britain they usually recruited locally. However, the army in Britain was augmented by soldiers from elsewhere. These were often Germans and Gauls, but might include men from other areas including the middle Danube and Africa. Auxiliary soldiers received Roman citizenship on

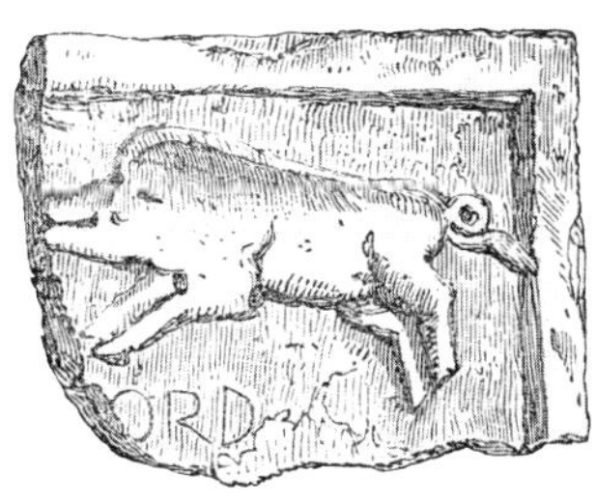

Fragment of a stone found at Maryport showing the boar, the symbol of the Twentieth Legion.
(178 x 203 mm)

The tombstone of an archer found at Housesteads. (1.14 m high)

The tombstone of a standard-bearer found at Carrawburgh. (1.16 m high)

retirement, and it seems probable that the number of citizens in such regiments grew as sons of citizen soldiers joined their father's unit.

The auxiliaries were normally protected by mail shirts and armed with swords and spears and carried oval shields. There were six different types of regiments: cohorts of infantry and *alae* of cavalry, nominally either 1,000 (milliary) or 500 (quingenary) strong, with some cohorts (*cohortes equitatae*) containing a cavalry component of either 240 or 120 men in addition to the infantry core. The cohort was divided into 10 or 6 centuries, each commanded by a centurion, an ala into 24 or 16 troops (*turmae*) each commanded by a decurion. The milliary cohort was normally commanded by a tribune; the quingenary cohorts and all cavalry regiments by a prefect. Tribunes and prefects were members of the lower nobility, and normally held their posts for about three years. The centurions and decurions, as in the legions, had risen from the ranks and were supported by junior officers and specialist staff. The length of service was 25 years, apart for the centurions and decurions who appear to have had no formal retirement age.

Under Hadrian there were as many as 63 or 64 auxiliary units known to have been serving in Britain, most in northern Britain. Their paper strength was about 38,000 men, though documents demonstrate that this was rarely achieved, leading to a more realistic estimate of about 30,000 for the total number of men. Between 110 and 127 the army of Britain was supplemented by the arrival of the Fifth Cohort of Gauls, but at about the same time three cavalry units left Britain, two for Lower Germany and the third for Noricum (modern Austria). The relationship of such troop movements to events in Britain is not known.

The British Fleet (*classis Britannica*) was the naval branch of the army. Based on the English Channel, its forces were employed to protect the empire's coasts from hostile action. There is no clear evidence that it was involved in supply: this was normally carried out by civilian contractors. The fleet may have contained its own engineering and building corps, like the army, hence its soldiers being brought north to aid with the construction of the Wall. A building inscription of the fleet dating to the governorship of Platorius Nepos has been found in the granaries at Benwell, while two others record work in the Birdoswald area, though neither is dated.

The auxiliary units were supplemented by a different type of unit known as a *numerus*, which is first attested on the Wall about 200. The *numerus* was a regular army unit, but of lower status than the auxiliary regiment and usually formed from tribes in the frontier areas. Some may have been commanded by officers drawn from the tribal leaders, such as Notfried's regiment based at Housesteads.

The *Notitia Dignitatum* shows that many of the units based on the Wall at the very end of Roman Britain had the same title as their predecessors 200 years before. Over the intervening years, however, the units had changed in many ways. Documentary evidence indicates that each unit was probably only about a quarter of its earlier size. Substantial barrack-blocks were still being constructed in the fourth century, though how many soldiers occupied them is uncertain. There is also evidence that commanding officers now normally rose from the ranks, though the large house at South Shields indicates the scale of accommodation still provided. Certainly, the Roman army was still a significant force, capable of defending the empire during the fourth and into the fifth century.

Something is known of the officers in the army of Britain during the reign of Hadrian. The governor was Aulus Platorius Nepos, a senator who had held the consulate in 119, three years prior to his arrival in Britain, which was shortly before 17 July 122. Before Britain he had been governor of Thrace (modern Bulgaria) and Lower Germany. He was accompanied to Britain from Germany by Pontius Laelianus, tribune of the Sixth, and possibly by Publius Tullius Varro, who was legate of the legion about this time: his brother had also been consul with Hadrian in 119. A few years later, the Twentieth was commanded by Aemilius Papus whose father was a friend of Hadrian.

Personal connections with the emperor may also be seen amongst the commanding officers of the auxiliary regiments. Marcus Maenius Agrippa, tribune of the First Cohort of Spaniards at Maryport, was described on an inscription erected at his home city of Camerinum as the host of Hadrian. He had previously commanded a Cohort of Britons on the lower Danube and was to serve as prefect of the British fleet later in Hadrian's reign. We can date precisely the service in Britain of two auxiliary commanding officers to the governorship of Nepos: Fabius Sabinus commanded the First Cavalry Regiment of Pannonians, *Tampiana*, on 17 July 122 while Marcus Iunius Claudianus was prefect of the First Cohort of Sunucians on 16 September 124; both were recorded on diplomas issued to retiring soldiers on those days.

The recording of the work of building the Wall through the practice of legionary centurions signing both ends of the lengths that their soldiers had constructed with 'centurial stones' has resulted in the names of about 150 such officers from the three legions of the province being known. However, in the vast majority of cases we know only their names, often abbreviated too. Quarries have yielded names and ranks carved on rocks, but these mostly probably date to after Hadrian's reign. The ranks include *optio* and *imaginifer* (standard-bearer).

This writing tablet found at Vindolanda is a list of food including, on lines 3-7: condimen[torum] (of spices); capream (goat); salis (of salt); porcellum (young pig); pernam (ham); lines 9-10: frumen[ti] of corn; ceruin[am] venison).
(675 mm high)

The Vindolanda writing tablets furnish a vivid picture of life on the northern frontier in the years immediately preceding the construction of the Wall. Many of the documents are about food and other supplies. They list a wide variety of food including, wheat, barley, bread, pork, ham, bacon, bacon-lard, pork-fat, roe-deer, venison, chickens, fish-sauce, oysters, gruel, apples, eggs, honey, oil, peppers and spices, as well as wine and beer. There are also references to the ox herds at the wood, Candidus in charge of the pigs, and the brewer. Amongst the clothes recorded are robes, vests, tunics, an overcoat, boots, sandals, socks and underpants. Blankets, a coverlet and a bedspread are listed, as are plates, dishes, bowls, vinegar bowls, bread-baskets, eggcups and a lamp. Supply could be a problem, with the state of the roads to Catterick in the winter being a cause of concern. Wagons are mentioned, and axles and spokes. Soldiers are recorded building a bath-house and a hospital, while amongst the raw materials listed are stones, rubble, lime, clay, lead and timber. Not all soldiers in the regiment based at the fort were there all the time. A report on the current strength of the unit, prepared in the 90s, records soldiers being at *Coria* (Corbridge) and as far away as London. Other soldiers were sick, wounded or suffering from inflammation of the eye, a common complaint. Only a third of the unit was at Vindolanda and fit for service. Several tablets are requests for leave, while one is a letter of recommendation. Amongst the writing tablets found at Carlisle one concerns the issuing of wheat and barley to the 16 decurions of the cavalry regiment stationed there, while another is about missing lances.

The writing tablets also cast light on those people normally almost invisible to us, women, children and slaves. The correspondence of two commanding officers' wives, Claudia Severa and Sulpicia Lepidina, has produced the earliest known example of writing in Latin by a woman. Two lines from Virgil's *Aeneid* are probably part of a child's exercise: archaeological evidence indicates the presence of five or six children aged between two and ten in the commanding officer's house.

At least two slaves are mentioned by name at Vindolanda, and it is well known that soldiers as well as officers owned slaves. Some slaves might be freed, such as Victor the Moor, the freedman of Numerianus, cavalryman in the First Cavalry Regiment of Asturians based at South Shields, a site which has also yielded a tombstone to Regina of the Catuvellauni, the freedwoman and wife of Barathes of Palmyra. Such references indicate the cosmopolitan nature of society on the north-west frontier of the Roman empire.

HEIGHT ABOVE SEA-LEVEL OF PRINCIPAL POINTS ON THE WALL

These are taken from Ordnance Survey maps of Northumberland and Cumbria

	metres	feet
Wallsend	28.95	95
Newcastle Keep	28.65	94
Newcastle Bridge	7.01	23
Benwell	126.50	415
Chapel House	103.38	371
Rudchester	138.91	449
Harlow Hill	139.87	495
Down Hill	203.05	666
Halton	185.82	610
MC 23 (Stanley)	261.12	860
St. Oswald's	227.07	745
Chesters	73.15	240
Limestone Corner	250.85	823
Carrawburgh	208.98	785
Sewingshields Crags	325.52	1,068
Housesteads	259.08	850
Hotbank Crag	327.15	1,074
Cat Stairs	294.32	900
Winshields	370.90	1,230
Great Chesters	210.31	690
Mucklebank Crag	261.12	860
Carvoran	182.88	700
Willowford Bridge	99.70	360
Birdoswald	156.97	515
Pike Hill	164.90	541
Hare Hill	130.15	427
King Water	42.67	140
Walton	75.59	248
Castlesteads	53.95	177
Newtown of Irthington	67.97	223
Stanwix	33.53	110
River Eden	10.67	35
Beaumont	22.86	75
Burgh-by-Sands	19.81	65
Drumburgh	21.37	70
Bowness-on-Solway	16.46	54

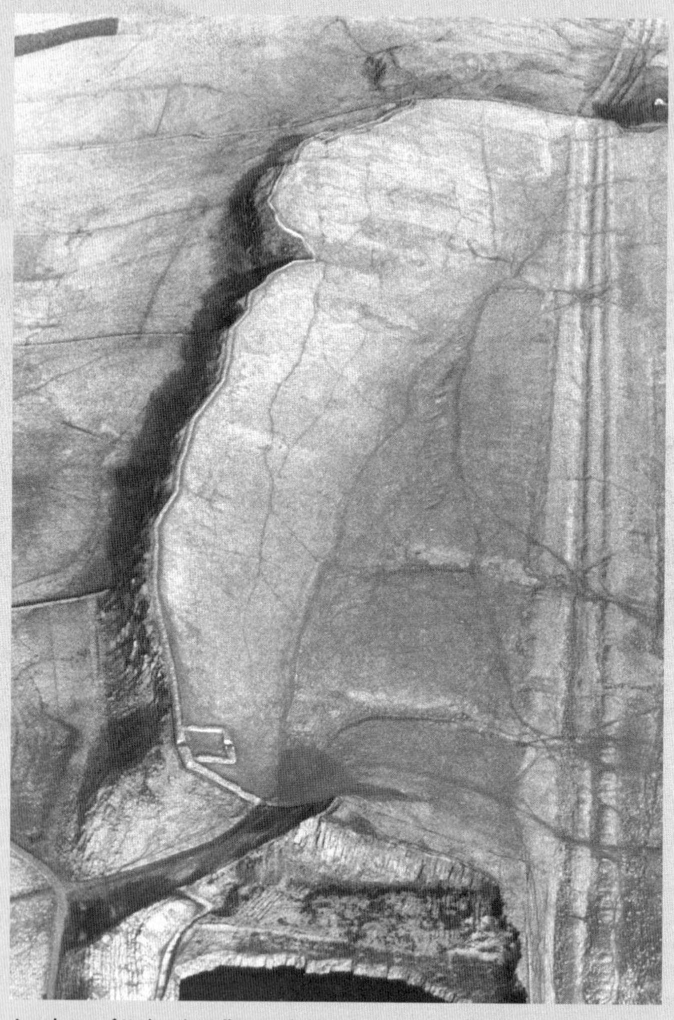

Aerial view of Hadrian's Wall at Cawfields looking east. The Wall follows the line of the crags to the left, while the Vallum takes the lower ground to the right.
In the foreground is MC 42 (Cawfields). The quarry, now disused, has removed a section of the Wall.

CHAPTER 2

A GENERAL ACCOUNT OF THE WORKS

THE STANEGATE

Well before the construction of the Wall, forts existed on the Tyne-Solway isthmus. In a strategic position at the head of the Solway Estuary lay Carlisle. Tree-ring dating has indicated that the timbers used to build this fort were felled in the winter of 72/3. The foundation of the base at Corbridge where Dere Street, the road from the south, crossed the River Tyne is not so closely dated: excavation has demonstrated that it was occupied during the years 75-90. These two forts were linked by a road now known by its medieval name, the Stanegate. The base at Corbridge was succeeded by a fort a little over a kilometre to the east (this site is now in the care of English Heritage) in or shortly after 85. About the same time a fort was established at Vindolanda. Pottery would also support the erection of a fort at Nether Denton, roughly half way between Carlisle and Vindolanda, in the late first century. The spacing between these four forts, 22 km (14 miles), was roughly a day's march. An additional fort at Carvoran between Vindolanda and Nether Denton was probably related to its position at the head of the road known as the Maiden Way.

There is evidence for rebuilding at Corbridge, Vindolanda and Carlisle in or shortly after 103-5, while about the same time new forts were placed on the isthmus. One was at Brampton Old Church roughly halfway between Nether Denton and Carlisle. It has been argued that it ought to have been balanced by another installation at Newbrough between Corbridge and Vindolanda but no fort of the right date has been located and none may ever have existed. Two other additions were rather different, the 'small forts' at Haltwhistle Burn and Throp. The former is more extensively excavated and contained several buildings but insufficient to hold a complete unit. West of Carlisle, Kirkbride dates to this time and perhaps one of the large forts at Burgh-by-Sands strategically placed beside an important ford across the Solway estuary. To the east of Corbridge, Washingwells at Whickham, undated but with two periods of defences revealed by aerial photography, faced east rather than north.

There are also four stone towers known on the isthmus, two later incorporated into the Wall as T 45a (Walltown) and Pike Hill tower: both may date to the early years of Hadrian's reign. The other two, at Mains Rigg between Throp and Nether Denton and at Birdoswald, are both undated. There is a distinction between these sites in that the latter two are surrounded by a rampart and ditch, while Pike Hill and T 45a stand alone. This has led to the suggestion that these two towers were part of the original plan for the Wall, perhaps being constructed separately in order to provide early lookout posts.

The greatest concentration of towers, small forts and forts lay in the relatively short sector of 29 km (18 miles) from Vindolanda to Brampton Old Church: the reason for this is not known. It was perhaps recognition of the failure of existing arrangements on the isthmus which led to the construction of the Wall. Several forts were abandoned when the Wall was built, including Kirkbride, Brampton Old Church, Haltwhistle Burn and Throp, though Carlisle, Vindolanda, Corbridge and perhaps others, continued in use.

HADRIAN'S WALL

Hadrian's Wall had a complicated building history. The first plan appears to have been for a stone wall, 10 Roman feet (3 m) wide, from the lower Tyne to the River Irthing, a distance of 49 Roman miles (72 km), and a turf rampart 20 Roman feet (6 m) wide for the remaining 31 miles (45 km) to Bowness-on-Solway. At every mile (1.6 km) there was a fortified gate (a milecastle) and in between two towers or turrets. Together with a tower over the north gate of each milecastle, these formed a line of watch-towers 1/3 Roman mile, i.e. 495 m (540 yards), apart. This linear barrier and its attendant structures formed the system of frontier control. No forts were placed on the linear barrier in this phase, forts being retained on the Stanegate, though it is probable that this plan included outpost forts. The milecastles and towers are known to have continued beyond the west end of the Wall at Bowness down the Cumbrian Coast for about 32 km (20 miles), but with no wall.

While work was still in progress, it was decided to make two significant changes to the Wall. The first was to erect a new series of forts along the whole line, on average 11.6 km (7⅓ miles) apart. The first forts were mainly built astride the Wall; later ones lay behind, though still attached. Probably at the same time it was decided to add an earthwork, the 'Vallum', behind the Wall from Newcastle to Bowness. Both the position of the forts astride the Wall and the Vallum are unique features not replicated on any other Roman frontier. A further change probably flowed from these actions, the decision to reduce the width of the Stone Wall from 10 Roman feet (3 m) to 8 feet (2.4 m) or less.

Hadrian's Wall, for 100 km (66 miles) of its length, lies on the northern slopes of the valleys of the Rivers Tyne and Irthing which together form the Tyne-Solway gap. Its eastern end, Wallsend, lies 10 km (6 miles) upstream from the mouth of the River Tyne, at the bend where the Long Reach turns sharply south into the Bill Reach. The Wall then cuts across the wide loop of the river from Wallsend to Newcastle. Here it turns sharply north to run up a long ridge in a west-north-west direction heading for Limestone Corner (misnamed because the rock here is actually dolerite), its most northerly point, in a series of straight stretches, never more than 5 km (3 miles) long, changing direction slightly on each high point. At Limestone Corner, the Wall turned southwards, heading west-south-west for Stanwix and the crossing of the Eden at Carlisle. However, the countryside through which it passed was far from uniform. At Sewingshields (33) the Wall moved onto the crags and utilised them for 21 km (13 miles): here its line became sinuous. West of Banks (52), the Wall runs along the ridge overlooking the Irthing Valley to the south and the open country dropping down into Eskdale to the north. After crossing the River Eden, the Wall swings north, zigzagging across the low lying ground, and then the marshes behind the River Eden and the Solway Firth. Its termination at Bowness was probably to control as many fording points as possible.

Examination of the eastern end of the Wall, from Benwell to the River North Tyne, suggests that the line of Hadrian's Wall was largely planned from east to west. Within that, it appears to have been set out in a series of alignments usually from 1.6 to 4.8 km (1 to 3 miles) long. Particular features in the landscape caused some deviations from these straight lines.

The Wall passed through different types of countryside, and it might be expected that this was reflected in the local vegetation when it was constructed. The discovery of plough marks beneath the Wall and the existence of considerable evidence for settlement, farming and other human activity in the area of the Wall for centuries before the Romans, together with the testimony of pollen analysis, indicate that most of the Wall was erected through an open, farmed landscape, with relatively few trees. The very fact that part of the Wall was constructed of turf emphasises the existence of many acres of pasture, presumably grazed by cattle and sheep. The lack of available timber may have played a part in the decision to construct the Wall in stone or turf, unlike the 550-km-long German frontier which was a timber palisade.

It may be presumed that the Wall was built through land which was already owned. While the army may have requisitioned this land, it may also be assumed that it was paid for: the Emperor Domitian (81-96) compensated farmers for the loss of their crops when he constructed the frontier in Germany.

THE STONE WALL

The Stone Wall is not of a uniform width. Both 'broad' and 'narrow' gauges have been recorded and appear to date to the reign of Hadrian. Later repairs resulted in an even narrower Wall. The Stone Wall was built from a northern setting out line and narrowing always took place on the southern face.

The foundations of the Broad Wall are normally about 3.20 m (10 ft 6 in) wide (though variations from 2.97 m/9 ft 9 in to 3.50 m/ 11 ft 6 in have been recorded) and consist of a layer of rough flat flags bedded in clay. They can be set on the ground or placed in a shallow trench perhaps 10 cm (4 in deep). Where the Wall was to be constructed on a north-south slope, an attempt was often made to create a level terrace. In spite of such measures, the superstructure sometimes settled with catastrophic results which included the collapse of one or both faces of the Wall. Indeed, the foundations were so slight for the superstructure which rested on them that the flags sometimes cracked on the line of the front and/or rear face of the Wall.

Above the foundations one or more footing courses were laid. An offset on each face then reduced the width to an average of 2.90 m (9 ft 6 in) though varying in width by up to 30 cm (1 ft): this was close to 10 Roman feet (*pedes monetales*). The offset occurred either after the first course (standard A), or third or fourth course (standard B).

The Narrow Wall is usually 2.29 m (7 ft 6 in) wide, though 1.98 m (6 ft 6 in) has been recorded. It is possible that it was intended that this Wall should be 8 Roman feet (2.4 m) thick, the width recorded by Bede. The foundations, commensurately wide, were of rough stones set in clay and sealed by a layer of clay. East of Newcastle foundations vary from 2.29 m to 3.10 m (7 ft 6 in to 10 ft 2 in) in width, though are normally about 2.44 m (8 ft) wide, and the Wall above 2.29 m (7 ft 6 in).

Table 2: Normal widths of the foundations and Wall

	Foundations	Wall
Stone Wall		
Broad	2.74 m-3.20 m/9 ft-10 ft 6 in*	2.74 m-2.97 m/9 ft-9 ft 9 in
Narrow	2.39 m-2.69 m/7 ft 10 in-8 ft 10 in	2.13 m-2.36 m/7 ft-7 ft 9 in
East of Newcastle	2.29 m-2.64 m/7 ft 6 in-8 ft 8 in°	2.22 m/7 ft 3 in
Wallsend fort-river	2.29 m/7 ft 6 in	1.98 m/6 ft 6 in
Turf Wall sector		
MCs 49-54	2.44 m-2.74 m/8 ft-9 ft	2.31 m-2.44 m/7 ft 6 in-8 ft
MCs 54-80 (Intermediate Wall)	2.55 m-3.20 m/8 ft 4 in-10 ft 6 in	2.44 m-2.90 m/8 ft-9 ft 6 in
Very narrow ('Severan')		1.52 m-1.90 m/5 ft-6 ft 3 in

*At MC 27 (Brunton) foundation widths of 3.35 m (11 ft) and 3.50 m (11 ft 6 in) were recorded. The sector MCs 22-27 has also produced some of the narrowest widths of between 1.68 m and 1.96 m (5 ft 6 in and 6 ft 5 in).
°Near St Francis Community Centre foundations 3.10 m (10 ft 2 in) wide were recorded.

The Wall (and most of its attendant structures) was not built to a high standard. Its masonry may be described as squared rubble. The stones usually measure about 15 by 25 cm (6 by 10 in), though much larger blocks occur in places between MC 7 and the North Tyne. The relative lack of masons' chippings indicates that the stones were mainly dressed elsewhere, presumably at the quarry. The facing stones were tapered at the back to aid the building work. The core could be of clay, or soil and stones: the original core was rarely mortared. It would appear that only the facing stones were bedded in mortar, and then not always: a light brown mortar of poor quality was used. Sometimes evidence has been recorded for layering of the core material while at times its stones were placed in herring-bone style. Evidence also exists for the Wall having been built in horizontal stages, about 1.5 m (5 ft) deep separated in places by a thin course of stones. In general, the courses follow the contours of the ground, but on steep slopes they remain horizontal, being stepped down the slope.

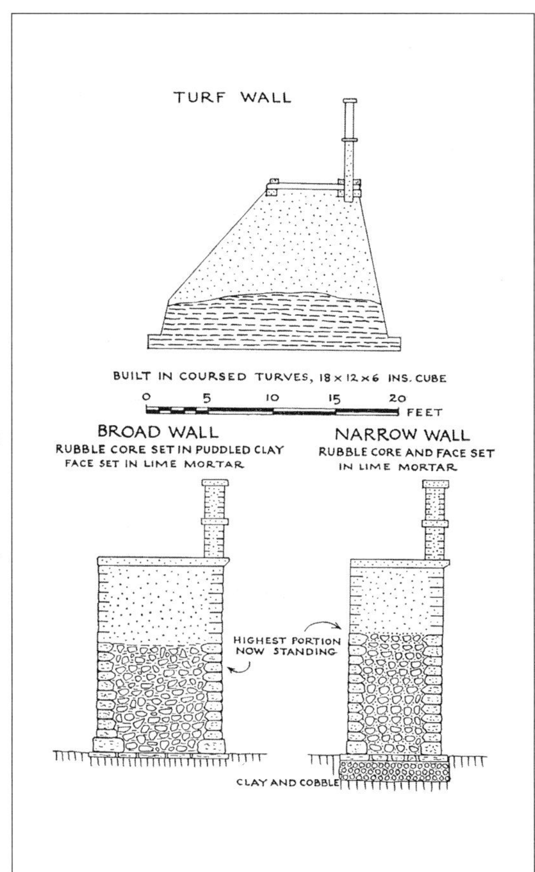

Schematic sections though the Turf and Stone Walls, drawn by I. A. Richmond.

Evidence has been found in various places which suggests that the bare appearance of the Wall was changed by the application of plaster. At Denton, a cream-coloured lightweight mortar was used, either to provide an overall render or flush pointing. At Heddon, flecks of white mortar can still be seen on the faces of several stones. Some mortar still adhered to the outer face of the north wall of MC 64 (Drawdykes).

Archaeological evidence from the central sector suggests that the Wall here may have been lime-washed, though the possibility of lime leaching out of the mortar cannot be ruled out. The application of a render to stone walls was common in the Roman period, and sometimes red lines to simulate stone work were applied.

The steps at MC 48 (Poltross Burn) offer the best evidence for the height of the Wall: 3.66 m (12 ft) on the inside and, owing to the slope of the ground, 4.27 m (14 ft) on the outside. Bede, who lived close to the eastern end of the Wall, recorded that its height was 12 feet (3.66 m). Chamfered stones such as might have been used as a projecting string-course have been found in several locations but in themselves do not prove the existence of a wall-walk, the evidence for which is discussed below. The erection of a wall of this height would have required scaffolding, as would the individual structures.

The Broad Foundation is recorded throughout the whole length of the Stone Wall, though not continuously. East of T 6b (Benwell Hill), the distinctive foundation normally associated with the Broad Wall was found in front of the Mining Institute in central Newcastle in 1952, but only the south face was located, while in the area of T 0b (St Francis) the Wall conformed to the width of the Broad Wall, but was erected on the clay-and-rubble foundations used on the Narrow Wall: the width here may be due to later repairs following subsidence, but could equally be original. The Broad Foundation appears to be present from West Benwell (6b-7), and probably central Newcastle, through to the River North Tyne. It is generally surmounted by the Broad Wall: while narrower widths of 2.23 to 2.59 m (7 ft 4 in to 8 ft 6 in) were noted by antiquarians in this sector, none has been recorded in modern excavations and it is possible that they relate to later rebuilding. Between Portgate (22) and the North Tyne (27) several points of reduction from broad to narrow gauge are known. In the sector between the Rivers North Tyne and Irthing the Broad

Foundation is found much more sporadically, with only a few stretches of Broad Wall recorded towards the western limit of this sector. It appears that all the milecastles and turrets were planned to have been erected to broad gauge (T 44b (Mucklebank) is the exception), though some were completed to narrow gauge.

The points of reduction from broad to narrow gauge could be either horizontal or vertical. These changes allow us to determine the order of construction. The foundation was, naturally, laid first and this operation included the laying of drains through the Wall, at least at Planetrees (26-26a). The milecastles and turrets were begun early in the sequence, to be linked by the Wall. The gates were the first elements to be erected at milecastles. The lack of Broad Wall in the central sector suggests that the Wall builders had fallen some way behind the foundation and structure gangs. Before the Wall could be completed to the broad gauge, the order came to reduce its thickness and complete it at a width of about 8 Roman feet (2.4 m).

These differences allow further conclusions to be reached about the building sequence for the Wall. Work in the sector 7-22 appears to have been most advanced before the decision to narrow the Wall, and this section was therefore presumably started first. Dere Street lies at the west end of this sector and it seems possible that this is where the legionaries started building: this is the point where, marching from the south, they first reached the Wall (and where later the distances marked on milestones were measured from). Not all the 24 km (15 miles) from 7 to 22 were built in Broad Wall: some milecastles and other parts of the Wall were completed or rebuilt to a narrower gauge.

The eastern terminus was obviously Wallsend, but the absence of Broad Wall east of Newcastle led to the argument that the original intention was to end the Wall at Newcastle, it only later being extended 14.6 km (4.5 miles) downstream to

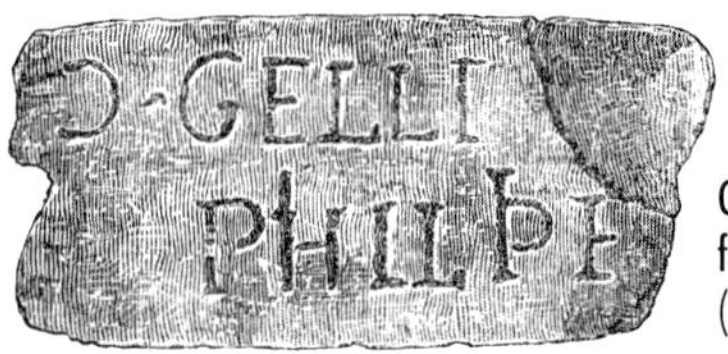

Centurial stone of Gellius Phillipus found at Sewingshields.
(172 x 381 mm)

Wallsend. A review of the evidence in 2001, however, led to a suggestion that the termination was always planned to be at Wallsend, though this eastern sector was not completed until after the Wall had been narrowed.

Inscriptions not only indicate that the Wall was built by soldiers from the three legions of Britain but also demonstrate how the work was organised. Stones marked with the names of centuries, cohorts and, occasionally, legions have been found along the Wall. Analysis of these "centurial stones" has led to the suggestion that centuries built lengths of about 41 m (45 yards) each; this, however, is going beyond the available evidence in view of the complexity of the building process. There is, for example, no evidence that the one century built the whole of a particular section of the Wall from bottom to top: perhaps the centurial stones relate only to one horizontal building layer. The distance of 112 or 113 feet (34.14 and 34.44 m) occurs on other building stones.

In many places the Wall was later rebuilt, often to an even narrower gauge, using a hard white mortar: this rebuilding is generally ascribed to the Severan period, and this date is supported by late-second-century pottery associated with the repairs. The extent of this rebuilding may help to account for the late Roman sources which attribute the construction of the Wall to the Emperor Septimius Severus.

THE TURF WALL

The Turf Wall, from Harrow's Scar (MC 49) to Bowness, was 6 m (20 ft) thick at base and formed of cut turves laid in courses. It is not clear why this sector was built in a different material from the rest of the Wall. It is usually related to the absence of limestone, which was used to make mortar, west of the Red Rock fault which occurs just west of T 53b (Craggle Hill). However, the Wall could have been bonded with clay as certainly occurs further east, so arguments based on the lack of limestone may be discounted. The poor quality of the 'soft' Cumberland sandstone has been advanced as a reason for the use of turf. However, it may be noted that the towers were of stone rather than timber while the local stone was used later when the Wall was rebuilt in stone. A requirement to complete this section urgently has been argued, but cannot be substantiated. It may be noted that it is only north of the turf sector of Hadrian's Wall that outpost forts are known at this time, which might be related to a requirement for extra defence, though their presence has alternatively been linked to the possibility of this area being occupied by part of the Brigantes, separated from the rest of the province by the construction of the linear barrier. The question relating to the use of turf may be turned on its head. It was more normal to build frontiers in timber, earth or turf: Hadrian's Wall is unusual in having so much of its length constructed in stone. This may have been a personal decision on the part of Hadrian who wished that the great Wall would serve as a memorial to himself and his frontier policies. The use of stone, alternatively, may reflect a lack of available timber, or indeed of good turf.

A section dug at High House (MC 50) in 1927 revealed that the turf rampart was placed on a base three to four layers of turf high. Above the base, the front sloped at an angle of about 4 to 1 (75%) while the back appears to have been almost vertical in its lowest courses, though it is thought to have then changed to a more gentle slope. The best estimate is a height of 3.66 m (12 ft) for the Turf Wall. Excavations below the upcast mound north of the ditch and below the Vallum mounds have demonstrated that these areas had been previously stripped of turf, presumably to build the Wall.

At T 70a (Beaumont) and at MC 72 (Burgh-by-Sands) and running thence westwards for 500 m (⅓ mile), the Turf Wall was erected on a raft of cobbles 5.64-5.79 m (18 ft 6 in-19 ft) wide framed by kerbs of slightly larger stones. A similar foundation of cobbles was found under the north wall of MC 53 (Banks Burn). It is possible that these features result from the activities of one legion building on the Wall rather than responses to local circumstances. In boggy ground the Turf Wall appears to have been underpinned by piles.

The replacement of the Turf Wall in stone appears to have taken place in two stages with the sector from the River Irthing to just west of MC 54 (Randylands) being built during the reign of Hadrian, and the remainder replaced after the return from the Antonine Wall: this is indicated by comparison of the pottery from the Turf Wall structures and their replacements. The new Hadrianic Stone Wall was about the same width as the Narrow Wall, but with no offsets. It was on the same line as the Turf Wall except from Harrow's Scar (49) to Wallbowers (51), where the Stone Wall took a course further north. The reason may have been to provide further space on the plateau behind Birdoswald, though it has also been suggested that the new line was to bring this stretch into visibility from the new fort at Birdoswald.

The rest of the replacement Stone Wall appears to be a little wider and is generally termed the Intermediate Wall, that is intermediate between Broad and Narrow Walls. This section appears to have been rebuilt after the re-occupation of the Wall in the 160s, though a date as late as the reign of the Emperor Septimius Severus (193-211) has been suggested.

In some places, by MCs 73 (Dykesfield) and 78 (Kirkland), the Stone Wall was erected immediately behind the demolished Turf Wall. Elsewhere it sat on the demolished remains of the Turf Wall. The Stone Wall was normally placed about 1 m (3 ft) back from the front of this turf base. Two explanations have been offered: that it was for structural reasons, this location

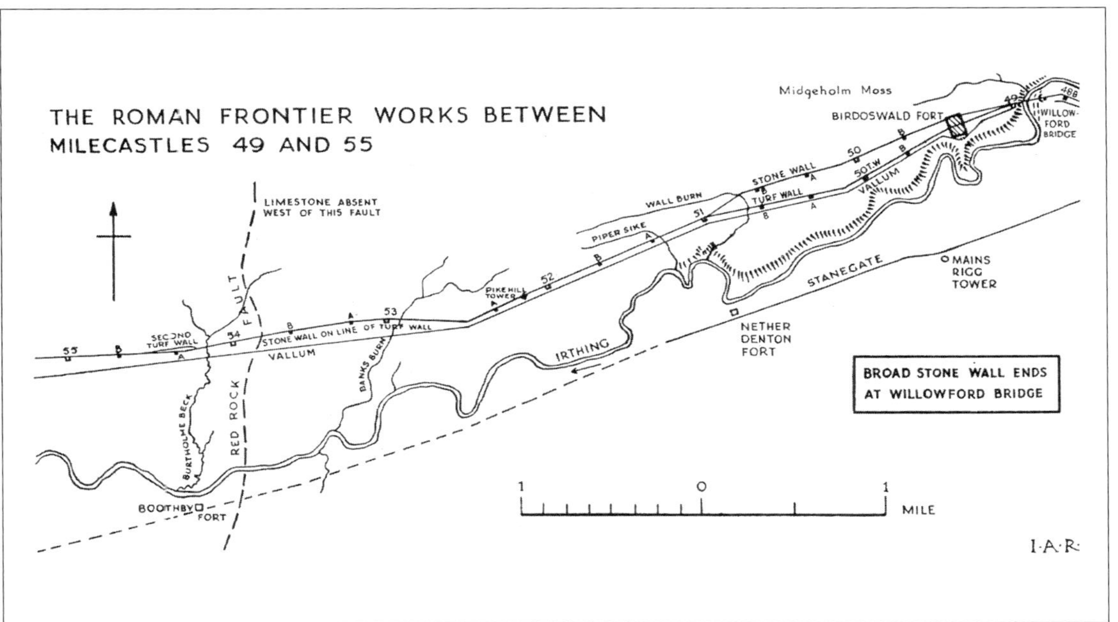

Map of Hadrian's Wall between MC 49 and MC 55, drawn by I. A. Richmond.

placing the Stone Wall firmly on the most compacted, and therefore stable, remains of the Turf Wall; or that it was to line up the top of the Stone Wall with putative doors giving access from the first floors of the turrets onto a wall-walk. Variations are known: at MC 72 (Fauld Farm) the Stone Wall was only 30 cm (1 ft) behind the front of the cobble foundation of the Turf Wall while at T 52a (Banks East) the north face of the Wall is flush with the north face of the turret. The turrets which had formerly been encased within the Turf Wall now projected to the south of the replacement Stone Wall in the same manner as the other Stone Wall turrets.

THE DITCH

A ditch was excavated north of the Wall for much of its length. It is only absent where there are crags, though there it reappears in the gaps, along the Solway marshes and probably also along the bluff above the River Eden west of Carlisle, unless here it has been eroded away. V-shaped, the average width is 8.23-8.53 m (27-28 ft) and depth 2.74 m (9 ft), as indicated by well-preserved sections excavated below forts. There are, however, considerable variations and it would appear that the ditch was cut as steep as the subsoil conditions permitted. Sometimes one side was markedly steeper than the other. Little evidence exists on the details of the construction of the ditch. Two sectors where the ditch was unfinished offer some guidance. At Limestone Corner (MC 30), the work seems to have been proceeding eastwards, but on Winshields (MC 40) in the opposite direction.

The contents of the ditch were tipped out onto the north side and generally smoothed out to form a broad mound, 10-15 m (30-50 ft) wide, tapering gently to the north. This has been called a counterscarp bank, upcast or outer mound, but perhaps glacis would be a more correct name. In some areas the soil was heaped up into a triangular-shaped mound (Wall miles 26-29, 32-33, 47-48). This usually occurs where the land is falling away to the north, and the intention appears to have been to heighten the north lip of the ditch. In the crags sector, where the ditch re-appears in gaps, the spoil is often formed into a small bank. At Limestone Corner (MC 30) and at High House (MC 50 SW) a low mound has been identified running along the north lip of the ditch: it may have been a marking-out mound though it could also be the debris from later cleaning of the ditch. There are many places where the excavation of the ditch and the smoothing of the counterscarp bank was not completed. This includes Limestone Corner (MC 30) and Cockmount Hill and Allolee (T 43a-b). West of Portgate (MC 22) and at Appletree (T 51b) the material lifted out of the ditch in baskets survives as a series of small mounds, never smoothed out by the Wall builders. In some places the stone dug out of the ditch was probably used in the core of the Wall.

Little excavation of the upcast mound has taken place. At Tarraby, near Carlisle, two phases of construction were recorded.

The berm (the space between the Wall and the ditch) on the Stone Wall is normally about 6 m (20 ft) wide. On the Turf Wall the width of the berm is generally about 2.44 m (8 ft) wide, but varies from 1.82 m (6 ft) to between 9 and 11.3 m (29-37 ft) at MCs 65 (Tarraby) and 72 (Fauld Farm) and 12 m (40 ft) at MC 54 (Randylands).

At several places, including Wallsend, Byker and Throckley (0-12), pits have been found on the berm. There were three rows of pits at Byker, each pit holding two stakes, and showing evidence of later re-cutting, perhaps in order to remove the stakes. The stakes provided extra obstacles such as forked branches to hinder illicit intruders. At Throckley the line of pits turned inwards towards the site of the turret (T 11b). This suggests that the berm narrowed at this point and the same phenomenon has been noticed at T 26b (Brunton), where it is still visible, and at a number of turrets in the eastern sector of the Turf Wall.

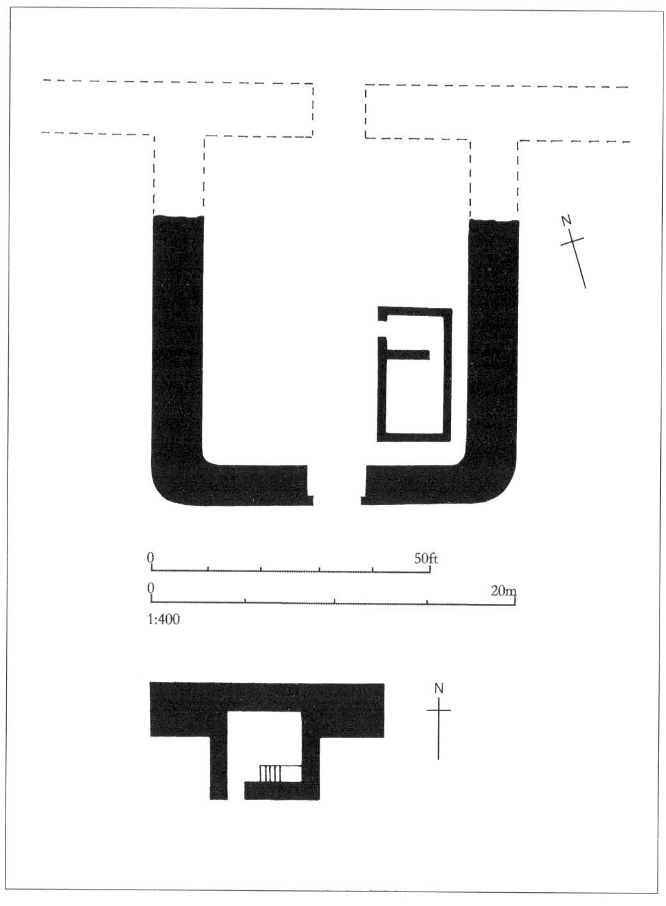

Milecastle and turret to the same scale:
MC 9 (Chapel House) and T 18a (Wallhouses East).

MILECASTLES

A gateway through the Wall was provided at every Roman mile (1480 m), though the distance is subject to variation depending, for example, upon the terrain or, it would appear, the need for communicate back to the forts on the Stanegate. The gate was protected by a small defended enclosure known since the early eighteenth century as a milecastle. These were usually 60 by 50 Roman feet (17.76 by 14.80 m), with an internal area of about 270 m^2. The main axis could run north-south (long) or west-east (short). The walls were laid out from a marking-out line, which might be the inside face or the outside face of the milecastle side walls. The original plan appears to have been for the side walls to be broad, so if the exterior marking-out line was used and narrow walls built, the interior space would be larger than 60 by 50 Roman feet. It is also clear that the north gate, and perhaps the south gate, was built first. The external southern corners of milecastles were always rounded: the interiors are usually squared.

Two milecastles, 47 (Chapel House) and 48 (Poltross Burn), were larger than all others on the Stone Wall, measuring 70 by 60 Roman feet (20 by 17.76 m = 395 m^2). The reason for this is not known. The Wall ditch is unusually large in this sector, while the adjacent Turf Wall milecastles to the west are also large, hinting at a specific problem, perhaps of security, hereabouts. An alternative suggestion is that these two were built first, the size of milecastles being reduced thereafter.

Both long- and short-axis milecastles are known on the Turf Wall. The space within one milecastle on the Turf Wall, MC 52 (Bankshead), exceeds all others by 20% while its stone successor was over twice the normal size. The proximity of an extra tower at Pike Hill between T 52a (Banks East) and T 52b (Banks), and the need to provide additional accommodation for the soldiers based there, has been taken to explain this.

Milecastles on the Stone Wall were provided with stone walls, while those on the Turf Wall were enclosed by turf ramparts. When the Turf Wall was rebuilt in stone, the turf milecastle ramparts were similarly replaced, though the walls of their Stone Wall replacements did not always respect the position of their turf predecessors, sometimes lying to one side rather than on top of the turfwork. The ground might be specially prepared by the laying of a platform, of clay at MC 9 (Chapel House) and gravel and turf at MC 79 (Solway House), or the interior levelled as at MCs 40 (Winshields) and 78 (Kirkland).

Nine milecastles have provided evidence for internal buildings (MCs 9, 35, 37, 39, 47, 48, 50, 54 and 79). The usual arrangement seems to have been for at least one small building, of stone on the Stone Wall, timber on the Turf Wall, measuring about 7.62-9.14 m (25-30 ft) by 3.66-4.57 m (12-15 ft) and containing two rooms. The building is usually a little larger than the two-roomed *contubernium*, the barrack-room of an auxiliary barrack-block. It is presumed to have served the same purpose. A military treatise describes how eight soldiers occupied a tent during campaigning and accordingly about the same number may have lived in a barrack-room. The large MCs 47 (Chapel House) and 48 (Poltross Burn) contained two buildings, one on each side of a central road. Each building is about twice the size of the block in the other milecastles and the number of soldiers based here may have been commensurately larger, perhaps 32 as opposed to eight. It has been suggested that not only was the size of later milecastles reduced, but so also was the number of troops based in each, resulting in smaller internal buildings.

The other features which have been found in milecastles include hearths and ovens, and, in MC 48 (Poltross Burn), a staircase with three steps surviving and part of a fourth; this will have provided access to the tower over the north gate or a wall-walk, or both. Not surprisingly, the largest quantity of finds at milecastles are objects associated with cooking and eating: quern stones, pottery (especially storage jars) and knives. Weapons, mainly spearheads, have been found at several milecastles but are relatively rare. Objects associated with writing are not present, with the exception of part of a writing tablet at MC 50 TW (High House). Gaming boards and counters are found in small numbers. Two milecastles, MC 40 (Winshields) and MC 48 (Poltross Burn), have produced harness pieces and if horses were quartered in some milecastles, the amount of space available for soldiers would have been reduced.

Both gateways of each milecastle were of the same plan. There was presumably a tower over the north gate in order to provide a continuous chain of towers along the Wall. As the south gate is always of the same plan as the north (with the single exception of MC 50 TW (High House)), there may also have been a tower over the south gate, though the fact that this would have been superfluous renders its existence unlikely. It has been suggested that the existence of more timber posts at the north gate of MC 50 TW (High House) than at the south indicates that there was a tower over one and not the other, but the six posts at the south gate would have been sufficient for a tower if one was required.

Different gate plans have been long recognised in the stone milecastles of Hadrian's Wall. They all conform to three basic types, type IV being a variant of type II. The variants appear to relate to the different legionary gangs constructing the Wall. Five inscriptions have been found at milecastles, two at MC 38 (Hotbank) which suggests that each gate was surmounted by a record of its construction.

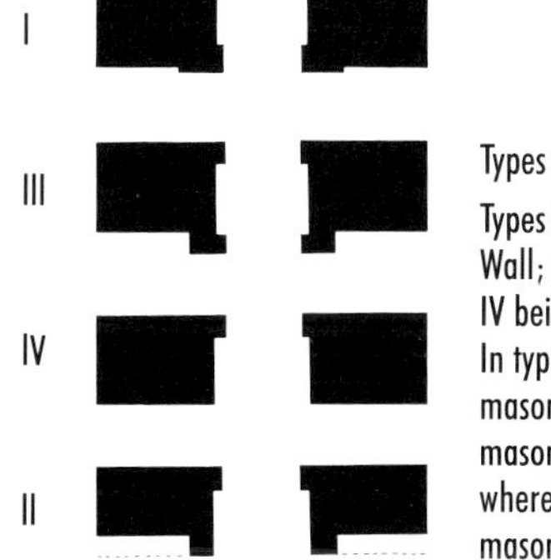

Types of milecastle gates

Types I, III and IV were all built for the Broad Wall; type II, at the bottom, is a variant of type IV being found only on the Narrow Wall. In type I the piers and passage walls are in large masonry; in type III the piers are in large masonry but the passage walls in small masonry, whereas in types II and IV all are in small masonry.

Five milecastles (9, 23, 25, 29 and 51) are known to have had ditches: others may yet be found through geophysical prospection or excavation. A causeway across the ditch can be seen in front of MCs 25 (Codlawhill) and 50 TW (High House) while archaeological evidence suggests that one formerly existed at MC 54 (Randylands) before being removed. No other causeways survive today. A recent survey has, however, suggested that vestigial remains hint at the prior existence of causeways at several milecastles indicating that they were originally provided at all, only to be later removed. The placing of forts on the Wall and the construction of the Vallum, which channeled movement through gates at forts, would be an appropriate time to remove crossings at milecastles, but we cannot be certain.

At the end of the first period of occupation many milecastle gates had their pivots broken. This suggests that the gates were removed when Hadrian's Wall was abandoned for the Antonine Wall. The gates were replaced when the Wall was re-occupied, often entailing renewing the thresholds. Later, the entrances of many milecastles were narrowed in width: the lack of wear on the western collar of the north gate of MC 10 (Walbottle Dene) suggests that here only one leaf had normally been used. Milecastles often continued in occupation into the fourth century.

There were some gates in other parts of the Wall. At Portgate, where Dere Street (the modern A68) passed through the Wall, part of a gate has been found, and a second presumably lay on the road leading north from Carlisle. A gate was also later created at the Knag Burn beside Housesteads.

TURRETS

Between each milecastle lay two turrets, an average 495 m (540 yards apart). Whether on the stone or turf sections of the Wall, all were of stone. However, those on the former were bonded with the Stone Wall, while the latter were erected as free-standing structures, subsequently completely embedded in the thickness of the Turf Wall. In the turf sector, the north and south turret walls were wider than the east and west walls, but were narrowed at a plinth course, presumably to reflect the slope of the Turf Wall itself.

The turrets normally measured about 5.79 m (19 ft = 20 Roman ft) square, 3.67-3.96 m (12-13 ft) internally. Differences between turrets have been noticed, including the width of their walls (0.81-0.91 m/2 ft 8 in to 3 ft and 1.09-1.22 m/3 ft 7 in to 4 ft), the position of the door (to east or west), and type of threshold (monolithic or not). Some differences appear to relate to the different legionary builders.

The walls were normally mortared, the use of clay in T 19b (West Clarewood) being an exception. The foundations were not especially deep, unlike those at the Pike Hill tower. The doors opened outwards: sometimes paths have been recorded leading to the door. Floors were normally of clay in the first period, usually being flagged thereafter. Evidence that the floor was covered in straw has been found in one turret (T 51b (Lea Hill)) and also a tower on the Cumbrian Coast (T 16b (Mawbray Sandpit)). Many turrets contained, in either the south-west or south-east corner, a stone platform (a platform has also been found in two of the Cumbrian Coast towers), though often these are secondary. The platforms measure 2.13-2.44 m (7-8 ft) by 0.91 m (3 ft); the five steps at T 18a (Wallhouses East) suggest a height of nearly 1 m (3 ft). The steps also point to the purpose of the platforms, the bases for stairs leading to the upper floor(s), placed at right angles to the axis of the platform: stairs are more probable than ladders. At some turrets, an area of flagging lay against the north wall. It has been suggested this was where soldiers slept or ate.

Hearths are a common feature, and might be placed anywhere in the turret, but ovens such as are known at milecastles are not found in turrets. Rather strangely, at two turrets the hearth overlay the door threshold. Inability to close

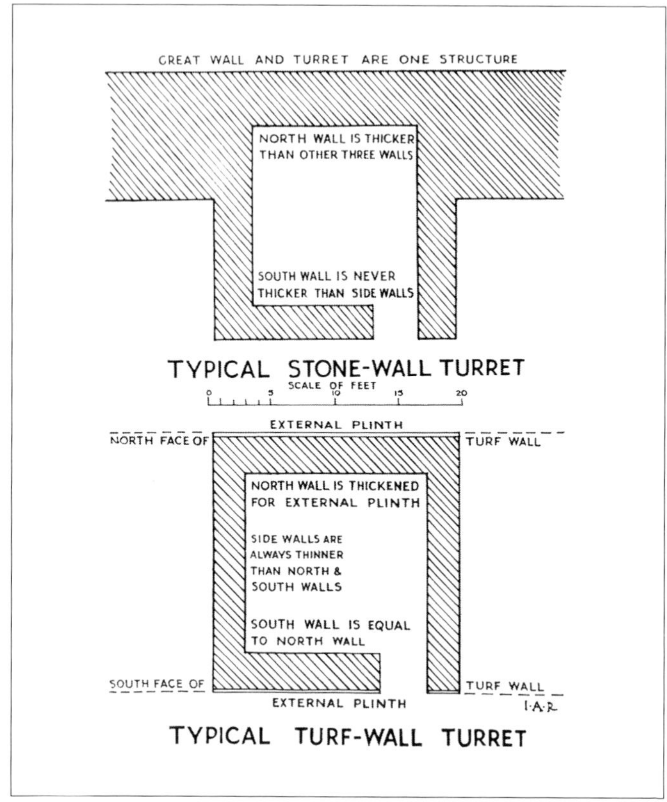

Schematic drawing of turrets, drawn by I. A. Richmond.

(rather than open) the door suggests confidence on the part of the occupants. No keys have been found at turrets, though there are two from towers on the Cumbrian Coast. At three turrets (7b (Denton), 35a (Sewingshields Crags) and 51b (Lea Hill)) small stone boxes set into the ground have been recorded. Turrets have produced a wide range of objects: quern stones, pottery including mixing bowls, cooking pots, jars and *amphorae* (large jars which held a range of products including wine and olives), brooches, gaming boards, counters, knives, spearheads and metal edge bindings probably for shields, but only one arrowhead and three catapult bolts. Bones are known but have been rarely recorded. The finds at some turrets are unusual, such as the fragments of about 50 flagons at T 25b (St Oswald), while Ts 18b (Wallhouses West) and 26a (High Brunton) were used for industrial activity.

At some turrets, stones from door arches or window heads have been found, and, at five, fragments of window glass. The location of pottery outside the east wall of T 7b (Denton) and gaming counters outside the west wall of T 25b (St Oswalds) have been taken to suggest the position of lateral windows. The range of artefacts found at turrets does not include several items such as box fittings and furniture which are found in milecastles and forts and suggests that soldiers did not live there permanently. Rather, the impression is that soldiers were based elsewhere, perhaps at milecastles, and came out to the turrets on rotation. Many excavators have noted the untidy interiors of turrets.

Little evidence survives for the nature of the roof, or indeed the upper parts of turrets. A few stone slates have been found. Tiles are notable for their absence, except the odd fragment. In view of the lack of evidence it is possible that the roof was of an organic material such as shingle or thatch, pyramidal shaped to throw off water. Many turrets have produced no evidence for nails, and when they do occur they tend to be neither large nor numerous; wooden pegs may have been used to secure timber roofs. Flags at Ts 29b (Limestone Bank), 34a (Sewingshields Crag) and 44b (Mucklebank) – 60 cm (2 ft) square and 7-10 cm (3-4 in) thick at the latter – were interpreted as the flooring of the upper storey, flat roof or wall-walk.

The purpose of the turrets was presumably to provide an elevated observation platform rather than just a sentry box. That platform may have been an upper window or a balcony as on the contemporary towers depicted on Trajan's Column, rather than the roof. In order to provide appropriate elevation, it might be expected that the towers were three storeys high. Several milecastles and turrets are not in their theoretical position and it has been argued that they were moved in order to aid communication back to sites on the Stanegate, which, if accepted, emphasises their observation role. The size of the structures and the nature of duties suggest that there may have been four or six soldiers based at each turret.

The later placing of forts on the Wall reduced the importance of the turrets, though none is known to have been abandoned under Hadrian and all appear to have been re-occupied after the withdrawal from the Antonine Wall. Later in the second century, however, most of the turrets in the central sector were abandoned, though elsewhere many are known to have continued in occupation. Those that had a lengthy occupation have often exhibited a distinction in the build-up between the first and second floors, which never contains masonry debris, and that between the floors in the later periods which generally contains masonry debris and ash. While ascribed to enemy action in the past, the greater quantities of building debris may otherwise point to a more thorough rebuilding of these structures later in their lives.

LEGIONARY STYLES OF BUILDING

The plotting of the different types of milecastle, turrets and Wall leads to distinctive patterns. Thus, the 24 km (15 miles) from about MC 7 (Benwell Bank) to MC 22 (Portgate) divides into three 8 km (5 mile) stretches where, in each section, milecastles, turrets and Wall are all of the same type. Further west, the pattern is less distinct for the original arrangements are obscured by subsequent changes. All the known structures from T 22a (Portgate) to T 36a (Kennel Crag) are of the same type. The 19 km (12 miles) from T 36b (Housesteads) to the River Irthing appears to be broken into two sectors at MC 43 (Great Chesters).

Table 3 Legionary styles of building on the Stone Wall

Legion	Wall mile	MC axis	Gate	Setting out line	Turret	Wall
A	12a-17	short	I	internal	broad walls east door	A
B VI ?	7b-12 22a-36a	long	II/IV	internal	narrow walls east door	A
C	17a-22 47-Irthing	long	III	external	narrow walls west door	B

On the Turf Wall the known milecastles of the eastern 8 km (5 miles) from MC 49 (Harrow's Scar) to MC 54 (Randylands) are all long axis, while the turrets here have east doors; T 54a (Garthside) had a west door. MC 64 (Drawdykes) has a short axis while MC 73 (Dykefield) is long. At the west end of the Turf Wall two short-axis milecastles are known at MCs 78 (Kirkland) and 79 (Solway House). This evidence would allow a 5-mile pattern as on the Stone Wall.

Table 4 Legionary styles of building on the Turf Wall

Legion	Wall mile	MC axis	Turret
A	78-79	short	-
B	49-54 -64-	long	east door
C	54a-?	-	west door

The inscriptions discovered at several milecastles and turrets have all been found in those areas where work was disrupted following the decisions to add forts to the Wall line. It is therefore not certain whether these inscriptions relate to the original builders of the structures. As a result we cannot relate any type of structure with confidence to any legion. Notwithstanding that cautionary statement, it is tentatively suggested that type B on the Stone Wall may be the work of the Sixth Legion in view of the discovery of a building stone of that regiment at T 33b (Coesyke), a turret with narrow walls and an east doorway. This is supported by the discovery at T 26b (Brunton) of fragments of pottery probably made by the Sixth Legion near York in the early 120s.

FORTS

In the original plan for the Wall, no forts lay on the Wall line. Some lay close behind on the Stanegate, others on the main roads leading south. During construction of the Wall, there was a radical re-thinking of the way in which the frontier would operate and as a result forts were added to the Wall. They were placed on average just 11.6 km (7⅓ miles) apart. This distance, which is found on other frontiers, was probably chosen because it is half the normal daily march of about 22.4 km (14 miles). The distance was, however, varied to suit local conditions. Thus Benwell was a little east of its correct location, presumably so that it could take advantage of the high point of Benwell Bank, and Chesters was also moved a short distance to the east of its correct position so that it lay beside the River North Tyne.

The recognition of a pattern based on spacing allows the primary series and the additional forts to be differentiated. The relationship of each site to the Wall enables further details of their relative chronology to be elucidated. The known relationships are:

Halton Chesters and Rudchester: Wall begun and ditch excavated across fort site; former demolished and latter filled in.

Chesters, Housesteads, Great Chesters and Birdoswald: Wall foundation laid, turret started at Chesters (27a), Housesteads (36b) and Birdoswald (49a); milecastle begun at Great Chesters (43); ditch excavated across Chesters and Birdoswald and subsequently obliterated. The Narrow Wall abuts Chesters and Housesteads and bonds with Great Chesters.

Wallsend: bonds with Narrow Wall.

Carrawburgh: overlies the Vallum and may bond with Narrow Wall.

Newcastle: artefacts indicate a post-Hadrianic date for construction.

Inscriptions demonstrate that Benwell and Halton Chesters were constructed during the governorship of Platorius Nepos. A building stone at Great Chesters gives Hadrian the title *pater patriae* (father of his country) which he formally accepted in 128, though there are a few instances of the use of the title before that date.

Many of the main series of forts were placed astride the Wall. These include the forts from Wallsend to Chesters, Birdoswald and Burgh-by-Sands. It is probable that the original intention was to have all the forts so positioned where topography allowed. At Housesteads, the ridge ran west to east and this dictated the alignment of the fort. Carrawburgh was a late addition and was attached to the rear. Great Chesters was a primary fort but was built late in the sequence: it does not project even though the lie of the land would allow it. Modifications at Birdoswald during construction work led the Wall to be moved and the fort to change from lying astride to being attached to the rear of the Wall.

Taken together, all this evidence leads to a possible sequence for fort building, Rudchester, Halton Chesters and presumably Benwell, being constructed first. Great Chesters and Carrawburgh, late in the sequence, do not project (none of the forts on the later Antonine Wall, it may be noted, project). Housesteads and Chesters, each overlying a turret and earlier than the Narrow Wall, probably occupy an intermediary position.

The relationship between the forts and the Wall, especially when compared with the Antonine Wall in Scotland, indicates that the forts were built as separate entities and did not closely relate to the Wall, other than in one important respect. Where the fort lay astride the Wall, an extra entrance was provided at both ends of the *via quintana* (the minor cross-road). This was presumably to aid mobility, for otherwise there would have been only one gate south of the barrier, the *porta decumana* (the back gate), as well as to assist normal lateral traffic. The desire for additional mobility, as reflected in the unique arrangement of gates, may also help to explain the reason for the addition of the forts to the original plan.

In the first plan for the Wall, units would have had to move across country from the bases on the Stanegate or further south and pass through a milecastle gateway in order to operate north of the Wall. This restriction on movement would equally operate if the forts were placed wholly north of the Wall, though in reverse. The particular – and unique – position of the forts astride the Wall with the equivalent of six milecastle gates opening to the north and four gates to the south suggests that mobility was foremost in the minds of the military authorities. There may, however, be a more prosaic explanation, that the army considered this the best way to deal with a situation they had not encountered before: relating free-standing forts to a linear barrier. This particular fort plan seems to have resulted in an over-provision of gates. Several appear to have been unfinished (the east portal of the north gate and the south portal of the east gate at Housesteads and the north portal of the east gate at Chesters), while the lack of wear on several gate thresholds similarly points to a lack of use; however, the same phenomenon has been observed at Carlisle, not a Wall fort.

It has been assumed that the units placed in the new forts were transferred from their predecessors immediately to the south, but excavation at several sites on the Stanegate has suggested continuing occupation during Hadrian's reign. These forts include Corbridge, Vindolanda, Carvoran and Carlisle, and thus it would appear that the units based in the Wall forts were drawn from further afield, Wales and northern Britain, where several forts were abandoned at this time.

The River Tyne cut off communication between the east end of the Wall and the rest of the province. As this was the first stretch of the barrier to be constructed, the separation of the army from the Wall would have first been obvious in this sector, and it is therefore not surprising that the earliest forts to be placed on the Wall were here.

Certain rules governed the alignment of Roman forts. They should face the enemy, as did most forts on the Wall, or, second-best, the rising sun, as at Housesteads. Others faced the point they were protecting, such as a bridge, Corbridge being an example of this.

The Wall forts followed the normal plan, even though their size might vary from 1.2 to 2.4 ha (3 to 6 acres): only Stanwix is larger. They were generally shaped like a modern playing card, with rounded corners. Ditches, ranging in number from one to four, lay beyond the rampart. This was of turf on the Turf Wall and of stone backed by earth on the Stone Wall. At the fort of Worth in Germany the stone wall stood 4.27-4.87 m (14-16 ft) high to a wall-walk which was fronted by a parapet 1.5 m (5 ft) high.

All the fort buildings were laid out within a fairly rigid framework of roads. The *via praetoria* led from the main gate (*porta praetoria*) to the main entrance of the headquarters building where it met, at right angles, the *via principalis* which crossed the fort between the two side gates, the *porta principalis dextra* and the *porta principalis sinistra*. That part of the fort which lay between the main gate and the central range was known as the *praetentura*. Behind the central range of buildings lay the *via quintana*. Uniquely, in those forts which lie astride the Wall there was a gate at each end of this road. The back gate (*porta decumana*) was reached by the *via decumana*. The rear part of the fort was called the *retentura*. A road, the intervallum road or *via sagularis*, also ran round the full circuit within the defences.

All the main gates in the Hadrianic forts contained two portals, though often the lack of wear on the sill of one gate suggests that only one entrance was normally used. A stone from Maryport depicts a gate with two portals below an upper storey lit by five round-headed windows (page 402). Ovens

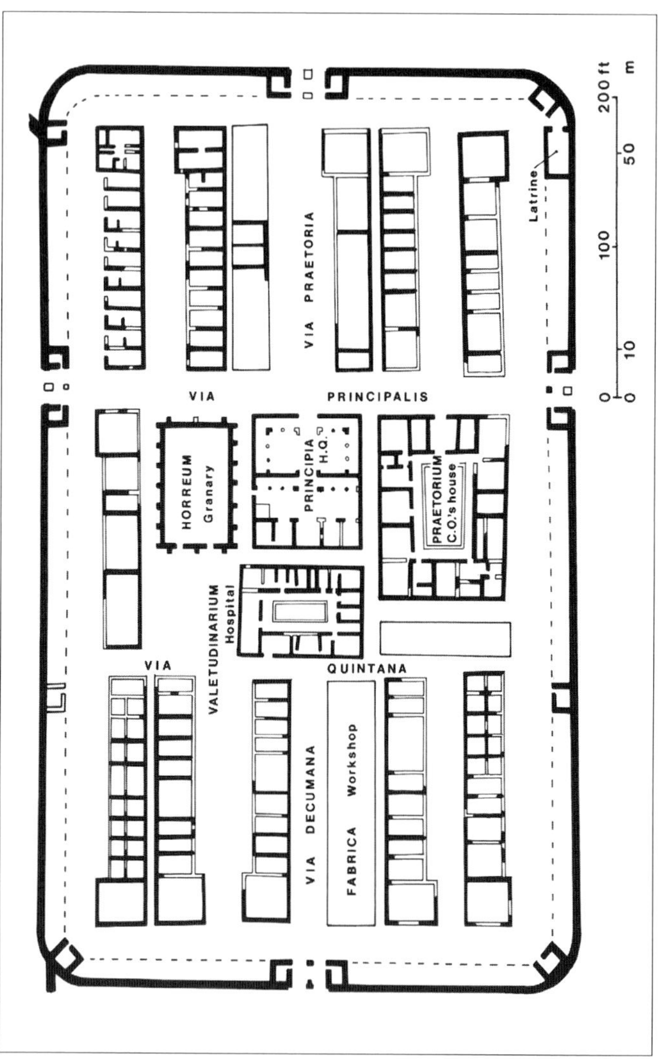

Plan of a Roman fort based upon Housesteads in the Hadrianic period with the names of the principal buildings and roads.

were often placed in the lower rooms of towers, or tucked into the rampart backing.

All the internal buildings visible today are stone built, but many were originally of timber. Perhaps all buildings in the Turf Wall forts were of timber; timber barrack-blocks have also been noted at Chesters and Wallsend and in the earliest fort at South Shields. Only the bare walls of buildings survive today, but excavation has demonstrated that when constructed they would have been plastered inside and out and many painted too.

In the centre of the fort lay the headquarters building (*principia*). It contained a courtyard, surrounded on three sides by a verandah and it is possible that notices were posted here. The courtyard often contained a well. A door led into a hall aligned across the width of the building in which stood a platform, presumably for the commanding officer. This hall was probably lit by upper windows. Opposite the entrance, a room known as the temple (*aedes*), held the standards of the unit and a statue of the emperor. Often a stair led down from here into a strongroom, designed to hold the chests for pay and regimental savings, and presumably located here because the temple was constantly guarded. To each side of the temple were two rooms, used by staff.

The house of the commanding officer (*praetorium*) was normally placed to the right of the headquarters. A large courtyard building of Mediterranean type, this provided accommodation for the commander, his wife and family, and his slaves. To the other side of the headquarters lay the fort's granaries (*horrea*), recognisable from the buttresses which supported their side walls. The granaries in Hadrian's Wall forts vary considerably in their plans and it is even possible that some had two storeys.

Other significant buildings included the hospital, latrine, workshop and storehouses. The remainder of the fort mainly contained barrack-blocks. These were originally probably of timber while the principal buildings were of stone, or at least had stone foundations. It would appear that during the second half of the second century timber buildings started to be replaced in stone. Even so, many continued to have roofs of thatch or shingle, while tiles were used for the main buildings.

It is probable that an infantry century occupied a single building. Each barrack-block was divided into an officer's suite and ten double rooms: the double room is called a *contubernium*. On the basis of a reference to eight men occupying a tent on campaign it is assumed that the same number of men occupied each pair of rooms in a permanent barrack-block. The ten double rooms of an infantry barrack could accordingly accommodate 80 men, which, one military treatise states, was the total number of men in a century.

The situation is not so clear for the cavalry. The identification of stables has long been a problem, but it was considered that eight-roomed barrack-blocks provided accommodation for two troops of 32 men each. Excavations in Germany, however, revealed evidence for horses sharing a barrack-block with men, and now such buildings have been recognised at South Shields and Wallsend. In these cases it would appear that a single troop and its horses occupied one block.

At one end of each barrack-block - usually by the rampart - lay accommodation for the senior officer, a centurion in the case of the century, a decurion for a troop. Both centurions and decurions were supported by junior officers. It would appear that all the regimental junior officers were distributed amongst the centuries and troops; certainly no special accommodation for junior officers has definitely been identified. However, several documents attest that regiments could be up to 25% under strength so accommodation was perhaps not as cramped as often assumed, while at all times some soldiers would have been away from base.

Outside the fort lay the regimental bath-house. Five bath-houses are known to have been built to the same plan

(Benwell, Chesters and Carrawburgh on the Wall and the outpost forts at Bewcastle and Netherby). The plan is unusual in that the rooms are arranged in two adjoining rows (a 'block type') rather than in one long row. Water for the various facilities within the fort as well as the bath-house might be brought to the fort by aqueduct. In later centuries, bath-houses were sometimes located within the forts, such as at Halton Chesters and Housesteads.

It would appear that each fort on Hadrian's Wall was designed for a single regiment. Each regiment was a highly organised and large 'family'. Its commanding officer not only had authority over his men but perhaps also over the civilians in the settlement outside the fort gates. He presumably was also responsible for patrolling and maintaining peace within an area of land. However, how he co-operated operationally with his fellow regimental commanders is unclear.

It would be surprising if forts did not change over the nearly three centuries they were occupied. Generally the basic plan remained, but internal buildings as well as defences might be radically remodelled or rebuilt. In some forts extra space was required so the rampart backing was removed to be replaced by buildings, while elsewhere roads might be built over. In two forts (Rudchester and Halton Chesters) it has been argued that some buildings were demolished, perhaps in the late third century and the first half of the fourth, and not replaced for decades. An inscription at Great Chesters records rebuilding of the granary, ruinous with age, in 225, while one at Birdoswald records the rebuilding of the commanding officer's house, which had been covered with earth and fallen into ruin, the headquarters building and the bath house between 296 and 305.

Some buildings retained the same general plan over centuries. The basic plan of the headquarters building, for example, continued, but there were modifications in detail: the construction of walls dividing the verandah into separate rooms and the insertion of hypocausts (under-floor heating) into rear rooms, for example. Headquarters buildings newly constructed in the late second or early third century tended to be smaller with no courtyard and only three rooms at the rear. The status of commanding officers changed in the late third century and it has been argued that large houses were no longer required, though a new, large courtyard house was erected at South Shields about this time. The plan of this fort was also amended in the fourth century from the earlier tripartite arrangement to a configuration based on a cross, the interior thus being divided into four quarters.

The arrangement of barrack-blocks changed more radically. Significant changes occurred in the third century. At South Shields, Wallsend and Vindolanda, barracks erected in the early third century depart considerably from earlier buildings in the smaller number of *contubernia* (five or six compared to eight to ten), the construction of the *contubernia* in separate buildings rather than conjoined in one long structure, and the provision of a passage leading from the front of the building to the back room. These features thereafter appear more regularly in other forts, though the details might vary considerably.

Finally, we may note that all the structures on the Wall interpreted as Christian buildings have been found within forts: the room containing a table altar in the headquarters building at South Shields; the apsidal building in the commander's house at Vindolanda; the possible apsidal building and long cist burial at Housesteads; and the apse in the centurion's quarters at Birdoswald.

CIVIL SETTLEMENTS

Civil settlements are known to have existed outside several forts and it is presumed that they once lay outside all. These villages or towns included temples, inns, workshops, shops and the like, and also houses. Soldiers were not allowed to marry according to Roman law until at least the early third century, but they could marry according to local law, and such unions were recognised retrospectively by the State. It has long been believed that there was a strict division between military and civilian, soldiers living in the forts, civilians outside. There is, however, increasing evidence for women and children in forts and it is not impossible that some lived there rather than in civil settlements, while other soldiers may have stayed with their families outside the fort.

A civil settlement could cover an extensive area, often as large or larger than the fort itself. Those at Housesteads and Vindolanda have been most explored through excavation but some evidence exists at most forts. Our knowledge of them has been significantly increased through geophysical survey. This has demonstrated extensive areas of settlement outside the forts at Halton Chesters, Carvoran, Birdoswald, Castlesteads and Maryport. In several cases the buildings of the settlement spread along one or two sides of the fort wall, over the infilled ditches and also formed a ribbon development along one of the roads leading away from the fort. This can be seen at Vindolanda, where the buildings line the road leading out of the west gate and spread to each side.

The civil settlements at Vindolanda and Housesteads offer a variety of plans, including ‘strip houses’ with shutters separating the interior from the street: these were probably shops. Such houses are the main style of building plan revealed by geophysical survey. Larger, and more complex, houses are known, for example, at Benwell, Vindolanda, Maryport and Corbridge. Some have been interpreted as inns for official travellers (*mansiones*), but they are similar in plan to other large houses and may be no more than grand private dwellings.

Only Housesteads has produced evidence for early, that is Hadrianic, occupation of a civil settlement, and here it lay some distance from the fort, south of the Vallum. Perhaps earlier evidence, probably in the form of timber buildings, lies beneath the later settlements. Most evidence for civil settlements dates to the third century, though often this peters out about 270. This may relate to a decline of activity in forts, including the reduced number of troops stationed in them. Apart from at Housesteads there is little evidence for occupation in civil settlements in the fourth century.

An important new discovery has been that some civil settlements, Wallsend, Housesteads, Castlesteads and Maryport, were surrounded by ditches. Whether these were defensive in intent or merely defining the limit of the settlements is not clear. A second important discovery is increasing evidence for buildings north of the Wall (Wallsend and Birdoswald in addition to earlier references to possible Roman buildings north of the Wall at Chesters), but not sitting within a defended enclosure. Geophysical survey has also led to the identification of fields, usually defined by ditches, in close proximity to civil settlements.

There is little evidence for connections between the civil settlements and the rural settlements of the north. While it has been suggested that the people of the civil settlement came from the surrounding countryside, it is perhaps more probable that they were first established by the camp followers who had accompanied the soldiers to their new homes from their previous bases.

THE VALLUM

Behind the Wall and its structures lay a great earthwork known as the Vallum. Its name is erroneous. Bede, writing shortly after 700, considered the Vallum to be a turf earthwork and used the correct Latin word, *vallum*, to describe it and to distinguish it from the Stone Wall or *murus*. Bede's name has stuck.

The Vallum has not been found between Wallsend and Newcastle but otherwise ran the whole length of the Wall. The Vallum consisted of a ditch with the earth placed symmetrically on each side in continuous mounds. The whole measured about 120 Roman feet, that is 1 *actus* (35.52 m) across. The ditch appears to have been intended to be 6 m (20 ft) wide at the top and 3 m (10 ft) deep, while steeply sloping sides reduced the width at the bottom to between about 1.22 m and 2.44 m (4-8 ft); dimensions, however, varied according to the local soil conditions. Where necessary, the ditch sides and the mounds were revetted by turf or stone cheeks.

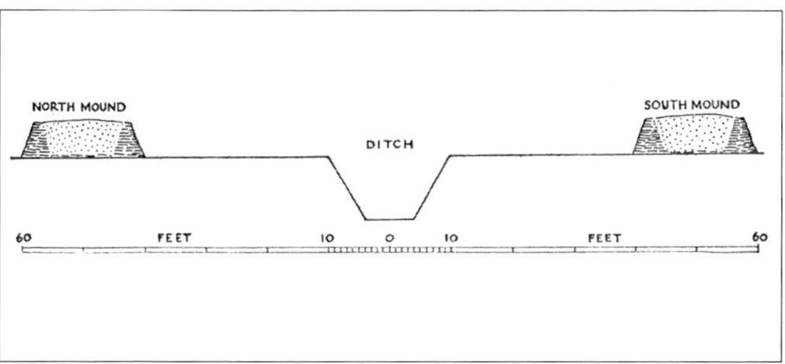

Schematic cross-section of the Vallum as originally designed, drawn by I. A. Richmond.

The material taken out of the ditch was normally piled in two mounds originally set 9 m (30 ft) back from each lip of the ditch. Where necessary, and when the material was available, the mounds, 6 m (20 ft) wide at base, were revetted with kerbs of turfwork, though stone kerbs have been found in two places. The north mound, but not the south, was broken by a gap at each milecastle. The south berm has yielded, in several places, evidence for a metalled track, but it was not consistently provided; such a track has also been recorded on the north berm in two locations. The track was probably original and would have been the only path along the Wall before the construction of the Military Way.

At several forts (Benwell, Housesteads, Great Chesters and Birdoswald), there was a break in the Vallum: both mounds were broken by a gap while a causeway of undug earth, revetted by stone, was left in the ditch: this was surmounted by a gate closed from the north, the fort side. Presumably such causeways existed to the south of every fort. These were the only places where the Vallum could be crossed, though at MC 50 TW (High House) and MC 51 (Wall Bowers) the Vallum ditch was interrupted by an original causeway revetted in stone together with a gap in the north mound but not in the south. Observation on the ground indicates the existence of causeways opposite every other milecastle where the Vallum is well enough preserved to retain such evidence, but, where excavation has been undertaken, it has been demonstrated that they are secondary.

A small number of inscriptions, placed on both the north and the south mounds, have been found. A group of five were recovered at Denton in the sector T 7b – MC 8, one recording work by the First Cohort of Dacians. These stones tend to be thinner than the legionary building stones on the Wall. Similar thin stones discovered elsewhere also record work by auxiliary units.

The Vallum was laid out in long straight stretches. This is especially noticeable in the central sector where the Wall hugs the crags and the Vallum stays well to the rear, occupying the bottom of the slope. Elsewhere, the Vallum runs so close to the Wall that when it approaches a fort it is forced to deviate round it, demonstrating the building sequence. West of Birdoswald, the Vallum diverges round MC 50 TW (High House), while the north mound was omitted throughout the mile to the east.

The Vallum was clearly seen as an important part of the suite of installations for its ditch was completely excavated where the Wall ditch was not, as at Limestone Corner. Its purpose is best explained as a means of defining the limit of the military zone; in effect, it was the second-century equivalent of barbed wire. Access to the zone between Vallum and Wall was only through the gate erected on the causeways left across the ditch at forts. Thus the construction of the Vallum reduced the number of crossing points through the Wall from an original 80 to about 16 and increased military control of movement across the frontier. Its construction may have been a response to resentment at the building of the Wall. Many other explanations have been offered for the construction of the Vallum over the centuries. A recent proposal is that it was an extra obstacle to frustrate the activities of mounted raiders.

Secondary gaps in the mounds and secondary crossings over the ditch can be seen in many sectors. These relate to a systematic slighting of the earthwork, at intervals of about 41 m (45 yards), though they can vary from 36.60 to 45.70 m (40 to 50 yards). The intervals in the long Wall mile 7 are longer, suggesting that the order may have been to make 35 breaks through it in each mile. Observation on the ground today demonstrates that this task was not completed for in places there are no crossings, no gaps, or incomplete gaps and crossings. Frequently, the gaps in the mounds seem to be insufficiently large to provide enough material to form the crossing in the ditch. Excavation at Cockmount Hill in 1939 suggested that between 5 and 15 years had elapsed between excavation and infilling. The slighting of the Vallum has therefore been related to the abandonment of the Wall in the 140s in favour of the Antonine Wall.

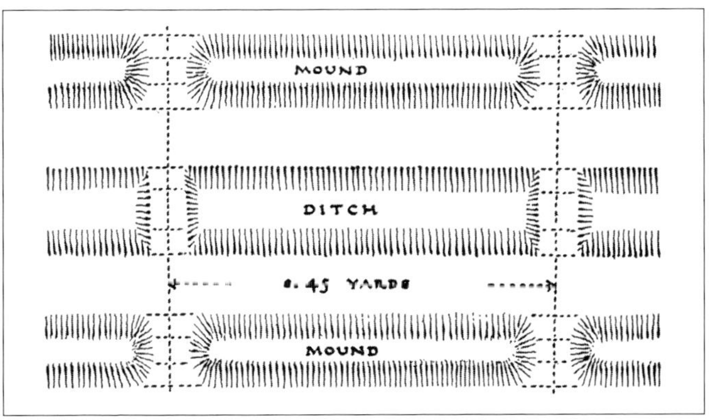

The Vallum crossings, drawn by I. A. Richmond.

In many sectors an additional mound may be observed, the marginal mound. This normally lies on the south lip of the ditch, but occasionally on the north too. It is usually assumed that the marginal mound results from cleaning out the ditch on the return from the Antonine Wall, but excavation has demonstrated that the situation is more complex. Often the marginal mound comprises silty material cleared from the ditch, although near MC 42 (Cawfields) it is mostly clean soil while at Limestone Bank its clean nature was attributed to the necessity to remove the results of frost action from the newly rock-cut ditch. The similar soil profiles beneath the marginal mound and the Vallum south mound at Black Carts and Appletree has led to the suggestion that the two mounds are contemporary.

Whether the Vallum was ever brought back into full operation on the return from the Antonine Wall is unlikely for both crossings and gaps in the mounds remain visible today in many areas, though elsewhere the ditch was recut and the gaps infilled. In some sectors the marginal mound appears to block the crossing opposite the gap in the south mound suggesting that it is later than the slighting of the Vallum. In short, the evidence appears to be mutually contradictory, pointing in places to a Hadrianic date for the marginal mound but more generally to a later date.

Near forts there is some evidence which bears on the length of use of the Vallum. At the causeway at Benwell, the pivot stone was replaced while the road through the gate was resurfaced three times. Close to the causeway, pottery indicated a late-second-century date for the infilling of the ditch, and this may be supported by the contemporary date of an altar in the temple of Antenociticus, erected between the Vallum and the Wall. At Birdoswald, disuse seems to have occurred unusually early for late Hadrianic pottery was found in the fill of the ditch while the gateway of the Vallum causeway had been dismantled. This action presumably allowed civilian buildings to expand into the former military zone.

THE MILITARY WAY

The final linear feature is a road, the Military Way. In many areas this runs along the top of the north mound of the Vallum and is clearly not primary: elsewhere, and seemingly always to the west of the River Irthing, it lies between Wall and Vallum. It was, however, built before the turrets were abandoned in the second century for some were connected by roads to the Military Way (and connections are known to milecastles). The Military Way was therefore presumably constructed when or after the Wall was re-occupied on the abandonment of the Antonine Wall. It seems probable that no road was provided in the original plan owing to the existence of the Stanegate supplemented in places by additional tracks.

The Military Way is usually about 6 m (20 ft) wide, cambered up to 46 cm (18 in) high, and formed of large stones surfaced with gravel. It is well engineered and can be followed today with ease in the central sector, though Bruce argued that it was not intended for wheeled traffic, and this has been confirmed by recent survey in Wall miles 40 and 41 where gradients of 1:4 and even 1:3 can be found in short stretches. Some milestones are known on the road: they usually take the form of large columns. In the third century the distances appear to have been measured westwards from Dere Street.

In the eighteenth century a track was noted behind the Wall at various places in the sector between MCs 28 (Walwick) and 34 (Grindon) but it was not recorded by MacLauchlan nor by modern surveyors. In 1980 a track immediately behind the Wall at Denton (Wall mile 7) was found to have been resurfaced twice and continued in use into the third century, while in 2003 two tracks were recorded between the Wall and the Military Way about 1.5 km (1 mile) to the east.

BRIDGES, CULVERTS AND DRAINS

The major rivers were each crossed by a bridge, for example the North Tyne at Chesters and the Irthing at Willowford.

In both cases the walk-way over the original bridge appears to have about 3 m (10 ft) wide. Before the end of the second century both were replaced by more substantial structures intended to carry the Military Way. These two bridges are amongst the most remarkable feats of engineering along the whole line of the Wall.

Streams were allowed through the Wall in culverts. At other places drains were let through the Wall. They are only found irregularly on the Stone Wall, whereas on the rebuilt stone sector of the Turf Wall they are placed at regular intervals of about 7 m (23 ft) suggesting that insufficient numbers were provided in the original plan.

TEMPORARY CAMPS

In the vicinity of the Wall, and along Dere Street, lies an important collection of temporary camps. These enclosures served different purposes. Some along the Wall line may have been used by construction gangs: these include several beside the Haltwhistle Burn and those adjacent to MC 68 (Boomby Gill) and MC 71 (Wormanby). Camps lie close to MCs 29 (Tower Tye), 30 (Limestone Corner) and 34 (Grindon) and may have sheltered their builders. Others, in particular those along Dere Street, were erected by the army on the march, which was trained to protect itself each night by throwing up such simple earthworks. It is possible that some camps were constructed during manoeuvres. The final group consists of small practice camps erected in different forms of training exercises, and again there is an example at Haltwhistle Burn and others south of MC 34 (Grindon).

The defences of the camp consisted of a ditch with the earth thrown on to the inside to form a rampart which was surmounted by stakes carried by the army for this purpose. The entrances were protected either by a detached section of rampart and ditch (*titulum*) or a curved section of rampart and ditch springing from one side of the entrance (*clavicula*).

The gates were obviously the most difficult element to construct and it is not surprising that the small practice camps contain relatively little rampart and ditch, but, usually, a gate in each side. Within the defences, leather tents were arranged in rows, 8 soldiers to each tent 10 Roman feet square, with that of the commanding officer at one end. The soldiers placed their armour and equipment in the space in front of the tent. This arrangement would appear to have been repeated in the fort barrack-room.

MATERIALS AND LOGISTICS

The requirements of the army for material were prodigious. Stone, turf, timber, nails, clay, limestone, sand and water for mortar were all basic necessities and all needed to be transported from their points of origin to the Wall. Tools were required to work these raw materials. Hammers, axes, chisels, wedges, picks, trowels, tongs, a saw and turf cutters have all been found on the Wall.

The Wall and most of its associated structures were built of squared rubble. Few stones were dressed to a high quality: those used in the gate on the Vallum causeway at Benwell and the west gate at Birdoswald are among the best dressed.

Stone could be won locally. Several quarries have been found within the Wall zone, some bearing the names of Roman soldiers or their doodles. Wedge marks are still visible on some rock faces. In Cumbria, the known quarries which supplied the Wall are generally further away than those in Northumberland, though at Cambeck and at Bleatarn the soft red sandstone available on the spot was used. The ditch might be a source of stone for the core, and of clay for use in the foundations and core. The making of mortar would have involved the burning of limestone, usually where both limestone and fuel could be brought most easily together, and slaking, where water was available, perhaps close to the Wall, as at the kiln at Housesteads.

For the production of good turf, open and preferably well-grazed, land is required. A Roman military manual states that turves should measure 18 by 12 by 6 inches (45 by 30 by 15 cm). A rampart 6 m (20 ft) wide and 3 m (10 ft) high would necessitate the cutting of turf from a strip of ground at least 400 m (1/4 mile) wide along the whole length of the Turf Wall.

Oak was the preferred timber for building, but by the time of the Roman conquest most of the trees had already been removed from the north of England and oak was relatively scarce. Therefore alder, hazel and willow would also often have been used. Wood was also required for scaffolding and as fuel.

It is possible that nails and other fittings were imported from southern Britain. Some structures required metal-working on site, such as the clamps in the bridges, and this material may have arrived as ingots.

Slates, tiles, shingles and thatch may all have been used for roofing. Some items could be won from the ground, but tiles had to be made. Tile kilns are known in northern Britain but not in connection with the construction of the Wall.

All these materials required transporting from their point of origin to the Wall. Carts and wagons would be available, as well as mules and horses – and the soldiers themselves. Both carts and wagons are depicted on the contemporary Trajan's Column in Rome, pulled by oxen as well as mules. The grazing of these animals governed the length of the working day. Transport of material to the crags sector would have been particularly difficult and may have slowed progress in that area.

Inscriptions provide ample evidence that the three legions of the province were responsible for the task of building the Wall, though they received aid from auxiliaries and sailors. Each legion contained its own engineering corps, well used to the erection of forts and other military installations. There is no evidence for civilian participation in the building of the Wall, though some inscriptions attest work by the civilian communities of southern Britain, perhaps in the fourth century.

It is not known how long the Wall took to construct. The way the Stone Wall was divided up into blocks of work has led to the suggestion that the aim was to complete the original plan in three years. Another review of the evidence, taking into account the scale of all the requirements, together with the length of the working year – about 200 days – has led to the proposal that the length of time needed for the completion of this plan would have been closer to seven years, but this is not certain.

MEASUREMENTS AND STANDARDISATION

Hadrian's Wall was built to a remarkably standardised plan. The Stone Wall was to be 10 Roman feet wide and, it would appear, 15 Roman feet high. The Turf Wall was 20 Roman feet wide. Turrets were 20 feet square externally, milecastles 60 by 50 Roman feet internally on the Stone Wall, 60 by 60 on the Turf Wall: even MCs 47 (Chapel House) and 48 (Poltross Burn), larger than usual, are 70 by 60 Roman feet. The dimensions of the ditch may be surmised therefore as being planned to be 30 Roman feet wide by 10 feet deep. The Vallum also followed suit: an *actus* (120 Roman feet) across with standardised measurements for mounds, berms and ditch. The bath-house at Chesters has walls 3 Roman feet thick, with the rooms laid out using multiples of 10 Roman feet: the other Hadrianic bath-houses appear to have followed the same pattern. Such broad concepts of standardisation were extended to the forts, and to the spacing of all structures.

THE CUMBRIAN COAST

From Bowness westwards the Solway coast faces Scotland. Fortlets and towers, in the normal pattern and the usual spacing, have been traced for about 32 km (20 miles) from the end of the Wall as far south as T 25b (Fothergill) at Flimby. Various proposed fortlets and towers stretching as far south as Ravenglass have not been proved.

The milefortlets of the Cumbrian Coast are built of the same materials as the milecastles of the Turf Wall, turf or clay ramparts and timber buildings, with front and rear entrances, and measure about 60 by 50 Roman feet (17.76 by 14.80 m) within a rampart normally about 6 m (20 ft) wide, providing an internal area of about 370 m². MFs 15 (Beckfoot Beach) and 16 (Mawbray) were not protected by ditches, though other fortlets were. MF 5 (Cardurnock) and MF 9 (Skinburness), located by the north and south entrances to Moricambe Estuary, are larger than their contemporaries, measuring 42.67 by 36.57 m (140 by 120 ft) and 33.53 by 24.38 m (110 by 80 ft) internally respectively.

Only three fortlets have been extensively examined internally, and the arrangements are all different. MF 1 (Biglands)

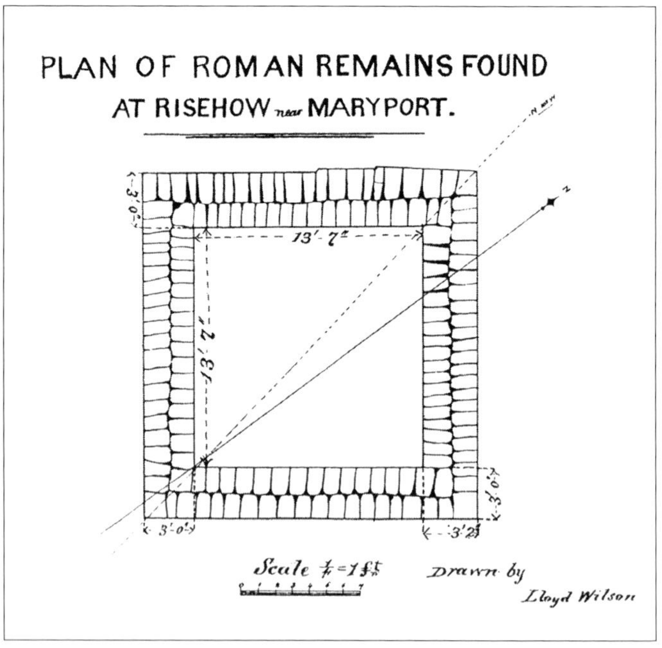

T 25b CC (Fothergill, formerly Risehow), drawn by Lloyd Wilson in 1880.

and MF 5 (Cardurnock) each contained two timber buildings, but of greatly different size. At MF 21 (Swarthy Hill) the southern area was divided into three buildings, while a single structure occupied the northern part. Hearths have been recorded in some milefortlets. Beside the normal types of pottery vessels, artefacts include spearheads, knives, brooches, gaming boards and gaming counters, though not at the same site.

The towers are similar in size to those on the Wall and were uniformly built of stone. Their foundations were substantial where they were erected on sand. In these instances four layers of cobbles interleaved with clay created foundations between 0.91 and 1.52 m (3 and 5 ft) wide and about 1.07 m (3 ft 6 in) deep. Above this, two layers of thin flags normally formed the footings on which the walls were erected. Evidence had been found to indicate that some at least had their facing stones bedded in mortar, though the core was of clay or earth and stones. In two towers, 13b (Wolsty) and 16b (Mawbray Sandpit), platforms were located, 1.83 by 1.22 m (6 by 4 ft) at the former and a little smaller at the latter. The floor, often apparently of sand, was usually at the level of the top of the footings. In two towers, a gravel floor had been laid down and, in a third, one of thin flags. The discovery of a possibly merlon cap from a crenellation at both Ts 16a (Cote How) and 16b (Mawbray Sandpit) may suggest that the towers had flat roofs, though other explanations are possible. No window glass has been found at any tower. In only two cases has it been possible to record the position of the door, in both towers to the right of the rear wall: in two other instances there is circumstantial evidence for an entrance to the left side.

Hearths have been found in many towers. Two towers have produced considerable quantities of bones. Animals and fish represented include pig, sheep, cattle, oysters, mussels, whelks, winkles and cockles. Fragments of quern stones were found at two sites. Spearheads are known from two towers and a knife also. The range of pottery includes samian ware, cooking pots, *mortaria* (mixing bowls) and *amphorae* as well as a little glass. Part of a gaming board was retrieved from T 25a (Risehow).

The zone containing the fortlets and towers in the more northern stretch of the Cumbrian Coast, from Bowness to Cardurnock on the north shore of the Moricambe Estuary, has been found to have been delineated by slight ditches. There is an indication from excavations at T 2b (Campfield) and T 4b (Cardurnock) that these sites were more complex than those south of Moricambe Estuary. Interestingly, too, in its second phase MF 5 (Cardurnock) was reduced to the same size as MF 9 (Skinburness). These three factors raise the possibility that the coastal installations were laid out in two stages, Bowness to Cardurnock first, followed by the southerly sector.

The relationship between the small installations and the forts is not known, though it has been argued that Maryport is earlier than the milefortlets and towers. The spacing is greater than on the Wall. Beckfoot is 17.5 km (11 miles) from Bowness; Maryport lies 16 km (10 miles) beyond Beckfoot and Moresby another 17.5 km (11 miles) on: in between lay Burrow Walls, probably a fourth-century addition. Moresby has produced an inscription giving Hadrian the title *pater patriae* (father of his country), which therefore ought to date to 128-138.

No tower and very few milefortlets have produced any other pottery than Hadrianic. They all appear to have been relinquished when the Antonine Wall was built; one or two towers appear to have been purposely demolished. Structural changes indicate that some milefortlets were re-occupied on the return to Hadrian's Wall, but these appear to have been abandoned before the end of the second century: none was rebuilt in stone.

Later material has, however, been found at some sites: two late-third-century coins at T 2b (Campfield) and late-third- or fourth-century pottery at T 16a (Cote How) and MFs 5 (Cardurnock),

12 (Blitterlees) and 20 (Low Mire). A rough tower was erected on the demolition debris of T 16b (Mawbray Sandpit). It is possible that some sites were re-occupied in the face of the threat posed by the Scots from across the Irish Sea.

OUTPOST AND HINTERLAND FORTS

North of the Wall in the Hadrianic period lay three outpost forts, Birrens, Netherby and Bewcastle: no forts are known to have been occupied on Dere Street north of the Wall at this time. Bewcastle and Netherby are known to date to Hadrian's reign from inscriptions, Birrens from pottery, though a Hadrianic inscription has also been tentatively assigned to this fort. The purpose of these forts may have been to give advance warning of attack, but alternatively they may have protected part of the Brigantes cut off from the rest of the province by the construction of the Wall. A dedication to the goddess Brigantia found at Birrens has been taken to support the latter conjecture. It was, however, erected by an *architectus*, who is likely to have been a legionary from York. Consequently the goddess may be an import rather than a local deity and therefore have no bearing on the political affiliations of the people of Lower Annandale.

The Hadrianic fort at **Birrens** lies beneath its Antonine successor, the fort platform of which survives to this day. It measured 140 by 119 m (460 by 390 ft), and covered 1.68 ha (4.15 acres). The ramparts were of turf, 6.70 m (22 ft) wide, with one ditch known. The fort would appear to have had stone principal buildings and timber barrack-blocks and storehouses; it apparently faced south, which is somewhat surprising. The fort lay at the northern end of the second route of the Antonine Itinerary which gives its name as *Blatobulgium*, which probably means "the flour sack".

The most distinctive feature about **Bewcastle** is its shape, hexagonal, conforming to the plateau on which it sits. Its area extended to 2.42 ha (6 acres). The Roman name of the site was

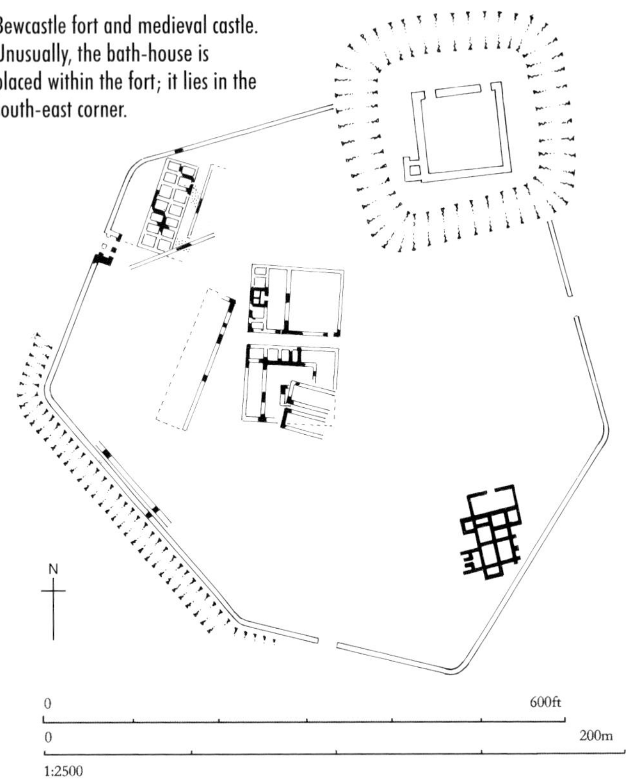

Bewcastle fort and medieval castle. Unusually, the bath-house is placed within the fort; it lies in the south-east corner.

probably *Fanum Cocidii*, a name which appears in the *Ravenna Cosmography*, and which means the "shrine of Cocidius"; several dedications to the god are known from here. The fort had a rampart revetted with turf, timber internal buildings, though probably a stone headquarters, while the gates may also have been of stone. A dedication slab records building by the Second and Twentieth Legions under Hadrian. An altar to Jupiter, dedicated by the First Cohort of Dacians, has been tentatively assigned to the Hadrianic period as the regiment lacks the epithet *Aelia*, which is first recorded in 146.

Netherby lies under the eighteenth-century house of that name. An inscription records the construction of a fort here by the Second Legion under Hadrian; as the governor Platorius Nepos is not named, it may be presumed to date to 127-138. The bath-house was drawn in 1732 and is of the same Hadrianic plan as found elsewhere on the Wall; in the cold room was found an altar to Fortuna dedicated by Marcus Aurelius Salvius, tribune of the First Cohort of Spaniards, the unit recorded here in the early third century. The Antonine Itinerary, also dating to the early third century, records the name as *Castra Exploratorum*, "the fort of the scouts".

Birrens and Netherby were both connected to the frontier by the road which led north from Carlisle and Stanwix. Bewcastle was linked to Birdoswald by a separate road. Visibility between the two forts was provided by two towers, Robin Hood's Butt and Barron's Pike. The former is 5.79 m (19 ft) square externally, 3.96 m (13 ft) internally, with no door at ground level, and is surrounded by a ditch broken by a causeway to the east leading to the road.

Only Birrens is known to have continued in use during the occupation of the Antonine Wall. At this time the fort was rebuilt: in 158 the Second Cohort of Tungrians, a thousand strong and part mounted, was based here. On Dere Street to the east lay the sites of two forts previously occupied in the first century. A new fort was built at this time at High Rochester under Quintus Lollius Urbicus, governor from 138 to 142, by the First Cohort of Lingones, who were probably then stationed here. Risingham, between the Wall and High Rochester, has produced Antonine pottery and may also have been re-occupied.

Following the abandonment of the Antonine Wall, probably in the early 160s, some forts in the Scottish Lowlands continued in occupation for a decade or two. Thus Birrens, rebuilt in 158, appears to have remained in use until about 180, as did Newstead in the Tweed valley, and with Newstead presumably went Cappuck 16 km (10 miles) to the south. Archaeological investigations have revealed that Bewcastle was reoccupied on the abandonment of the Antonine Wall, being provided with stone walls.

Under Severus and his son Caracalla, building is recorded at Netherby, Risingham and High Rochester. The inscriptions record the presence at all three sites of thousand-strong mixed regiments of infantry and cavalry, supplemented at the latter two by scouts (*exploratores*) and by another unit at Risingham certainly and High Rochester probably. The Roman name of Netherby, *Castra Exploratorum*, reflects its function as the base for scouts. Two tribunes are attested at Bewcastle, which ought to indicate that a thousand-strong cohort was also based there, unless the officers had travelled to the site to dedicate to Cocidius.

The visible fort at **Risingham** dates to the early third century: it measures 122 by 137 m (400 by 450 ft) and covers just over 1.6 ha (4 acres). A vast dedication slab, now in the Museum of Antiquities, Newcastle, erected in 213 furnishes the name of the fort: *Habitancum*. An inscription found at the south gate recorded that the First Cohort of Vangiones "restored from ground-level this gate with its walls, which had fallen in through age" in 205-7. The gate was single portal with projecting seven-sided towers. At this time, the fort faced south so this was the main gate, but in the early fourth century the fort was re-aligned to face west, the headquarters building being rebuilt.

High Rochester's Roman name was *Bremenium*, as given by Ptolemy, the Antonine Itinerary and the *Ravenna Cosmography*; it translates as "the place of the roaring stream". The fort measured 148 by 136 m (485 by 445 ft), just over 2 ha (5 acres), and was occupied by the First Cohort of Loyal Vardullians recorded here in 213. It faced north, which is appropriate as for over 100 years this was the most northerly known fort of the Roman empire. It sits at the point where a road leading to the mouth of the Tweed meets Dere Street.

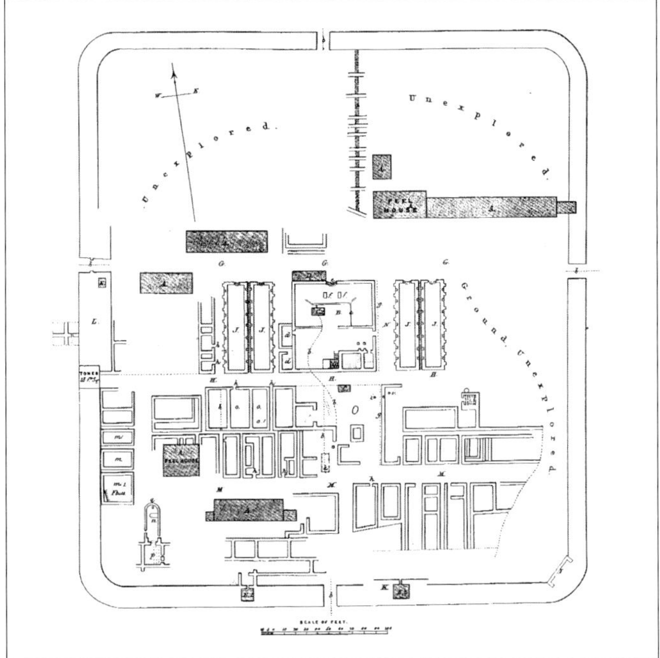

Plan of the 1852-5 excavations at High Rochester.

The regiments based at these two outpost forts have left records of their activities even further north. Two third-century inscriptions have been found at Jedburgh beyond the Cheviots and close to the fort at Cappuck. One is an altar dedicated to Jupiter Best and Greatest which might be thought to indicate a unit in residence. They record the presence of the First Cohort of Vardullians, based at High Rochester, and a detachment of the Raetian Spearmen from Risingham. The *Ravenna Cosmography* lists a group of sites north of Hadrian's Wall under the heading of *diversa loca*, "miscellaneous places". "*Loca*" has been interpreted in a technical sense to mean meeting places agreed between the Romans and their neighbours, but this interpretation has been challenged.

The units in the outpost forts were probably withdrawn in the early fourth century, perhaps as a result of the Emperor Constantine's postulated visit to Britain in 312 in order to gather troops for his final campaign against his rival Maxentius. The frontier scouts continued to operate down to the Barbarian Conspiracy of 367, in the aftermath of which they were abolished.

South of the Wall, a network of forts extended across the hinterland of Hadrian's Wall in northern England. Many forts had been established in the early years of the conquest: some (Hardknott and Ravenglass) were Hadrianic foundations. Most forts lay on the main roads leading north. In the early third century several of these were the bases of cavalry units, perhaps so positioned as to be able to support the troops on the Wall. Two major bases lay at York, the home of the Sixth Legion, and Chester, the base of the Twentieth Legion. The Wall was thus one element in a deep military zone, stretching over 240 km (150 miles) from the most northerly outpost fort at High Rochester to the southern Pennines.

THE ORDER AND DATE OF THE WORKS

Excavation over the last 100 years has provided considerable evidence on the order of construction of the Wall and its structures. A schedule can now be drawn up:

Original Plan:

10 Roman feet (2.90 m) wide Stone Wall and 20 Roman feet (5.94 m) wide Turf Wall with ditch and milecastles and turrets. It seems probable that the original intention was to divide the Wall into lengths of roughly 8-9.6 km (5-6 miles), each to be constructed by one legion, perhaps in one season. It has been long assumed that work on the Stone Wall commenced at Newcastle, the soldiers working westwards. However, a case has been made for work starting at Dere Street, the point at

which the legionaries probably reached the line of the Stone Wall, with the 24 km (15 miles) to the east being the first stretch to be constructed. Broad Wall foundations and structures have also been found between the Rivers North Tyne (T 27a) and Irthing (48b/49), while the unusual features of MCs 47 and 48 and Ts 48a and b have led to the suggestion that these were erected early in the programme.
Milefortlet and towers down Cumbrian Coast for at least 32 km (20 miles).
Three outpost forts to the north.
Existing forts to the south retained.

Revised Plan:
Forts built at a module of about 11.6 km (7⅓ mile) intervals, where possible astride the Wall, and along the Cumbrian Coast at wider intervals. Later forts (Great Chesters and Carrawburgh) built behind the Wall, though still attached to it.
Vallum.
Wall narrowed to 2.44 m (8 ft) or less.
Some forts and all small forts on the isthmus behind the Wall abandoned.

These plans overlapped. Forts were added to the Wall before the original scheme was finished. Some Broad Wall milecastles were completed with narrow side walls. At Birdoswald work ceased for some time, probably a few years, on building a replacement fort in stone, while west of Great Chesters, the Broad Foundation appears to have been overgrown when the building gangs returned to construct the Narrow Wall, which they placed beside it, and in Peel Gap a deep layer of peat and silt had developed between the laying of the Broad Foundation and the erection of the Narrow Wall. The impression is gained of a vast building site stretching across north Britain with the Wall, its milecastles and turrets, ditch, forts and Vallum all proceeding at different paces and at various stages of completeness at any one time. It was presumably to speed up the work that the Wall was reduced in thickness, and standards of workmanship lowered, as evidenced by the gates at Chesters, Housesteads and Birdoswald and at MCs 10, 37 and 42. The possibility has to be considered that some parts of the frontier were never finished and that the reason it is not possible to trace the Cumbrian Coast sites beyond Risehow is because their construction petered out at that point, though on topographical grounds this is a good place to end the series of milefortlets and towers.

Hadrian visited Britain in 122 and ordered the building of the Wall. He came to the island from Lower Germany and about the same time from the same province came A. Platorius Nepos: it may be assumed the two came together. Nepos arrived shortly before 17 July 122 when his presence is attested on a military diploma. With Hadrian and Nepos may also have travelled the Sixth Legion, formerly based in the same province and first recorded in Britain building in the Wall area.

It is not known how long Nepos was governor of Britain, but his successor was in office by 20 August 127. By that time, the second phase had been implemented for Nepos appears on inscriptions recording work on the forts at Benwell and Halton Chesters as well as completing milecastles in the central sector. Inscriptions record work at Great Chesters and at Moresby after 128, and at Carvoran as late as 136-8. Archaeological evidence points to the rebuilding of the most easterly 8 km (5 miles) of the Turf Wall still within Hadrian's reign, the remainder being completed later in the century.

One of the major changes in the building programme, the placing of the forts on the Wall line, appears to have resulted from experience gained during the early life of the new frontier and a desire to improve its operation. Warfare in the north may also have played a part. If the *expeditio Britannica* did take place in the mid-120s, it seems likely that the building programme was disrupted. Such warfare, as much as a lengthening building programme, may have led to a fall in the standard of workmanship, the narrowing of walls and even the construction of the Vallum.

THE LATER HISTORY OF THE WALL

Hadrian's Wall was abandoned when the Antonine Wall was constructed in the 140s. Broken pivot stones at some milecastle gates suggest the removal of the doors. The Vallum was slighted by the cutting of gaps through the mounds, and the creation of crossings over its ditch. Thus was the Wall thrown open to movement. However, it would appear that some forts, including several on the Stanegate, were retained.

Hadrian's Wall was re-occupied on the abandonment of the Antonine Wall. A lost inscription records rebuilding of the curtain in the area of Heddon in 158 and other inscriptions attest regiments in Wall forts in the 160s. Milecastles and turrets appear to have been re-occupied, but several turrets, particularly in the central sector, were abandoned later in the century: they had long been superfluous owing to their position on the crags and the presence of forts on the Wall. At unknown dates, many milecastle gates were narrowed. In some cases unusual items, such as hypocaust pillars, were used in later repairs.

An invasion from the north about 180 appears to have led to changes on the Wall. New units appear at several forts; north of the Wall, Birrens was abandoned but to the east new outpost forts were established at Risingham and High Rochester. It was probably now that extra units and scouts were assigned to the four forts beyond the Wall.

It appears to have been under the Emperor Septimius Severus (193-211) that major rebuilding took place on the Wall itself. Certainly the work of his army is attested by inscriptions at the forts of Chesters, Housesteads and Birdoswald, while the rebuilding of South Shields as a supply base has been demonstrated to date to this time. Action on the Wall itself has been most closely observed in the central sector where the new, narrow Wall was not now bonded in clay but in a hard white mortar. Severus may have had to order a thorough re-build following the wear of 80 years on a construction of inferior workmanship.

Modifications continued throughout the third and fourth centuries. During the early decades of the third century the facilities at forts were improved, for example by the construction of aqueducts. New style barrack-blocks were constructed at South Shields, Wallsend and Vindolanda. At the same time, civil settlements grew in size outside forts. After the middle of the third century, it is rare for rebuilding to be dated, as at Birdoswald where an inscription of 296-305 survives. In the fourth century some forts seem to have had less accommodation, which would match the smaller size of units recorded in the documents of these years, but at others the number of buildings was increased. On the Cumbrian Coast some sites were re-occupied, presumably in the face of invaders from across the Irish Sea. The pressure on the frontier attested in the literary sources did not lead to the construction of massive walls such as protected the Saxon Shore forts in southern Britain. Changes can be recognised, however, such as the remodelled fort at South Shields which appears to reflect typical late-Roman fort planing. There is little archaeological evidence for the "Barbarian Conspiracy" of 367 on the Wall. Coins certainly indicate occupation continuing into the late 390s. More forts are furnishing evidence which implies occupation continuing after the end of Roman Britain about 410, including Birdoswald.

Following its official abandonment by the Roman authorities, the Wall entered into a long period of decay which continued into the last century. Its stones were removed in order to build castles, houses and churches; farmers wreaked their havoc with plough and stock. In the eighteenth century the government ordered the construction of a new road from Newcastle to Carlisle, which partly used the Wall for its foundations, in spite of protests from antiquarians. Even beneficent landowners such as John Clayton might allow his tenants to remove Roman stones from buildings once he had excavated and planned them: indeed the agricultural revolution of the eighteenth and nineteenth centuries had a bad effect on the Wall through the removal of stone to build new farms and field walls. However, Clayton also restored the Wall and protected its remains by purchase, while the passing of the first Ancient Monuments Act in 1882 heralded a new age of protection through legislative action. It was not until 1943, nevertheless, that the quarries on the Wall were bought out and the landscape of the most scenic sector protected.

THE PURPOSE AND OPERATION OF HADRIAN'S WALL

In the first edition of this *Handbook*, John Collingwood Bruce offered the first modern statement of the function of Hadrian's Wall: "the Roman Wall ... is a great fortification intended to act not only as a fence against a northern enemy, but to be used as the basis of military operations against a foe on either side of it". This neatly encapsulates the two primary functions of Hadrian's Wall: frontier control and military defence. The main vehicle of the former was the linear barrier itself, while the regiments based on and around the Wall performed the latter duty. The very size of the Wall and the nature of the materials used in its construction offer the clear impression that defence was foremost in the minds of its builders, yet the contemporary frontier in Germany was no more than a stout fence.

In constructing Hadrian's Wall - and the contemporary frontier in Germany - Hadrian was making a definitive statement. He was declaring that the empire should stop expanding, should stay within its established limits. His frontier adopted types of installations long used by the army, fortlets and towers, and even ramparts and walls were part of siegecraft: the new distinctive contribution was to incorporate them into a linear barrier to create a tight system of frontier control.

An anonymous biographer writing more than two centuries after the construction of the Wall stated that "Hadrian was the first to build a Wall, 80 miles long, to separate the Romans from the barbarians". The Wall certainly did provide a clear boundary marker but the plentiful provision of gates at milecastles indicates that movement across the frontier was envisaged. This may have been primarily military in nature: the gates facilitated army mobility. They may also have been used by civilians whose movements would have been thereby controlled. Such control is known on other frontiers. Writing about 100, Tacitus recorded that in Germany the Tencteri complained that they could only enter the empire if they were unarmed, under guard and after paying a fee, while the Hermanduri had the unique privilege of being allowed to trade within the province without guards. It would have been convenient to collect such fees – and customs-dues – at the milecastle gates, though we know little of trade between the empire and its northern neighbours and nothing of trade routes. A distinct problem is the lack of causeways over the ditch at milecastles, though it is possible that they had once existed to be later removed, perhaps when forts were placed on the Wall and the Vallum constructed for now milecastle gates were redundant. Inscriptions from Lower Pannonia (modern Hungary) erected two generations later during the reign of the Emperor Commodus (180-192) record the construction of towers and forts along the Danube "to prevent the secret crossings of petty raiders", another purpose of Roman frontiers. Inscriptions from Hadrian's Wall refer to military operations across the frontier and the slaughter of bands of barbarians. These references form a narrow base on which to build a picture of military life on Hadrian's Wall, but they do indicate that there were defensive activities other than dealing with major invasions from the north.

The existence of outpost forts demonstrates that Hadrian's Wall was not the provincial boundary but took a particular line for topographical reasons. While that line often offered a military advantage, that was not necessarily the primary purpose and there were several sections where the view to the north was restricted, for example at Great Chesters and for the eastern 5 km (3 miles) of the Turf Wall. Sometimes for little extra work a 'better' line could have been chosen but that was apparently not of consequence to the builders. This is underlined by the existence of structures immediately north of the Wall: buildings at Wallsend and Birdoswald, aqueducts at Great Chesters and Halton Chesters. We may presume that the Romans were confident not only through their superior military power, but also because they had treaties (recorded in 197/200 and in 360) with some of the tribes beyond the Wall. Scouts operated to the north while on at least one occasion peace was bought with money.

While through treaties, diplomacy, scouting, patrolling and, when necessary, fighting, the Romans sought to control affairs beyond the frontier, the Wall was carefully planned to ensure a tight system of observation and frontier control. In the central sector, where the evidence is clearest, the aim appears to have been for soldiers on duty in the towers along its line to be able to communicate back to the units in the forts on the Stanegate. Milecastles and turrets were moved out of their measured positions to improve such communication. This adaptability is in contrast to the otherwise rigidity of the planning of the Wall and its structures and indicates an intention to ensure that there was to be a 24-hour watch along the frontier, with the emphasis on observation.

No indubitable evidence has been found to prove that there was a walk along the top of the Wall. It was not required as a line of communication along the Wall: that could have been more safely undertaken at ground level, and the discovery of a path behind at least parts of the Wall may be noted in that connection. It was not necessary to aid observation: that could be effectively undertaken from the closely-spaced turrets.

It would have been superfluous and inappropriate for an offensive force such as the Roman army. Roman soldiers could and did on occasions have to defend their camps and forts but it is fair to state that they were not equipped with defensive weapons and preferred to seek a military decision in the field where their training, discipline and weapons gave them a distinct advantage. Few arrowheads, ballista bolts, ballista stones and other such weapons have been found in milecastles and turrets. We may also note that no other frontier is known to have had a wall-walk. These were provided on fort walls, but Hadrian's Wall was a very different structure. Moreover, in the first plan for the Wall there were to be very few men on the Wall line, far too few to operate in any military capacity from such a position.

Nor will the evidence on the ground unambiguously support the existence of a wall-walk. The bridges at Chesters and Willowford are exactly on the line of the Wall and may have taken a path across the river, but this in itself does not confirm the existence of a wall -walk. The stairs, which have only been found at MC 48 (Poltross Burn), may have provided access to the tower presumed to exist above the gate rather than to a parapet. There is no necessity for the turrets to serve an additional role of providing access to the top of the Wall, as has been suggested. Interestingly, when T 54a (Garthside) was rebuilt, the Turf Wall was re-aligned and the replacement turret became free-standing. In the Turf Wall sector, the location of the Stone Wall a little behind the front of the rampart it replaced has been interpreted as indicating the existence of a door at a high level leading onto a walk-way. An alternative proposal is that it was placed here to use the firm bed of the demolished Turf Wall. The building up of the turret recesses may have been to strengthen the Wall so as to carry a walk-way, but it may also have been to strengthen the Wall at a weak point. That said, none of this evidence is conclusive either way.

The placing of forts on the Wall, and more particularly the

construction of the Vallum, heightened control along the frontier line. Travellers now were restricted to only 16 or so crossing-points instead of the original 80. The reasons behind this additional control can only be surmised. The placing of forts on the Wall also blurred the distinct functions of frontier protection undertaken by the soldiers in the forts and frontier control exercised by the soldiers in the milecastles and turrets. It is not clear whence the latter came. The forts which were built on the Wall itself all seem to have been provided with sufficient accommodation for whole units: in other words no allowance was made for the possibility that some men might have been permanently outposted elsewhere along the Wall. Inscriptions recording auxiliary (and legionary) soldiers have been found at some milecastles and it is possible that the task of manning the milecastles and turrets was allocated to a number of regiments. While the artefacts found in milecastles are broadly comparable in quality and quantity to those in forts, the objects recovered from turrets tend to be slightly different. They lack items such as box fittings, furniture, instruments (apart from the occasional tweezers) and bone pins which indicate a settled occupation. The range of objects from turrets suggests that soldiers stayed there on rotation, for longer than a day, but nevertheless for a short period. With only one exception, part of a writing tablet at MC 50 TW (High House), no items associated with writing are found at milecastles, though some might be expected in view of their role as entry points and their possible function as customs posts.

No overall commanding officer for the Wall is known. Within the Roman army there was no mechanism known to us for one officer to assume command over others of equal rank, either on the basis of the seniority of his own commission or that of his unit, except by a specially created and temporary appointment. The only officers senior to the tribunes and prefects on the Wall were the legionary legates at York and at Chester.

Yet later it can be seen that there was order to the military dispositions, even if we cannot always understand the reason. In the later second century, some of the largest units in the provincial army occupied the outpost forts, in effect screening the front of the Wall. The cavalry units, both on and behind the Wall, were grouped around the main roads leading to these forts at Portgate in the east and at Carlisle in the west. These not only provided strong strike forces but also were located close to open country suitable for cavalry. In the centre of the Wall lay most of the infantry regiments, forced to operate over rougher country. The work-horses of the army, the 500-strong mixed infantry and cavalry units, were placed elsewhere. The disposition of forces was noticeably strong in the central sector. This follows an earlier pattern in that the milecastles from 47 (Chapel House) to 54 (Randylands) are the largest on the Wall while before the construction of the Wall the weight of installations lay in the same area, from Haltwhistle Burn to Brampton Old Church. This implies a common reason, but what? This section of the Wall lies opposite the sparsely populated country including what is known today as Spadeadam Waste. Here, only the army could keep watch and ward, whereas to east and west, on the densely populated Northumberland Plain and in the valleys of the River Annan and its tributaries, it was in the interests of the farmers and the leading men to maintain peace with the Roman army and inform them of any disturbances or potential disturbers of that peace: when the Romans were crossed, their retaliation could be terrible.

The careful arrangements for defence imply a strong enemy to the north. Certainly the literary sources record disturbances on the northern frontier at regular intervals during the second century and again during the fourth century. In about 180 and in 367 the Romans suffered severe defeats losing a general on each occasion, while the troop losses under Hadrian were so serious as to cause comment two generations later. In earlier years, Rome responded by retaining a large army in the province, commanded by experienced generals. In the later fourth century, the British army had to be supported by troops sent over from the continent, until at the very end of the century a field army was based in the island. Yet we know little of the fighting tactics of Rome's enemies. Tacitus records that in the first century they still used chariots, but fought on foot. Cassius Dio and Herodian mention chariots in the early third century, with the foot soldiers armed with a shield, spears, swords and daggers. Equally interestingly, the Caledonians used hit-and-run tactics. One of the Vindolanda writing tablets offers a valuable account. A report states that "the Britons are unprotected by armour (?). There are very many cavalry. The cavalry do not use swords nor do the wretched Britons mount in order to throw javelins".

Hadrian's Wall offers a fascinating insight into the military mind. Often portrayed as inflexible, certainly the Roman military mind was not that. This indeed should cause us no surprise for the Roman army remained a powerful fighting machine for centuries. The building of Hadrian's Wall indicates that problems arose during construction and were dealt with. It was presumably because the Wall itself was soon shown to restrict army mobility that troops were moved onto the Wall line. As a unique solution to this so far unique problem the forts were placed astride the Wall and additional gates provided to aid movement. When it was seen that these elaborate arrangements were not required, the later forts were built behind though still attached to the Wall; elsewhere some fort gates were left unused. The Vallum was an unusual initiative, never repeated on other frontiers. In one sense it created little more than a continuous annexe all along the rear of the Wall. But it was presumably more than that in offering protection to the whole military zone. Understanding the building of Hadrian's Wall is not merely an intellectual academic exercise but a window into a past civilisation and its operation.

South Shields from the air looking west. The granaries are clearly visible together with the reconstructed west gate. The partially reconstructed commanding officer's house and barrack-block lie towards the bottom left corner.

Wallsend from the air looking south-east. The headquarters building sits in the centre of the fort with the commanding officer's house to its left and the granaries and hospital to its right. To north and south lie barrack-blocks and store-houses. The reconstructed bath-house is top right.

CHAPTER 3

A DESCRIPTION OF THE WALL

SOUTH SHIELDS (*ARBEIA*)

Although it was not thought necessary to extend the Wall east of Wallsend, a fort was erected at **South Shields** overlooking the mouth of the River Tyne. It is generally accepted that South Shields was the *Arbeia* of the *Notitia Dignitatum*, where was stationed the *numerus barcariorum Tigrisiensium*, a unit of Tigris bargemen. The identification, however, is based upon this being an appropriate location for a unit with a specific riverine function. As the names of Roman regiments do not necessarily describe the function of the unit, some doubt must surround this identification. Various derivations have been proposed for the name *Arbeia*: "the place of the Arabs", or "the stream where wild turnips grow". Inscriptions attest the Fifth Cohort of Gauls here in 213 and 222, while lead sealings infer its presence from before 209. An ornate tombstone records the burial here of Victor the Moor, freedman of Numerianus, a trooper in the First Cavalry Regiment of Asturians.

The fort lay on the Lawe, a low hill on the south side of the Tyne estuary, occupied perhaps for over 4000 years before the arrival of the Romans. In the last centuries before Christ, a round house was erected and the land around it cultivated. Spelt wheat and barley were grown. After the house was burnt down the settlement moved elsewhere though cultivation continued on this site.

The fort, known from the sixteenth century, was first excavated when remains were discovered during house building operations in 1875. Part of the site, including the headquarters building and some granaries, were subsequently preserved within the 'People's Roman Remains Park', the first acquisition and presentation of a Roman fort in Britain to the public. Excavations in 1949-50 were followed by the building of a museum in 1953. The demolition of the 1875 houses after a life of a little less than 100 years resulted in further excavations in 1966-7, and the present programme of investigation which commenced in 1975. This has produced a vast increase in knowledge about the fort as well as the exposure and consolidation of many buildings. A replica of the west gate was erected in 1988, and two further buildings, the large courtyard house and the adjacent barrack-block, in 2000-1.

The **fort** as recorded in 1875 measured 188 by 113 m (616 by 370 ft), with an area of 2.1 ha (5.16 acres). However, it was discovered in 1978 that this fort was created by extending an earlier fort to the south. The earlier enclosure measured 148 by 113 m (485 by 370 ft), covered 1.67 ha (4.1 acres) and was surrounded by two ditches, except to the west which was protected by three. The primary fort has been dated to the 160s, and the extension to about 208. Even earlier were timber buildings which seem to belong to a civil settlement outside a fort not yet located, but possibly lying on the higher ground to the south of the known fort. An area of cobbling beneath the fort extension has been interpreted as a parade-ground.

The earliest known fort was probably designed for a small cohort of 480 infantry and 120 cavalry. The headquarters building, a double granary and possible accommodation block of this fort are laid out for display. In the southern part of the fort lay four timber barrack-blocks, later widened and rebuilt either in whole or part in stone. The front room in each of the nine *contubernia* contained an under-floor urine-pit demonstrating that these were combined accommodation for horses as well as men. The living space at the rear was entered through the stable. An inscription of the Sixth Legion cut into one of the stones used in the headquarters building may indicate the builders of this fort.

The next changes were of more than local significance: the creation of a **supply base**. The south wall was demolished and

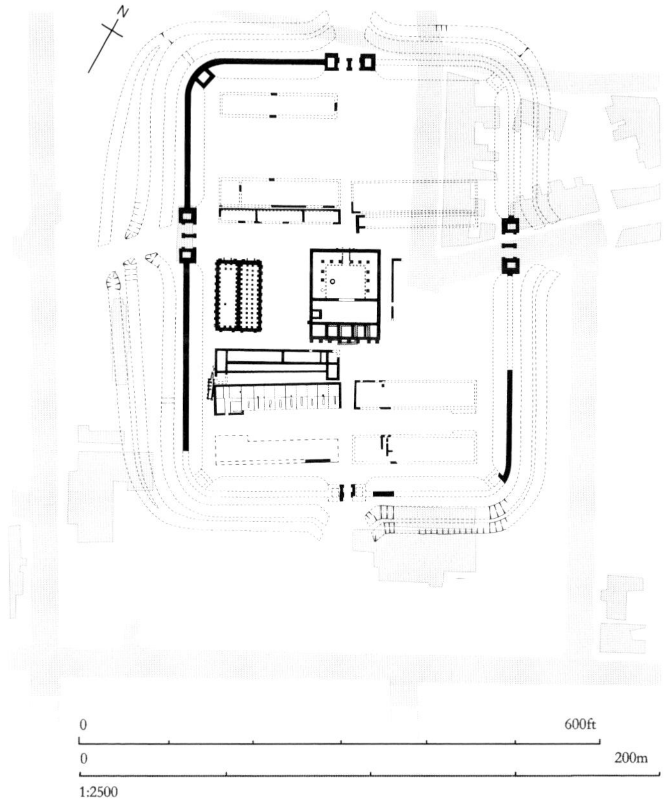

South Shields in the Antonine period, about 160.

the fort extended southwards. A wall was erected internally dividing the new fort into two almost equal parts. To the south lay accommodation and granaries for a regiment, probably the Fifth Cohort of Gauls: the four barrack-blocks are unusual both in their shortness and the mixture of both stone and timber walls. To the north, 13 granaries were erected, replacing all the buildings with the exception of the existing double granary; the headquarters building was rebuilt to face south and reduced in size, and a granary erected behind it. Before this scheme was completed, the dividing wall was demolished and the number of granaries was increased to 22 by the addition of a further six, while new barrack-blocks were inserted into the south-east corner of the fort. In order to fit the barracks into the limited space, each was split into two separate buildings. The Severan campaigns into north Britain, which commenced following the arrival of the imperial family in 208, and the subsequent planned occupation of Scotland, were presumably the occasion for this major rebuilding. How the emendation of the original plan related to historical events is not clear. As the supply base continued in use after the end of the Severan campaigns, it presumably had a function in relation to the supply of Hadrian's Wall and other forts in north Britain.

The new headquarters building was soon demolished to make way for another granary, its replacement being erected to the south. This was smaller than its predecessor, having no courtyard. At the same time, the barracks were rebuilt but to the same pattern. They were soon replaced by five barracks arranged at right-angles to their predecessors. Each contained an officer's suite and five *contubernia*. The walls were clay-bonded and within the rear rooms lay hearths for cooking and heating, while ovens were regularly placed in the front rooms. An inscription of 222, now in the museum, records the installation of a water supply for the Fifth Cohort of Gauls; this may have been the occasion for either of these actions.

Sometime during the years on either side of 300, the fort was destroyed by fire, though the cause is not known. The fire was fiercest at the east end of the barracks, but that may have been because of the chimney effect of the rampart. The burnt debris contained a mail shirt (on display in the museum), three gold objects and pottery. Subsequent changes were far-reaching and radical in plan. Sufficient survived of eight granaries in the southern part of the fort for them to be converted to barrack-blocks by the removal of their floors and

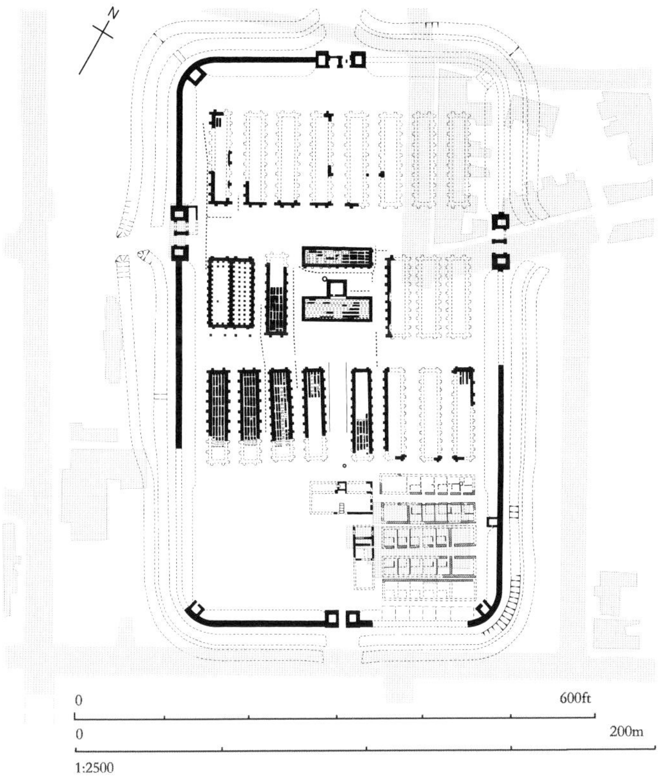

South Shields in the early third century.

the insertion of partitions, while at least two new barrack-blocks were erected. Each barrack-block contained five *contubernia*; allowing six or eight men in each would result in a unit strength of 300 or 400. A large courtyard house was placed in the south-east corner of the fort. The fort buildings were arranged around two wide streets, which effectively divided the southern area of the fort into four quarters: the road leading from the south gate focussed on a new headquarters building erected on the site of its second-century predecessor. This is the only known example in Britain of a common type of late Roman fort plan. These changes may be associated with the arrival of the unit of Tigris bargemen. Eight granaries survived in the northern sector of the fort, indicating continuation of part of the former function of the site.

Modifications to the fort continued throughout the fourth century and into the fifth. One structural change was the demolition of the original double granary: the area was then occupied by two tile kilns. John Leland, writing in the mid-sixteenth century, recorded that "the monks of the Tyne say that there was a city on the further bank of the mouth of the River Tyne, Caer Urfe by name, where King Oswin had been born" in the early seventh century.

The River Tyne was used by the Roman army for the transport of both soldiers and goods, and evidence for this is provided by the discoveries at South Shields. A shield-boss of a soldier of the Eighth Augustan Legion was dredged up in about 1866 from the Herd Sand on the south side of the estuary. This area has also produced over 64 coins, a helmet cheek-piece, parts of three metal cooking pots and several brooches. It has been suggested that these were the result of one or more shipwrecks. Harbour installations, though sought, have not, however, been found.

The fort has also produced the second largest British collection of lead sealings, small tokens used to seal packages.

A lead sealing found at South Shields bearing the heads of the Emperor Septimius Severus and his two sons, Caracalla and Geta. (actual size)

They are of particular interest because of the large number bearing seal impressions of the Severan imperial household. The seals include one stamped CVG, *cohors V Gallorum*, another AVGG dating to 198 to 209 when Severus and his son

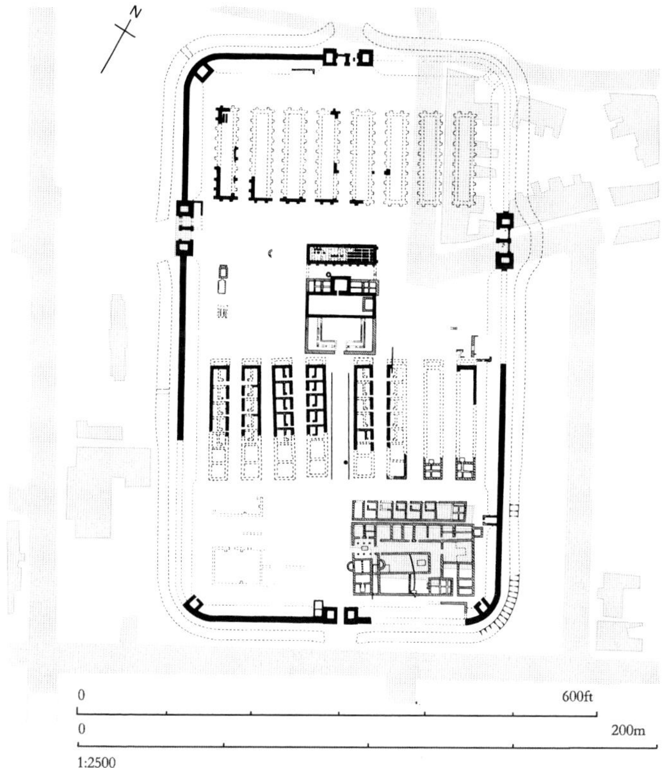

South Shields in the fourth century.

Caracalla were joint emperors, and a third AVGGG reflecting that Geta joined his father and brother as emperor in 209.

Entrance to the fort is by the site museum situated adjacent to the reconstructed west gate on Baring Street.

The north-east corner of the fort, together with the east gate located in 1875, still lies under houses, but otherwise most of the circuit of the defences can be seen. The **fort wall**, built from local sandstones, is generally reduced to its foundations 2.5 m (8 ft) wide or to the lowest course. At the south-east corner, the second course of the outer face is chamfered, reducing the width of the fort wall to 1.83 m (6 ft). Behind the wall stood an earth backing up to 5 m (16 ft) wide, below which lay masons' chippings from the final dressing of the fort wall. In places, evidence survived for additions to the earth backing. Inside the rampart lay the *intervallum* road, in places twice resurfaced.

The fort **ditches** are only visible at the west gate. Here the butt-ends of the three ditches of the original layout were recreated when the replica west gate was constructed. In the Roman period, the ditches were re-dug several times, finally, in the late fourth or early fifth century, being replaced by a single large ditch, itself later filled with debris from the fabric of the gate.

The replica of the **west gate**, the *porta principalis sinistra*, was opened in 1988 and is faithful to the known evidence for both the structure and from elsewhere on the Wall and the Roman empire. It contains information about its construction and the history of the fort, including two models. The window heads are based on those found at the site; two are displayed inside the gate, one with scored lines to represent voussoirs and found near the east gate in 1875 and the other with painted lines recovered from the late Roman west ditch. Also inside the tower is a putative merlon cap from a crenellated wall and a stone from a projecting string-course, both found in the late west ditch. The hemispherical stones over the tower doors are based on an original from Housesteads, now in Chesters Museum. The modern inscription over the entrance portals ascribes the building of the fort to the governor Calpurnius Agricola for the Emperors Marcus Aurelius and Lucius Verus, that is 161-3.

The original gate was constructed of a mixture of white magnesian limestone and sandstone, but only the lowest course survived. Excavations in 1966 revealed that the north tower of the gate had received an extension which contained an *amphora* sunk into the floor, perhaps serving as a urinal.

The west gate partly collapsed, or was demolished, after 388. The south portal was rebuilt in timber, the road running out of the fort over the filling of the late ditch. Burials across the line of the road mark its disuse in the fifth century.

The northern third of the fort has been examined through small-scale excavation, but nothing is now visible apart from the fort wall with the severely robbed **north-west corner tower**. The only surviving floor within the tower, of flags, appeared to date to the early third century. The **north gate** was constructed of magnesian limestone. Its eastern tower contained two floor levels, each supporting a small hearth, and both retaining evidence for industrial activity. The gate itself shows signs of repair and change at various periods. The west portal was blocked at the outer arch, while the south wall of the adjacent tower was removed and covered by a paved surface: pottery dates these modifications to the early third century. Following resurfacing of the road through the east portal, a timber post was erected to support the arch, probably also in the early third century. This post was soon replaced by a sandstone pier, of which the lowest stones still remain. Drains exited through both portals, the west being original, the east debouching through a hole in a large sandstone slab.

Along the **east wall** of the fort is exposed the corner of the original mid-second-century fort with its angle-tower; the part buried by the later rampart backing is best preserved. To the north, original rampart backing had been removed to allow the insertion of two bread ovens, probably in the late second century. In 1961 and 1994 building stones of the Sixth Legion were found in the debris resulting from the collapse of the fort wall: one was a centurial stone bearing the name Paternus.

Beside the demolished angle-tower is the communal **latrine**, an early addition to the early-third-century fort. Originally 3 m (10 ft) long with a door in the east wall, it was later extended to 4.5 m (15 ft) with the door moved to the south wall, and, even later, rebuilt. In its later two phases it had seats for ten on each side of a central platform. The latrine was fed by drains leading from the fort while the sewage flowed through the fort wall into the ditch.

The **south-east angle-tower** of the fort is largely robbed. To the west, the rampart backing had been cut away to insert a building resting against the inside face of the fort wall. The single portal **south gate** has lost all its facing stones. To the west is a stone platform which originally had timber walls, replaced by modern replicas. The **south-west angle-tower** survives better, the inside wall standing as many as six courses high, with an offset at the third course. To one side of the tower is a water tank.

The first fort faced north. The **west gate** was accordingly the *porta principalis sinistra* and led on to the *via principalis*. Between the gate and the headquarters building, south of this street, lie the foundations of the double **granary** of the first fort, built of white magnesian limestone. There were doors to north and south, the latter opening onto the *via quintana* and protected by a portico represented by the four pillar bases. In the fourth century the granary was demolished. The area of the western half was used for two tile kilns: one is exposed and the other covered by a grass mound.

To the south of the double granary lie the lower courses of a long building with a projecting wing at each end. Excavation has demonstrated that several rooms contained a hearth (each now marked by a concrete pad) as if the building had a domestic function, but its purpose remains uncertain. The building is crossed by the remains of the dividing wall erected at the time that the supply base was constructed. Immediately to the west are the remains of a **settling tank**, partially overlain by a granary, and therefore presumably dating to the second century.

On the far, east, side of the double granary lies a Severan granary and beyond that the **headquarters**. This is a complex building. The original faced north. The walls of its five rear rooms are mostly reduced to their lowest courses or marked by cobbles, but the threshold to the central room, the shrine, survives. The tribunal at the west side of the cross-hall, internally deeper than the surrounding floor, may have served as a strongroom. Under Severus the cross-hall was replaced by a granary, the remains of which have been totally removed. To the north, lay the forecourt, containing a well 7 m (23 ft) deep. The lower part is timber lined. The courtyard was surrounded to west, north and east by colonnades. These rested on massive stone piers, two Roman feet (60 cm) square. The blocks used in the piers can be seen reused in several parts of the fort, particularly in the north gate, the latrine and the road leading from the headquarters; one bears an inscription of the Sixth Legion. The gutters lining the north colonnade survive below the granary erected over the northern range of the forecourt in the early third century: its eastern part survives best with a section of floor restored.

Throughout the third century the site was occupied by the two granaries but about 300 was returned to its original function as a headquarters. The forecourt granary was burnt

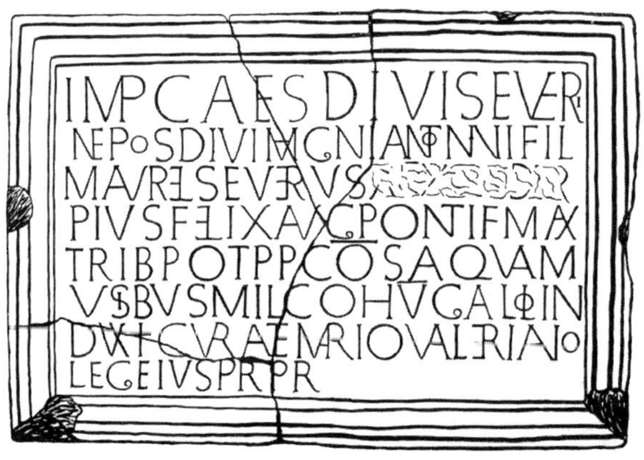

Inscription recording the provision of a water supply to South Shields fort in 222 under the Emperor Severus Alexander. (1.42 x 0.94 m)

and some of this burnt debris was used as the build-up for its successor. Grain found between the sleeper walls included spelt wheat and bread wheat together with some barley: the seeds of weeds recovered from the deposit suggest that the spelt wheat was grown locally.

The new headquarters building faced south. Its massive strongroom is worthy of close inspection for in the south wall is a rare survival, the sill of a window allowing light to percolate into the semi-subterranean vault. The large stones forming the walls of the strongroom were held together by wooden clamps. Steps led down into the vaulted chamber, where one rebate for the springing of the vault survives. In the floor is a sump. The strongroom is the largest known in Britain, which presumably relates to the special role of the fort.

The rooms to each side of the strong room were heated by hypocausts. The tribunal now lay at the east end of the cross-hall. The courtyard contains fragments of columns supporting the verandah, including two complete columns which have been repaired and re-erected. Here, in 1875, was discovered the remains of a small room or recess in which stood a small stone table, interpreted as a Christian altar. The keystone of the entrance arch bearing a bull's head was also found in 1875. It lay in front of the position of the south entrance to the courtyard. Both are now displayed in the site museum.

To the east of the headquarters building the lower, badly preserved wall, is probably the west wall of the original **commanding officer's house**: on top has been erected a granary. A further two granaries, located in 1875, lay beyond, but are not now visible.

South of the road are visible all or part of six **granaries** forming part of a row of eight. In several, the dwarf walls are overlain by the partitions related to their later reuse as barracks. The new partition walls are especially clear in the granary immediately to the south of the headquarters building. Each barrack-room appears to consist of a front and rear room, the latter entered by means of a passage running along the side of the front room. The upright slabs in the granary to the west mark the position of doors.

The road leading south from the headquarters building is lined by a colonnade on both sides. It crossed the site of the early-third-century headquarters building, which is now exposed. Visible are the strongroom, entered by a steep staircase, two of the other rear rooms and part of the cross-hall; outside the latter stands a replica altar. To the north, in the road, is a well, apparently dug during the modifications of about 222.

In the south-east corner of the fort are two replica buildings, a barrack-block of the type in use in the third century and part of the large **courtyard house** of the commanding officer erected about 300, the remainder being represented by lines of cobbles. The original house had been erected on foundations of clay, cobble and broken sandstones on which were constructed mortar-bonded walls. Most of the building had been robbed to foundation level after Roman times.

Access to the house is through a small entrance-court, its six columns flanking a central water tank or basin. This opens onto a colonnade running along the north and east sides of the main courtyard. The north range included residential rooms with *opus signinum* floors, two heated by hypocausts. The main room in the east wing was the dining room, and the colonnade beside its entrance was decorated with figurative wall-plaster. This was the summer dining room. The rooms have been decorated in the style of the wall plaster found in the house and furnished to represent the range of activities which would have taken place in such an important fine building. The reconstruction offers an excellent indication of the sumptuousness of a senior officer's house on the northern frontier of the Roman empire in the fourth century.

The unreconstructed south range contained a hypocausted room which was possibly the winter dining room. The three rooms between the two dining rooms presumably served as the kitchen area: the separate entrance to these rooms is paralleled in similar continental houses. A large room in the south range is a stable. In the south-west corner of the house was a small bath-suite containing cold, warm and hot rooms.

The replica **barrack-block** belongs to an earlier phase than the house, that destroyed by the fire. This barrack-block is one of the new styles of such buildings developed in the third century, containing only five rooms for the soldiers and an officer's suite. The replica is based upon structural evidence recovered from the barrack-blocks at South Shields. The walls are of clay-bonded stone with an external rendering of mud-plaster with a lime wash. The internal partitions are of wattle and daub, also lime washed. Both front and rear rooms of each of the five *contubernia* contain hearths indicating that both rooms were used as living quarters. The rooms have been restored in different ways to indicate the range of possible internal arrangements in barrack-blocks. Roman buildings did not have gutters and the reconstructed building shows clearly what happened in such circumstances: the water dripped off the roofs and splashed back onto the walls to create a dirty band.

The site **museum** contains inscriptions and sculpture, a lead ingot, pottery, glass and quern stones from the site, including the two splendid tombstones of Victor the Moor and Regina the wife of Barathes of Palmyra. She was a Catuvellaunian, bought by Barathes, freed and married by him. The Barathes buried at Corbridge is perhaps her husband. The museum displays several burials from South Shields. There are also many items of military equipment, including a sword applied with the figure of Mars, and the mail shirt found in 1997 in a barrack-room destroyed by fire about 300, and important collections of jet objects, amber beads and engraved gemstones. Outside the museum are displayed many more of the stones found in the fort.

The tombstones of Regina and Victor the Moor. (1.25 m and 1 m high)
Drawn by Miriam Daniels

Civilian buildings and two stone-lined wells have been recorded west of the fort in the area of the modern school: occupation here ended before the late third century. One building appeared to be a courtyard structure. Building plots here may have been defined by gulleys. North of the fort, altars and a statue excavated in 1959 were interpreted as lying beside the parade-ground, but perhaps more likely relate to a shrine. A road led south-west from the fort to join the main road leading south from Newcastle at Chester-le-Street: it is known as the Wrekendyke.

A **cemetery** examined 240 m (270 yards) south of the fort in 1993-4 and 2003 contained both cremations and inhumations extending in date from the early second century to the mid-fourth century. This was where the tombstones of Victor the Moor and Regina had been found in the nineteenth century. An isolated burial has also been found east of Baring Street.

JARROW TO WALLSEND

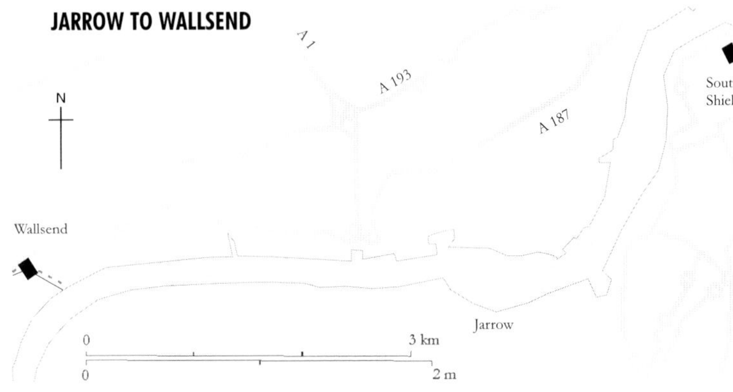

No Roman military installation has been discovered between South Shields and Wallsend on either side of the River Tyne. The discovery of pottery and coins at Jarrow has led to the suggestion that a military structure may have been located there, though no physical remains have been found. Jarrow Church has produced two fragments of an inscription which includes the name of Hadrian. It has been argued that the inscription is from a monument commemorating either the building of the Wall by Hadrian or, on the basis of the formula used, the size of Hadrian's name and the style of lettering, its reconstruction by Septimius Severus 80 years later, referring back to the original builder.

One of two stones found in 1782 in Jarrow Church: this includes the name HAD[RIANUS] on the second line. (600 mm square)

WALLSEND (*SEGEDUNUM*)

Wallsend acquired its modern name owing to its location. To the Romans it was *Segedunum*, which may mean "strong fort" or perhaps "victory fort". Wallsend commands extensive views in every direction, not least downstream along the Long Reach and up water along the Bill Reach. Today the river is wide and deep, but 200 years ago, before dredging, it was only 40 m (130 ft) wide and 3 m (10 ft) deep at low water. Excavations in the 1970s and in 1998 revealed traces of cultivation under considerable areas of the fort, including three or more sets of plough marks cut into the subsoil, within several fields.

The fort measures 138 by 120 m (453 by 393 ft), an area of 1.66 ha (4.1 acres). The Second Cohort of Nervians is attested here in the second century and in the third and fourth centuries the Fourth Cohort of Lingones, a mixed unit of infantry and cavalry, also recorded at *Segedunum* in the *Notitia Dignitatum*.

Almost the whole area of the fort was excavated from 1975 to 1984 following demolition of the modern buildings on the site. Further excavation preceded laying out of the fort for display in 1999.

Wallsend would appear to be one of the first series of forts on the Wall. This is indicated by its projection north of the Wall together with the fact that the fort and the Wall are bonded together indicating construction at the same time, as was discovered by tunnelling in 1929. Unusually, the north face of the Wall and the north face of the south tower formed a straight face of continuous masonry further emphasising that they were built at the same time: normally in projecting forts, the Wall met fort gates at about the middle of the south tower. There was an unusually wide berm of 7 m (23 ft) on all sides between the fort wall and the inner ditch, the same width as on the adjacent stretch of Wall. There were two ditches to north and east, but three slighter ones to the south. Internal buildings were either of stone (granaries, presumably headquarters and

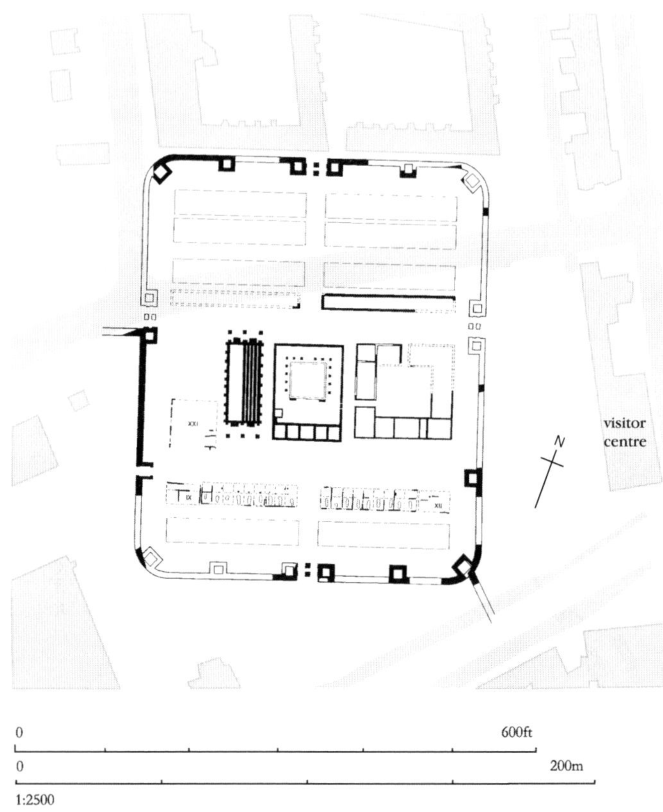

Wallsend in the Hadrianic period.

commander's house, possibly storehouses) or timber (hospital, barracks). Two barrack-blocks in the rear part of the fort contained nine *contubernia*, eight of the front rooms with an under-floor urine pit, indicating their use as stables. On the assumption that the adjacent two barrack-blocks were of the same type, the whole of this area appears to have been occupied by four cavalry troops. Six barrack-blocks lay within the front section of the fort thus completing the

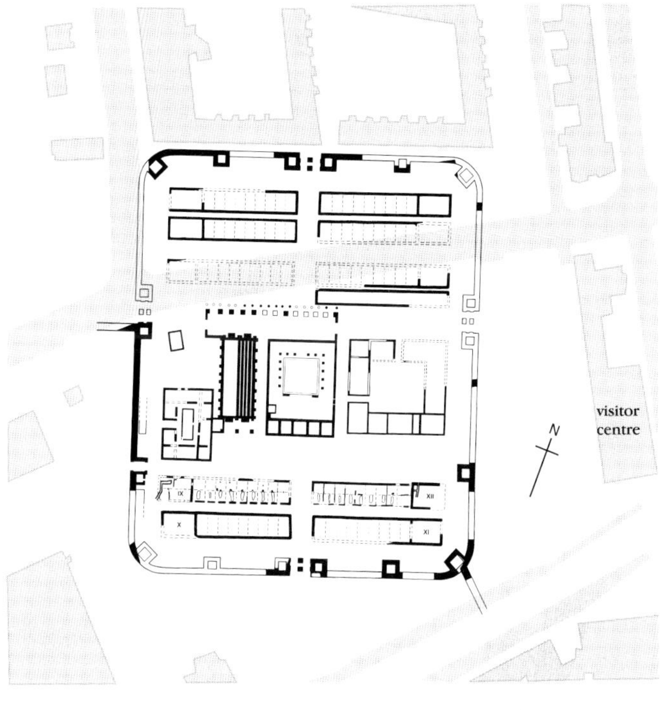

Wallsend in the later second century.

accommodation for a mixed infantry and cavalry unit nominally 500 strong. One peculiarity, however, is that the infantry barracks only contained nine *contubernia*, at least when they were rebuilt, not the ten that would be expected.

There is no evidence that the fort was abandoned when the Antonine Wall was occupied. Later in the second century a start was made on replacing the timber buildings in stone. A forehall was added to the headquarters, while two rooms were attached to the west side of the granaries, to be removed when the hospital was later remodelled. The last action appears to have been to allow access for carts from the minor west gate to the northern entrance of the granaries: this interpretation is supported by the deep ruts cutting into the street recorded during excavation.

In the early third century there were modifications to the defences. A third ditch was added to the east, and possibly to the north and west sides of the fort. The south gate was blocked and the ditches, now reduced in number to two, extended across its frontage. Another rampart with ditches now protected a wider area beyond the south-west defences of the fort, presumably an annexe or a civil settlement.

The second quarter of the third century saw major changes in the fort. All the barracks were demolished and replaced. The eastern pair in the rear part of the fort, which had faced each other, was replaced by two barracks, attached back-to-back and with only five *contubernia* apiece. The pair of barracks to the west was separate but conformed to the same general arrangement. Stone-lined drains survived in several rooms of two of the barracks suggested their continued use as stable-barracks. It may be that it was at this time that the barrack-blocks in the forward part of the fort were replaced by buildings broadly similar to those in the rearward area. The general implication would appear to be that the number of men stationed at Wallsend was reduced, but perhaps the cavalry component was increased in relation to the infantry. At the same time, or soon after, the hospital was demolished to be replaced by timber buildings, possibly barracks, which extended into the space south of the granaries. The presence of vessels appropriate to African cooking styles has led to the suggestion that a unit of Moors may have been at Wallsend in the third century.

Minor amendments to the buildings continued throughout the third century and into the fourth. These included the

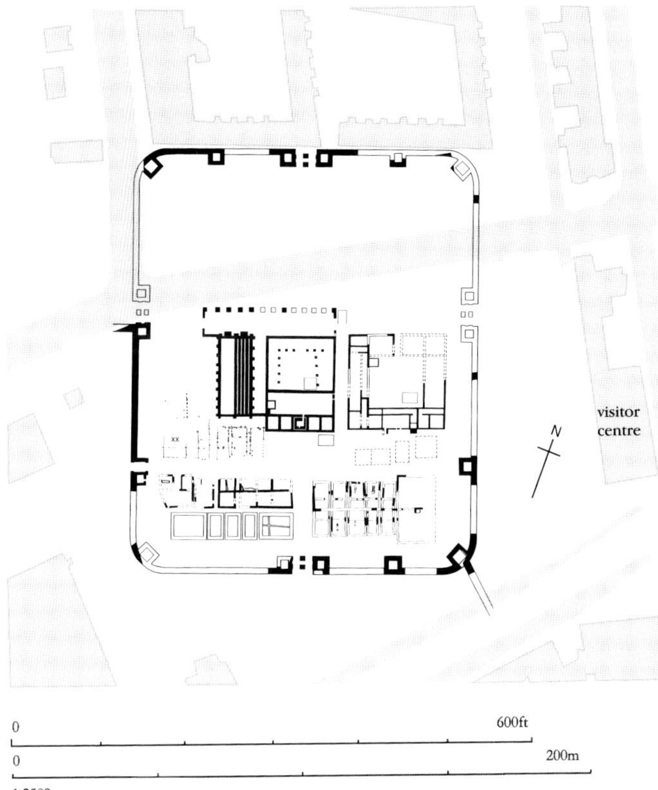

Wallsend in the second half of the third century.

reopening of the south gate – surprising in view of the abandonment of the civil settlement by the late third century – and the relaying of the road at the minor west gate: the considerable number of coins within and beside the gate points to the existence of a market there throughout most of the fourth century. In the early fourth century the outer ditches were refilled and the inner ditch recut to form a single large ditch. Within the fort, the timber building south of the granaries was demolished, and the remodelling of the buildings to the north may date to this time, rather than the mid-third century. Unfortunately the later Roman levels had not survived subsequent agricultural and industrial activities. The latest coins from the fort are slightly worn issues of 367-75, suggesting occupation continuing into the last quarter of the fourth century at least.

Much of the full circuit of the **fort wall**, the north, south and east gates, part of the west gate, the minor west gate, several towers and part or all of 14 buildings may now be seen, though several buildings are only marked in outline by setts and others only represented by their foundations or the lowest course. The defences and some of the central-range buildings are Hadrianic in date, but the others displayed date to later in the second century, when the earlier timber buildings were rebuilt in stone. The visible remains are supplemented by many visitor facilities including a **museum** and viewing tower and a reconstructed **bath-house**, based upon that at Chesters, not actually on the site of the Wallsend bath-house; it provides an excellent impression of such a building, surprising the visitor by the size and scale of its rooms.

The four main double-portal **gates** and the minor single-portal west gate are of basic type. The west gate was bonded with the Narrow Wall. The Military Way entered the fort at the minor west gate and showed much sign of use. A short stretch of Wall, now crossed by a modern path, ran from the south-east corner of the fort down to the river. In the early nineteenth century, as recorded by Bruce, John Buddle the Younger had often seen the Wall foundations extending far into the river when swimming there as a boy. In 1903 part of this section was removed when the Swan Hunter shipyard was extended. It was returned in 1991 to the site and rebuilt close to its original location.

The **headquarters building** is of the normal plan, with a courtyard, cross-hall and five rooms at the rear, the central containing a sunken strongroom. No well has been found, though the courtyard contained a water tank. To the west was a double granary, with the dwarf walls running north-south in the eastern half. It had entrances at both ends, each protected by a portico. To the north of both the headquarters building and the **granary**, and straddling the street, was a **forehall**, erected at the end of the second century and continuing in use throughout the life of the fort. Such structures are often interpreted as covered exercise halls, though possibly they were used for parades or ceremonial occasions. Its construction at the end of the second century led to the removal of the north granary portico, though this entrance clearly continued in use for in the third century the southern doors were blocked by buildings and the southern portico demolished.

To the west of the granary was a large **cistern** apparently provided in the early third century, and, south of that, a courtyard building normally interpreted as a **hospital**. This was not original, but replaced a Hadrianic timber predecessor later in the second century. The room in the south-west corner was a latrine. Part of a stone toilet seat was found reused in it; the seat is displayed in the museum. The hospital was demolished in two stages in the third century. The **commanding officer's house** lay to the east of the headquarters. It consisted of four ranges of rooms built round a courtyard; a bath-suite was a later addition.

The remainder of the fort contained ten **barrack-blocks** and two possible stores buildings. The barrack-blocks are of the normal pattern, with a block for the officer at the end of a row of double rooms for the men. It is unusual, however, for both infantry and cavalry barracks each to have nine *contubernia*. Two buildings are particularly interesting. These are the two northerly barracks in the rear part of the fort, both dating to the later second century. In the front room, long pits collected waste from horses; these have been marked on the site in grey.

Most of the rooms behind contained a hearth, marked in red. It has been argued that each of the nine rooms at the front was occupied by three horses, with the troopers in the rear room, giving a total of 27. This is close to the number of 30 or 32 which, according to several sources, was the theoretical strength of each cavalry troop, though there is clearly a discrepancy between the evidence of excavation and that of the documentary sources. At one stage, the eastern stable-barrack was occupied by the troop of Pruso, as intimated by an inscription on an item of horse harness. The fragmentary stone walls overlying these two buildings are the remains of mid-third-century barrack-blocks.

North of Buddle Street, setts and paving stones mark the lines of the fort wall, rampart backing, streets, north gate, towers and parts or all of five buildings, all probably infantry barrack-blocks.

The **civil settlement** lay west and south of the fort, where, for example a bath-house was recorded in 1814, "a little above high-water mark". Two or three streets were noted by early visitors and a temple, erected by a centurion of the Sixth Legion, is attested by an inscription. More recent excavations have led to the discovery of parts of stone and timber buildings south of the fort. 50 m (160 ft) west of the fort, three ditches and the traces of an earth bank have been found running north-south. Ditches have also been found along the riverside. They date to the third century and had been recut. In both periods, the ditch terminated in a butt-end, suggesting an access point to the river. The ditches to west and south of the fort have been interpreted as the defences of an annexe or civil settlement, the east side being formed by the spur wall between fort and river. The civil settlement appears to have been abandoned by the 270s. A timber building was found outside the east gate of the fort, and therefore north of Hadrian's Wall. This was demolished to make way for a road which was in use in the early third century.

WALLSEND TO NEWCASTLE

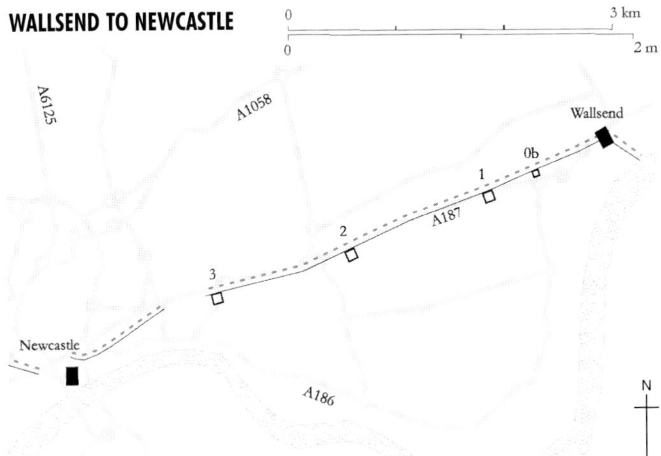

The Wall from Wallsend to Newcastle, wherever it has been found, was narrow, about 2.3 m (7 ft 6 in) thick, on a foundation averaging 2.44 m (8 ft) wide formed of rough quarried sandstone pieces with occasional water-worn boulders set in clay, except at Stott Road, where the foundation was wider. For the first 3 km (2 miles), the Wall runs in a straight line.

Fifty metres (160 ft) west of the fort, on the north side of Buddle Street, a stretch of the foundations survive with up to two courses of wall in places. A section of Narrow Wall rebuilt in 1993-96 to full height stands immediately to the south. To the north, on the berm, which is about 6 m (20 ft) wide, small pits were found in three rows, with nine pits in the longest row; each pit had held one post, now replaced by modern replicas. These were presumably sharpened stakes intended to impede access to the Wall. The pits terminate immediately north of where the ditches meet the Wall to the south. Debris found over the pits suggests their abandonment in the early third century. At the west end of the modern compound, the Wall, up to eight courses high and crossed by a culvert, has subsided southwards into a small valley. It was repaired twice, the first time after the middle of the third century when sculpture and architectural fragments, possibly from a shrine, were used.

To the west, the streets and houses cut across the line of the Wall, though the pedestrian way called the Roman Wall, running to the right of the houses, roughly follows the line of the Wall to The Avenue. Here the Wall was noted still standing over a metre high during alterations to the road in 1973. In 1999 the ditch was sectioned and found to have remained open into the 1890s. On the west side of George Road two altars dedicated to Jupiter Optimus Maximus were found in 1892-3, together with fragments of two carved stone plaques dedicated to Mercury: they probably stood beside the Military Way. The ditch here was still visible as a hollow 9 m (30 ft) wide in 1930.

At the junction with Stott Road, the presbytery of St Francis Catholic Church, formerly the Grange, is the site of a structure variously described as being "like a cellar" or "a square tower", recorded during construction of the house shortly before 1886. This has been interpreted as both a milecastle and a turret, though the description better supports the latter identification, in which case this would be **T 0b** (St Francis). In 1978, east of St Francis Community Centre, excavation found that a single course of stone survived, mortar pointed, but fronting a clay-and-cobble core. The Wall foundation, formed of clay and cobbles and flag-stones, was 3.10 m (10 ft 2 in) wide, both east and west of the Community Centre. In the eastern trench it was discovered that the facing stones had subsided and tilted away from the core allowing fissures up to 25 cm (10 in) wide to develop behind and parallel to the facing stones. To the west of the Community Centre, a pronounced north-facing camber in the foundations also hinted at subsidence. Here, though, a new foundation 3 m (9 ft 9 in) wide had been laid to the south of and partly overlying the primary foundations. This consisted of sandstone rubble set in clay and faced on both sides with water-rounded boulders. A section cut in 1928 a little further west revealed the foundations to be 1.88 m (6 ft 2 in) wide.

MacLauchlan observed the line of the Military Way about 90 m (100 yards) south of the Wall. This was confirmed in 1964 when it was located 5.18 m (17 ft) wide, constructed of two layers of mixed sandstones and river cobbles, on Tumulus Avenue, and overlying plough marks. West of Stott Road, the Wall is lost below Finchley Close and Crescent and Vauxhall Road, beyond which lay **MC 1** (Stott's Pow) within the recreation ground, Miller's Dene. The milecastle, recorded by Horsley and MacLauchlan, stood on the west side of the Stott's Pow, now covered over. MacLauchlan recorded that both MCs 1 and 2 appeared to be short-axis milecastles. Investigation in 1928 revealed "occupation debris" at both sites but no structural evidence. At about Coutts Avenue the Wall converges with Fossway which runs mainly on the ditch as far as Byker Hill.

The site of **MC 2** (Walker) ought to be about opposite the entrance to the Brough Park Stadium on Fossway: a slight mound was still visible in the late nineteenth century. Investigations in 2004 failed to find any trace. On Byker Hill the Wall turned slightly towards the north and ran on a line parallel with Shields Road, immediately south of which the Wall

Bronze stud decorated with a tiger, found ncar Walker.
(actual size)

foundations were found in 2000. Set in a trench 2.44 m (8 ft) wide, the foundations were constucted in two layers, the lowest of clay and cobbles and the upper largely of clay bounded by sandstone blocks. Across the foundations was a change in construction style, presumably reflecting the junction of two building gangs. The cracking in the foundation stones indicate a width of 2.3 m (7 ft 6 in) for the Wall. On the berm were three rows of oval pits, the inner and outer row running along the line of the berm with the middle row aligned at right angles. They held stakes, probably two per pit placed at each end, which provided further obstacles to access to the Wall. The pits showed evidence for recutting, when the square shape of the original pit was changed to a bowl-shape; this may indicate removal of the stakes by the Roman army. Between the northern row and the ditch was a low mound. Similar pits were recorded 220 m (243 yards) to the east in 2004.

Several antiquarians recorded a milecastle on the east side of the Ouse Burn, including Stukeley who provided an illustration: this ought to be **MC 3** (Ouseburn). A small altar dedicated by the priest Julius Maximus was found at the junction of Shields Road and Stephen Street, just short of Byker Bridge, the presumed location of the milecastle, while two large chiselled stones have also been recovered from hereabouts. Investigations in 1979, however, failed to reveal any evidence for either Wall or milecastle. Horsley's measurement places the milecastle on the west bank of the Ouse Burn.

On the west side of the valley, the line is picked up again a little east of Crawhall Road. Investigations from here to central Newcastle traced its line in 1928-30. The Wall passes under the south wall of St Dominic's Church. The ditch was 8.53 m (28 ft) wide and 3.2 m (10 ft 6 in) deep from the modern surface, with the berm 5.9 m (19 ft 6 in) wide in front of the Wall foundations about 2.44 m (8 ft) wide. In 1981 the Wall was again located. The foundation trench, 10 cm (4 in) deep, varied in width from

2.30 to 2.65 m (7 ft 6 in to 8 ft 8 in), and contained clay-bound sandstone rubble. The Wall, offset to the rear, was 2.20 m (7 ft 3 in) wide, bonded with clay.

At the junction of Grenville Terrace and Blagdon Close the foundations were 2.57 m (8 ft 5 in) wide, and this was confirmed in 1978. Stepney Lane and Melbourne Street follow the line of the Wall, but at a distance of some metres to the north. Pits have been found on the berm at Melbourne Street. West of Blagdon Close only the ditch has been found. At first, it runs almost straight to the Sallyport Gate, where it turns slightly northwards (slight traces of the Military Way were noted here in the eighteenth and nineteenth centuries). Between here and All Saints Church the valley of the Pandon Burn, now simply a great hollow, intervenes. At All Saints the ditch was located in six sections in 1928 on Silver Street to the north. In the most westerly section, to the north-west of the church, the line turned slightly northwards.

Two sections excavated in 1929 located the ditch, 2.90 m (9 ft 6 in) deep, at Painterheugh on the west side of Pilgrim Street immediately north of the railway before it ran out on the slope, presumably owing to later ground disturbance. A fourth-century mixing-bowl was found in the ditch fill, implying that it had remained open. The pottery found here in 1929 and 1930 was interpreted as evidence for the location of MC 4 but that identification cannot be substantiated. This line for the ditch continued the swing north from its alignment on Silver Street. This might have been in order to aid the progress of the Wall across the Lort Burn, now occupied by Dean Street, where the Wall has been sought but not found. A southwards turn must now be allowed to bring the alignment onto that recorded in 1929 and 2004 to the west of the castle. Stukeley stated that the Wall approached "the castle where the stairs are". These are assumed to be the Dog Leap Stairs which ascend beside the railway line from Dean Street, because no others are known. Excavation in 1929 failed to confirm this line.

NEWCASTLE UPON TYNE (*PONS AELII*)

The *Notitia Dignitatum* places the First Cohort of Cornovians at *Pons Aelii* (*Pons Aelius* is also possible). *Aelius* was the family name of Hadrian, but it was also the name taken by his successor and by his adopted grandson, a span stretching from 117 to 180. An inscription found in 1979 erected in 213 to the Dowager Empress Iulia Domna is one of a series of loyalty dedications erected to the Emperor Caracalla and/or his mother Iulia Domna at forts on the northern frontier in that year, and it reveals that the fort had been constructed by that date. It records that the unit at that time was the First Cohort of Cugernians, which had originally been raised in the Lower Rhineland.

The location of the bridge is now not known. It has been suggested that three inscriptions found in the river by the nineteenth-century Swing Bridge came from a shrine on the Roman bridge, though this cannot be proved. Twin altars, dedicated respectively to *Oceanus* and to *Neptune* by the Sixth Legion, it has been proposed, commemorated the safe arrival

Altars to Neptune and Oceanus found in the River Tyne at Newcastle.
(both 1.12 m high)

of the legion in or shortly after 122 when it came from the province of Lower Germany to help build the Wall. These are the same gods to which Alexander the Great had sacrificed at the River Hydaspes on the Indus over four centuries earlier. It has therefore been suggested that Hadrian himself was present and chose the deities. However, it is by no means certain that the bridge was in existence when the legion arrived, or that it was erected immediately thereafter. Moreover, the placing of the dedication on the capital of each altar is indicative of a third-century date. This would more closely coincide with the date of the erection of the fort. The third inscription was a dedication to Antoninus Pius by a detachment drawn from all three legions of Britain apparently being sent to the army of the two Germanies during the governorship of Julius Verus, that is about 158. Some of the coins found in the river were, no doubt, offerings to the gods.

The **fort** lies under the Castle Keep upon one of the ridges between the streams which flow into the River Tyne. It is likely to have been free-standing and not attached to the Wall. The fort was located in 1929, but most of our knowledge about the site stems from the excavations undertaken between 1976 and 1992. The north and south defences have been located. The south ditch lay between the Keep and the Bridge Hotel and contained some Roman stones and a samian mixing bowl not manufactured before the late second century. The north wall was 1.7 m (5 ft 7 in) wide, with no earthen backing. The best estimate is that the fort measured about 95 by 67 m (360 by 220 ft), covering 0.64 ha (1.53 acres), which is too small to hold either regiment attested here. It is possible, however, that the fort was related to the topography and was polygonal in shape, thus providing more accommodation space.

The fort was not built until the late second or early third century. The only known fort on the road leading south from the bridge, Chester-le-Street, also appears to date from the late second century. Newcastle breaks the normal Hadrianic 11.6 km

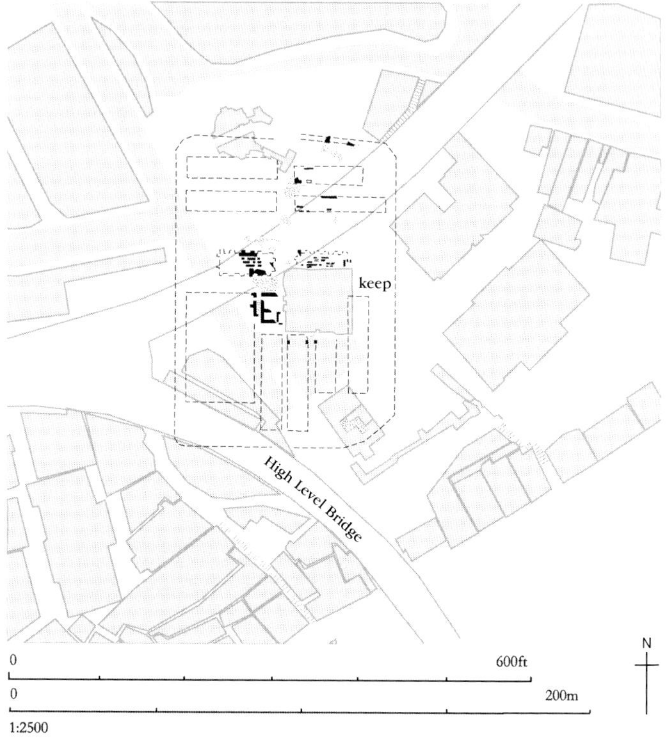

Newcastle fort.

(7⅓ miles) spacing of forts along the line of the Wall. Fragments of the headquarters building, commanding officer's house and granary are visible under a railway arch beside the keep.

The **headquarters building** contained only a cross-hall and three rooms at the rear, the central room with a strongroom. The absence of a courtyard and the small size of the rooms may be explained by the size of the fort. A hypocausted building was found in 1929 immediately to the south-east of the headquarters and may form a later addition to it. The **commanding officer's house**, which contained at least one heated room, lay to the west of the headquarters; only the north-east corner was available for investigation. The north wall of the headquarters together with the commanding officer's house were rebuilt in the second quarter of the fourth century; the *via principalis* was resurfaced at the same time. Later in the century that part of the house was again rebuilt, and the *via principalis* resurfaced.

Two **granaries**, smaller than usual, were aligned east-west and end-to-end along the north side of the *via principalis*. In the second half of the fourth century, the floor of the west granary was removed, the sleeper walls reduced in height and the space between filled. It is possible that industrial activity of some kind now took place within the building. The east granary was treated in the same way, though the date could not be determined. Fragments of buildings have been found in the southern part of the fort and in its north-east quadrant, but their function cannot be identified.

Across the fort, from the headquarters to the north wall, 143 coins were recovered during excavations, far more than might be expected. These range in date from the 270s down to 364-75, with a concentration in the 330s, 340s and 350s. Trade in this part of the fort has been advanced to explain the coin

A relief of Mercury found in 1847 south of the castle while preparing the foundations for the High Level Bridge. Mercury holds a money bag in his right hand while a goat reclines by his right foot. (432 x 230 mm)

A dedication to the Mother Goddesses of his native land overseas by Aurelius Juvenalis, found in St Nicholas Churchyard, Newcastle. (457 x 660 mm)

loss, and, if this is the case, Newcastle is unlikely to have been operating as a normal fort through much of the fourth century. The latest coins from the site date to 388-402.

Two stone coffins, one containing a pot dating to the late second to third centuries, and skeletons were found at Clavering Place on the south side of Hanover Square in 1864, 160 m (530 ft) south-west of the fort: they may indicate the location of the **cemetery**. Material found in 1990 to have been dumped on the river bank during the Roman period may be connected to the bridge or the quayside. Across the river finds indicate the existence of a settlement or a fort.

The **cathedral**, located just to the north of the fort, contains an effigy of John Collingwood Bruce: a plaque on Percy Street marks the site of his school. No visitor should leave Newcastle without seeing the internationally important **Museum of Antiquities** in the Quadrangle of the University of Newcastle. This contains many inscribed and sculptured stones and other material from Hadrian's Wall and its outpost forts. The museum also contains a model of the Wall and others of its component parts, together with a full-scale replica of the temple of Mithras at Carrawburgh.

NEWCASTLE TO BENWELL

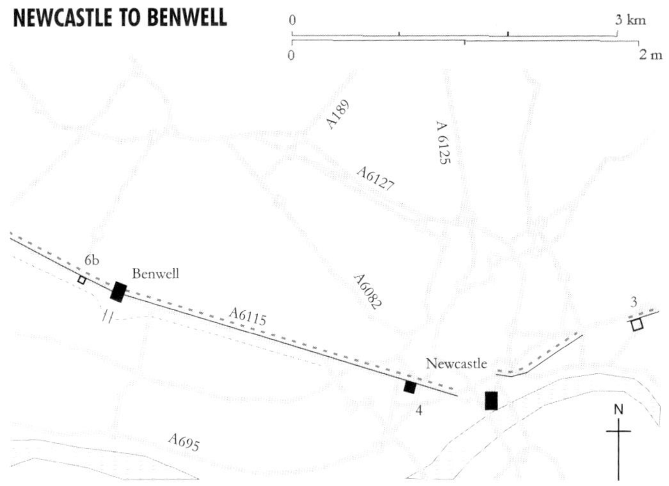

West of the castle, several excavations, all in limited space, have established a line for the Wall and its ditch. In 1929, the northern half of the ditch was located behind the St Nicholas Buildings. It was 3.66 m (12 ft) deep, with a Roman shoe at 3.35 m (11 ft) down. Close by, in 2004 the normal flagstone foundations of the Broad Wall were recorded, supporting one course of large sandstone blocks, clay-bonded and with a clay and rubble core. This line continues past the Mining Institute, Neville Hall. The south face of the Wall was found here in 1952. Even part of the flagged footings were robbed out, but on them survived the first course of the Wall, offset, with one stone of the second course, also offset. The line is marked by a strip of red concrete and an inscribed plaque. The north lip of the ditch was recorded in front of the Literary and Philosophical Society in the same year. The ditch was located a little further west in 1934, just north of the Stephenson monument. Westgate Road then takes the line of the Wall westwards out of central Newcastle with the road lying partly north of the ditch and partly over it.

The **Vallum** starts at Newcastle. The junction of the Vallum and the river is believed to have been by Redheugh Bridge, whence it cut uphill to Elswick Road. However, there is no record, either by observation or excavation, of the Vallum between Elswick Road and the river. An inscription recording work by the First Cohort of Thracians of the type used by the builders of the Vallum discovered in Clavering Place on the south side of Hanover Square in 1864 lay to the east of the most easterly credibly recorded point on Elswick Row about 100 m (300 ft) south of Westgate Road.

An inscription of the First Cohort of Thracians found at Clavering Place, Newcastle.
(254 x 353 mm)

Much uncertainty surrounds the spacing and location of milecastles and turrets from Newcastle to MC 9. In 1985 the south-west corner of a milecastle was found on the site of the Newcastle Arts Centre at 67-75 Westgate Road: it has been argued that this is **MC 4** (Westgate Road). It would appear to be a long-axis milecastle measuring 14.90 m (49 ft) across and probably 18 m (60 ft) north-south. The south wall of the milecastle, bonded in clay, was 2.70 m (9 ft) wide with the foundations of the south and east walls 2.90 m (9 ft 6 in) wide formed of flags, which are normally associated with the Broad Wall. There was some evidence to suggest that the south gate had been blocked, but the pottery indicated that the milecastle had been abandoned in the later second century or shortly after. The Roman masonry on display has been lifted and rebuilt at a higher level.

Excavations at various locations between the milecastle and Blandford Square in 1929 and in the 1990s have confirmed the line of the ditch and indicated a slight change in the line of the Wall, probably at the milecastle.

Horsley fancied that he saw some signs of a milecastle – **MC 5** (Quarry House) – at the junction of Westgate Road and Corporation Street by the cemetery, but spacing indicates a location on the summit of Elswick Hill. No trace has been found of **MC 6** (Benwell Grove), whose measured position is the Church of the Venerable Bede. The Wall ditch was found in 1992 to lie under the southern edge of the Rutherford School playing field 200 m (216 yards) east of Benwell fort. The **Vallum** lies about 10 m (33 ft) south of Westgate Road.

BENWELL (*CONDERCUM*)

The fort at Benwell occupies a magnificent natural position, on a level hill-top, from which the ground falls away gently to the north and more steeply on the other sides; it overlooked the Denton Burn to the west. The Roman name of the fort was *Condercum*, which probably means "a place with a wide view".

In the second century the First Cohort of Vangiones was stationed here, and, about 180, a cavalry regiment. Under the Emperor Antoninus Pius (138-61), Liburnius Fronto, centurion of the Sixth Legion, dedicated an altar to Jupiter, which may suggest that a detachment of the unit was based here, perhaps during the occupation of the Antonine Wall. Through the third and fourth centuries, and recorded in the *Notitia Dignitatum*, the unit in residence was the First Cavalry Regiment of Asturians. During the reign of Gordian (238-44), the prefect T. Agrippa made a dedication to the three Mother Goddesses of the Parade-ground.

Most of the fort north of Westgate Road was destroyed with the construction of a reservoir in 1863-64, while the southern area was built over between 1926 and 1937 when rescue excavations took place. There is therefore some doubt about the exact size of the fort: the latest discussion gives the measurements as 170.69 by 120.7 m (560 by 396 ft), an area of

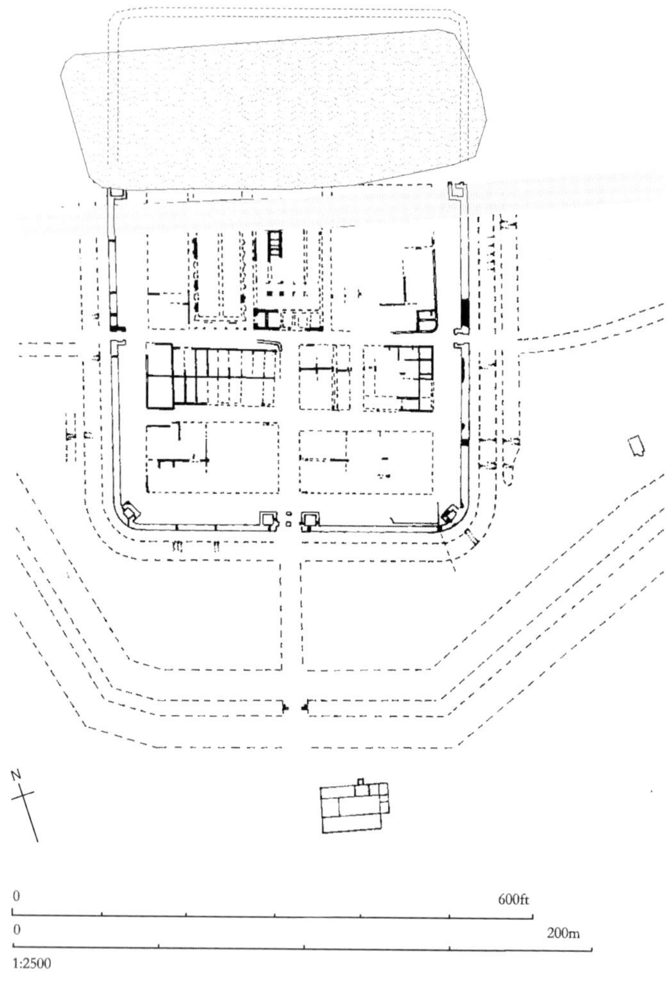

Benwell fort and the Vallum in the Hadrianic period; a road leads from the fort's south gate to the Vallum crossing. To the east of the fort sits the temple of Antenociticus while to the south of the Vallum lies a large house. The northern part of the fort is covered by a reservoir.

2.06 ha (5 acres). The fort wall, whose foundations of clay and rubble were 2.08 m (6 ft 10 in) wide, was backed by a clay bank with a width of 4.57 m (15 ft). To east and west lay two ditches, but only the inner continued round to form the south ditch, the outer ditches ending at the southern corners of the fort. Post-Roman activities on the fort site has removed much stratigraphy but left the plan. Pottery, however, indicates occupation continuing into the late fourth century.

The central range of the fort contained, from east to west, the commanding officer's house, headquarters, a double granary and a workshop or forge. The regimental strongroom was placed in the room to the east of the temple in the rear range of the **headquarters**: it was cut into the rock, decorated with wall-plaster and lit by a splayed window in its south wall. The courtyard contained a settling tank divided into five aeration chambers. The water was probably brought from the north, where Denton Hill Head is the nearest point where water emerges at a higher level than the fort.

Little remained of the large **commanding officer's house**, though hypocausts for heating were observed both in 1761 and 1926, when a silver spoon was discovered, while a well was found in its courtyard in 1959: its contents included pottery of the second half of the fourth century.

The loading bay for the double **granary** lay to the south, on the *via quintana*. In 1937 its dedication slab was found face downwards in the portico and shattered by the fall; it can be translated as "For the Emperor Caesar Trajan Hadrian Augustus, under Aulus Platorius Nepos, the Emperor's propraetorian

Inscription recording building work by the British fleet under Hadrian and the governor A. Platorius Nepos. (0.56 x 1.5 m)

legate, a detachment of the British fleet (built this)". It dates the dedication of the granary, and by implication the whole fort, to the governorship of Platorius Nepos (122-about 126). The inscription is now in the Museum of Antiquities, Newcastle. In 1990 it was recorded that the northern part of the eastern half of the granary had, at an unknown date, been demolished and metalled over.

The **workshop** was divided into several rooms. It yielded a mass of sweepings from a forge or blacksmith's shop, including scale from heated iron and local coal, heaped against its east wall.

The road behind these buildings, the *via quintana*, ran between the minor east and west gates, the latter located in 1937 and leading to causeways over the ditches. To its south, and east of the *via decumana*, lay a courtyard building, usually interpreted as a **hospital**, and another small building of uncertain purpose. Part of a bronze torque (a decorated necklace) was recovered from it in 1937. West lay two **barracks**, arranged back to back with a joint wall. Each contained an officer's suite and nine rooms: perhaps accommodation for cavalry. The rest of the space was occupied by two more double buildings, presumably either barracks or stables.

The **Vallum** took an asymmetrical diversion round the fort. Opposite the south gate the mounds were broken by gaps while a causeway crossed the ditch. This, the only visible causeway, may be seen at the foot of Denhill Park Avenue. The natural causeway of undisturbed subsoil is revetted on both

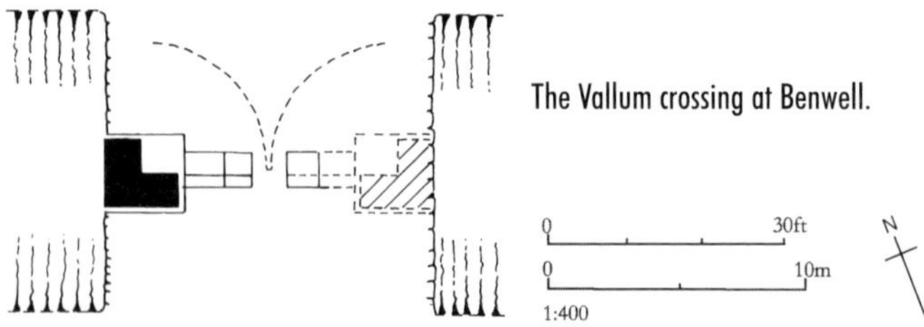

The Vallum crossing at Benwell.

sides: it supported a monumental gateway, larger and wider than a normal fort gate, 3.56 m (11 ft 8 in) as opposed to 3 m (10 ft). The stones which survive on the west side are the best dressed of any Hadrianic work on the Wall, exceeded only by the reused masonry built into the west wall at Birdoswald. The threshold indicates that the gate was closed from the north and thus access to the zone between the Wall and the Vallum was controlled from the fort. A road, resurfaced three times, passed over the causeway. By the railings lies the secondary pivot stone from the west side of the gate, also indicating a long life for the crossing. The Vallum ditch has been refilled since excavation to about half its original depth. A culvert through the causeway indicates that water drained from east to west.

Excavation has demonstrated that the ditch on each side of the causeway was filled with clay in the late second century, over which a stone building was erected to the east of the gate. Other buildings followed, being erected over the infilled ditch to both east and west of the causeway. Pottery indicates occupation of them continuing into the third century. Immediately beyond the south mound and to the east of the causeway lay a large house, often interpreted as an inn for official travellers (*mansio*), though other possibilities include an aisled barn or a farmhouse in the style of a villa.

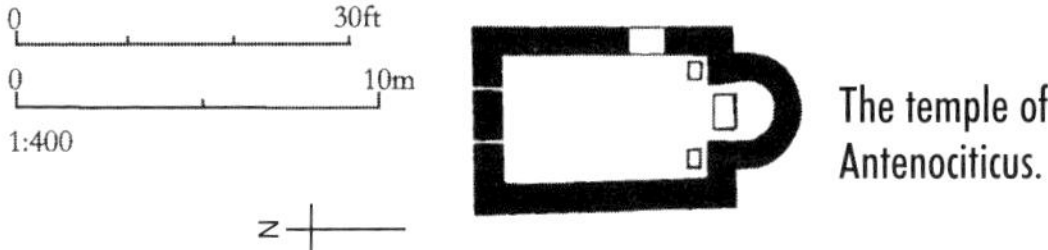

The temple of Antenociticus.

The **temple of Antenociticus** may be seen in Broomridge Avenue, opening first right out of Weidner Road to the east of the fort. It lies between the Wall and the Vallum. The temple is rectangular, 4.88 by 3.05 m (16 by 10 ft) internally, with an apse to the south. In 1862, when the temple was discovered, some traces were noted of a door in the north wall, but these have

The head of Antenociticus. (300 x 200 mm)

now disappeared, the only surviving door lying in the east wall. The apse held the stone cult-statue, of which the head, ovoid in shape, with wild hair and Celtic neck-torque, and part of an arm and leg, are now in the Museum of Antiquities, Newcastle. The apse is flanked by casts of two original altars in the same museum. One, gracefully carved, is dedicated to Antenociticus and the deities of the emperors, by Aelius Vibius, centurion of the Twentieth Legion. The other has an inscription referring to the promotion of its dedicator, which may be translated "To the god Anociticus, Tineius Longus (set this up) having, while prefect of cavalry, been adorned with the (senatorial) broad stripe and designated quaestor, by the decrees of our best and greatest Emperors, under Ulpius Marcellus, consular governor". Marcellus was governor by March 178 when there were two emperors, Marcus Aurelius and his son Commodus. A third altar, not copied at the temple, was dedicated to Antenociticus by the First Cohort of Vangiones. Other finds in the temple included two brooches, two silver coins, some bronze coins and the handle of a box or chest.

The collapsed walls of the temple were associated with burnt timber and roof-tiles suggesting destruction; the few coins point to a date in the late second or early third century, though at whose hand is not clear. Antenociticus is otherwise unrecorded within the Roman empire; he was either a local deity or imported by the Vangiones. Three burials in the apse may have been post-Roman in date. A stone-lined grave containing a lead coffin for a child was found 50 m (160 ft) south-west of the temple, immediately north of the Vallum. "A few yards west of the Roman chapel" were found two Anglo-Saxon brooches, one dating to the sixth-seventh centuries. There is a hint from the find-spots of inscriptions and sculpture that other temples lay hereabouts.

The **bath-house**, found about 270 m (300 yards) south-west of the fort in 1751, and carefully drawn by the landowner Robert Shafto before destruction, is of the regular Hadrianic plan. A drain was traced in 1926 through the south-east corner of the fort southwards for about 60 m (200 ft); walls of stone buildings were also recorded here. To the west, on Denton Bank, seams of coal once came to the surface and these have been shown by analysis and comparison with the coal found in the fort workshop to have been exploited by the Romans.

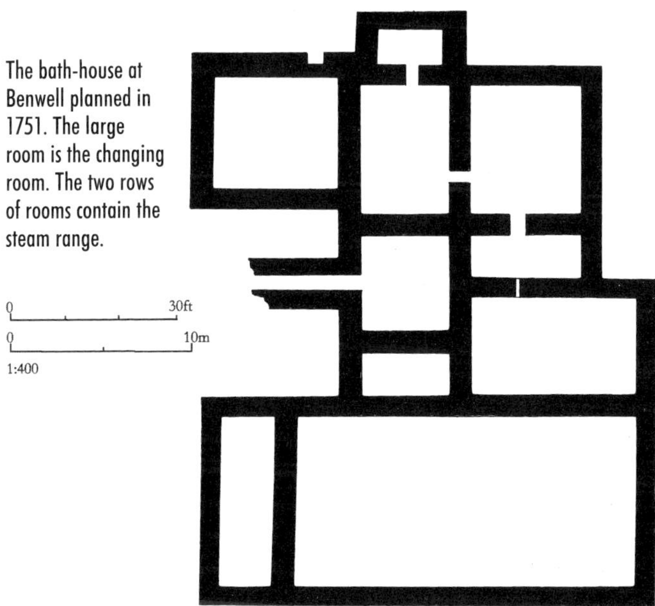

The bath-house at Benwell planned in 1751. The large room is the changing room. The two rows of rooms contain the steam range.

BENWELL TO RUDCHESTER

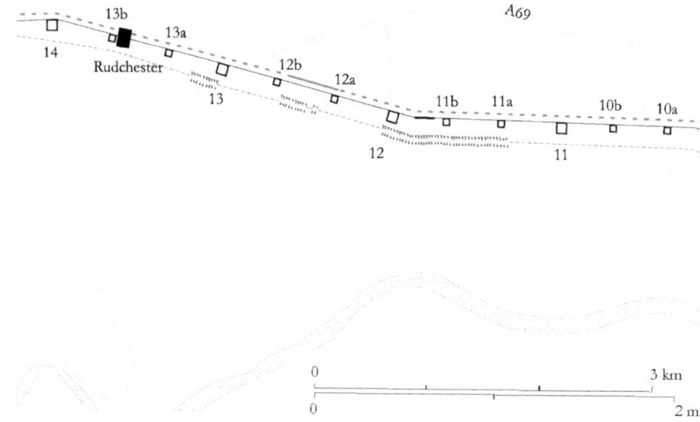

In 2003 the Military Way was located 170 m (560 ft) west of Benwell fort and about 50 m (160 ft) south of the Wall. It was 7.76 m (25 ft 6 in) wide and bordered on the south side by three rock-cut ditches. Two narrower metalled tracks lay between the Wall and the Military Way.

A structure "about 4 yards square" (3.66 m) was recorded by Robert Shafto in 1751 during construction of the Military Road. It lies 280 m (308 yards) beyond the fort, just east of Two Ball Lonnen, and is normally interpreted as **T 6b** (Benwell Hill) (measurement from MC 4 (Westgate) suggests it might be T 6a). In 2003 the Wall, at least 2.1 m (6 ft 11 in) wide, was located a little to the west, with the north face built of large blocks. **MC 7** (Benwell Bank) has not been located. The Wall was found beneath the steps of the Methodist chapel at the foot of Denton Bank in 1953. Three centurial stones found in the area of Wall mile 7 record work by the Second Legion. Their style suggests a late-second-century date, implying that the Wall in this sector required repair at that time.

The **Vallum** ran straight for 5.4 km (3⅓ miles) from Benwell fort to Walbottle Dene. South of Wall mile 7 the crossings were

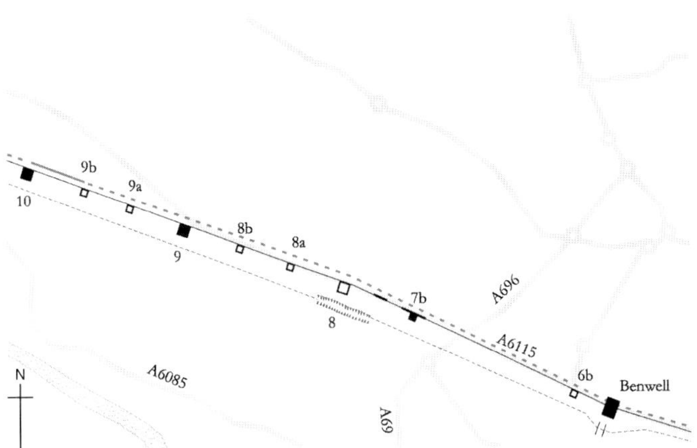

55 m (60 yards) apart rather than the normal 41 m (45 yards), perhaps because this mile is longer than normal and there was a need to retain a standard number of crossings (35?) between each milecastle. The Vallum between T 7b and MC 8 was destroyed in 1938. Centurial stones, one recording work by the First Cohort of Dacians, were found set into the faces of the mounds looking onto the berm.

In the forecourt of the petrol station at the south-west side of the roundabout at the junction of the West Road and Denton Road lies the first fragment of the Wall to be seen west of Newcastle: it is part of the south face. 20 m (6 ft) on is a further length up to three courses high, 2.77 - 2.87 m (9 ft 1 in - 9 ft 5 in) wide above a foundation of rough flat slabs and clay about 3.20 m (10 ft 6 in) wide. Excavation in 1927 revealed a concrete core. More recently, excavation uncovered foundations 3 m (9 ft 10 in) wide at 717 West Road. The exact dimensions of the Wall could not be determined, but it was at least 2.75 m (9 ft) wide. The facing stones were laid on mortar beds and pointed with mortar, but the core was of clay. Masons' chippings indicate that here the final dressing took place on site.

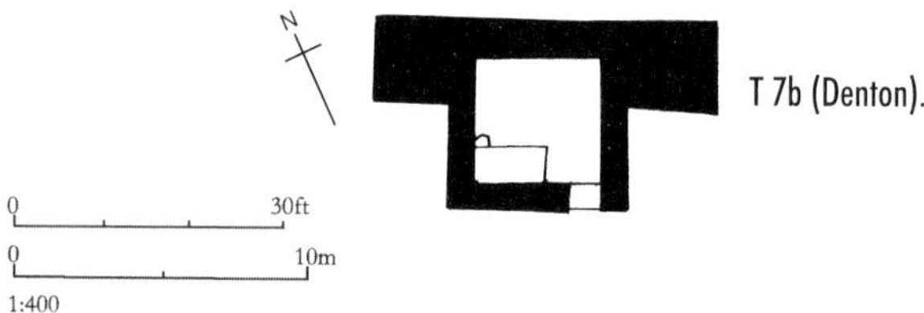

T 7b (Denton).

T 7b (Denton) sits within a length of Broad Wall, formed, like the turret, of large stones: it was excavated in 1929. The turret stands up to six courses high. It is recessed 1.52 m (5 ft) into the Wall and its walls are nearly 90 cm (3 ft) thick. The doorway is on the east side of the south wall. The original pivot hole survives to the front of the doorway on the east side; to the west there is a socket in the top stone which may have been intended to hold a bar. A heap of pottery found outside the centre of the east wall of the turret was taken to indicate the position of a window.

The original floor of the turret, 30 cm (1 ft) thick, was of clay containing fragments of building stone. On this rested a platform in the south-west corner and beside it a small square box formed of flags, partially surviving. A stone bowl was found sitting on the box. One hearth lay beside the stone box and the platform, a second in the centre of the north wall of the turret. The floor was repaired, with flagging laid round the stone box. Within the material used to repair the floor was found a spear-head and the binding from a shield.

The threshold of the doorway was raised 60 cm (2 ft) and a new floor laid over a quantity of debris. The southern part of the turret was flagged and this layer covered the platform. Its successor was placed in the south-west corner, but against the west wall. Again there were two hearths, one beside the south wall and the other near to the centre of the turret. The threshold of the turret was subsequently raised again and pottery indicates occupation continued into the fourth century. Much later, a building was erected in the turret; it was associated with eighteenth-century pottery.

A little beyond T 7b the Newcastle Western Bypass (A1) cuts through the Wall, the line of which was investigated in 1988-89. The Wall itself was severely robbed and only a few stones of the south face survived fronting a core of clay and rubble, the latter probably won from the ditch. There had been some attempt to create a level terrace for the foundations, 3.02 m (9 ft 11 in) wide, but they still sloped southwards at an angle of 3.5°. The resulting pressure had caused the foundation slabs to snap 20 cm (8 in) from their southern edge. This uneven support for the superstructure had also led to the collapse of the south face. The south-facing stones had fallen and, although they had been subsequently removed, the mortar from the joints between seven courses of stones survived. This plaster was cream-coloured and lightweight, different from the grey mortar here used as bedding between the facing stones. It would appear to represent either an overall render to the Wall face or flush pointing. The collapse apparently occurred during the Roman period, the fallen facing stones then being removed to use in the repair of the Wall.

Behind the Wall, on the original ground surface, was a strip of metalling up to 8.40 m (27 ft 7 in) wide marked by wheel ruts. After patching and being covered by clay, a new surface was laid; this contained a coin of the Emperor Septimius Severus dating to 202-210. Under and on each side of the Wall were found plough marks representing several different phases of activity. It is possible that the last ploughing was undertaken in the season before the construction of the Wall.

The rock-cut Vallum ditch was 2.44 m (8 ft) deep, 5.70 m (18 ft 8 in) wide at the top and 2.85 m (9 ft 4 in) at the bottom with sides at an angle of 75-80°. It was found to have silted naturally. The clay and sandstone rubble forming the mounds was revetted with clay blocks. The north mound was 5.95 m (19 ft 6 in) wide and the south 6.80 m (22 ft 3 in); the north berm was 8.15 m (26 ft 9 in) wide and the south 9.5 m (31 ft 2 in).

Beyond the bypass, on the Ramparts immediately south of West Road, is a length of Broad Wall uncovered in 1947. Up to three courses of large facing stones survive, 1.22 m (4 ft) high. Southway leads to Wallington Drive where the Vallum is still well preserved with crossings visible in an open strip of ground.

MC 8 (West Denton) probably lies just short of Sugley Burn. Excavation in 1928 failed to locate any structures, but pottery and "occupation earth" were found. Two Romano-Celtic heads were found nearby in 1969 and 1980. The burn passed through the Wall via a culvert 60 cm (2 ft) square recorded in 1864. A footpath leads south along the burn and across it, climbing the west bank where a short section of the Vallum is obscured by the undergrowth. On the site of West Denton School the Vallum was found in 1961 to be rock-cut, 3.66 m (12 ft) deep and almost 3.35 m (11 ft) wide across the top and 2.36 m (7 ft 9 in) at the bottom. The berms were 10.67 m (35 ft) wide and the mounds turf-revetted. Between Wall and Vallum lay the Military Way, 7.31 m (24 ft) wide, with a bottoming of large stones. Here the Wall and Vallum are about 180 m (200 yards) apart; they then slowly converge, until at Walbottle Dene they are only 54 m (60 yards) apart, and thereafter keep nearly parallel until they approach Rudchester.

At West Denton the Wall has been destroyed by the dual carriageway. Lost in this stretch are **T 8a** (West Denton), sought in 1928, but its location only implied by the discovery of pottery and "occupation earth", and **T 8b** (Union Hall), which stood two courses high with a door in the east side of the south wall. Beyond the roundabout the Vallum is faintly visible in the first field on the left of the B8528.

The low platform of **MC 9** (Chapel House) is just before Blucher village; it was excavated in 1929 and partially re-examined in 1951 and 2000. It is a long-axis milecastle measuring 18.29 by 14.88 m (60 by 48 ft 10 in) with side walls 2.74 m (9 ft) wide but a narrower south wall. The core of the east wall was of clay and rubble but the facing stones, formed of large blocks, were mortared. Seven stones on the base course of the south wall were numbered, five with VIII and one each bearing VIIII and IX, possibly cut at the quarry. Its type IV north gate was located in 1951. The road passing through the milecastle led to the Military Way, at least 5.49 m (18 ft) wide, 9.75 m (32 ft) to the south. A layer of yellow clay was noted below the milecastle in 2000; it may have been laid down as a building platform. In the eastern part of the milecastle was a two-roomed stone building, with clay-bonded walls. The door led off the road into the smaller northern room. After patching, the floor was raised by 55 cm (22 in) and the door threshold lifted while the building was extended to the north. In the western area of the milecastle, two rows each of three post-holes were found, 2.13 m (7 ft) apart. A stone building was later erected here but was very badly preserved. Pottery and a coin of the Emperor Valentinian I dating to 364-75 indicates that occupation continued into the final third of the fourth century.

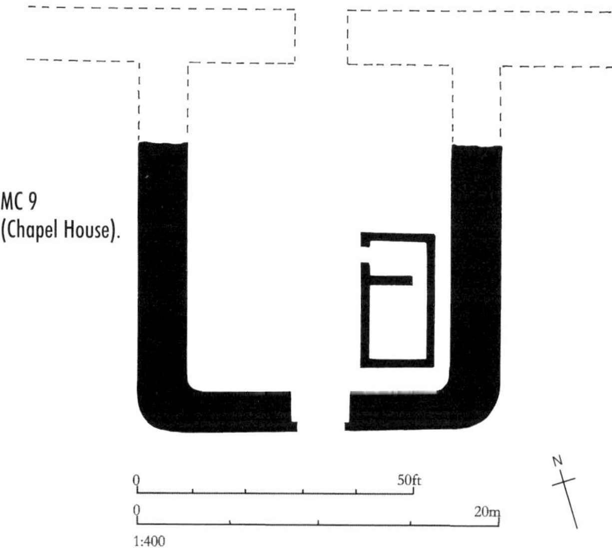

MC 9 (Chapel House).

Other finds included a gaming board, a sword scabbard chape and part of a relief of a female figure.

Beyond the south-east corner of the milecastle a flagged surface was recorded in 2000 and, to the east, a ditch. In 1929, outside the south wall of the milecastle, about halfway between the gate and the south-west corner, the headless skeleton of a person of about 17 years was found, with the bones of an adult man and a woman of about 20 nearby. The body could have been buried in either the Roman or the post-Roman period.

T 9b (Walbottle) is at the west end of St Cuthbert's School. It was built of the same massive masonry as T 7b with the door in the same position. To the south, the line of the Vallum is not built over. The ditch is visible in the grounds of the Walbottle Campus. **MC 10** (Walbottle Dene), opposite Dene House, was excavated in 1928 and re-examined in 1999-2001. It measured 17.69 by 14.76 m (58 by 48 ft 6 in) internally with broad walls 2.98 m (9 ft 9 in) wide. The threshold of its north gateway, with jambs in large masonry, lies at the south-east corner of the front garden of Dene House. It has been observed, though no longer visible, that the eastern iron collar is worn but the western is not, suggesting that only one leaf of the gate was usually opened. Both gates appear to have been of type IV. Little is known of the internal arrangements of the milecastle, though excavation in the south-east corner revealed evidence for a hearth or oven. Just before crossing the dene, both Wall and Vallum turn about 20°, to aim for the Great Hill at Heddon.

T 10a (Throckley East) lies in Throckley, just east of Callerton Road. Excavated in 1980, it was found to have been erected on ground which had previously been cultivated. The turret had walls 1.07 m (3 ft 6 in) wide, the facing stones mortar pointed but with the core formed by clay and sandstone blocks. The entrance lay in the south-east corner. The door threshold was overlain by a series of hearths: there were also hearths against the north wall. There were two floor levels, both of clay; on the upper surface some stones in the south-west corner may be the remains of a platform. The finds included a spearhead and four worked flints. With the exception of one sherd, all the pottery dated to the Hadrianic period. Although the turret had a short life, the recess was not built up.

T 10b (Throckley) has not been located. A little to the west, the Wall foundation 2.8 m (9 ft 2 in) wide was recorded in 2004. The underlying soil contained some burnt wood and plants which may represent preliminary clearance of the ground.

Throckley and District Bank Top Club is the computed site of **MC 11** (Throckley Bank Top) but investigations on three occasions have failed to locate it and it may have been destroyed. In 2002 a metalled surface of two levels was recorded north of the presumed site of the milecastle. Near this point a hoard of over 5,000 silvered coins of 244-75 was found in 1879 secreted in a pot just behind the Wall and below the main road. Further west, the Wall was recorded as 2.59 m (8 ft 6 in) thick with a clay core. From just east of the presumed site of MC 11 to T 11b, 145 pits were traced along the berm for a distance of over 1 km (⅔ mile) in 2002. Some pits retained the impressions of two upright stakes.

T 11a (Heddon Hall) has not been found. At the end of the houses on the right the ditch starts to become visible; to the left there are faint traces of the Vallum. **T 11b** (Great Hill) lies on the east side and towards the summit of Great Hill, its location only surmised in 1928 by the discovery of pottery and "occupation earth". The line of the pits planned in 2002 turned towards the Wall at this point, suggesting that the berm narrowed at the turret. The Broad Wall was removed from here in 1926; it was found to have been bonded with tough white mortar. The **Vallum** was examined in 1893 when the toolmarks of the Roman diggers were recognised on the south side of the ditch, both sides of which were revetted with masonry between the out-cropping bed rock. There is no marginal mound on the south berm. The Vallum changes direction on top of the hill, but the Wall turns further west on the downhill slope, within the English Heritage enclosure to the south of the modern road. At this point, the north mound of the Vallum is only 20 m (66 ft) behind the Wall.

Within the English Heritage enclosure a stretch of Broad Wall stands up to 1.52 m (5 ft) high. Some of the stones of the south face, which survives up to seven courses high, retain traces of white mortar, which is usually assigned to the Severan period. Insufficient remains, however, to prove that these represent more than over-pointing of the joints, or even a surviving indication of where the masons mixed their mortar beside the Wall. The foundations are 3.23 m (10 ft 7 in) wide and the Wall is 2.92 m (9 ft 7 in) thick; its core was of clay before consolidation. At the west end of the stretch a kiln was later built into the back of the Wall. Also, at the west end, the south lip of the ditch survives.

MC 12 (Heddon) lay under Town Farm; its north gate is recorded as having been found in 1926. A large hoard of Roman coins in wooden boxes was found here in 1752. Another small hoard discovered at or near Heddon about 1820 comprised coins of emperors from Maximian (286-305) to Arcadius (383-408), the latest being one of 394. Finally, two inscriptions were discovered during the construction of the Military Road, and are presumed to come from the Heddon area. Both record the Sixth Legion engaged on rebuilding work (*Leg VI V P F ref*), and one bears the names of Tertullus and Sacerdos, consuls for 158.

Sixth Legion rebuilding stone of 158 found at Heddon.

The Military Way was found to lie on the north mound of the Vallum just west of Heddon.

From Heddon the Wall follows the B6318, the Military Road, westwards. The road lies on the line of the Wall with the ditch to the right, which was found in 1956 to be 8.23 m (27 ft) wide and 2.13 m (7 ft) deep, with an upcast mound 9 m (30 ft) wide. South of the road, the south mound of the Vallum is visible behind the houses as a ridge, having a commanding view to the north.

T 12a (Heddon West) was examined in 1930. It was so badly robbed that the existence of an internal platform could not be determined. Its mortared walls were 1.22 m (4 ft) thick, and the door lay to the east. **T 12b** (North Lodge), excavated the same year, was the same plan as its neighbour, though here the platform survived. At this point the B6318 diverges from the Wall line to cross the dual carriageway. Sections cut here in 1975 showed the Wall to be standing up to five courses high with a sandy clay core and resting upon a foundation of similar material 76 cm (2 ft 6 in) deep. The culvert carrying the Rudchester Burn under the Wall was seen in 1974: it was similar to that recorded by Bruce at West Denton Burn.

MC 13 (Rudchester Burn) is visible as a low platform south of the road 155 m (170 yards) beyond the burn. It is a short-axis milecastle measuring 15.24 by 17.91 m (50 by 58 ft 9in) with narrow side walls, 2.34 m (7 ft 8 in) wide; its north gate is of Type I. The threshold of the gate had been raised 23 cm (9 in); it was unworn. A single stone remained which related either to a third threshold or to the narrowing of the gateway. A pot containing a hoard of nearly 516 gold and silver coins, the latest dating to 168, was found here in 1776. The Vallum is also visible to the south.

T 13a (Rudchester East) was investigated in 1930: it was of the same plan as 12a and b, with the platform surviving as well as blocking within the doorway. A thickness of 2.82 m (9 ft 3 in) has been recorded for the Wall here.

RUDCHESTER (*VINDOBALA*)

The fort at Rudchester lies on the top of the flat ridge between the Rudchester Burn and the March Burn, 11 km (6¾ miles) west of Benwell and immediately to the west of the modern cross-roads. The name is *Vindobala* in the *Notitia Dignitatum* and *Vindovala* in the *Ravenna Cosmography*. The former might mean "white peak", the latter "white walls", which may be preferable. The *Notitia Dignitatum* records that *cohors prima Frixagorum* was based here. This is presumably the First Cohort of Frisiavones, which is attested on several second-century diplomas and as *Frixiav(onum)* on an altar dedicated by an *optio* (a junior officer) to Coventina at Carrawburgh. This regiment may have been at the fort during the third and fourth centuries. The fort measures 157 by 117.3 m (515 by 385 ft), covering 1.8 ha (4.5 acres), appropriate for a 500-strong unit of infantry and cavalry. To the north of the road a low platform

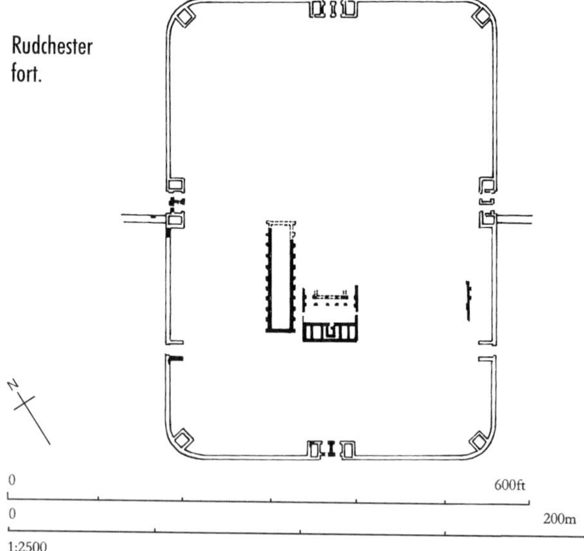

Rudchester fort.

survives; to the south, the west and south ramparts are clearer with the farm-buildings beyond.

The fort has been investigated twice, in 1924 and 1972. The earlier work concentrated on the gates and principal buildings. The **south gate** had been robbed to its lowest course, which displayed a marking out line for the main walls. The entrance to the western guard-chamber was, unusually, on the north side and from the fort rather than the entrance passage. The west portal had been blocked, the wall resting on the original threshold, in the second half of the second century: three layers of floor lay within the resulting room, a hearth on the lowest. At an unknown date, a second door was introduced at the rear of the east passage.

The **west gate** lay partly under the modern road; some walls were found to be well preserved, standing 1.83 m (6 ft) high. The threshold of the south portal showed no signs of wear before it was blocked. The north portal had also been blocked, probably in the later second century. The **minor west gate** was located together with the *via quintana* rutted by carts with an axle width of 1.60 m (5 ft 3 in). The road itself was found in 1972 to be at least 4 m (13 ft) wide.

In the centre of the fort lay the **headquarters building**. It was of the normal plan. A strongroom, entered by a flight of six steps, occupied much of the central rear room: it was clearly secondary. On the floor lay a considerable quantity of painted wall-plaster. The floors of the two rooms to the west were flagged and cement-rendered, and a flue broke through the partition wall.

It seems probable that the **commanding officer's house** lay to the east. Here were found a flagged floor above an earlier one of *opus signinum* (waterproof mortar) and a hypocaust. To the west was a single, large **granary**, fronting onto the *via quintana*.

Investigations in 1972 south of the central range revealed three successive buildings. In the small area examined, the earlier two buildings appear to represent barrack-blocks lying east-west. While both were of stone, the first probably had timber partitions. This building was burnt down, burnt pottery, charred wood, fired daub and window glass softened and distorted by heat all bearing testimony to this. The date appeared to be in the last third of the second century. It was replaced by a building with stone internal partitions. At an unknown date, this building fell into disrepair, a layer of soil covering its remains. Over this, a single stone containing two sockets for tenons on its upper face was interpreted as evidence for the erection of a timber-framed building, dated to the late fourth century.

Below the earliest building and the *via quintana* examined in 1972 were found plough marks in the clay subsoil. They appeared to relate to rigs some 1.5 m (5 ft) from crest to crest. It is possible that the area was being cultivated when the army arrived to build the fort.

The Vallum makes a slight southwards turn 700 m (800 yards) east of the fort to pass some 73 m (240 ft) to the south; no regular diversion was therefore required on this side. To the west, the Vallum takes a sharp dog-leg to avoid the fort. Its ditch was located south of the fort in 1898 and, nearest the fort, was largely filled with stones. Investigations in 2000 revealed a metalled surface running over the infilled ditch, together with gullies and ditches.

Several **shrines** are known outside the fort. A life-sized statue of Hercules was found in 1760 and is now in the Museum

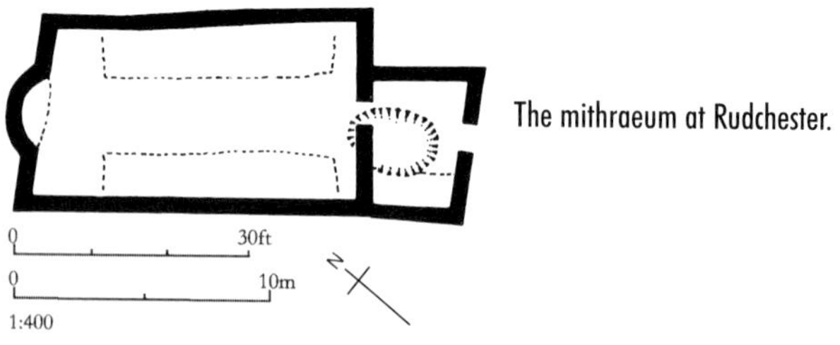

The mithraeum at Rudchester.

of Antiquities, Newcastle. In 1844, five altars to Mithras were discovered and his temple was excavated in 1953. It had been erected in the late second or early third century on the site of earlier buildings and seems to have lasted into the fourth, when it was deliberately destroyed. The first building, 13.12 by 6.76 m (43 by 22 ft), contained two long benches with an apse at one end, and a vestibule or narthex at the other, subsequently replaced. Four altars had occupied the sanctuary while five others, and a incense burner, were ranged along the benches. One altar was dedicated by a centurion of the Sixth Legion, two of the others by prefects, presumably of the local unit. Apart from some inscriptions built into the farmstead, a cistern known as the Giant's Grave, 3.66 m by 1.37 m by 60 cm deep (12 by 4 ft 6 in by 2 ft) with an outlet hole close to the bottom, is the only visible feature at Rudchester: it is well protected by nettles. When found in 1766 it contained many bones and an object described as being like a candlestick with three feet: this is now in the Museum of Antiquities, Newcastle. In the same year a hoard of 15 gold and 500 silver coins was found nearby.

Statue of Hercules holding a club and carrying a basket containing the Apples of the Hesperides. (1.22 m high)

RUDCHESTER TO HALTON CHESTERS

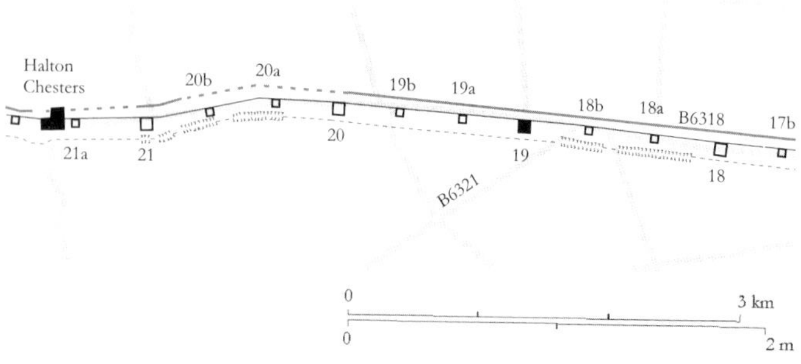

Excavation in 1924 at a point 3 m (10 ft) west of the fort revealed the north face of the Wall erected on a foundation course of coarse white stone. The first course was topped by an elaborately moulded plinth, a treatment not known elsewhere on the Wall. Perhaps there was a special inscription mounted here to mark work on the Wall. A chamfered stone was also found, presumably fallen from the top of the Wall.

T 13b (Rudchester West) ought to lie 73 m (80 yards) beyond the fort. The Wall bears left on the crest beyond the stream and immediately beyond **MC 14** (March Burn) survives as a low platform. Investigated in 1946, it was found to measure 18.29 m (60 ft) across, with broad walls and is presumably a short-axis milecastle. Examination in 2000 revealed that, in spite of the poor state of preservation, enough survived to indicate the existence of a building up to 5.11 m (16 ft 9 in) wide on the west side of the milecastle.

Horsley saw **T 14a** (Eppies Hill) on the knoll of that name where the Wall and Vallum are but 36 m (30 yards) apart. The Wall changes direction again on the hill and the ditch is visible running down on the right, and its upcast is clear on the summit. To the south, the Vallum ditch is faintly visible, very close to the Wall. Wall and Vallum soon draw apart, however, for the Wall stays with the high ground *en route* to Harlow Hill, while the Vallum cuts across country behind, taking a straight

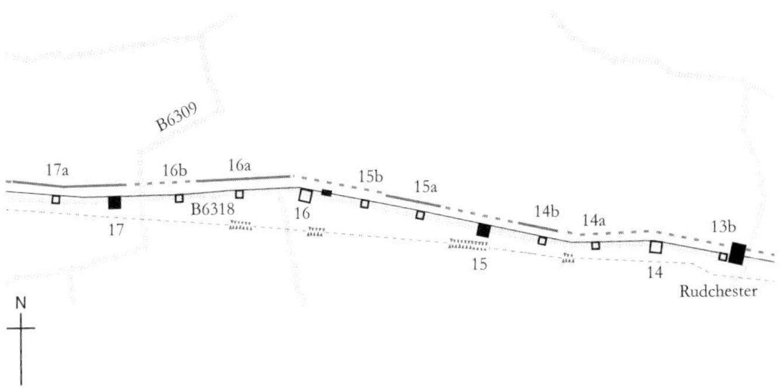

line from MC 15 for 8 km (5 miles) to Carr Hill. It is only intermittently visible, though often reflected in the field boundaries.

A bold platform and robbed walls identify **MC 15** (Whitchester) beside the field gate: it has not been excavated. **Ts 15a** and **15b** were located at the normal spacing in 1931. On Harlow Hill the road swings a little north of the Wall which is visible as a mound. Various widths have been recorded for the Wall here: 2.23 m (7 ft 4 in) and 2.44 m (8 ft) in the eighteenth century, 2.7 m (9 ft) in the nineteenth century and 2.79 m (9 ft 2 in) in 1929. The narrower widths may relate to narrowing during construction or to later repairs. **MC 16** (Harlow Hill) sits to the left of the modern road, just short of the minor road, but is not visible.

The Wall runs downhill past the site of the next two turrets to the reservoirs. Recent excavations at the reservoirs showed the Wall to have been completely removed by the construction of the road. On the rise beyond, the low platform of **MC 17** (Welton) may be seen. Measuring 14.93 by 17.68 m (49 by 58 ft), it was a short-axis milecastle with narrow side walls and a type I north gate. The crossing over the ditch does not appear to be original. A milestone formerly stood on the Military Way just east of the milecastle: it was erected in 213 during the reign of Caracalla.

About 174 m (190 yards) west of MC 17 a significant change in the construction of the Wall was discovered in 1931. Up to this point, one course was laid above the foundations and then the Wall reduced in thickness (standard A), but to the west the offset does not occur until above the third or, sometimes, fourth course (standard B). In addition, the stones used in the construction of the Wall tend to be smaller than those recorded between here and Denton. This change has been related to the work of different legions. Differences have also been recorded in the plans of the turrets. Those to the east as far as T 12a had east doors and thick walls. All examined between T 17a and T 21a have doors at the west end of the south wall, a platform in the south-east corner and narrow walls. **T 17a** (Welton East), excavated in 1931, also had a rectangular platform in the north-west corner. The only known find is a ballista ball made from whinstone.

MC 18 (East Wallhouses), also examined in 1931, was a long-axis milecastle measuring 18.14 by 16.36 m (59 ft 6 in by 53 ft 8 in), with its north gate of type I, though it was recorded as being of rougher construction than other gateways of that type. Although the north wall was broad, the side walls, of standard B, were narrow. These factors suggest that the building of the milecastle was started by one legion and finished by another. There is no sign of a causeway over the Wall ditch, though one used to be visible across the Vallum ditch.

The ditch now becomes better preserved. Excavation in 1999 revealed that it was 13 m (4 ft 6 in) across and from 2.74 to 2.96 m (9 to 9 ft 8 in) deep, with a U-shaped profile. The Vallum exhibits gaps in the mounds and crossings in the ditch. These features can be seen from just east of the lane to Wallhouses to the B6321 road leading south to Corbridge.

T 18a (Wallhouses East) was found to be well preserved in 1931. Four steps led to the top of a platform in the south-east corner. The turret also produced a ballista ball. The Vallum was examined a little to the west in 1980-1 in advance of the laying

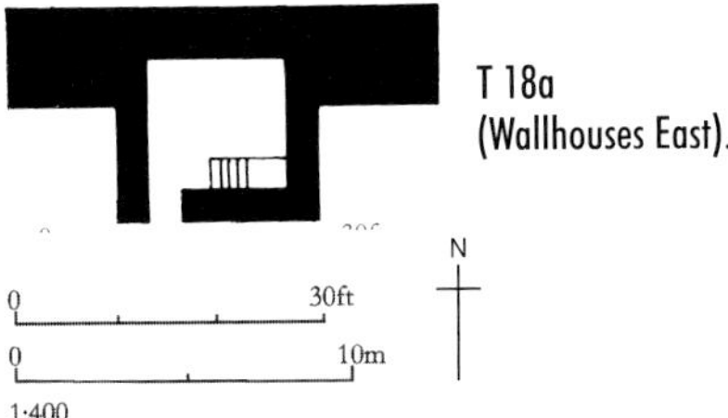

T 18a (Wallhouses East).

of a pipeline. The ditch averaged 8 m (26 ft 3 in) across, with a depth of 2.29 m (7 ft 6 in). Both mounds had been breached in the Antonine period and a causeway with a metalled surface laid across the ditch. The Military Way lay immediately to the north of the north mound. Plough marks were recorded beneath both mounds.

T 18b (Wallhouses West) was partly excavated in 1931 and fully in 1959. There was some evidence for a platform in both main periods of occupation. The floor was of clay and, as at T 10a, a hearth had been constructed in the doorway. Beside it, a small enclosure appeared to have been used as a coal store. The use of the turret as a workshop is suggested by the presence of a high-temperature hearth, about 1 m (3 ft) of ash, some heavily impregnated by iron oxide, and several iron objects. The latter included a shield boss and 60 hobnails suggesting, possibly, the repair of footwear. Other artefacts included a brooch, three items of copper, a bone plaque and a struck flake. The usual range of cooking pots was found. The cut of the bones of cattle, sheep and pig suggested that stew was a popular dish, while some remains of shellfish were also recorded. A layer of rubble separated the two main periods of occupation, which artefacts indicate dated to the second century.

The piers of the old gateway of Matfen estate mark the site of **MC 19** (Matfen Piers), a low platform to the south of the road. 17.20 by 16.26 m (56 ft 5 in by 53 ft 4 in), with narrow south wall and a type III south gate, it survives poorly. The presence of a small hearth in the north gate passage indicates that the gateway had been narrowed. Limited investigation in 1999 revealed evidence for a stone building to the east side of the milecastle and hard standing to the west. In 1931, immediately outside the south gate, in a level which appeared to date to the second century, was found an altar to the Mothers recording the erection of a temple by a detachment drawn from the First Cohort of Vardullians. Presumably the temple stood beside the milecastle. The discovery of this inscription led Eric Birley to suggest that the soldiers manning the milecastles and turrets were not drawn from the forts on the Wall but from units spread along the Wall for this purpose. The Vardullians were recorded at Corbridge in the 160s. Bruce recorded a width for the Wall here of under 2.44 m (8 ft). 27.5 m (90 ft) east of the milecastle, the south face was found to have an extra offset between the second and third courses, resulting in a slightly narrower wall: the standard of workmanship suggested that this was a later repair. To the south of the milecastle a causeway across the Vallum ditch was once visible.

T 19a (East Clarewood) was examined in 1932. It was of the same style as Ts 18a and b, with the important exception that the recess was built up, the walling resting on earlier occupation layers. Incorporated within the blocking was a door-jamb 1.5 m (5 ft) long, and a stone resembling a hypocaust pillar. No pottery later than the second century was found. South of T 19a the gaps in the south mound of the Vallum were formerly visible, blocked by an additional small mound like a traverse. **T 19b** (West Clarewood), built mainly with clay rather than mortar, yielded an uninscribed altar below the latest, flagged floor; it also was abandoned during the second century. The Wall here was rather wider than normal, 2.97 m (9 ft 9 in). Just east of Halton Shields isolated gaps may be seen in the south mound of the Vallum.

MC 20 (Halton Shields) lies in the gardens of the houses at the east end of the hamlet. It measures 17.98 by 16.56 m (59 by 54 ft 4 in); its side walls appear to be narrow. The north gate was of type III and the threshold was found in 1935 to have been raised and consist of ordinary facing stones. No evidence of narrowing or blocking of the gate was found. Just west of the gate passage four courses of Wall survived without an offset. The Vallum passes particularly close to the milecastle, the north mound as close as 1.5 m (5 ft). It is perhaps this proximity which forced the Military Way, somewhere between MCs 19 and 20, to move from its normal position between the Wall and Vallum onto the north mound, where it remained as far as Down Hill.

The modern road avoids the summit of Carr Hill, where the Wall was recorded 2.90 m (9 ft 6 in) wide at the point where it turned slightly on the summit of the rise. In 1936, **T 20a** (Carr Hill) was located just short of the hill and **T 20b** (Downhill East) beyond it. In the field to the west of Carr Hill Farm gaps in the south mound of the Vallum are visible.

The Wall passed straight over the top of Down Hill, with but a slight bend to the north, with its ditch cut through solid rock, while the Military Road also swings round to the north of the hill. The well-preserved Vallum moves in the opposite direction. As Bruce remarked, "If the Vallum had been constructed as an independent defence against a northern foe…an elevation which so entirely commands the Vallum would surely not have been left open to the enemy, especially as it would be just as easy to take the Vallum along the north flank of the hill as the south".

Excavation in 1893 demonstrated that the Vallum mounds had been revetted in stone instead of turf at one point. The gaps in the mounds are clear, as are the crossings in the ditch, and there is a marginal mound on its south lip. Investigations in 1952 revealed metalling on the south berm. The west side of Down Hill is pitted with quarries. The lime kiln lies close to the site of the unlocated **MC 21** (Down Hill) which may have been totally removed. **T 21a** (Red House) lies beyond, 73 m (80 yards) short of the fort at Halton Chesters.

HALTON CHESTERS (*ONNUM*)

Halton Chesters fort lies 12 km (7½ miles) west of Rudchester, almost exactly at the measured location, which ignores the existence of the Portgate on Dere Street 1.2 km (¾ mile) to the west, another indication that the forts were located according to their own 'rules'. Although the name of the fort was recorded on the *Notitia Dignitatum* as *Hunnum*, it was probably more correctly rendered as *Onnum*, the H being added by a scribe in the Middle Ages. The name may mean a stream, and the Fence Burn flows close by.

The only regiment attested at the site was Sabinius' Cavalry Regiment of Pannonians, recorded in the *Notitia Dignitatum* as the *ala Sabiniana*. A tombstone to a native of Noricum (modern Austria), first seen at Halton in 1600 and probably of

Halton Chesters, composite plan showing buildings of the second and third centuries.

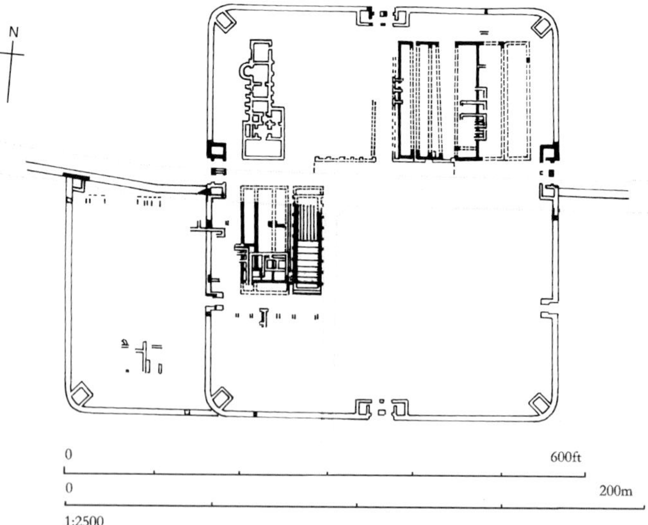

Inscription from Halton Chesters recording its construction by the Sixth Legion under the governor A. Platorius Nepos during the reign of Hadrian. (0.91 x 1.35 m)

third-century date, was erected by his brother, Messorius Magnus, a *duplicarius* (junior officer) in the *ala Sabiniana*. This was a 500-strong cavalry regiment. The Hadrianic fort was too small to hold such a unit; it measured 140 by 125 m (460 by 410 ft) and covered 1.74 ha (4.3 acres). In the early third century an extension was created, increasing the area to 1.94 ha (4.8 acres), and it was probably then that the cavalry regiment came to Halton. Today, only the fort platform is visible, the low remains of the south rampart and a wide southern ditch.

Three main campaigns of excavation have been carried out at the fort. The first, in 1935-6, was in advance of road works; the second two were research excavations undertaken in 1956-8 and 1960-1. Geophysical survey in 1995 and 1999 has considerably amplified our knowledge of the fort and its civil settlement.

The Wall and ditch, dug to full depth, crossed the site and were obliterated when the fort was built. The **west** and **east gates** were erected partly over the ditch and as a result the foundations of the northern towers were substantial, rising seven courses above a rubble platform placed in the bottom of the ditch. However, above this the superstructure had been badly robbed. The pivot-holes at the east gate showed much use, thereafter the south portal was blocked and the gap in the central spine built up. The pivot-holes at the west gate were unworn and both portals were blocked and the spine closed. Earlier, during building, it appeared that the north chamber served as a shelter for the builders for a hearth was found in it. A remarkable discovery in 1936 was the weathered building inscription found on the ground, face downwards in front of the central pier. The dedication stone records work by the Sixth Legion under the Emperor Hadrian and his governor A. Platorius Nepos.

The **north gate** was severely robbed, but on the west side of the west portal part of a secondary block of masonry, possibly a reducing wall, was found. The fort ditches in front of the gate were interrupted for a causeway. Behind the east chamber lay a large water tank; an aqueduct, no longer visible, led to the gate from a spring 1.5 km (1 mile) to the north-west. To the east, substantial foundations were interpreted as the base for a catapult platform, though other explanations are possible.

Four buildings are known in the central range. In front of the site of the **headquarters building**, a forehall, 48.77 m (160 ft) long and extending over the *via principalis*, was erected in the early third century. To the east, geophysical survey has revealed part of the **commanding officer's house** of the usual courtyard layout. To the west, the **granary** was of similar type to that at Rudchester. It had a massive foundation formed by a stone raft of flagging laid on clay, itself resting on packed broken limestone. In the southern half of the building the sleeper walls ran east-west, while in the northern half they were aligned north-south. The third building was similar in plan to the so-called **hospitals** excavated at Wallsend and Housesteads.

Inscription recording building work at Halton Chesters by the Second Legion. (0.56 x 0.84 m)

Originally partly built of timber, it was replaced in the early third century to a slightly different plan.

The north-east sector contained buildings of two periods. The first were aligned north-south. The five buildings of this period included a storehouse, double barrack-block and a stable. The last was identified on the basis of a 3 m (10 ft) wide door opening onto the *via principalis* and a deep layer of burnt straw. The second-period buildings encroached onto the *via praetoria*: these included barrack-blocks and stables. Although the foundations were of stone, the superstructures appear to be of wattle-and-daub for the drains were choked with such material.

In the western half of the *praetentura*, geophysical survey has revealed a further double barrack-block and a **bath-house**. The latter building was drawn by John Dobson, the architect, in 1823: it is likely to date to the third or fourth century. Geophysical survey has provided the outlines of two double barrack-blocks running west-east in the *retentura*. There may have been as many as 12 barrack-blocks in the original fort. The latrine appears to have lain in the south-east corner of the fort, its lowest point.

When the **extension** was added, the original fort wall was demolished down to the lowest courses. Evidence survived, however, for a chamfered plinth above the bottom course. The two fort ditches were infilled. This occurred in or shortly after the closing years of the second century. The extension contained a bath-house and sundry other buildings. Part of the rampart backing was removed, possibly in the early fourth century, to provide space for a new building.

In the fourth century buildings in the fort fell into ruin and certain areas became covered in soil. Some military presence would appear to have been maintained for the same regiment is recorded here in the third century and in the late fourth century. It would appear that occupation intensified in the late fourth century. At this time, timber-framed buildings were

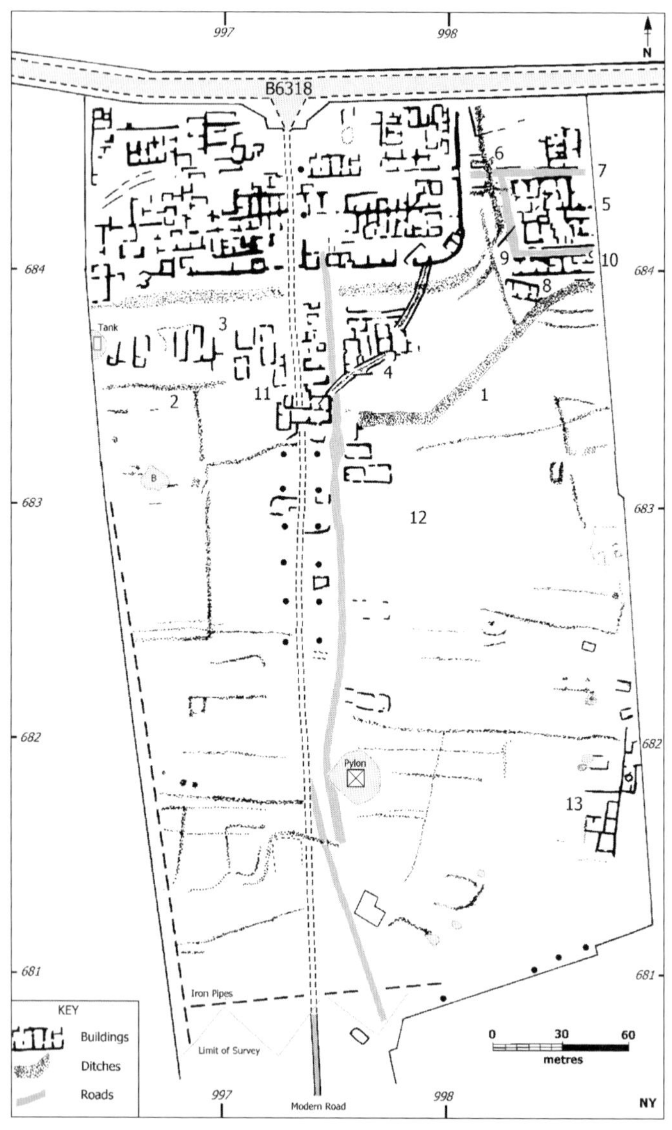

997
998
N
B6318
6
7
5
9
10
8
684
3
Tank
3
4
1
2
11
B
683
12
682
Pylon
13
681
Iron Pipes
KEY
Buildings
Ditches
Roads
Limit of Survey
Modern Road
0
30
60
metres
NY

erected, resting on stone sill-blocks socketed for the timbers.

The Vallum diversion has been traced round the fort. Recent geophysical survey has indicated the existence of a **civil settlement** between the fort and the Vallum. Buildings were of both stone and timber. Some relate to the Military Way which exited from the minor east gate; others straddled the road leading south and continuing beyond the Vallum. One large building, outside the fort's south gate, may be the Hadrianic bath-house, but most were roughly rectangular in shape measuring about 10-15 m (33-50 ft) long by 7-10 m (23-33 ft) wide. Finds show that quite elaborate jewellery manufacture, including the use of gold as well as local shale, was taking place, probably in the third century. Some buildings, set within their own enclosures, give the impression of being linked to farming: it has been suggested that the enclosures that lay to the east may be fields or paddocks. A small excavation in 1999 revealed the presence of some buildings beyond the area of the geophysical survey plan, though none produced pottery later than the late third century.

South of the fort and immediately north of the hamlet of Halton, at least one barrow is visible. Tombstones tell of Aurelia Victorina, mourned by her father, and a slave of Hardalio, whose stone was set up by the guild of his fellow-slaves. Another tombstone, probably dating to the later third century, is of a family group of father, mother and child: it is now in the Museum of Antiquities, Newcastle. A weathered altar stands in Halton churchyard, while the regular stones used in the church suggest a Roman origin.

Geophysical survey of Halton Chesters.
The southern part of the fort lies immediately to the south of the B6318. Beyond the defences are buildings, presumably of the civil settlement, with a distinct complex to the east: these all lie between the Vallum and the fort wall. Other buildings straggle along the road leading south. Ancient field boundaries are also visible.

HALTON CHESTERS TO CHESTERS

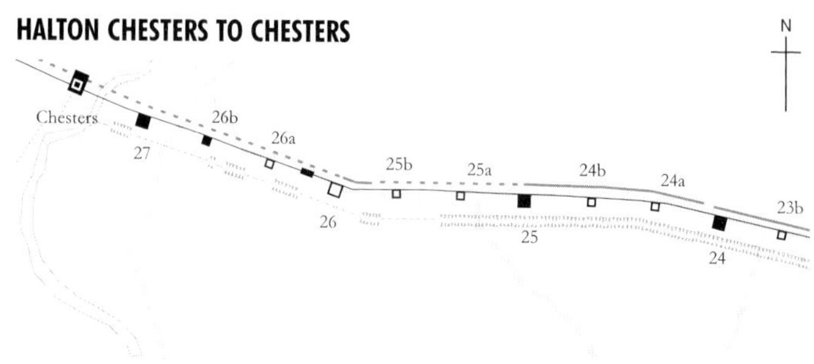

The Fence Burn lies on the west side of Halton Chesters. The modern road then cuts through a mound, the site of **T 21b** (Fence Burn). Gaps in the south mound of the Vallum are visible. **MC 22** (Portgate) survives as a platform a little short of the roundabout. Presumably a long-axis milecastle, it was 16.76 m (55 ft) wide with a type III north gate and narrow walls of standard B construction. The original pivot-holes were well worn. Only one of their replacements survived, that to the west. Over this was constructed a wall, 1 m (3 ft 3 in) thick, completely closing the north gate. The proximity of the milecastle to Portgate presumably led to the blocking of the gateway. In 1992, the eastern part of the south wall was found to survive up to five courses high. The Wall between the milecastle and the roundabout was 3.05 m (10 ft) wide.

At the point where the Wall crossed Dere Street leading northwards to Risingham and High Rochester, stood a gate known as the **Portgate**. Located in 1966, its north face was found to have been constructed of massive masonry and to project 3.05-3.66 m (10-12 ft) north of the Wall. The gate therefore sat astride the Wall and was probably a square or rectangular structure. It now lies immediately to the south-west of the roundabout on the north side of the old road line beside the Errington Arms. 5 km (3 miles) to the south lies the Roman town of Corbridge (pages 416-27).

The **Wall ditch** and the **Vallum**, about 73 m (80 yards) apart,

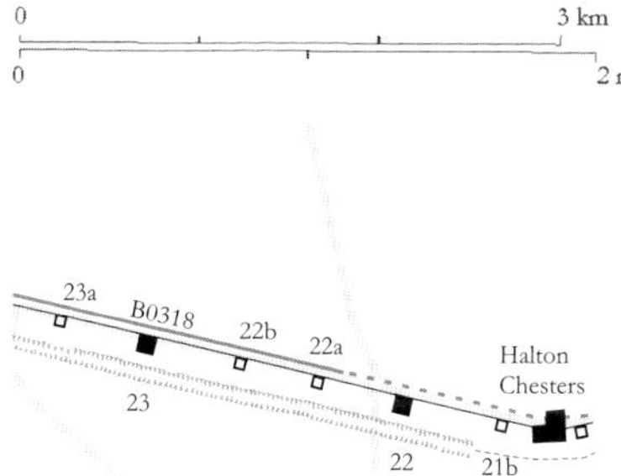

are very well preserved for the next 5 km (3 miles). The upcast mound on the north lip of the ditch is now clearly seen for the first time, though often obscured by gorse. The spoil has not always been smoothed out but in places lies on the north lip, rough and unlevelled, the task clearly having been left unfinished. At one point the mound is markedly pointed. Through the first fields, the north mound of the Vallum has gone but gaps in the south mound survive. Thereafter, there are also gaps in the north mound while crossings over the ditch survive in places.

T 22a (Portgate) lies nearly 182 m (200 yards) beyond the roundabout. It was of standard A construction and indicates a change in builder since MC 22. Widths of 1.83 m (6 ft) and 2.90 m (9 ft 6 in) have been recorded for the Wall. Hereabouts a stone was discovered in 1850 inscribed *Fulgar divom*, "the lightning of the gods": it had presumably been set up where a lightning bolt had struck. **T 22b** (Stanley) is beside the lane leading south. The excellent state of preservation of the **Vallum** caused William Hutton in 1801 to exclaim, "I climbed over a stone wall to examine the wonder … was fascinated, and unable to proceed; forgot I was upon a wild common, a stranger, and the evening approaching … lost in astonishment, I was not able to move at all".

MC 23 (Stanley) survives as a low mound south of the road. Examined in 1930, it was found to have a long axis, about 15.24 m

(50 ft) across, with broad east and west walls; the width of the south wall is not known. There are traces of an external ditch. There is a slight change of profile in the bottom of the ditch in front of the north gate and a gap, about 8 m (26 ft) wide, in the upcast mound to the north. Both are suggestive of the existence of a causeway, later removed. In 1952 the Vallum was examined. The south mound continues unbroken past the milecastle; excavation revealed that its northern edge was revetted by a stone kerb and its southern by a turf bank. Although the north mound appears to be unbroken, excavation revealed that former existence of a gap 2.44 m (8 ft) wide, revetted by turf kerbs, suggesting the previous existence of an original causeway, and that the visible causeway is secondary. Following infilling of the gap, the mound was revetted to north and south by stone kerbs. To east and west of the milecastle the marginal mound is visible. Just to the east of the milecastle the 1952 excavation revealed that the north edge of the marginal mound was revetted by three layers of turf. Crossings survive in Stanley Plantation, while tool marks may be seen on each side of the rock-cut ditch. **T 23a** (Stanley Plantation) and **T 23b** (Wall Fell) were both located in their correct positions in 1920.

On the summit of the hill, the ditch, 7.92 m (26 ft) wide and 3.35 m (11 ft) deep, is cut into rock. Again the upcast still survives in heaps as dumped by the excavators. A width of 3.17 m (10 ft 5 in) was recorded for the Wall when it was visible in the surface of the road, but it is not clear whether this was the foundation or the superstructure. The Vallum lies close, with the crossings and marginal mound clear. The Military Way runs on the north mound from just west of MC 23 to just east of MC 26, there being little room between Vallum and Wall.

In the north-east corner of the first arable field to the south of the road, **MC 24** (Wall Fell) is a distinct platform and was found in 1930 to be 15.24 m (50 ft) wide internally, with broad east and west walls. A gap in the rushes in the ditch may mark the location of a causeway subsequently removed. Two fields further on, at a dip in the road, is the site of **T 24a** (Green Field). The profile of the ditch is noticeably sharp at the bend in the road. **T 24b** (Tithe Barn) is opposite the ruined Tithe Barn. Crossings appear in the Vallum, blocked by the marginal mound.

The platform of **MC 25** (Codlawhill) is recognisable, opposite a gate in the field wall to the north of the road. The same size as MCs 23 and 24, it was protected by a ditch, no longer visible. There is a broad causeway, about 15 m (50 ft) wide, over the Wall ditch, now utilised by the modern access. To the north it appears as if an original gap in the upcast mound was later partially blocked by a small mound on the north lip of the ditch. There is also a causeway over the Vallum ditch. Thereafter, both mounds and the marginal mound are clear; slight depressions suggest that a start was made on cutting gaps in the mounds.

T 25a (Hill Head) probably lay a little east of the farm of that name. It was located in 1930 but could not be rediscovered by trenching in 1959. About half a mile south of this point, at Fallowfield Fell, a Roman soldier, Flavius Carantinus, inscribed

The rock of Flavius Carantinus from a Roman quarry south of T 25a and now at Chesters Museum.

his name upon the rock which he was quarrying. The inscription now sits outside Chesters Museum.

At Hill Head the road swings to the south and leaves the line of the Wall which runs through the fields to the north. The Vallum also crosses the road, which runs briefly on its south berm. North of the Wall is St Oswald's Church, which contains a Roman altar re-used as a cross-base, while by the roadside stands a wooden cross marking the traditional site of the battle of Heavenfield where Oswald, King of Northumbria, defeated the British King Cadwallon in 634; the battle actually took place about 12 km (7½ miles) to the south on the Rowley Burn.

T 25b (St Oswald's) is south-west of the church. The Wall here is between 2.90 m (9 ft 6 in) and 3.05 m (10 ft) wide with a core of clay and small stones. The walls of the turret were mortared. Outside them lay dumps of clay containing mortar, up to 76 cm (2 ft 6 in) thick. The floor of the turret was formed of the same material. The south-west corner was marked off by boulders as a working area; on it lay a hearth, renewed twice. Later a platform was constructed against the south wall and partly overlying the working area. The turret produced no artefacts later than the second century. There was a hint of the former existence of a wall filling the recess. Sherds from as many as 50 flagons were found during the 1959 excavations, and more *amphorae* sherds than normal. Five gaming pieces were found outside the north-west corner of the turret, which may indicate the existence of a window in the west wall. Other objects included items of copper and iron, one being an arrowhead. A path led from the turret and beside it, to the left, stood a wall.

West of the cross, the road swings southwards to cross the Vallum, which runs straight on behind the cottage, down the bank and through Planetrees farm. The Wall ditch descends the bank to the north of the road. Just east of the farm, the road swings north to cross Vallum and Wall at the site of **MC 26** (Planetrees), which was found in 1930 to have the same dimensions as the preceding three milecastles. There appears to have been a causeway over the Wall ditch here, though not necessarily primary. In 1956 two iron wedges for splitting stones, 260 and 270 mm (10¼ and 10½ in) long, were retrieved from the rubble and mortar core behind the north-facing stones of the Wall in a trench cut beside the farm.

South of the road, a section of Wall at **Planetrees** is

preserved by English Heritage. This was reputedly saved by the intervention of William Hutton in 1801 when he entreated the owner to stop ripping up the Wall for building materials. The section is exceptionally interesting since it preserves a junction between the Broad Wall on the east and a sector only 1.83 m (6 ft) thick to the west. To the south of the Narrow Wall lies the Broad Foundation with a drain sitting on it demonstrating, it would appear, that those laying the foundations also constructed the drains.

The road descends steeply into the valley of the River North Tyne, with a fine length of the Wall ditch on its south side. **T 26a** (High Brunton), opposite High Brunton House, was located in 1930 and examined in 1959. The Wall was 3.05 m (10 ft) wide at its base, narrowed to 2.64 m (8 ft 8 in) above the offsets, with a core of rubble set in some clay. The original floor of the turret was of clay and mortar, overlain in parts by stones. It was twice resurfaced with sand and twice with flags and each time a new hearth was created. Most lay close to the centre of the structure. A small area delineated by kerbs was retained in the north-west corner throughout the life of the turret, though its purpose could not be ascertained. There were no finds later than the second century. The excavations produced a large amount of evidence of bronze casting, including a crucible, a whetstone and animal bones within the building, but, in comparison with T 25b, fragments of only two flagons and one *amphora*. Fragments of pottery made by the Sixth Legion near York in the early 120s are an unusual find and may identify the builders of the turret. A trench cut in the garden of Middle Brunton House in 1975 demonstrated that the Wall had been robbed to its foundations, at least 3.3 m (10 ft 10 in) wide.

The road then swings to the north. Approached by turning left at the crossroads is **T 26b** (Brunton). Here is a fine stretch of Broad Wall, still 2.59 m (8 ft 6 in) high and exhibiting up to 11 courses of facing-stones. The faces have been reset in mortar, but the core was originally clay. The turret was excavated by

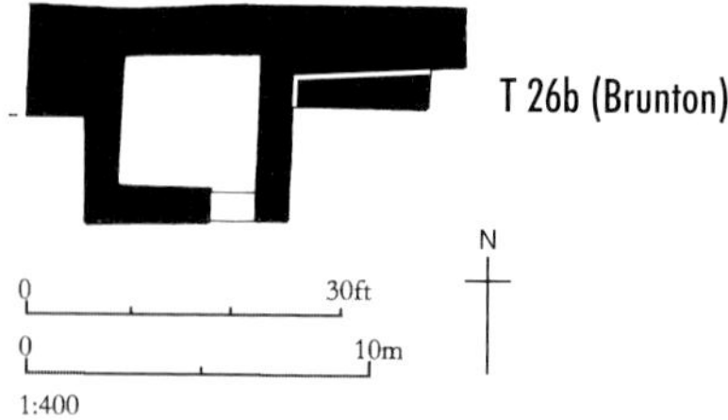

T 26b (Brunton).

John Clayton in 1878 and 1880. It measures internally 3.88 by 3.50 m (12 ft 9 in by 11 ft 6 in) with side walls 84 cm (2 ft 9 in) thick, being recessed into the Wall about 1.22 m (4 ft). It has a doorway with the threshold checked for monolithic stone jambs. The stones in the lower courses of the walls are larger than usual. The turret was laid out with wing-walls. That to the west is bonded with the Broad Wall and is no longer visible. On the east, the Broad Foundation approaches the turret but the Narrow Wall, 1.83 m (6 ft) wide and with its own foundation, rides up over the six courses of the broad wing wall to abut the turret. This suggests that the turret had only been built to a height of about 1.52 m (5 ft) before the decision to narrow the Wall. To the north, the ditch is well preserved. The berm narrows from 5 m (16 ft) to 3 m (9 ft) opposite the turret.

The Wall ends abruptly, but the north scarp of the ditch is visible to the end of the field. 50 m (55 yards) to the west of the turret, the Wall has been recorded as narrow. At about this point, an inscription was found in the tumble at the base of the Wall. It is marked on two faces, the one at right angles to the other, and had been used for sharpening knives. The two inscriptions are similar, recording the construction of 113 feet (34.44 m) by the troop of L. A. Fanus. The stone is unusual in recording building by cavalrymen and being marked on two faces, though a similar stone has been found at the minor east gate at Chesters. It is not clear how either stone fits into the Wall. An inscription from the fort at Carvoran records the construction of 112 feet (34.14 m).

From the turret the Wall runs straight across the fields to the river. Between road and river a low platform marks the site of **MC 27** (Low Brunton). Excavation in 1952 revealed this to be a long-axis milecastle set in the Broad Wall measuring 17.91 by 14.63 m (58 ft 9 in by 48 ft) with type IV gateways and broad side walls. The Broad Wall had a clay core, with the facing stones bonded in mortar. Its foundations were unusually wide, varying between 3.35 m and 3.50 m (11 ft and 11 ft 6 in). Between the milecastle and the disused railway a section of Vallum survives.

The modern road crosses the North Tyne on Chollerford Bridge, built in 1773. Beside the bridge is the path to **Chesters bridge abutment** (English Heritage), a remarkable structure. The abutment was uncovered by John Clayton in 1860, work continuing until 1863, and re-examined in 1982-3.

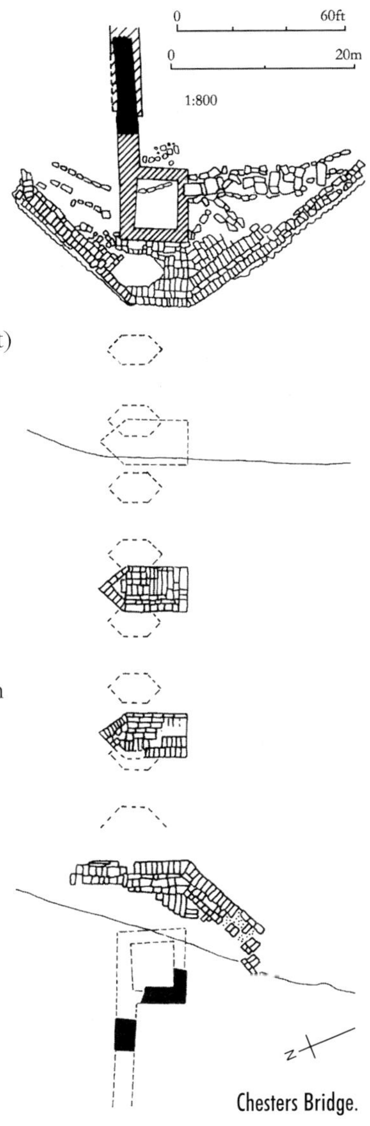

Chesters Bridge.

The Wall ditch may be distinguished running down to the river. The Narrow Wall, 1.93 m (6 ft 4 in) thick and up to 2.64 m (8 ft 8 in) high, stands on a broad foundation; indeed two courses of the south face of the Broad Wall also survive with a shallow offset between the two. The lower facing stones are noticeably large. The Wall terminates in a tower 6.71 m (22 ft) square standing upon the abutment. A water channel passing under the tower may have led to a mill further downstream. The river has moved approximately 15 m (50 ft) westwards since the Roman period, leaving the abutment dry.

The main face of the abutment is 6.71 m (22 ft) long with splayed sides about twice as long; the southern splay has been extended to check scour by the river. At the north end of the abutment five courses of facing stones stand nearly 1.80 m (6 ft) above the foundation course. Some are very large and come from Black Pasture Quarry, about a mile to the east. Most have a lewis hole cut to aid lifting. The facing stones along the central part of the abutment facing the river were held together by lead. Their distinctive feathered tooling will be noted; and a phallic symbol, for good luck, is carved on the northward water-face. Also visible are the marking out lines for individual courses. Halfway along the south wing of the abutment is a hole which, on examination in 1982/3 was found to contain the stump of an oak post. This has been interpreted as the bottom of a crane.

To the side of the abutment lie many carved stones, including those bearing evidence for a cornice, found at the site during its excavation. These are of two main types which formed part of the superstructure of the bridge. Analysis of these stones has led to the suggestion that there may have been platforms over the cutwaters. One reconstruction would place a shrine to the nymphs of the river on such a platform. This is based upon the discovery of the fragment of a base bearing a dedication to [*Nymp*]*his*, the Nymphs, by a detachment of the Sixth Legion.

A column with its attached base is one of four found at the site; the other three are fragmentary. The style of the base indicates that the column once adorned the parapet, while the tenon on the top indicates that it is but the lower half of the column which survives. It is possible that each column was surmounted by a statue. Another feature of the parapet may have been the inscription recording work under the supervision of Aelius Longinus, prefect of cavalry, found at the bridge. A third-century date has been suggested for this inscription.

The carved stones allow it to be calculated that this fine bridge, 58 m (63 yards) long, contained four arches while its carriageway may have stood over 10 m (33 ft) above the water.

Embedded within the abutment is a pier of an earlier bridge, several of its stones bound together with dovetail cramps.

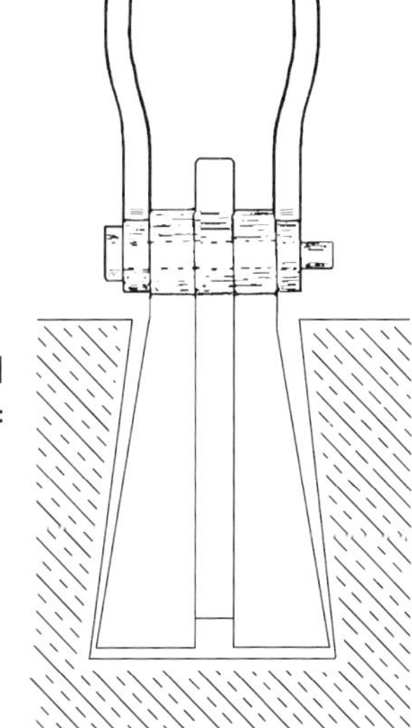

Diagram of a lewis hole mechanism.
The two triangular metal elements are dropped into the hole first, followed by the central piece: a bar across the top holds the three together, a hook allows the stone to be lifted.

The east abutment of this bridge lies under the tower. Only the cut in the ground surface for its lowest course was found in 1982; its location is now marked out. Between the abutment and the pier, a causeway was later laid. This bridge was probably carried on eight piers supporting stone arches.

The visible pier is 2.8-3 m (9 ft 2 in – 9 ft 10 in) long minus the cutwaters, the width of the Broad Wall. It thus appears that the original bridge only provided for pedestrian movement along the Wall; whether this in turn implied a walk-way along the top of the Wall is questionable. The bridge is at a slight angle to the line of the Wall to the east but shares the same alignment as the Wall to the west as far as Chesters fort; this may imply that the bridge was constructed by the soldiers operating from the west bank of the river.

At a date probably in the late second century this bridge was replaced by the visible, more substantial structure, which carried a road over the river. The road is now believed to have approached the bridge by a ramp placed to the south of the tower and subsequently removed. At this time, the Stanegate was probably re-aligned to cross the river at this bridge. Among the stones found at the bridge is a barrel-shaped object now in Chesters Museum; this is best explained as a rammer for compressing the subsoil and foundations and possibly also the road surface. The bridge would appear to have continued in use to the end of the Roman period.

When the river is low, two piers and the west abutment of the second bridge, drawn in the 1860s, may be glimpsed: the third pier lies under the modern river bank by the east abutment. Examination of the west abutment in 1990-1 revealed part of a tower in a similar relationship to the abutment as its partner on the east bank; the east wall of the tower has now been consolidated. Behind the tower, the road mound can be seen approaching at an angle from the west. The road is carried on a massive embankment of rubble retained by stone walls.

CHESTERS (*CILURNUM*)

Chesters lies almost 2 km (about a mile) east of its measured position: its location was presumably moved so that the fort could sit beside the river. Chesters is the *Cilurnum* of the *Notitia Dignitatum*. The name has traditionally been taken to mean "The Cauldron Pool", but which is inappropriate to the sluggish North Tyne at Chesters. The name has therefore been related to the Inglepool, which lay to the south-west of the fort until the early nineteenth century. An inscription recently found in the Asturias area of Spain, however, refers to a people called the Cilurnigi. It has been proposed that the Second Cavalry Regiment of Asturians, stationed at Chesters from the late second to the early fifth century, was recruited from the

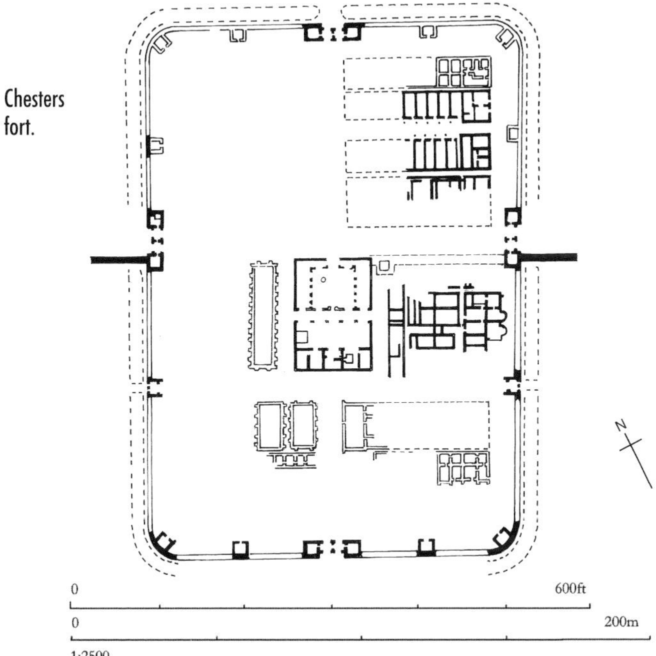

Chesters fort.

Cilurnigi country and named the fort after its homeland. If so, the site originally had a different name which is not known.

An inscription to Hadrian's Imperial Discipline found in 1978 reveals that the first unit to be based at Chesters was *ala Augusta ob virtutem appellata*, the Cavalry Regiment called Augusta for Valour. Further inscriptions record work at the fort in 139 by the Sixth Legion, about 180, 205-8, 221 and in 223. From the early 180s the Second Cavalry Regiment of Asturians was based here, though inscriptions of the First Cohort of Dalmatians and the First Cohort of Vangiones have also been found at Chesters.

For over 100 years from 1796 the fort and surrounding estate was owned by the Clayton family. In 1843 John Clayton began the series of excavations which resulted in the exposure of the buildings visible today. Not surviving are two granaries which formerly stood behind the headquarters building and were removed by Clayton as they were not original. Subsequent work has been limited in scope and has mainly related to elucidating the relationship between the fort and the Wall or to the consolidation of the existing buildings. In 1938 evidence for earlier structures was found below the visible headquarters building and commanding officer's house.

The **museum** was opened in 1903 to house Clayton's collection of finds from Hadrian's Wall. Its contents include altars and sculpture from Chesters, Carrawburgh (in particular the objects from Coventina's Well), Housesteads, Vindolanda and Carvoran as well as from milecastles, turrets and the curtain of the Wall itself.

The **fort** measured 177 by 131 m (581 by 430 ft) covering an area of 2.32 ha (5.75 acres) which forms a bold platform. The fort wall was 1.5 m (5 ft) thick, backed by an earth bank; only one ditch has been located beyond the rampart. There were six gateways.

The fort lies astride the Wall. Clayton recorded that the Narrow Wall abutted the fort at the south towers of its principal east and west gates. Examination of the north tower of the east gate in 1938 indicated that it had been built over the infilled Wall ditch, which had presumably crossed the site of the fort. In 1945 the Broad Foundation of the Wall, 3.61 m (11 ft 10 in) wide and formed of clay and massive cobbles, was traced across the fort from the east gate to the headquarters building where it had been removed. The foundations of **T 27a** were located immediately to the east of the north-east corner of the headquarters. It measured 3.36 m (11 ft) square within foundations 1.37 m (4 ft 6 in) broad. The turret yielded three fragments of a small cooking pot.

In 1921 the relationship of the east and west fort ditches to the Wall was investigated. Masonry found in the west ditch pointed to the subsidence and collapse of the south face of the Wall, though not necessarily in Roman times. Similar conditions were found to the east of the fort, though here the south face of the Wall had been rebuilt following the collapse, to an inferior standard and on narrower foundations.

The course of the **Vallum** is not known. One aerial photograph suggests that it avoided the fort by the usual diversion, another that it coincided with the fort's south ditch.

The visitor reaches the fort at the **north gate** (*porta praetoria*), which had two portals, separated by piers of masonry carrying arches at front and back. Each portal is about 3.66 m (12 ft) wide and was closed by double doors turning on iron pivots in socket-stones which are still to be seen behind the front jambs of the entrances. The west portal was still blocked when found, but it was then cleared down to its original sill-stone, which is still fresh and unworn, showing that the blocking took place at an early date. In the east portal, which was kept in use, are later sills and the central stop-block. A drain with cover-slabs of reused stones, some carved, passes under the threshold. On each side of the gate is the lower storey of a tower with doors opening into the entrance passages; that to the west has a flagged floor. A road leading out of the gate towards the river has been recorded in the past.

The north rampart, clearly seen as a mound running east and west, leads on the right to the north-west angle; and so to the main **west gate** (*porta principalis sinistra*), again with twin portals flanked by towers. The Narrow Wall, 2.13 m (7 ft) wide and on Broad Foundation (not visible), abuts the south tower of the gateway. Marking-out lines may be seen at the western central pier. The eastern face of the central pier is not dressed well. The sills of both portals are unworn, suggesting early blocking of the entrances; in the south passage, the original iron socket-cups of the pivots are still in place. In the north portal, a later paving of large stones has been left. At an unknown date, the rear entrances of both passages were also walled-up. When unearthed, the interior space was found to be filled with rubble.

The north tower contains the base of a settling tank fed by a stone channel which brought water through the fort wall. Tucked into the corner beside the tower is an oven. At the south tower two short lengths of wall lie diagonally to the gate, one section embedded within the gate structure at the junction of the tower and the Wall.

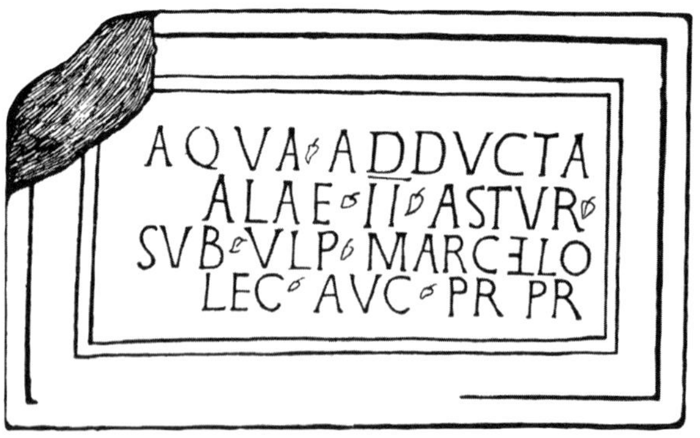

An inscription recording the bringing of water to Chesters under the governor Ulpius Marcellus, about 180. (0.58 x 0.99 m)

The outer face of the fort wall at the south-west corner of the fort is visible. Further along the south wall is an **interval-tower** with a central doorway and a flagged floor. In front of the door are a gutter and a column, probably from a barrack-block colonnade. Beyond the fort rampart lies a gentle depression caused by the ditch or ditches which surrounded the fort.

The **south gate** (*porta decumana*) has the usual two passages and towers. The piers separating the two portals are more complete than any other at Chesters. The gate still retains considerable evidence of its history. The west portal was blocked when still new, the blocking wall being removed in 1879 to reveal the unworn threshold. Part of a later road survives at the rear of the passage, immediately inside the modern gate. The east portal exhibits two phases. In the earlier, there are, unusually, thresholds at both ends of the passage. They are formed of inverted gutter-stones much worn by traffic. In the final phase, the floor in this passage was raised considerably by a mass of stones. It exhibits later pivot-holes and a stop-block for the doors. Lying in the gate passage is a fallen block from the central pier, pierced to receive the upper door pivots.

When the gate was excavated, painted wall plaster was found in the east guard-chamber, the colours being brown, black, red and yellow. In the same room, two layers of "wood ashes, sometimes as thick as three inches" were recorded. Here also was found much of a bronze tablet, a diploma, of AD 146, the recipient's copy of the official decree giving Roman citizenship to an auxiliary soldier on his honourable discharge after 25 years' army service and legalising his marriage, past or future, with any one wife. The original is now in the British Museum with a copy displayed in the Chesters Museum. A stone on which is faintly carved *leg VI Vi* (legion VI Victrix) can be seen on the upper course of the east wall of the tower.

Outside the gate is a gutter to take rainwater dripping from the roof, though it has been conjectured that this was a channel carrying water from the west gate to the bath-house. A road led south from the gate, aiming for Walwick Grange, and a junction with the Stanegate. A section cut in 1882 or 1883 revealed its width as 8.23 m (27 ft) with kerbs.

Further along the south rampart lie an **interval-tower** and the south-east **angle-tower**. Two infant burials were found in the interval-tower. The walls of the angle-tower stand about 11 courses high, enclosing an area 3.96 by 3.05 m (13 by 10 ft). To the north stand some columns, probably from a barrack-block. Northwards along the east rampart lies the single portal **lesser east gate** (*porta quintana dextra*). The pivot stones and door stop are secondary. In the passage is a broken panel: it may have borne a painted inscription. The large stone beyond may contain an upper pivot-hole. An inscription found in 1961 fallen from the southern wing wall of this gate records on two right-angled faces that the unit of Varius Paternus built a length of wall (*vallum*); the number of feet is no longer readable. From the gate the Military Way can be observed leading to the west abutment of Chesters Bridge. In 1897 an inscription recording the provision of an aqueduct by Ulpius Marcellus about 180 was found reused in a room west of this gate.

Next comes the main **east gate** (*porta principalis dextra*). This gate is one of the best-preserved fort gateways on Hadrian's Wall. The towers stand up to 11 courses high. Each portal has been arched both at front and back. The piers were formed of large stones. The northern piers show more skill and care than the dressing of the other parts of the gate. On the upper surface of the south-west pier are two small sinkings: their purpose is unknown. A drain is seen in the flooring of the south portal. Two quern stones sit on the outer pier of the spine. The Wall joins the south tower a little south of the portal. When disinterred by John Clayton, he recorded that "the two structures are obviously distinct and separate works", though the two now appear to be bonded.

The thresholds of each portal are unworn; the northernmost pivot hole was not cut; a square depression indicates where it was to be located. Two later levels were removed when the gate was excavated. The lower was a road just over 30 cm (1 ft) above the original; at this time the doors were provided with new pivot stones. Later, the doors were removed and the entrances blocked; at the same time the whole building – guard-chambers as well as the former passages – were filled with 90 cm (3 ft) of rubble over which a new floor was laid. Limited excavation in 1938 suggested that the north tower was erected over the Wall ditch which had been infilled with stone.

The **headquarters building** (*principia*) lies in the centre of the fort. It fronts on to the *via principalis* and faces down the *via praetoria* to the main, north gate of the fort. Its north half was a courtyard bordered on three sides by covered colonnades. It seems possible that notices detailing duties were posted in the colonnades. Bases of the piers which supported the columns remain, and the gutter-stones for their eaves-drips are in position. The court, which contains a fine well, is flagged, and on one paving stone is carved a large phallic symbol, a device much used in the Roman world to avert the evil eye.

South of the courtyard a large hall (*basilica*) extends across the building. In the centre was a monumental doorway, now removed, and to each side are additional openings. Then comes a north aisle, entered from the colonnade and also by side doors. The west side door was used by small wheeled vehicles, perhaps hand carts. At the east end of the hall are the foundations of a raised dais or tribunal, from which the commanding officer addressed his troops and administered justice. The remains of a doorway suggest that there may have been storage space below the platform: perhaps money was kept here before the strongroom was constructed.

On the south side of the hall lie five rooms. The front wall has two chamfered courses. Three rooms have wide, open fronts, once spanned by arches, the fallen stones from which lie near; the openings would formerly have been narrowed by the presence of stone screens surmounted by grilles. The central room, divided into ante-room and shrine, was the chapel (*aedes*) where stood the regimental standards and flags and, it is believed, a statue of the emperor. There would normally always have been a guard posted here. The other rooms served as offices. On slight evidence, the pair to the west are interpreted as being for the records staff and those to the east for the pay staff. In both instances the inner chambers could only be entered through the outer rooms offering more privacy, presumably to the senior officers.

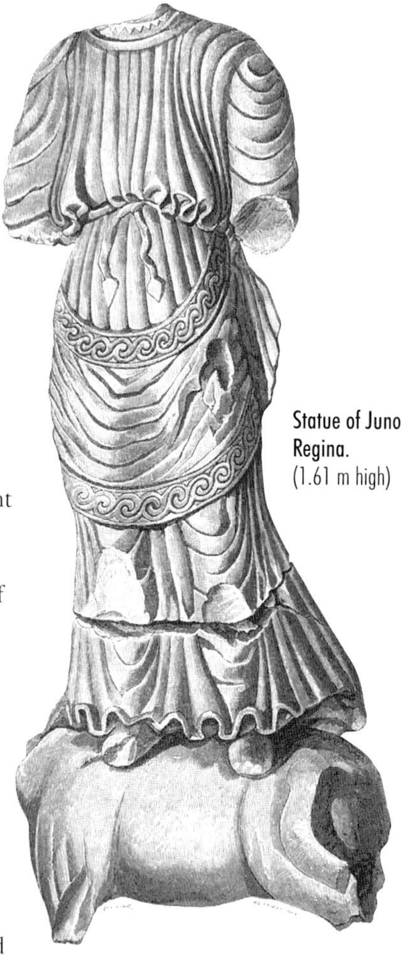

Statue of Juno Regina. (1.61 m high)

A flight of stairs on the east side of the chapel led down into the strongroom. One step was formed of a re-used building inscription of the First Cohort of Dalmatians. An oak door, bound and studded with iron, and opening inwards, was found at the entrance to the chamber, but fell to pieces shortly after being exposed. On the strongroom floor was found a number of forged *denarii*, copies of originals of the reign of Septimius Severus. The roof is constructed with three parallel arched ribs, the intervals between them being bridged by large slabs.

Two remarkable sculptures, now in the museum, probably once decorated the headquarters building. The first is the top of a relief depicting a trooper holding a flag inscribed in Latin which can be translated as "While the Emperors are safe, the Second Cavalry Regiment of Antoninus's Own Asturians is happy! The valour of the Emperors!" These loyal sentiments date to 221-2, when Severus Alexander became the colleague of Elagabalus, who is the Antoninus mentioned and later erased in disgrace. The second piece is a statue of Juno Regina standing upon a heifer. The hooves of another bovine animal, trampling a snake (standing next to Juno Regina in the museum), could be the surviving part of a matching statue.

To the east of the headquarters lies a jumble of walls. The main building here is the **commanding officer's house**. Originally there may have been a series of rooms opening onto a central courtyard, as at Housesteads, but in time the courtyard itself seems to have been filled with additional accommodation. The long, narrow western range, which exhibits two phases of building, may or may not have formed part of the house. As surviving, the house is considered to be of late date overlying earlier structures visible here and there. The southern range exhibits evidence for several modifications, including the insertion of hypocausts. At the east end lies the commander's bath-house. It is admirably built, with a moulded base-course on the external walls, though it was not the first building on the site and the hypocausts are patched with reused columns. In a ruined part of the north wall was found a fine recumbent statue of a river god which must once have adorned a bath. A pair of cold baths lay in one of the northern chambers. When first exposed they were still lined with red waterproof cement (*opus signinum*), now weathered away. Immediately to their south is the dressing-room; to the east an intermediate warm room led to a hot room with apse. The hot room has an earlier stoke-hole and retains some of the original tile columns and some (presumably reused) pillars. To the north of the bath-suite lies the wall and some intermediate partitions of another range or a separate building. When excavated in the 1840s some wall plaster still survived.

In the north-east corner of the fort lie parts of three **barrack-blocks** (a fourth, to the north, examined in 1889, is no longer visible): limited excavation has suggested that they are not the first buildings on the site. The main two buildings face each other across a street with a central gutter lined with numerous reused shafts of columns which formerly supported verandahs. Opening off the verandahs were rooms for the soldiers, probably housing eight to each, though it is believed that each room visible today was originally subdivided into two by a timber partition. At the rampart end of each block lay the officer's quarters, divided into several rooms, some paved, with a drain leading from one, possibly indicating the position of the latrine. The southern-most building exhibits at least two phases of construction.

Among the refuse from these buildings, the shells of oysters, mussels, cockles and limpets were noted; the Romans relished sea food, and, though Chesters is 50 km (30 miles) from the sea, the regiment found means to procure it. The bones of red deer, roebuck, an extinct ox, wild boar, and sheep were also found. Other artefacts found in the barracks included spear-heads, daggers and millstones.

Excavations in the nineteenth century revealed barracks in the southern part of the fort and two small **granaries**, presumably late in date. Geophysical survey in 1992 established the existence of two granaries to the west of the headquarters building, that is in the more normal location of such buildings, and additional barrack-blocks in the north-west quarter of the fort.

Between the fort and the river lies the regimental **bath-house**.

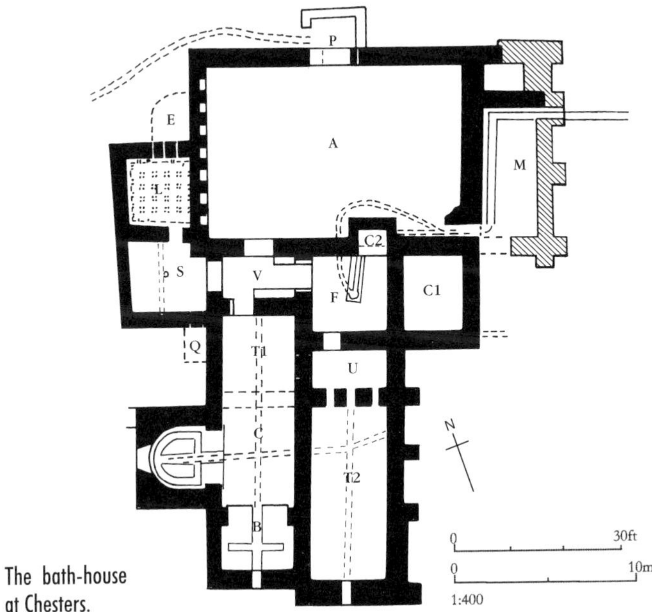

The bath-house at Chesters.

The baths were provided for the use of all the soldiers in the regiment stationed at Chesters. Two forms of bathing were on offer: the hot dry treatment (the modern sauna) and steam bathing, now called a Turkish bath, as the Turks inherited this form of bathing from the Romans when they conquered Constantinople.

Originally built under Hadrian, to a plan used elsewhere on the Wall, the bath-house was subsequently extended. Today, entrance is gained through a small porch, P, itself an addition. This leads into the changing room (*apodyterium*), A, paved with flagstones, themselves secondary, on which the bases of central pillars supporting the roof were found: when excavated, the floor was completely paved. Its west wall contains seven round-headed niches of a kind known in other Roman baths, but of uncertain use. The top stones may have been reused window-heads. Built into this wall at a lower level is the stone support for a bench. From the east side of the room opens a latrine, M, carried on a massive buttressed foundation on the steep river bank. It was flushed by the main outflow drain from the whole of the baths.

A door in the south wall of the dressing room leads to a vestibule, V, where the floor and the steps to adjacent rooms are much worn. Here the bather, turning left, entered the cold room (*frigidarium*), F, in the middle of which stood a basin for douching: its base is still visible and two drains, belonging to different periods, run away from it. At the far end is the large cold bath, C1, first reduced in size and then disused and replaced by a much smaller bath, C2, to the north. A door opened from the cold room into the first warm room of the steam range, suggesting that the bather might start with a cold bath.

To the west of the vestibule lie two rooms, both additions at different times to the original building. They provided hot dry heat. Here, as elsewhere in the building, are fine door jambs of stone. The first room, S, was originally the hot dry room (*sudatorium* or *laconicum*) but was subsequently rebuilt as an ante-room to a new hot dry room, L. Within the interior of the west wall of S may be seen a blocked window and on the outside a blocked door; the furnace is at E. The floor is now mainly replaced by modern flags. Particularly noteworthy are the fragments of the stone wall-jacketing, which formerly covered the walls, and the replaced metal T-pieces which held the jacketing in place. The hot air which circulated under the floor seeped up the gap between the jacketing and the walls in order to add to the heat of the room: it escaped at the top, perhaps through chimneys.

The south door of the vestibule led into the first room of the steam range. The rooms lying to the south have all been modified at various stages in their long life and a description of this part of the building is accordingly more complicated.

The building is more difficult to understand because of the loss of the original floors in most of the rooms, though the thresholds to the doors remain and give an indication of the original floor level. All the rooms were heated by hot air circulating under the floor and, in the hotter rooms, flowing upwards between the walls and the wall-jacketing. The single furnace was at the south end of the building, though for a time an additional furnace was provided at Q. The bather would progress through the rooms, each hotter than the last, and then return through a different warm room to the cold bath to close his pores before returning to the fort.

The first room, T1 (*tepidarium*), provided gentle heat. This room was later amalgamated with its neighbour to the south, but originally a door, later blocked, led eastwards into an ante-room, U, perhaps serving as an *unctorium*, where the bather's skin was rubbed with oil. Three apertures below floor-level in the south wall of this room admitted hot air into its hypocaust from that of the room beyond. Later in the history of the building, these hypocausts were dismantled and the chambers filled up with sand (now removed).

The bather then passed into the long room, T2, which was a second warm room. Its east wall is strengthened on the outside by four buttresses. Its south wall has no buttresses but is 1.37 m (4 ft 6 in) thick and shows evidence for being erected in stages. Originally the room ended at the third buttress, but later it was extended and a furnace provided in its south wall. In this room an altar was found dedicated "To the goddess Fortuna the Preserver, Venenus, a German willingly and deservedly set this up". The front bears a carved figure of the deity.

On clearing the soil from outside the east and south walls of these rooms 33 human skeletons were found, together with the skeletons of two dogs and a horse.

From the second warm room the bather passed through another west door, later blocked, into the hot room (*caldarium*), C. This was the place where bathers sweated, washed in hot water, and were scraped with a strigil, a curved knife, to remove dirt and oil. Hot water was provided from a boiler which presumably was placed over the furnace to the south of the stoke hole. A hot bath rested on the mass of masonry, B, at the south end of the room, under which ran a flue from the furnace beyond. The apsed bay projecting westwards, contained the warm bath, now removed, though the duct for its outlet pipe remains while some of the dark-red water-proof wall plaster (*opus signinum*) is still visible on the apse wall. There is also a splayed window outside which window glass was found.

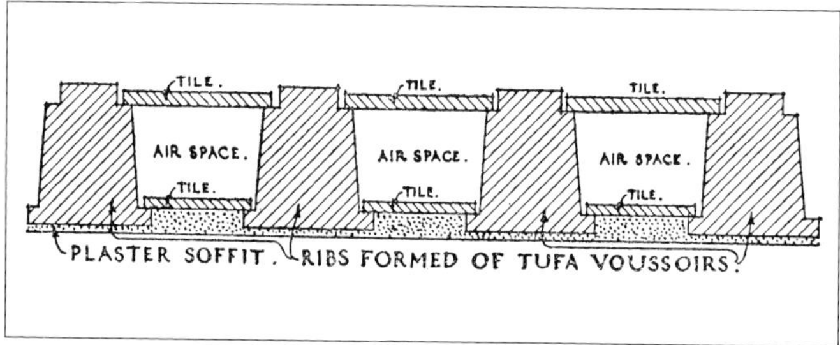

Schematic section through the roof of the bath-house at Chesters.

In excavating the hot room numerous small blocks of a light stone, calcareous tufa, were found: they are now piled outside the south wall of the hot bath. Wedge-shaped, these formed the ribs of a barrel-vault, the intervals being bridged by tiles placed in the nicks in the upper and lower edges. A roof formed in such a way would have been light in construction and at the same time provided insulation. A second type of voussoir stone is now used as a step in some of the rooms.

In the lowest course of masonry in the east wall of room C are two small stones lightly carved by a fanciful mason; one of them bears a phallic symbol for good luck; on the other is a bird and the word *Neilo* above it.

Traces of the buildings of a **civil settlement**, were recorded in the nineteenth century, stretching all round the fort from the road out of the minor east gate to the lawns of Chesters House to the west. Aerial photography and geophysical survey have confirmed the existence of an extensive **civil settlement** covering perhaps 15 ha (37 acres). A stone bearing the number 343 or 344, found immediately to the west of Chesters House may be a boundary marker, though an altar to Regina Caelestis was found even further west in 1891.

Within the settlement, analysis of the aerial photographs has led to the suggestion that the road pattern is thought to fossilise the line of the Vallum diverging round the fort. Most of the buildings appear to be strip houses, though several larger structures have been revealed by geophysical survey between the east side of the fort and the river. Here also survey has revealed a large circular feature, about 50 m (160 ft) in diameter, overlying an earlier road leading from the bridge to the minor east gate. Hutchinson in the late eighteenth century observed buildings north of the Wall: it is not impossible that these were Roman in view of the discovery of such buildings elsewhere.

One **cemetery** lay along the road leading south-west from the civil settlement. Several tombstones from here are in the museum. One is "sacred to the spirits of the departed and to Fabia Honorata: Fabius Honoratus, tribune of the First Cohort of Vangiones, and Aurelia Eglectiane made this for their most sweet daughter". Another was erected by a German, Lurio, to his daughter Ursa, wife Julia and son Canio. A single cremation, found in the construction of the railway on the other side of the river in the middle of the nineteenth century, may indicate the location of a second cemetery, perhaps beside the Military Way.

On the River North Tyne, about 2.4 km (1½ miles) above Chollerford, stands Chollerton Church. The columns of the south side of the nave are of Roman origin, probably from Chesters, as is the Roman altar once inscribed to Jupiter Optimus Maximus and inverted for use in the church as a font.

CHESTERS TO CARRAWBURGH

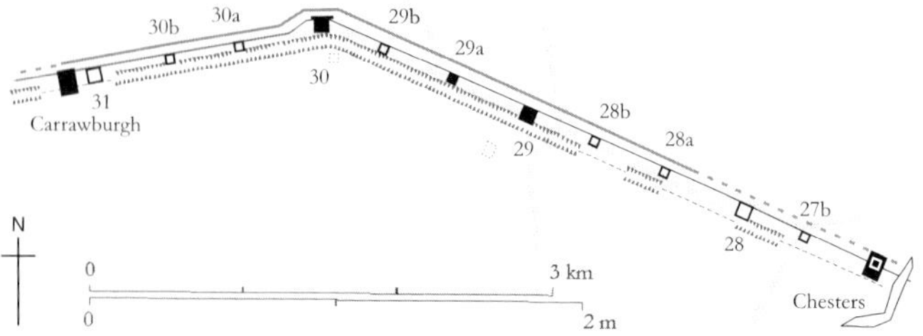

For 460 m (500 yards) west of the fort, the Wall runs through the private grounds of Chesters House, where, at one point, it is visible four courses high. On leaving the grounds of Chesters, it once more coincides with the Military Road, and climbs the hill which leads to Walwick. In 1928 the Wall here was found to be 2.31 m (7 ft 7 in) wide, the Broad Foundation extending another 66 cm (2 ft 2 in) beyond it on the south. The Vallum crosses the field on the left. Where the road veers south-west, off the line of the Wall, the platform of **MC 28** (Walwick), apparently of long-axis type, lies just beyond the farm-track running south, but is not visible. The view from Walwick is exceedingly fine, commanding the valleys of the North and

The Wall visible in the road at Walwick in 1862.

South Tyne Rivers, with the Iron-Age fort of Warden Hill between them; the distant view is closed by Hexham with its priory church.

Ascending the hill, the road lies on the north berm of the Vallum with the north mound to the right. The Wall ditch is at first obscured by trees, but it becomes clearer in the middle of the first field on the right. On the summit, the road swings into the Vallum ditch, but soon leaves it for the north mound. Immediately beyond the wood to the north, the remains of **MC 29** (Tower Tye) are very distinctly marked by the hollows made in robbing its walls. This long-axis milecastle is one of the few milecastles known to have been protected by a ditch still to be seen. A causeway crosses the ditch opposite the south gate. Beyond, but offset to the east, is a break in the north mound of the Vallum; there is also a causeway over the Vallum ditch. A bulge in the south lip of the Wall ditch may represent collapsed stonework from the north gate. A slight rise in the floor of the ditch may reflect the former existence of a causeway, but the topography is complicated by the possible existence of a later track here.

The temporary camp **Walwick Fell** lies 300 m (330 yards) to the south of the Vallum, in a plantation. 75 m (250 ft) square and enclosing 0.5 ha (1.4 acres), traverses are still visible at three of its four gateways.

The Wall now comes into view to the north running parallel to the road for a considerable distance. In this stretch lies **T 29a** (Black Carts), severely robbed on the south side, but standing 11 courses high in the recess. It was excavated in 1873, 1912 and 1971. Coins of Vespasian, Trajan, Hadrian and Constantine have been found here, more than are usually recovered. The only other recorded finds were fragments of millstones. The turret has wing-walls to fit the Broad Wall. The doorway with a thick threshold stone, cut by slots for the stone jambs and a pivot-hole to hang the door, is at the east side. One centurial stone was found within the turret and another in

T 29a (Black Carts).

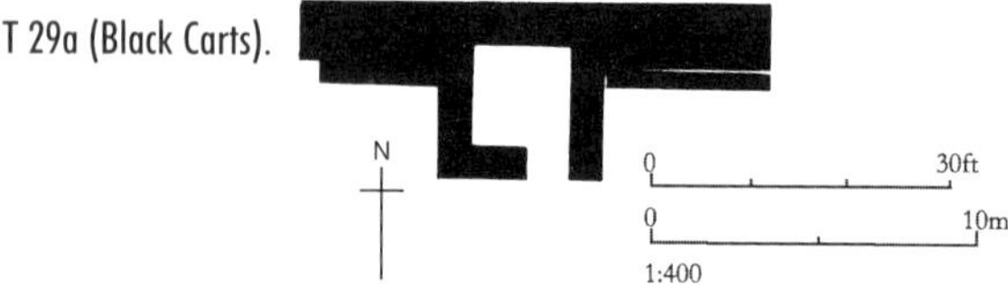

debris on the north side of the Wall: both are in Chesters Museum. Opposite the turret, the marginal mound and gaps in the south mound of the Vallum are very clear.

Excavation in 1998 revealed that the Wall **ditch** was only 3.5 m (11 ft 6 in) wide and 2.8 m (9 ft 2 in) deep, cut through whinstone. The upcast mound consisted of a bank on the northern lip of the ditch and, further north, a series of low mounds formed of split whin boulders and stone chips. It has been suggested that these are the result of surface quarrying for whin rather than debris from the ditch. Analysis of pollen from below the mound revealed a heathland landscape followed by a more sedge-dominated vegetation immediately before its construction. The pollen from below the south mound of the **Vallum** and the marginal mound indicated an open grassy environment; both mounds sealed plough marks impressed with hoof prints. The bottom 1.3 m (4 ft 3 in) of the 2.8 m (9 ft 2 in) deep ditch was cut through bedrock. Metalling was recorded on the north berm of the Vallum: wheel ruts on its surface are not certainly Roman.

A little further west, a modern road runs north to Simonburn through the Hen Gap, beyond which the Wall has rather larger facing stones than usual. Halfway up the hill, the grass-grown remains of **T 29b** (Limestone Bank) are immediately to the east of a hawthorn tree. Excavated in 1912, the turret had wing walls and a door similar to that at T 29a. Amongst the debris inside the turret were a number of broken roofing-slabs, many pierced for nails. Three larger and thicker flags, it was argued, might have been from the floor of an upper chamber. Below the masonry debris, two occupation levels were each marked by about 15 cm (6 in) of burnt rubbish. The later floor was of flags, the original of beaten clay. On the later floor stood, in the south-west corner, a masonry platform while by the east wall an *amphora* had been set in clay and cobbles. A hearth lay against the west wall. The artefacts found during excavation include a shield boss, spearhead, brooches and a melon bead, a gaming board, fragments of millstones and two flints. The pottery reveals that the occupation of the turret did not extend beyond the close of the second century. The turret was approached by a branch road, 3.35 m (11 ft) wide, leading off the Military Way, thereby helping to date the construction of this lateral line of communication.

South of the plantation and about 90 m (100 yards) from the road, on the summit of the hill and a little to the east of MC 30 is a temporary camp, **Limestone Corner**. It is about 50 m (150 ft) square, enclosing an area of 0.2 ha (0.6 acres), with rampart, ditch, gateways and traverses all visible. Pottery found during the 1912 excavation dates to the second century and to the late third-early fourth century. A farmstead, now merely a series of banks, was later built within the camp.

The ditch of the **Vallum** is cut through the very hard quartz dolerite all the way up the hill, though today somewhat overgrown with trees. Secondary crossings are seen at every 41 m (45 yards), many apparently half-finished. There are also gaps in the south mound. Unusually, the marginal mound, containing much whinstone, is present through much of this length. It is occasionally broken at a crossing, but some or all of these gaps may be relatively recent in date. The rock removed from the ditch has mostly been broken up small and packed into the mounds, but some large stones lie on the south berm as they were brought out of the ditch. The Vallum continues in this fashion after the plantation, with great boulders lying on both north and south berms. There is a causeway south of MC 30, which excavation demonstrated in 1950 was secondary. The next crossing is missing, apparently never created. The profile of the Vallum ditch, beyond the section cut through dolerite, is more gentle than the normal original slope, suggesting re-cutting, perhaps to provide stone for the Military Way. The marginal mound, which continues up to Carrawburgh farm, was formed of dark silty earth, unlike the clean material in the north and south mounds.

To the north, the Wall **ditch** exhibits a different history. Immediately north of the trigpoint the ditch is unfinished with only part of the topsoil removed. Further west, huge blocks still sit in the ditch, with others lying on its northern lip. One immense stone is now split into three by frost, but when first removed, presumably by means of a crane, it must have been one single block weighing not less than 13 tons. In the ditch itself, a comparable mass still remains, and its upper surface reveals the method of dislodgement, as it exhibits a number of holes for the insertion of wedges. These holes are all made along the thin veins of quartz which intersect the dolerite, where iron wedges, when driven in, would promote cleavage. Two such iron wedges found in the Wall core at MC 26 have steel-faced tips and soft heads for hammering: they were probably used for splitting small stones. The quarrying, by means of such wedges, and lifting, by means of cranes, was heavy work, but Roman legionary engineers were accustomed to it. It is noteworthy that while the Wall ditch is left unfinished, the Vallum ditch is fully dug: for the Vallum the ditch was essential, while to the Wall this feature was an accessory.

At **Limestone Corner** the northward view is magnificent across North Tynedale, with Chipchase Castle on its north bank, to the Simonside Hills and Cheviot. **MC 30** (Limestone Corner) lies where the stone field-walls meet on the summit. In 1951 excavations at the milecastle, beyond the wing-walls, revealed that the Narrow Wall, 2.29 m (7 ft 6 in) wide to the west and 2.36 m (7 ft 9 in) to the east, sat upon Broad Foundation. The line of the Wall follows the edge of the escarpment, presumably in order to provide a better location for the milecastle.

An alternative, but less likely, suggestion is that the Vallum had already been excavated before the Wall foundation builders arrived. To the west of the milecastle, a double turn brings the Wall onto its new westerly line.

Both faces of the east wall of the milecastle, about 1.83 m (6 ft) wide, may be seen towards the north corner. For the first time, the **Military Way** can plainly be detected, coming up to the south gate of the milecastle and then swinging away to run westwards. A hundred yards beyond the milecastle it passes obliquely under the modern road and climbs on to the north mound of the Vallum, which it occupies as far as Carrawburgh farm house. Excavation has shown that the gaps in the north mound had been filled to carry the Military Way. Crossings over the ditch are still visible. Across the modern road, the Wall ditch's upcast mound becomes sharper owing to the steeper fall of the ground surface to the north.

T 30a (Carrawburgh East) was located in 1912. It lies mostly under the road, 36 m (40 yards) west of its measured position, as calculated from MC 30, though it is in the correct relationship to T 30b. This may suggest that work on the turrets started first, with the extra distance caused by moving the site of the milecastle forward to the brow of the hill. **T 30b** (Carrawburgh West), also located in 1912, is marked by a mound beside the field wall 40 m (43 yards) beyond the track to Carrawburgh farm. Here the marginal mound, which has been running along the south lip of the Vallum ditch, stops, and several crossings are seen in the ditch. **MC 31** (Carrawburgh) lies immediately to the east of the car-park. It was sought in 1934, though only a coin of Victorinus was found. The robbed west wall of the milecastle was located in 1964 during excavations undertaken in advance of the construction of the car-park. Also revealed were two small buildings, one either a small temple or a substantial funerary monument, both dating to the second century. Lingard reported the discovery of bones between MC 31 and the fort in the early nineteenth century.

CARRAWBURGH (BROCOLITIA)

The site of this fort, only about 4.6 km (3½ miles) from Chesters, is a bold platform. The fort measures 140 by 112 m (460 by 366 ft) and covers about 1.6 ha (3.9 acres). Its Roman name was *Brocolitia* which may have a connection with badgers, "brocks". A building inscription of the First Cohort of Aquitanians probably dates to the governorship of Sextus Iulius Severus (130-?3), and this may have been the first unit stationed at the fort. A second inscription records building by the First Cohort of Tungrians. The First Cohort of Batavians was building here in 237, being stationed at Carrawburgh from at least the early third century, its presence also noted in the *Notitia Dignitatum*. Other regiments are attested, dedicating to Coventina, but they may not have been based here.

The **fort** is well outlined by its rampart and ditches, two still being visible to the west: the single, wider south ditch is probably a fourth-century replacement. A probable third ditch between the east gate and the Wall was discovered in 1964. The positions of the east, south and west gateways are visible; excavation in 1969 demonstrated that the south gate was blocked at a late date. Stonework of the south tower of the **west gate**, an **interval-tower** on the west rampart, both examined in 1871, and buttresses of the **granaries** may be seen. A centurial stone found in the upper course of the interval-tower and now in Chesters Museum, states that "the Thruponian century (built) 24 feet" (7.22 m). The stone is of particular interest in that Thrupo is a German name and its rendering as an adjective indicates that he had been the century's last commander and had not yet been replaced.

The fort is an addition to the original sequence for, uniquely, it overlies the Vallum, as demonstrated by excavations which have located the Vallum ditch running under the fort. Investigations in 1934 under the modern road suggested that the north-west angle tower was recessed into the Wall, implying

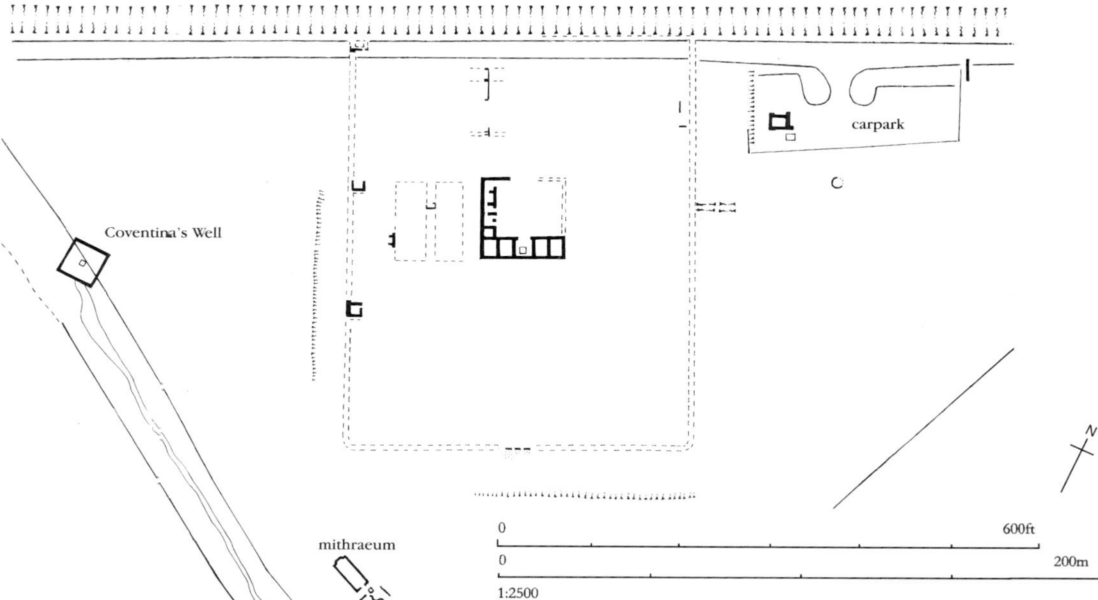

Carrawburgh fort, Coventina's Well to the west, the mithraeum and shrine of the Nymphs to the south-west and the cemetery to the east, under the car park

A building stone recording the construction of 24 feet by the Thruponian century. (213 x 305 mm)

that the fort and the Wall in this area were contemporary. The west wall of the fort stood five courses high, resting on a chamfered plinth. No causeway across the Wall ditch is apparent in front of the position of the north gate. The fort was presumably added to break the long gap between Chesters and Housesteads.

Excavations within the fort from 1967 to 1969 located barrack-blocks and the **headquarters building**. The latter was of the usual form, with five rooms at the rear, the central containing a strongroom, a cross-hall with dais to the west, and courtyard, under which lay the Vallum ditch. In its last phases, a well had been inserted into the courtyard and the adjacent west verandah divided into three rooms. Below the rear rooms was located the ditch of an earlier enclosure, possibly part of a temporary camp, a native settlement or a shrine. Even earlier were plough marks, in two directions, cut into the yellow clay subsoil, a witness that agriculture had been practised here in pre-Wall times.

Within the valley to the west and south of the fort several buildings have been found including a **bath-house** excavated by Clayton in 1873. No attempt was then made to distinguish periods in its life, but some of the walling belonged to the late third or fourth century since coins of the Emperors Claudius II (268-70) and Tacitus (275-6) were found in its core. The plan of the bath-house conforms to the Hadrianic blueprint, being a smaller version of the original plan of Chesters, and thus underlining the Hadrianic date of the fort. Tiles of the Sixth Legion were used for the hypocaust pillars. Later repairs included the use of tombstones as paving slabs. The site of the building is now lost, but it probably lay on the slope west of the fort and between its west gate and south-west corner.

Part or all of three temples is still visible in the valley. The most complete is the ***mithraeum***, a temple to the eastern god Mithras. Found in 1949 and excavated the following year, it was subsequently consolidated, with replica altars and statues replacing the originals which are now in the Museum of Antiquities, Newcastle, and concrete replacing the timber uprights and wattles. These grey objects give no hint that the altars would originally have been brightly painted. The layout as presented today represents the final stage of the building.

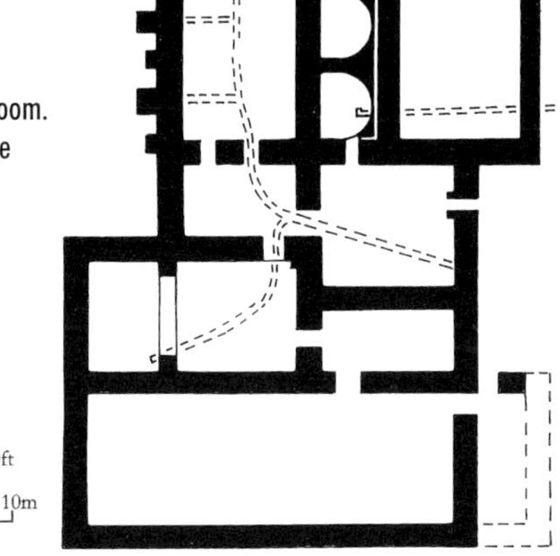

The bath-house at Carrawburgh. The large room is the changing room. The two rows of rooms contain the steam range.

Mithraism was introduced into the Roman world from Asia in the first century BC. Mithras, god of light, was the intermediary between men and eternity. In a cave, Mithras killed the bull from whose body sprang all goodness. The *mithraeum* imitated the cave, and, usually, at one end stood a sculptural depiction of the sacrifice. There were seven grades to the religion: raven, bridegroom, soldier, lion, Persian, courier of the sun and father. Movement from one grade to another was accompanied by a special ritual, including ordeals by fire and water, heat and cold, fasting and journeying. The mysteries also included the ritual use of bread and water, perhaps why Mithraism was singled out by Christians for opprobrium.

The first *mithraeum* was built in the early third century and continued in use for about 100 years, during that time undergoing several modifications. The original building measured 7.92 by 5.56 m (26 by 18 ft 3 in) with clay-bonded walls. It had a small narthex or vestibule, separated from the main body of the temple by a timber screen. Here, benches for 12 worshippers flanked the nave.

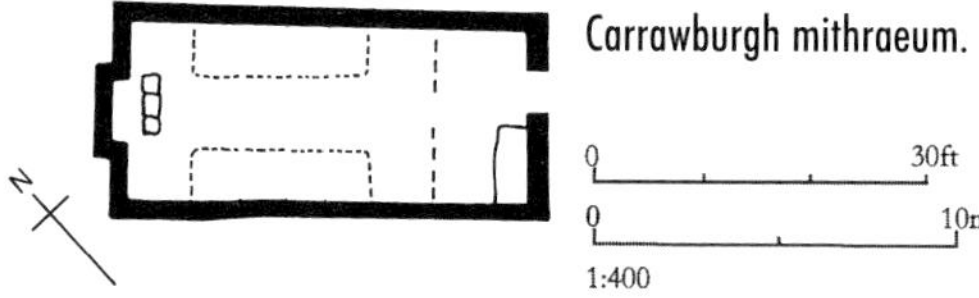

Carrawburgh mithraeum.

The *mithraeum* was extended to 12.19 m (40 ft) with an apse projecting a further 1.68 m (5 ft 6 in), and an enlarged narthex. The internal arrangements of this temple were twice modified before it was radically altered in the early fourth century. The walls were largely rebuilt, the door narrowed, the narthex extended and the apse reduced in size. Coins and pottery suggest that this phase in the life of the *mithraeum* was not long. On its abandonment, the roof was removed, some of the statues broken and the central sculpture of Mithras killing the bull removed altogether: only one small fragment was found. This may indicate action by Christians. The first recorded clash between Christianity and Mithraism was in 324, and such a date for the end of this particular temple would not be inappropriate. The *mithraeum* had suffered from flooding during its life: now it became submerged beneath peat. The waterlogged conditions helped to preserve organic material, such as the wattles retaining the benches and the heather from the floor.

Excavation revealed some evidence for the mithraic ritual. Pine cones used in worship and in ritual deposits were from the Mediterranean stone pine, a tree not native to Britain. A beaker placed in a pit under the altars included pine cone charcoal and the skull of a chicken. A fire-shovel also retained traces of pine cones.

The narthex appeared to be the area where the initiation rites were conducted which allowed worshippers to move on to the next grade. To the left, in the second phase, lay a bench and hearth, perhaps connected with the preparation of ritual meals. Fragments of 19 drinking vessels and several platters were recovered from the building during the excavations: pork was the most common meat eaten, followed by lamb, while many chicken bones were found in the nave. A pit, possibly for ordeals, was later inserted beside the hearth, its location suggesting ordeal by heat during an initiation ceremony. To the right was found a statuette of a mother goddess, brought here from elsewhere.

The nave of the temple, beyond the partition wall, is flanked to left and right by low benches on which the worshippers knelt or reclined: remnants of the rear wall of the original temple are embedded in the benches. Against each bench there are two small altars, personal dedications to the god, while the two attendants Cautes and Cautopates stand at the end of the benches. Cautes survives, except for his head, but of Cautopates only his feet were recovered in the excavation.

Beyond the nave is the temple sanctuary with its three altars, each dedicated by a prefect of the First Cohort of Batavians. The central altar was dedicated by L. Antonius Proculus during the years 213-222, as indicated by the appearance of *Antoniniana* in the regiment's titles. That on the left, by M. Simplicius Simplex, shows Mithras as charioteer of the Sun and was pierced so that a lamp placed in its rear recess would shine through the god's radiate crown. Simplex probably came from the Rhineland. The altar to the right was dedicated by

Aulus Cluentius Habitus whose home was the city of Larinum in Italy, abbreviated on the stone to L: a Cluentius of this city had been famously defended by Cicero. Behind and above the altars is a stone shelf on which the great relief showing Mithras killing the primeval bull once stood.

Immediately outside the door of the building was a small **shrine** to the Nymphs and the *Genius loci* – the spirit of the place. Excavation in 1960 revealed a semi-circular bench facing an altar with a well to one side: only one of the four slabs protecting the well is now visible. The dedication by M. Hispanius Modestinus, prefect of the First Cohort of Batavians, was placed on opposite faces of the altar for the convenience of passers-by: it probably dates to the early years of the third century. The altar is now in the Museum of Antiquities, Newcastle. The shrine appears to have gone out of use and been demolished by the early fourth century.

The statuette of a dog resembling an Aberdeen terrier found in Coventina's Well. (actual size)

At the bottom of the slope, to the north-west of the *mithraeum*, is the swampy source of a strong spring, in a rectangular basin within a fenced enclosure just west of the field wall, **Coventina's Well**. The basin, about 2.45 m (8 ft) square and at least 2.13 m (7 ft) deep, sat withi an enclosure about 12.20 m (40 ft) square with a doorway to the west, beyond which other foundations were noted. When the structure was excavated in 1876, the top was choked with stones. Below came a mass of coins, followed by carved stones, altars, more coins, jars and incense-burners, pearls, brooches and other votive objects in an indiscriminate mass. In total, Clayton retrieved 13,487 coins, four of gold, 184 of silver and the rest of bronze, ranging from Mark Antony (died

Incense burner found in Coventina's Well.
The name "Coventina" is inscribed on the left-hand panel.
(230 mm high)

31 BC) to the Emperor Gratian (367-83). Even this number of coins, however, only represented a portion as the site was heavily pillaged at the time of discovery "by thoughtless people". The objects recovered from the well are in the Chesters Museum; the coins are in the British Museum.

The well was dedicated to a water-goddess named Coventina who was portrayed either singly or in triplicate to express her power. The latter is a well-known Celtic trait. Coventina's recorded worshippers mostly came from the lower Rhineland, but links between the goddess and Spain and Provence have also been suggested.

While the peak period of activity, as indicated by the coins, was in the late second and early third centuries, depositions continued into the fourth century. Several of the stones of the upper courses had been removed from their position and placed on top of the material which filled up the well, apparently with the object of concealing and protecting it. The stones had to be broken before they could be removed. It would appear that the well was not abandoned gradually but as the result of a single act of careful concealment, perhaps in the face of the edicts against paganism. It seems probable that the blocking of the spring led to the flooding of the valley which in turn led to the preservation of the temples within it.

Several tombstones were recovered in the 1870s, including at least three from the bath-house. One was to Aelia Comindus, the wife of the decurion Nobilianus, who died at the age of 32. Two others commemorated a standard bearer and a trumpeter of the First Cohort of Batavians. All are now in Chesters Museum.

CARRAWBURGH TO HOUSESTEADS

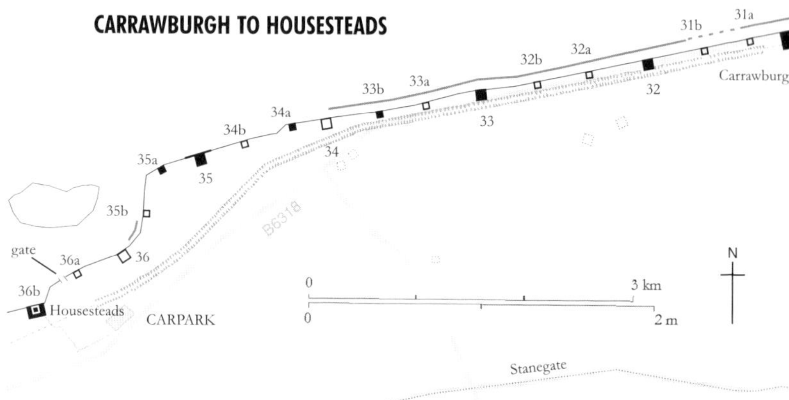

From Carrawburgh the Vallum can be seen climbing the hill towards Carraw Farm with some crossings faintly visible. The modern road here runs on the berm between Wall and ditch. In 1966 small-scale excavation failed to locate **T 31a** (The Strands) but did find **T 31b** (Carraw East) which lies just to the east of the farm. It has an east door with a raised threshold and side walls 1 m (3 ft 3 in) wide. 365 m (400 yards) past the farm the platform of **MC 32** (Carraw) is visible south of the road. It is of long-axis type; although severely robbed, excavation in 1971 produced pottery of fourth-century date. Immediately in front of the centre of the milecastle the shallow Wall ditch deepens and continues westward at this new size: this may indicate the previous existence of a causeway.

The site of **T 32a** (Carraw West) is at the normal distance beyond MC 32. Nearly half a mile to the south, a small Roman camp called **Brown Dykes** occupies a small hilltop with an extensive prospect. It is 67 m (223 ft) square with four gates each protected by a traverse and covers 0.4 ha (1.1 acres). A smaller camp, 274 m (300 yards) to the east-north-east, is hardly visible. **T 32b** (Brown Moor) has not been located.

Now the mounds and ditch of the **Vallum** and the **ditch** of the Wall are very grand and very close to each other. Some crossings are visible in the Vallum ditch, including opposite MC 33, but the gaps in the south mound were not completed. The Military Road lies on the north mound. The Wall swings first slightly north and then a little southwards following the higher ground presumably to provide a better location for **MC 33** (Shield-on-the-Wall), now a bracken-covered mound. The milecastle has a long axis and narrow walls. Its north wall, standing up to seven courses high, is in a good condition, as is the north gate of type II, constructed of large stone blocks and with larger backward-projecting passage-walls than usual. A raking joint in the north wall may indicate that the gate had been built and a start made on the north face of the Wall before there was a break in the building programme. A fragment of stone with a well-cut string-mould, ornamented with a pattern of leaves, was recorded at the gate in about 1930. South of the estate wall, slight remains of the south gateway are to be seen, including its monolithic threshold.

The berm, ditch and upcast mound have all been damaged by quarrying and it is not now possible to determine from surface observations whether the narrow and assymetrical causeway is Roman in date. Some of the sharpness of the upcast mound may also relate to the quarrying. Otherwise, the distinct low profile of the mound is retained.

For the next mile or so, the Wall survives as a mound. To the south, the deserted cottage of Shield-on-the-Wall sits within the Vallum. Ahead, the ridge of the Whin Sill, an outcrop of dolerite, along which the Wall runs in the central part of its length, comes boldly into view. Soon the modern road departs from its accustomed position between Vallum and Wall, swinging to the left across the Vallum. The Wall and Vallum also part company, the Wall, which has so far run in a series of straight stretches, now following the sinuous line of the crags, while the Vallum passes along the southern 'tail' of the hill so that its ditch need not be cut into the hard whinstone. At the same point the Military Way leaves the north mound of the

Vallum and runs more or less parallel to the Wall. For the next 21 km (13 miles), until Carvoran is reached, the Military Way is almost everywhere visible.

Beyond Shield-on-the-Wall gaps appear in the south mound of the **Vallum** and continue for 3 km (2 miles) with the marginal mound unbroken. Gaps in the north mound start after T 33b, though not always regularly and become even more intermittent after MC 34, until gaps in both mounds end.

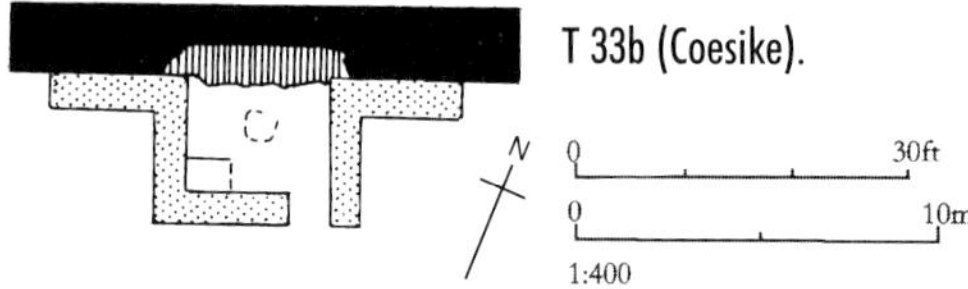

T 33b (Coesike).

Just beyond the point where the Wall and Vallum separate stands **T 33b** (Coesike). The turret has an east door and side walls 0.90 m (3 ft) wide. The wing-walls, of standard A, were 3.10 m (10 ft 2 in) wide; running over them was the Narrow Wall 1.90 m (6 ft 3 in) wide. Within the turret was a platform in the south-west corner and a hearth in the centre: debris from the hearth was dumped outside the east wall of the turret. The hearth was twice replaced, with burnt debris spilling out over the surrounding floor, which itself was raised and partly flagged: at the same time the threshold of the door was lifted. Bones of cattle, sheep and pig were recovered, mostly from young animals and all heavily butchered. Most of the pottery found at the site consisted of jars and cooking pots dating to the Hadrianic period. However, the turret was reoccupied after the abandonment of the Antonine Wall before the door was blocked. Finally, the turret was demolished down to the bottom four courses and the south face of the Wall rebuilt across the site of the recess into which it subsequently subsided. This blocking wall included a reused building inscription of the Sixth Legion, presumably the unit which erected the turret.

At this point, we move into a different landscape. As William Hutton remarked, we now "quit ... the more beautiful scenes of cultivation, and enter upon the rude of Nature, and the wreck of Antiquity".

Ascending the ridge, the ditch is most pronounced where it begins to mount the hill, but 60 m (200 ft) past **MC 34** (Grindon), marked by a clump of trees, it ends abruptly, the height of the cliffs rendering it unnecessary. The gates of MC 34 were of type II. A discontinuity in the bottom of the ditch to the north may indicate the former presence of a causeway. To the south, an excavation in 1947 revealed a lightly-metalled track on the south berm of the Vallum, which had grassed over before the marginal mound was formed. Beyond the Vallum lie the slight traces of two camps, **Coesike East** and **West**. The former measures 50 by 45 m (160 by 150 ft) and encloses 0.2 ha (0.4 acres); the other is 55 m (180 ft) square.

T 34a (Grindon West).

At the next field-wall beyond MC 34 is the site of **T 34a** (Grindon West), located in 1913 and re-examined in 1947. The door is to the east, and the walls are narrow with a mortar core. The wing-walls, unusually short, and the Wall, have a core of large whin blocks. The worn and cracked threshold stone survives with the seatings for the stone jambs while the pivot-hole is also visible. Excavation revealed three hearths in the first period of occupation, later replaced by one. Outside, a path of small stones and *amphora* fragments led to the door. After occupation in the second century, the turret went out of use and the recess was built up. Part of the recess has been removed to reveal the original north wall of the turret.

The farmhouse of **Sewingshields** is built out of Roman stones, **T 34b** lying under its buildings. It is possible that the turret formed the core of the original farm. A centurial stone is preserved here, reading "The century of Gellius Philippus". Examination of the Wall to the east of the farm in 1999 revealed the Narrow Wall 2.5 m (8 ft 2 in) wide with no Broad Foundation. Beyond the wood, excavations in 1978-9 uncovered Broad Foundation ranging in width from 3.23 to 3.6 m (10 ft 7 in to 11 ft 10 in) and formed of whinstones bonded with clay, though foundations were not provided where the Wall was laid directly on the bedrock. The Narrow Wall, about 2.44 m (8 ft) wide, sat on top, often with its own foundation. The Wall was laid in single courses with the core of dolerite blocks placed between and bonded with mortar. Over some parts of Sewingshields Crags Hodgson in the early nineteenth century had noted the construction of the core of the Wall in stages of about four courses with mortar binding each stage but the intervening rubble being left almost dry. The Wall was found to vary between standard A and sections with a second offset, the two styles being separated by vertical junctions. Above stood the Extra Narrow Wall 2.13 m (7 ft) wide and bonded with hard white mortar. A burial cist found here, tucked into the back of the Wall, had contained the skeleton of a male.

Cat's Gate is a narrow chasm by which, says local tradition, the Scots crept under the Wall. On each side of the gap, a series of small stake-holes were recorded in 1978-9 on the northern edge of the foundations; they probably represent a marking out line. The Narrow Wall here moved onto the southern edge of the Broad Foundation so as to negotiate the gap more easily.

MC 35 (Sewingshields) was completely excavated between 1978 and 1982 and found to be badly robbed: much of the east wall and eastern half of the south wall had gone. It is a long-axis milecastle, measuring 18.30 by 15.25 m (60 by 50 ft) within broad side walls: the south gate is type IV. Along the north wall ran the Broad Foundation, composed of blocks of dolerite and levelled by a layer of clay: it was surmounted by the Narrow Wall bonded with yellow mortar. No evidence for a north gate was

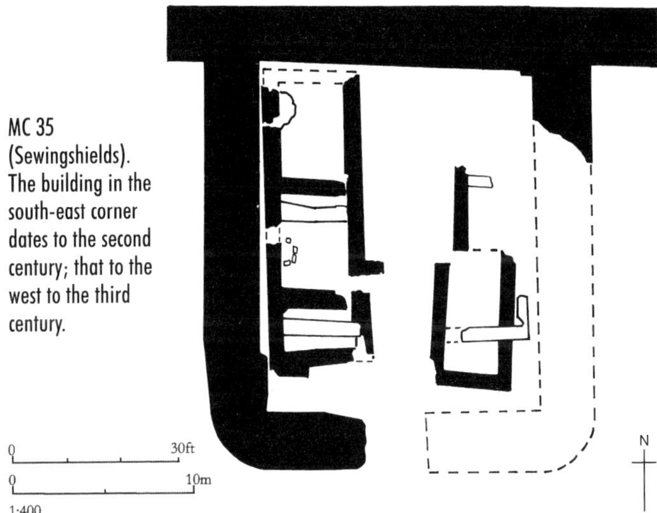

MC 35 (Sewingshields). The building in the south-east corner dates to the second century; that to the west to the third century.

found during the excavation and the excavator argued that none had existed. The Broad Foundation continued across the site of the north gate uninterrupted, but that is not unique for it also occurs at MC 37 (Housesteads), for example. Later repair or rebuilding of the north wall may have removed earlier evidence for a gate.

Following the construction of the side walls, the southern part of the interior had been levelled up with clay and rubble up to 25 cm (10 in) thick, over which sandstone flags had been laid. Within the milecastle, to the east and west of the central road, lies a jumble of buildings. The original two-roomed building in the south-east corner measured 7.45 by 4.25 m (24 ft 6 in by 14 ft) and was entered by a doorway in the north end of the west wall. The building was reflagged before it was replaced by a slightly larger structure in the third century. The west half of the milecastle was now occupied by a building for the first time: it measured 5.5 m by at least 14.5 m (18 by 47 ft 6 in). This new arrangement may have survived for as long as a century, though in that time the eastern building was dismantled and the western refurbished.

After a period of decay, new buildings were erected in the fourth century, that to the west measured about 6.5 by 5.5 m (21 ft 4 in by 18 ft). To the east lay a slightly smaller and less well-preserved structure: both were to be replaced by similar sized buildings. In the fourth century the eastern half of the milecastle was used for the smelting and casting of copper alloys and, on a smaller scale, the smithing of iron. Three successive metal-working hearths were found in the south-east corner of the milecastle, while in the south-west corner as many as nine successive metal-working hearths were uncovered. In the north-west corner lay an oven; earlier, an oven lay outside the east wall of the milecastle. The final, and seventh, phase of occupation was represented by a small building in the south-west corner. Pottery and a coin of the Emperor Valentinian I (364-75) indicated that occupation continued into the final third of the fourth century. The considerable number of finds included: 22 coins, most of fourth-century date; eight spearheads, an artillery bolt-head, a dagger and other pieces of military equipment; brooches, finger rings and other items of clothing; millstones and whetstones; several fragments of window glass; a gaming board; and a seal marked C I T, presumably either the First Cohort of Tungrians (based at Housesteads in the third and fourth centuries) or the First Cohort of Thracians. In the Middle Ages a farm was built on the site. South of the milecastle, between the Wall and the Vallum, terraces constructed for agriculture may date from the Roman period.

In a particularly steep dip beyond the milecastle, the Wall is stepped down on one side while it rises with the contours on the other. In some places the Broad Foundation is as wide as 11 Roman feet (3.3 m). A hundred metres before the summit of the hill comes **T 35a** (Sewingshields Crag), located in 1913 and examined again in 1947 and 1958. It had an east door and

T 35a (Sewingshields Crag).

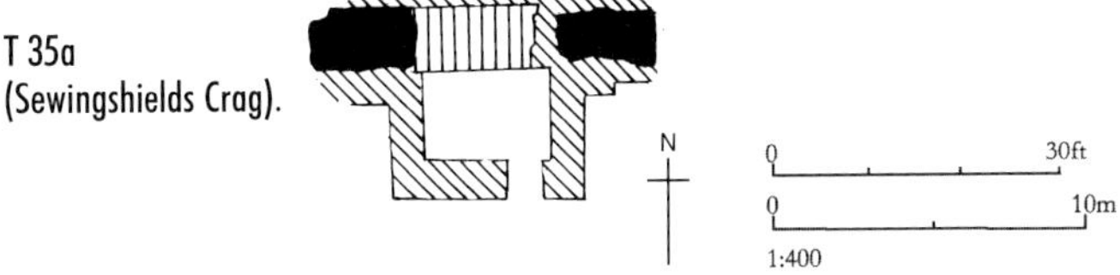

narrow walls with a hearth against the east wall and a small stone box set into the ground in the south-east corner. There was a path in front of the south wall of the turret. Evidence was found for working bronze and masonry. Finds included a brooch, knife, sword chape, bronze binding from a sword or shield as well as cooking pots, jars and tankards. Occupation only occurred in the second century after which it had been almost completely demolished and the recess built up: the blocking masonry has been partially removed to show the original north wall of the turret. From the summit can be seen Broomlee Lough (to the west) and the smaller Grindon Lough (to the south of the Military Road). To the north, the Whin Sill outcrops in a series of shelves. Some of the outcrops appear to have been quarried, probably by the Romans. On the north face of Queen's Crag, north-west of T 35a, the names of three officers are recorded: they are cut on the rock face under an overhanging outcrop about 20 m (60 ft) east of the massive detached stone known as the 'Rabbit Stone'. Faintly cut in the rock are the names of two centurions, Saturninus and Rufi[nus], and Henoenus, an *optio*.

T 35b (Busy Gap), investigated in 1947, like the others in this sector, had narrow walls, an east door and had gone out of use in the second century. West of the turret comes Busy Gap, where the Wall ditch reappears, as at all such breaks in the escarpment. In later centuries, a drove road passed through this gap.

MC 36 (King's Hill), a long-axis milecastle with narrow side walls, stands on a steep slope. The north wall, 2.13 m (7 ft) thick, was Narrow Wall on Broad Foundation. The north gate had been completely reconstructed in post-Hadrianic times to a reduced width and subsequently blocked; quarrying has destroyed the south gate. A road connected the milecastle to the Military Way. Next follow in rapid succession two narrow and rather steep gaps without names, and Kennel Crags, on whose summit stood **T 36a**, just east of the Knag Burn. Excavated in 1947, it had narrow side walls and an eastern door, the threshold of which had been raised at an unknown date. East of the wood, the **Vallum** ditch is cut through rock, still visible on its northern side. The Vallum is no longer visible west of the wood, but in 1950 the ditch was located on the eastern bank of the burn.

In the bottom of the valley is the **Knag Burn gateway** discovered in 1856, one of the very rare gates through the Wall other than at a milecastle or a fort. The single passage is flanked by guard-chambers, and pivot-holes at back and front show that there were two sets of doors. A particular implication has been drawn from this, namely that travellers could be admitted for examination in small groups and also, perhaps, to pay customs dues. The construction of the gate has generally been dated to the fourth century, but the discovery of late-second-century pottery on the surface of the road leading out of the north gate of the nearby fort of Housesteads led to the suggestion that the gate went out of use at that time and that the Knag Burn gate was built to replace it. To the south of the gate lies a stone 1.1 m (3 ft 7 in) long containing what appears to be a pivot-hole. The size of the stone suggests that it may have been an upper pivot stone from the gateway.

The Knag Burn passes under the Wall in a culvert, as it presumably did in Roman times. Between the burn and the fort are traces of extra-mural buildings and the Military Way may be seen winding up to the fort's east gate. The Wall from the Knag Burn to Peel Crag, including Housesteads fort, the Knag Burn gateway and MC 37, is owned by the National Trust; the fort is in the care of English Heritage.

HOUSESTEADS (*VERCOVICIUM*)

The ancient name of Housesteads is abbreviated in an inscription to Ver, and this establishes *Vercovicium* in preference to the *Borcovicium* of the *Notitia Dignitatum*. Translations offered include "hilly place" and "the place of the effective fighters".

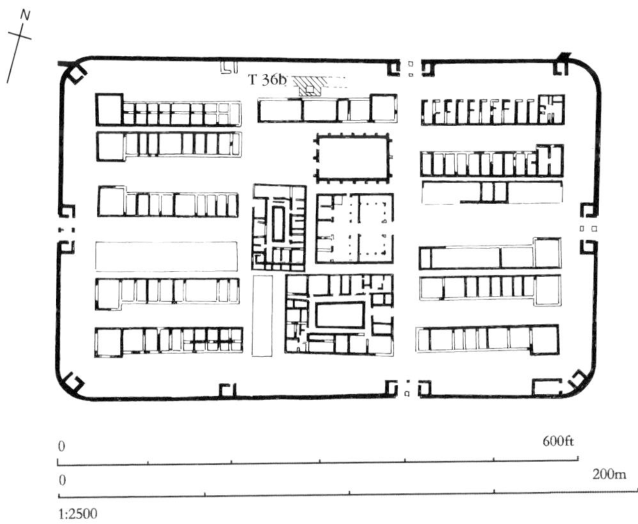

Housesteads fort, showing the original line of the Wall and the site of T 36b, the visible buildings and others extrapolated from the 1898 plan.

The size of the fort suggests that the unit originally based here was a milliary cohort. The First Cohort of Tungrians, a thousand strong, is attested at Housesteads not only in the *Notitia* but also in the third century, and may have arrived earlier. Also recorded here in the third century are the *cuneus Frisiorum*, a formation of Frisian cavalry, and the *numerus Hnaudifridi*, Notfried's regiment. It is not known whether all these units were based in the fort at the same time. Two undated inscriptions record soldiers of the Second Legion on garrison duty at Housesteads and a soldier of the Sixth Legion dedicating an altar to Cocidius and the spirit of the garrison. Other inscriptions include fragments of a dedication to the Emperors Septimius Severus and Caracalla (198-209) found in the headquarters building and the granary and part of a stone probably recording building work under Diocletian and Maximian (296-305).

The **fort** lies 7.6 km (4¾ miles) from Carrawburgh and covers 2.02 ha (5 acres). It measures 112 by 186 m (367 by 610 ft) with its long axis running from east to west, because the fort is planted at the very edge of the cliff on a narrow ridge which itself slopes sharply southwards. A better site to the west was sacrificed, perhaps in order to locate the fort closer to the Knag Burn.

Housesteads is one of the classic forts of the Roman empire. Although excavations took place as early as the 1830s, it is thanks to the wide-ranging investigations of R. C. Bosanquet in 1898 that the layout of the fort is well known. Work over the last 45 years funded by English Heritage and its predecessors has led to a large body of new information, improved interpretation and more buildings to view. The **museum** is the best starting point for a visit. The building itself was constructed in the 1930s as a replica of a Roman civilian building found in the settlement outside the fort.

Before the fort was built, the foundations of the Broad Wall, together with **T 36b**, were laid across the site on the true crest of the escarpment. It is possible that a little more of the turret than merely the foundations was erected for within it lay a reddened stone, taken to be a hearth, though this may merely indicate that the enclosed space was a convenient place for soldiers to cook. In addition, a cremation burial with a coin of Hadrian was found in the north-west corner of the fort: it probably also dates to this time as burial within settlements was forbidden. When the fort was constructed the turret was demolished to its lowest courses, which are still visible.

In order to gain more space on the ridge, the north wall of

the fort was sited a little beyond the earlier planned line, on the very edge of the crag. After the fort's construction, the Narrow Wall was completed, butting against its rounded north angles. Inside the north-east angle the tower was built up to its seventh course, bonded with the fort wall, before it was abandoned and demolished. A new tower was erected a few metres to the north at a point from which soldiers would be able to see over the Wall. The foundations of the original tower are not visible, though the patching executed when its walls were pulled away from the fort wall can still be seen.

A single ditch is known but only along the short stretches north of the west and east gates. The ditch to the east runs out on the slope down to the Knag Burn, but that on the west was cut through the Broad Foundation and ended just short of the Narrow Wall. Hodgson in 1833 noted a triple barrier of ditches and ramparts before the west gate: traces of the banks are still visible, while the ditches have been recorded in geophysical survey.

The full circuit of walls is visible together with the four gates. The walls, which stand up to 11 courses high, show evidence for repair, though this is not dated. Housesteads is unusual for a Wall fort in that it faces east, that is towards the rising sun, the normal alternative to facing the enemy if that was impractical. All four gates are exposed and are well worth detailed examination, not least in relation to the standard of workmanship which varies from high quality (the sub-foundations of the north gate and the north-west pier of the west gate) through average (most of the south, north and west gates) to very poor (the central spines of the south, north and west gates).

Visitors enter the fort by a modern field gate and are recommended to proceed to the **south gate**. In the seventeenth century a house was attached to the east tower on its southern side and a corn-drying kiln placed within the tower. The gate is of normal type, but the east portal was clearly blocked at some time for the road approaching the gate is aligned on the west portal only: the blocking wall was removed in the nineteenth century. That the gate threshold had already been replaced suggests that the blocking did not happen early in the life of the fort.

Statue of Victory from Housesteads. (1.39 m high)

The **east gate** was the front gate to the fort. Its north portal shows considerable signs of wear and two successive cups for the door-pivots survive. The width of the ruts corresponds closely to the British standard railway gauge. The local legend is that George Stephenson took his gauge from this gateway. His standard, however, had been reached by averaging the wheel-gauge of a hundred carts before the gate was uncovered. The south portal was not finished as demonstrated by the fact that the pivot-hole was not cut. The passage was blocked and used as a coal-store in which nearly a cart-load of coal was found in 1833. A relief of Victory was found in the street on the inside of the gate in 1852. A second sculpture of Victory found at the site is now in the Museum of Antiquities in Newcastle.

The **north gate** allowed access beyond the Wall. The embanked roadway which led from it has been removed to display the substantial foundations of the gate. Excavations have demonstrated that the pivots for the doors in the east portal had not yet been fitted when a wall was built across the entrance. A secondary threshold in the west portal, about 1 m (3 ft) higher than the original one, has been removed: one of its pivot-blocks lies at the back of the gate. The west tower was rebuilt in Roman times: its walls included part of an altar to Jupiter, now in Chesters Museum. Outside this chamber is a large water-tank. Its stone sides, themselves of reused material, were run in with lead in vertical slots at the joints and cramped with iron at the top. The tops are worn by sharpening swords or by washing clothes. Many tanks at Housesteads are related to the towers, collecting water from their roofs.

The **west gate** is one of the finest on the Wall. Its north pier remains to full height, ready for the cap and arch. Of particular importance are the marking-out lines scored by the masons on the large foundation stones. At the back of the outer central pier, bolt-holes for the bar of the doors and slots for its manipulation are visible; they go with corresponding holes behind the imposts. In spite of its fine appearance, the gate shows evidence that the upper courses are not finished as well as the lower courses. This may indicate a wish to speed the construction of the Wall at some stage during the building programme, through reducing the quality of the workmanship, or a change in the gang building the gate is possible. The existing threshold and stop-block in the south portal are replacements. Both portals were eventually blocked at front and rear: the masonry in the northern portal was the better and this work may therefore have been earlier. When the gate was cleared in 1833, several slates and iron nails were found within.

The eastern and western thirds of the fort mainly contained barrack-blocks, the ten that were required for a thousand-strong cohort. In the central range lay the headquarters building (*principia*) flanked to the north by the granaries (*borrea*) and to the south by the commander's house (*praetorium*), while behind was the hospital (*valetudinarium*). A workshop lay in the western part of the fort.

The **headquarters building** was of the normal plan, with a courtyard, cross-hall and range of five rear rooms. The building sits on an artificial platform retained by a substantial south wall built of large blocks laid as headers, many nearly 1 m (3 ft) long. This wall was partially restored at the close of the 1898 excavation. The entrance lies to the east, at the junction of the *via principalis* and the *via praetoria*. A sculpture of Mars was found on the opposite side of the street and may once have adorned the arched entrance. The large bases in front of the entrance were placed there in modern times.

The bases for a colonnade round the courtyard survive and many fragments of columns were recovered in 1898. The colonnade was later closed by walling and a series of rooms created: a hearth lay at the eastern end of the northern room. The roofs were stone-slated and projected 75 cm (2 ft 5 in) over the pavement as the eaves-drip demonstrates.

An entrance in the west wall led into the cross-hall. The pivot-holes for the door, which was closed from the inside, remain, and a paved area led across the room to the regimental shrine. The rest of the floor was composed of clay renewed periodically. Along the east wall lay an aisle. Walls were later added to each side of the entrance passage and a hearth was placed in the southern of the two corners thus created. At the north end of the hall stood a dais for the commander and, beside it, a flight of steps leading onto the side road.

The five rooms at the rear of the building show evidence for reconstruction and their excavation in 1898 was particularly illuminating. Originally the southern four rooms had wide doors: the fifth room to the north was entered from its neighbour. The central room retains its threshold which reveals evidence for the former existence of screens which would have narrowed the entrance. The floor of the room was formed of stones covered with clay; below this was found an early mortar floor. This room would have held the standards of the unit and probably a statue of the emperor, guarded by soldiers.

The floors of the rooms to the south were of clay, renewed at least twice. The rooms themselves were modified; the door of the northerly room was narrowed, and that of its neighbour blocked. The wall between them was removed and a new wall built at right angles towards the back of the new, large room. This may have screened a passage leading to a door in the south wall, contained a latrine or supported a stair to an upper storey. At the same time a new flagged floor, with a hearth, was laid.

The door to the room to the north of the central room was also narrowed and then blocked. At this point, the two northerly rooms were only accessible through the central room and one may have served the purpose of a strongroom. On excavation, these rooms were found to be filled with debris, including flue-tiles, which was interpreted as having fallen from an upper floor. Below this debris was a layer of slates and below that more than 800 arrowheads were found together with many nails and other iron objects. The excavator thought that there was some evidence that the arrows had been arranged in bundles. It would appear that in the last period of its use this area was an arms store.

South of the headquarters building is the **commanding officer's house**. This is a substantial courtyard or peristyle house of Mediterranean type facing inwards and is the largest building in the fort. It was built in two stages: the north and west ranges first. The steep slope necessitated an unusual form of construction. The outer walls were erected first and the interior of the building filled with clean material (blocks of whinstone and clay), then the partition walls added: they can be seen to butt against the outer walls. The south wall of the building was particularly substantial with alternating headers and stretchers as it had to take considerable pressure.

The entrance to the building is from the *via principalis*. A passage or vestibule insulated the occupants from the activities of the surrounding fort and is a normal provision in this type of house: it led to the courtyard. Part of its paved floor survives and this was surrounded on all sides by a colonnade. Most rooms opened off this colonnade, though some could only be entered from their neighbour. Stone steps aided movement round the building. It is not possible to determine the function of most rooms. Along the north range lay, from east to west: a kitchen still containing the base of an oven; a passage; a large room probably serving as a dining-room; a hypocausted room probably only converted into a heated room in the mid-fourth century; two rooms which appear to have been redesigned as a self-contained flat with an entrance leading off the *via decumana* at an unknown date. Such a back entrance is a common feature in a house of this type. The west range contained a latrine with its drain running along the outside face of the west wall of the house, and a heated room in the south-west corner. A water-trough and drains have led to the identification of the two large rooms in the south-east corner as stables; there may have been accommodation for the household slaves above.

To the west of the headquarters lay a second courtyard building, normally identified as the **hospital**, though this cannot be certain. The method of construction followed that of the commanding officer's house with the outer walls erected first and the partitions added later. Again care was taken to strengthen the lower, southern side of the building, in this case by the construction of two walls, the inner apparently being intended to retain the internal levelling material.

The entrance is towards the north end of the west wall and this leads into a colonnaded courtyard. A large room in the north range has been interpreted as an operating theatre. The other three ranges were divided into a series of rooms; some were small, possibly intended to hold medical supplies.

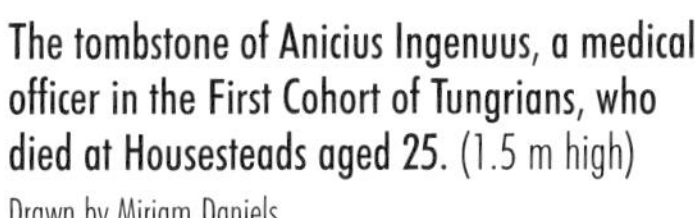

The tombstone of Anicius Ingenuus, a medical officer in the First Cohort of Tungrians, who died at Housesteads aged 25. (1.5 m high)
Drawn by Miriam Daniels

A latrine lay in the south-west corner. Several of the rooms, and the courtyard, were modified during the life of the building, which continued until at least 330.

North of the headquarters building lie two **granaries** side by side. These are buttressed buildings, whose floors, no longer present, rested on joists supported by rows of piers, thus creating a ventilated basement. Joist-holes are seen opposite each row of piers in the south wall of the north granary. The object of this arrangement was to raise the floor off the ground and thus keep the food dry and fresh, and perhaps restrict the activities of rodents. Doors at the west end, bolted from the inside, opened onto platforms, now removed, up to which carts could be backed for unloading food. Grain formed a major part of the diet and was probably stored in sacks.

Although now two buildings, there is evidence to indicate that the granaries once formed one large structure. The two middle walls butt against the end walls. This may be a building technique, though the existence of the bases and capitals of a dismantled colonnade lying between the walls, and possibly from an earlier central support for the wide roof, suggests that they are secondary. In the south granary, a post-medieval corn-drying kiln has been inserted.

Within the north-east corner of the fort, three buildings are exposed. None dates to the earliest phases of the site's history though they do incorporate earlier walls. The two northerly buildings are **barrack-blocks** of the fourth century. Each consists of a two-roomed officer's suite at the rampart end and seven or more individual rooms or 'chalets', one containing an oven. The fronts of the 'chalets' are open but presumably had wooden shutters which have since rotted. This barrack-block replaced an earlier building consisting of an officer's block and ten rooms of normal second-century type. The change of accommodation from a single building to a series of individual small buildings is probably related to changes in the structure of the regiment, but the details are not clear. It has been suggested that each 'chalet' was occupied by a family unit, but there is no evidence for this.

The third building, a **hall** or **storehouse**, was erected towards the end of the third century. It had three predecessors, apparently serving successively as a storehouse, barrack-block and storehouse again. The visible building, one of the largest buildings in the fort, was well constructed with its flags laid on a carefully levelled floor. It had a door in the south wall wide enough to allow access for carts and a second, smaller, entrance in the west wall. It was presumably a store-building of some kind. A centrally positioned stone block has been interpreted as a support for an upper floor. In the later fourth century the eastern end was demolished and a small bath-house erected there. There is a hot room, with a furnace to the north and a hot bath to the side, and a cold room with its own bath to the west. Voussoirs from its roof lie to one side.

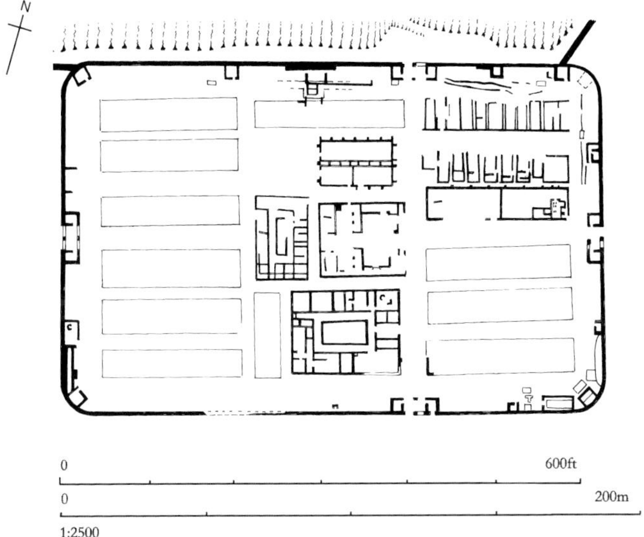

Housesteads in the fourth century.

One of the most important surviving buildings at Housesteads lies in the south-east corner, the **latrine**, not only because it is a fine structure in its own right, but also because it reminds us of the attention the Roman army paid to hygiene. This was a communal latrine, providing facilities for several men at any one time. The original entrance lay in the east wall, but at some stage this was blocked and a new doorway created in the west wall. The corbels and joist-holes to hold the wooden seating over the main sewer can still be seen. This sewer was flushed by water running along stone channels leading from water tanks: this main drain exited through the fort wall, discharging at a point as yet unknown. The channel in the floor carried running water to allow the soldiers to wash the sponges, placed on a stick, which were used instead of toilet paper. The two stone basins may have been for washing hands. Part of a sculptural composition of Neptune and a sea creature was found in the north sewer: it is now in Chesters Museum.

In spite of its well-ordered appearance, the latrine was not well designed. The adjacent angle-tower cut off the access to the sewer, forcing the visible complicated arrangement of water channels to be constructed. Water was collected in three cisterns. The main cistern, beside the angle-tower, was formed of ten large slabs and, when excavated, the bottom was found to have been lined with cement. The sides of the stones are grooved and run with lead and secured on the top with dove-tailed cramps. Two coping stones remain. The outlet is on the downhill side of the tank. The stone slabs of the more northerly tank are also jointed and fastened together by lead cramps: the interior was waterproofed with puddled clay. The wear on the top of the side slabs has been variously interpreted as resulting from washing clothes or sharpening swords and knives.

The **rampart backing**, at least along the north wall, had a complicated history, being removed and replaced at different times. At various places buildings can be seen erected against the inside face of the fort wall. These appear to date to the third and fourth centuries. In places there are interval-towers, often also of late date. West of the north gate, south of the east gate and in the south-west corner, staircase ramps are attached to the inner side of the fort walls. Just to the west of the latrine sits part of a possible staircase. Of earlier date, but no longer visible, were bakehouses and ovens. Immediately south of the western interval tower on the north wall Bosanquet found in 1898, above a layer of dark soil, an area of paving with the remains of an apse at the west end. This has been interpreted as a Christian church. Beside it, and still visible, is a water tank showing evidence for a later long cist burial within it.

Immediately beyond the south gate of the fort (and accessible through the field gate) are several buildings, representative of a **civil settlement** examined during the 1930s. Early visitors were astonished both at the extent of the buildings and at the number of inscribed and sculptured stones on the slopes and in the valley. One inscription, now in the museum, demonstrates that the occupants had self-governing rights. To the south-west of the gate are the massive foundations of a building examined in 1898; the other buildings were excavated in the 1930s and date to the third and fourth centuries. Only their lowest courses survive, though they were once half-timbered. One at least appears to have been a shop for the sill of its front wall is grooved for shutters. The buildings encroach on the access to the south gate, blocking the approach to the east portal. Excavation showed that the road continued in a southerly direction and crossed a causeway of undug rock over the **Vallum** ditch 100 m (300 ft) south of the fort: the Vallum lay far enough south of the fort as to require no deviation from its straight course. Excavation in 1934 revealed that the ditch, cut through bedrock, was later filled and obliterated by buildings of the civil settlement.

Between the fort and the first building, a road led eastwards along the fort wall. The first building had a shallow basement at the back, later filled in and occupied by an oven. A set of dice was found in this building, leading to the suggestion that it was a tavern. The most easterly building possibly had a timber predecessor, the floor of which was repaired four times before it was replaced by the present stone structure: a furnace lay towards its rear. Just outside it was found a mould for counterfeiting coins of the Empress Julia Domna (193-201). The most southerly house is known as the '**Murder House**'. Excavation here in 1932 led to the discovery of two bodies concealed within a thick clay floor in the back room. One skeleton was of a tall, robust man of middle age with a knife point in his ribs; the other was of a slighter individual, possibly a woman. The murder, for that is the obvious interpretation, was committed sometime in the fourth century before the abandonment of the civil settlement about 367.

These buildings yielded fragments of a distinctive pottery in

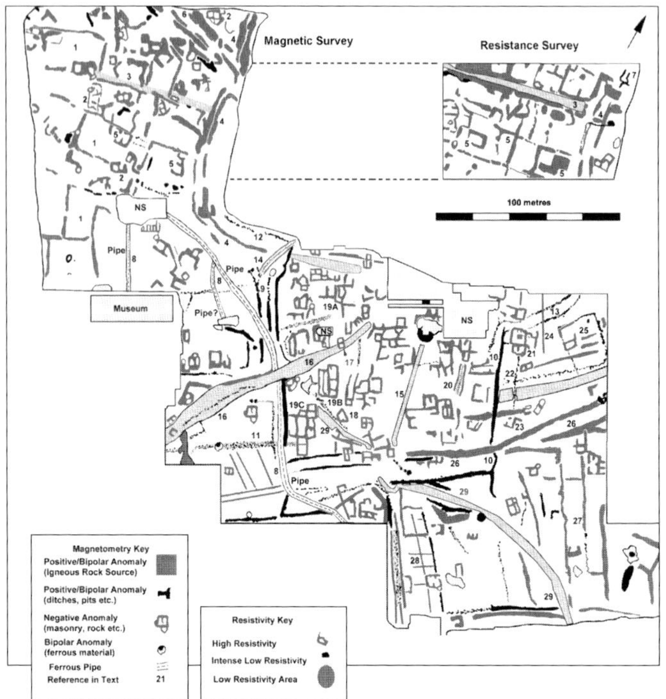

Geophysical survey of the area to the south and south-west of the fort.

a style known in Friesland in the northern Netherlands. It seems probably that members of either the *cuneus Frisiorum* or the *numerus Hnaudifridi*, or perhaps more likely their families, continued to make pottery in their traditional style when living at Housesteads in the third century. Similar pottery is known at Birdoswald, but again only from the civil settlement.

The excavated buildings are part of a more extensive civil settlement which stretched as far south as the Vallum. About 24 buildings were investigated in whole or in part during the 1930s. Most were more poorly constructed with walls, about

30 cm (1 ft) wide, consisting of a single line of stones. Geophysical survey in 2003 recorded these buildings and demonstrated that they were bounded east and west by ditches.

The ruins of the **bath-house** of the fort sit on a rocky shelf to the east of the Knag Burn, opposite the middle of the fort. It was discovered in the late eighteenth century but robbed of its stone: a flood in 1817 caused further damage. Nearer the Wall is a fenced spring, cased in Roman masonry, which seems to have supplied the bath-house. Opposite the baths, and to the west of the burn, was found a Roman lime-kiln. Following collapse of its dome, soil accumulated on the site: this contained late-third to mid-fourth-century pottery. To the north of the Wall and east of the Knag Burn gate, a distinct hollow has been interpreted as an amphitheatre.

South of the civil settlement and the museum is a series of **terraces**. These are long fields, with stone retaining walls built by the Romans, apparently, as early as the second century, though reused, perhaps in the twelfth and thirteenth centuries. Other fields to the south of the fort run north-south. These fields are a reminder that the whole landscape around Housesteads was farmed during the Roman period.

Between the fort and the car-park rises the ridge called **Chapel Hill**. Beyond its west end, close to an active spring, is the site of a half-underground temple dedicated to Mithras and first discovered in 1822. Excavations in 1898 revealed a long, narrow nave, flanked by benches for reclining worshippers. Beyond this was the sanctuary, which yielded fragments of the great bull-killing scene, a very notable relief of Mithras rising from the rock, surrounded by the signs of the Zodiac (the earliest example in Britain), so designed and placed that it would be illuminated from behind, statues of the attendant deities Cautes and Cautopates, and several altars. It has been suggested that the relief was smashed by Christians. Two altars were dedicated to Mithras, Lord of the Ages. One, dated to 252, probably marks a refurbishment of the temple some time after its foundation earlier in the century. Another was dedicated by Litorius Pacatianus, *beneficiarius consularis*, an officer from the governor's staff on detached duty. Most of the inscriptions from this temple are in the Museum of Antiquities, Newcastle; one is in Chesters Museum.

Relief found at the mithraeum at Housesteads showing Mithras emerging from the Cosmic Egg. (1.12 m high)

The large and imposing altars in Chesters Museum dedicated to Mars Thincsus were found on the north side of Chapel Hill. This German deity was attended by pairs of Alaisiagae, female spirits or Valkyries, whose names are given as Beda and Fimmilena, Baudihillia and Friagabis. Appropriately, one altar was dedicated by Germans in the unit of Frisians. The shrine also yielded a remarkable arched door-head, on which are carved the god and male attendants, represented as Mars, with Victories. Their worshippers belonged to the *cuneus Frisiorum* and the *numerus Hnaudifridi*, based here in the third century. Excavation in 1961 at the site of discovery revealed the foundations of a round shine, 4 m (13 ft) in internal diameter, and dating to the third century. Below lay traces of the second-century civil settlement.

Another group from Chapel Hill is a series of altars dedicated to Jupiter, Best and Greatest and the Spirit of the Deified Emperors, by the Tungrians under their commander. Such inscriptions are usually part of the official state cult, as practised by the army. Elsewhere lay an as yet unidentified temple to Nemesis. An unusual dedication was that to the gods and goddesses erected by the Tungrians according to the interpretation of the Oracle of Apollo at Claros, a religious sanctuary near Ephesos in modern Turkey. It is paralleled by nine similar inscriptions erected in other provinces. They all may relate to an appeal to the god for advice following the plague brought into the empire by the armies returning from the eastern frontier about 165.

Bosanquet in 1898 excavated a single trench in the low ground between Chapel Hill and the fort and found Roman walls, pottery, wood and earthwork preserved in the peat. Geophysical survey west of the fort in 2003 revealed fields occupying the area between the museum and the Wall, several containing a single building.

The **cemeteries** lay beyond the extra-mural settlement, one on each side of Chapel Hill and another to the west of the fort and south of the Military Way.

A large flat area lies about 400 m (430 yards) to the south-east of the fort. It has been suggested that this was a parade-ground.

The **museum** offers an interpretation of the fort and civil settlement and houses a small but interesting collection of objects, including the well-known relief of three deities, the *Genii Cucullati*, each wearing a long, hooded cloak, the *birrus Britannicus*, found in a temple in the civil settlement. Most of the earlier discoveries, however, are either in the Museum of Antiquities, Newcastle, or in Chesters Museum.

Housesteads was connected with the Stanegate by a road running south-east from the fort to the Stanegate at Grindon.

HOUSESTEADS TO GREAT CHESTERS

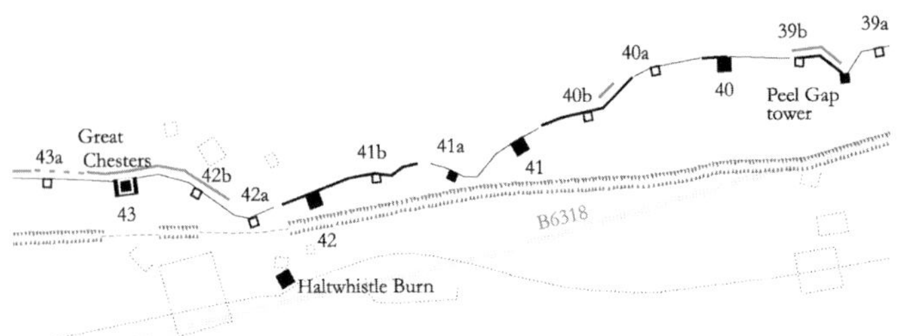

In walking westwards, those who wish to avoid fatigue should take the Military Way leading from the west gate of the fort. It is easily found, because all the field-gates are placed upon it. This road was still used by pack-horse carriers up to the building of the railway in the mid-nineteenth century.

Those who choose to walk along the Wall should leave the fort and walk round the west side to the north-west corner where a path runs through the wood along the south face of the Wall. This is one of the most beautiful and evocative stretches of Hadrian's Wall where, of anywhere along its whole line, it is possible to feel most empathy with the Roman soldiers maintaining watch and ward over the country to the north.

At various points along the south face there are vertical offsets. The purpose of these is not known but probably relates to later repairs. Over much of the Whin Sill the wall was rebuilt in the nineteenth century by John Clayton's workmen who replaced fallen facing stones. Today, these have often been mortared into place, but with the joints left open at the front.

MC 37 (Housesteads) lies just beyond the trees. It sits 46 m (50 yards) to the west of its measured position so that, it has been argued, it could maintain contact with Barcombe Hill, through whose observation tower communication was

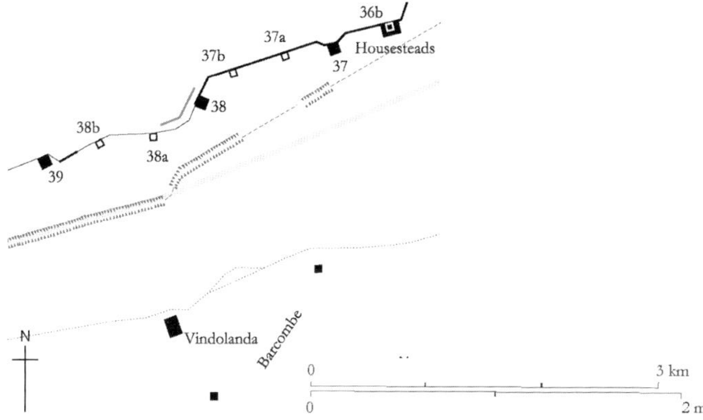

afforded with the fort at Vindolanda. The milecastle was excavated in 1853, 1907, 1933 and 1989-90. A short-axis milecastle, it measures internally 15.09 by 17.53 m (49 ft 6 in by 57 ft 6 in) and has side walls 2.59 m (8 ft 6 in) wide. The Broad Foundation was laid preparatory to the construction of the

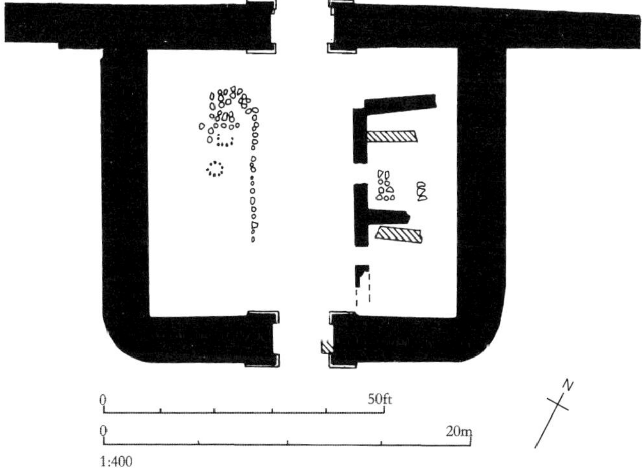

MC 37 (Housesteads).

north wall. At the north-west corner, one course of Broad Wall survives. The north gate was built to receive the Broad Wall, but to east and west the wall tapers to narrow gauge, a treatment not found anywhere else. The Narrow Wall is here 2.29 m (7 ft 6 in) wide, though it narrows to 1.98 m (6 ft 6 in) to the east of the milecastle. To the west of the gate an offset raking joint may be observed, marking the junction between Broad and Narrow Walls. The band of thin sandstone slabs in the north wall, occasionally seen elsewhere on the Wall, appears only in original Hadrianic work. Its purpose is unknown but it cannot have been a bonding course as it does not continue through the whole thickness of the wall.

The west wall of the milecastle is bonded with the north wall, but 60 cm (2 ft) south there is a joint, as if the Stone Wall and a short stub of the milecastle wall were built together. In the east wall a change of footings occurs 1.22 m (4 ft) south of the corner and may point to a similar arrangement.

Both gateways are of type I and of monumental masonry. A fragment of a building inscription of the Second Legion found reused in a later floor at the milecastle recorded its construction under A. Platorius Nepos. However, as the inscription would have been erected over the gate and there are two building phases, it is not known whether it was this legion which commenced the construction of the structure or completed the work.

The north gate exhibits two standards of workmanship. The lower courses are reasonably competently dressed, but the upper courses are rougher, the cap of the south-east pier being particularly bad. The gateway was re-examined in 1990. An original gate-stop remained, together with the pivot stones, but no road metalling had been laid within the gate. The entrance had been completely blocked by a clay-bonded wall before weathering of the stones in the passage walls had taken place. Investigations behind this blocking masonry revealed that the north piers had tilted out of position, probably due to subsidence of the

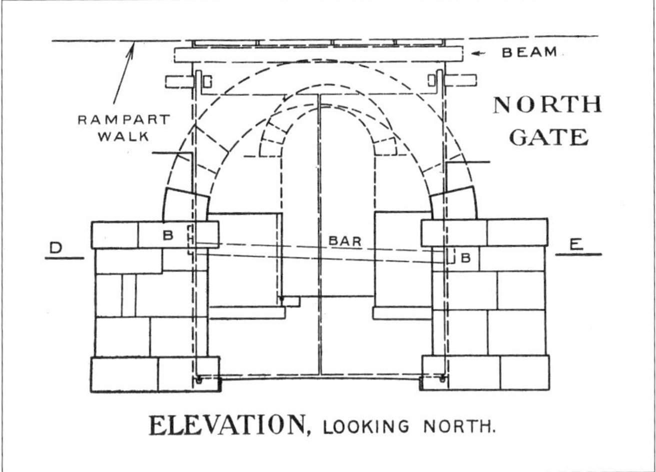

The south elevation of the north gate at MC 37 (Housesteads), drawn by F. G. Simpson.

inadequate foundations; this apparently had led to the collapse of the gate. MC 37 therefore joins MCs 22 and 35 in having their north gates completely blocked. However, at Housesteads a narrow alley was later cut through the blocking, its threshold 1.07 m (3 ft 6 in) above the original. Several arch stones have been replaced, the uppermost stones exhibiting the lewis holes by which they were lifted. The jambs, from the floor to the top of the impost, are a little under 1.89 m (6 ft) high, the arch giving an additional 1.52 m (5 ft) of head-room.

The south gateway does not survive so well but had also been reduced in width. A road, 3 m (10 ft) wide, led from the Military Way and passed through the south gate into the milecastle. To its east stand the walls of a building containing two rooms. This was presumably a small barrack-block. It is not clear whether a rear wall was removed during nineteenth-century excavations or whether the building would have been built against the milecastle wall. Two short walls, no longer visible, related to a later period. Some flagging and two hearths were found in the west part of the milecastle.

Finds included late-fourth-century pottery. At the foot of the cliff to the north was found an altar dedicated to the war-god Cocidius whose shrine appears to have been at Bewcastle.

At the west end of Housesteads Crags a length of Broad Wall foundation has been located. Here, and further westwards, it was constructed of whinstone boulders. At times, Broad Foundation and Narrow Wall diverge by as much as 2 m (6 ft 6 in). In the gap between Housesteads Crags and Cuddy's Crag the Wall ditch again appears, with a small mound to the north. From the top of Cuddy's Crag there is a well-known view eastwards to Housesteads and Sewingshields. Then comes Rapishaw Gap and Hotbank Crags. The Wall is stepped down the slope, using the protruding rock as a foundation. Immediately on gaining the ridge occurs the site of **T 37a** (Rapishaw Gap), found in 1911. This turret, like all others in the crags sector, was demolished in the late second century, the Wall being rebuilt and carried across its site. In the valley to the south, the Vallum is seen to be overlooked at close range by high ground on each side emphasising that it was not an earthwork to be manned and defended.

The view from the summit is extensive. To the north, all four loughs, Broomlee, Greenlee, Crag and Grindon, are in sight. A small temporary camp enclosing 3.6 acres (1.4 ha) sits on the ridge overlooking the southern shore of Greenlee Lough. Its full perimeter is visible, with north and south gates. Investigations in 1983 revealed a V-shaped ditch fronting a clay rampart. To the north-east lie the Simonside Hills and beyond them Cheviot. The heather-clad hill immediately to the south is Barcombe (see pages 428-9), running east from which is the gorge leading to the South Tyne. Vindolanda (pages 430-45) is also visible.

At the west end of the crag, beyond the site of **T 37b** (Hotbank Crag), located in 1911, Crag Lough comes into full view, adding much to the beauty of this wild and interesting region. Southwards, about halfway down the slope to Bradley Farm, lie the faint traces of an Iron Age farmstead.

As the Wall descends into Milking Gap, the ditch reappears. At first, only the top soil has been removed, but opposite Hotbank Farm it is more fully excavated.

In Milking Gap **MC 38** (Hotbank) is clearly visible, in the field opposite the farm. This milecastle, excavated in 1935, is of short-axis type, measuring internally 15.24 by 18.90 m (50 by 62 ft). Its gates, of type I, were of the same massive masonry as MC 37. They were later reduced in width: at this time a tombstone was used as a pivot-block. The milecastle was planned for the Broad Wall, but there is a point of reduction to Narrow Wall beyond the west wall. Part of a late building in the north-west corner, abutting the west wall, was located. Pottery of the late fourth century was found, indicating long occupation. This milecastle has produced two inscriptions recording building by the Second Legion under the governor A. Platorius Nepos for the emperor Hadrian, and therefore within the years 122 to about 126. The discovery of two inscriptions suggests that both the

Inscription recording the building of MC 38 (Hotbank) by the Second Legion during the reign of the Emperor Hadrian and governorship of A. Platorius Nepos.
(0.61 x 1.016 m)

north and the south gateways were adorned. Red paint survives in the letters of one inscription. All such items would have been highly decorated in antiquity.

At the bottom of the gap the Wall turns sharply to ascend the west crag. Broad Wall foundations have been found here. South of this point, between the Wall and the Vallum and just west of the farm track to the Military Road, low banks represent the remains of an **Iron Age farmstead**. As many as five round houses in and around the farmyard are visible. The plan of the settlement suggests occupation of some duration. Pottery found during its excavation in 1937 indicates that this included the second century, but does not confirm whether the settlement was requisitioned when the Wall was constructed or occupied after the Wall was abandoned in about 140. The complexity of the farmstead, however, points to a long life before destruction and therefore suggests the former scenario.

Just west of Milking Gap the Vallum takes a sharp swing south to avoid a large area of bog, which it skirts for the next 2 km (1¼ miles): gaps are visible in the mounds and crossings in the ditch. Excavation in 1949 revealed metalling on the south berm at Highshield, where the Military Road moves onto its south berm, parting at the Twice Brewed Inn south of T 39b.

T 38a (Milking Gap), located in 1911, is halfway up the ridge west of the gap, just beyond the end of the ditch. **T 38b** (Highshield Crag) is on the summit of Highshield Crag, above the west end of Crag Lough. Excavation has revealed the Broad Foundation descending the west brow of Highshield Crag. On it had been erected the Narrow Wall, sometimes up to two courses high with mortared facing stones but an unmortared core. This was surmounted by an even narrower wall, varying from 2.06 to 1.68 m (6 ft 9 in to 5 ft 6 in) wide, bonded with a hard white mortar. One section survives to a height of 3.3 m (10 ft), the highest known to date. The method of building the core is well seen. After a course of rubble had been placed slantwise a layer of mortar was laid and then another course of

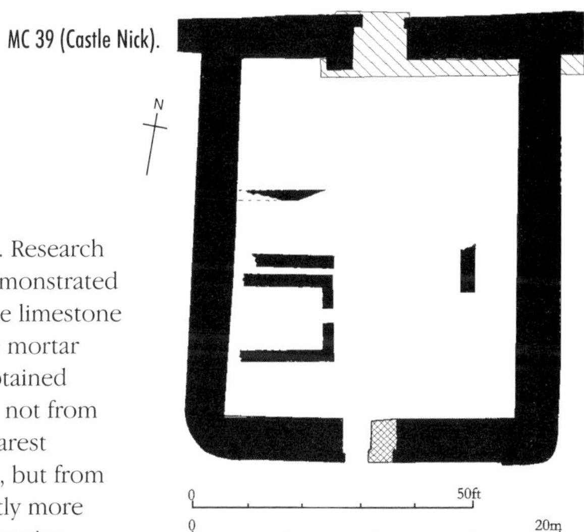

MC 39 (Castle Nick).

stones. Research has demonstrated that the limestone for the mortar was obtained locally, not from the nearest source, but from a slightly more distant point, carefully selected.

The Wall steps down the steep hillside into Sycamore Gap, named after the lone tree, which now has a successor planted close by. A dump of pottery on the north side of the Wall allows a repair at this point to be dated to the later second century. It has been argued that the repair and rebuilding with white mortar of considerable parts of the Wall was the work of the Emperor Septimius Severus. A coin hoard of the 350s was buried at the foot of the Wall and later covered by fallen stones.

Beyond is *Mons Fabricius* named in 1928 in honour of the great German frontier scholar Ernst Fabricius. On the top is a short length of Broad Foundation ignored by the later builders of the Narrow Wall. Also here, but behind the Wall, are two small sixteenth-century buildings.

From the summit, the Wall drops into the gap of Castle Nick, so named from the location here of **MC 39**. This lies 1,397 m (1,529 yards) from MC 38 and 1,650 m (1,806 yards) from MC 40, considerably more than a Roman mile. It has been argued that the milecastle was moved from its measured position on the hill to the west to render it more accessible while still retaining signalling contact with the tower on Barcombe Hill.

The milecastle has been examined on three occasions, 1854, 1908-11 and 1985-7. It is a long-axis milecastle measuring internally 18.90 by 15.70/14.93 m (62 ft by 51 ft 6 in/49 ft) with a type II gate later rebuilt without the internal projections. Broad Foundation underlies the eastern two-thirds of the north wall, the foundations four courses deep below the gate. The narrow side walls stand up to eight courses high. An almost continuous layer of masons' chippings covered the interior and below were some pits and post-holes. Little is known of the earliest internal buildings, though those to the west were of timber. Two subsequent periods of buildings, both leaning against the wall of the milecastle, were of stone. To the east, the later stone buildings were arranged in a row, encroaching on the central roadway. Only fragments of these buildings survive today. Occupation continued into the fourth century. Amongst the artefacts found here were a decorated dagger scabbard, a bronze sword chape, several gaming boards, spearheads and brooches.

The Military Way may be observed to the south as it negotiates the climb out of the gap to the east and west. As Bruce remarked, only pack-animals could have used it here.

After another small eminence, another break in the ridge occurs, called Cat Stairs. On Peel Crag the Wall is again in fine condition. During work here on the Narrow Wall between 1909 and 1911 by F. G. Simpson, 169 chamfered stones were found on the north side; these are believed to be from a strong-course on the upper part of the Wall. The presence of such a strong-course has been taken to imply the existence of a wall-walk, though there is no necessity to link the two.

T 39a (Peel Crag) was excavated in 1911. It had no wing-walls, which suggested that it was constructed with the Narrow Wall. The turret had narrow side walls and an eastern door; a path

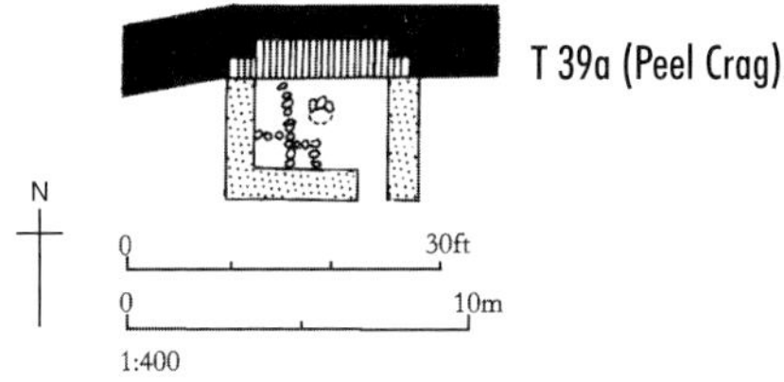

T 39a (Peel Crag).

led to the door. In the south-west corner of the turret was a platform. There were two internal floor levels, both formed of clay, with a hearth lying on the upper. Three coins of Trajan were found, together with samian ware, mixing bowls, cooking pots, jars and a mug. In the north-west corner of the turret there was a late grave containing two skeletons, a man of about 25, roughly 1.83 m (6 ft) in height, and an aged person, probably a woman, about 1.68 m (5 ft 6 in) tall. It seems that the bodies were already decomposed when the wall blocking the recess was erected over them for it did not subsequently subside.

The turret had been demolished in the late second century and its recess built up, unusually, with large well-dressed blocks: a small pillar lay in the filling. The blocking wall does not rise as high as the original north wall and the excavator suggested that this made it difficult to envisage a wall-walk being carried across the built-up recess. In the north-west corner between the Wall and the turret lay a hearth at foundation level, apparently used by the original builders.

The Wall continues over Peel Crag, where today it ends abruptly. At the bottom of the steep descent is a unique structure, an additional tower, **Peel Gap Tower**, discovered in 1987. This tower lies halfway between Ts 39a and 39b. This is the longest known interval between turrets on the whole of the Wall. It would appear that the builders regarded it as too long and plugged the gap with this extra turret; perhaps there was concern that the gap could not be observed from the adjacent turrets. It may be noted that the distances in this stretch of the

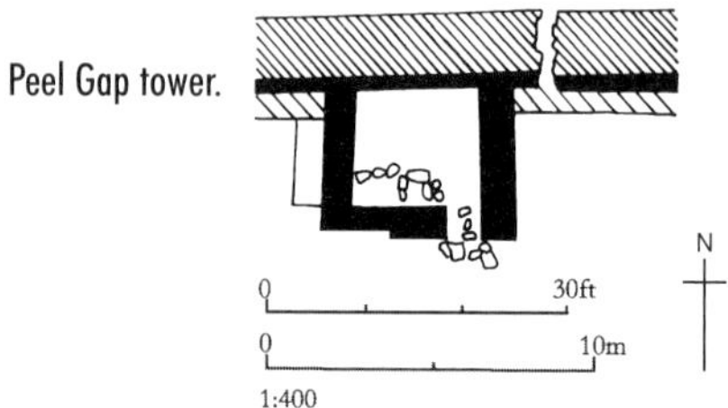

Peel Gap tower.

Wall are unusual, those between MCs 39, 40 and 41 being exceptionally long, measuring 1,650 m (1,806 yards) and 1,700 m (1,850 yards) respectively.

Broad Wall foundation had been constructed across the site of the tower together with a culvert and at least one course of wall before work was abandoned. By the time that it was resumed, the culvert had become blocked by a deep layer of peat and silt and the foundations had become overgrown. The undergrowth was cut down and burnt on site, the bonfire being placed on top of the existing wall foundations. The Narrow Wall was erected on top of these foundations and the tower subsequently added, abutting the south face of the Wall. Otherwise it was very similar to other turrets on the Wall, being of the same size and having the same history. Much of the interior was paved and some paving formed the base for a hearth. A platform stood in the south-west corner. The entrance was blocked and a platform added to the west: it has been suggested that this was to provide access to the Wall top or the upper floor of the tower. The turret was demolished when the Wall was rebuilt using hard white mortar, the latest pottery dating to 180-220. Finds included an artillery bolt-head and two piles of small rounded pebbles, perhaps sling shot. A chamfered stone found on the north side of the Wall was covered with lime, which may be evidence for white-washing or lime leaching from the joints.

At the tower the ditch begins again and runs as far as MC 40. Both ditch and Wall form a bold re-entrant, making the climb easier. It is likely that the low ground north of the Wall was a swamp in Roman times. As the ditch ascends the bank, it is reduced to a broad terrace. At the top of the bank is Steel Rigg car-park. Immediately on the west side of the road lies the site of **T 39b** (Steelrigg). Excavation in 1911 revealed that it was built with wing-walls. Inside there were two floor levels. Finds included the lower stone of a hand-mill set in the ground in the corner between the east wall of the turret and the Wall and the usual range of pottery. Following demolition of the turret, the recess was built up and the Extra-Narrow Wall has been traced from here to MC 40.

The Wall now leaves the dolerite crags and runs along a ridge of sandstone. At first it is in bad condition, but the **ditch**, with upcast mound to the north, is well preserved. The form of the ditch, however, gradually changes. 70 m (200 ft) east of MC 40 the ditch terminates in a butt-end. Thereafter, it would appear that only the top soil has been removed. The slight trough which should have been formed into the ditch eventually runs out to the north of the milecastle where the slope steepens. Shortly before the butt-end, the broad upcast is reduced to a mound, and then a stony bank.

Before reaching the top of Winshields, just beyond the field wall and where the ditch ends, is **MC 40** (Winshields), sitting on a slope of 1 in 10 (10%). Excavated in 1908, it was found to be a long-axis milecastle measuring 18.30 by 14.86 m (60 by 48 ft 9 in), with gateways of type II and narrow side walls: the east wing-wall survived two courses high. Uniquely, within the milecastle there is a 15° turn in the line of the Wall which occurs at the east jamb of the north gate. The east side of the gate passage is visible. In the late second century the gates were remodelled, the internal projections being removed and both gates narrowed. Further modifications occurred to the south gate, which exhibited four periods. In the last, the floor of the gate passage was of cement.

The uneven nature of the original ground surface led to the

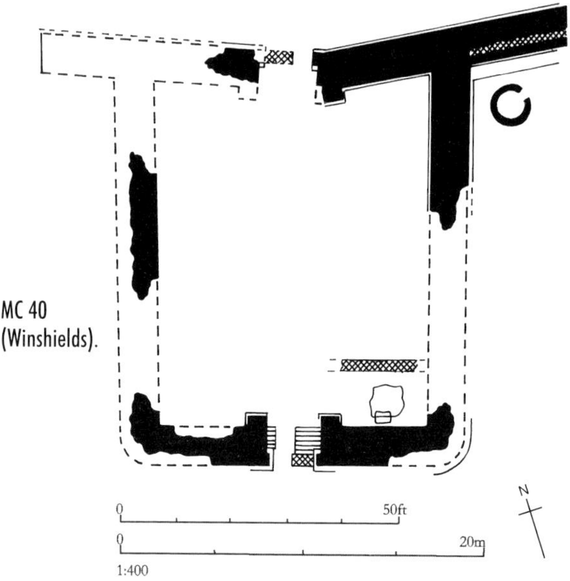

MC 40 (Winshields).

hollows being filled with large whinstone blocks. No buildings were located, just a fragment of walling in the south-east corner dating to the second century. Between this wall and the inner face of the milecastle's south wall lay a hearth: most of the pottery and many of the other artefacts were found in this area. An oven lay outside the milecastle in the north-east corner. Finds included 11 coins ranging in date from Trajan (a forgery of 114-7) to Constantine II (minted 320-4), fragments of possible roofing slabs and of two millstones, a gaming board, two whetstones, a knife handle, two brooches, a nail cleaner, two harness fittings and a wide range of pottery – samian ware, mixing bowls, jars and cooking pots continuing in date into the last third of the fourth century. A path led from the south gate towards the Military Way which is lost immediately to the south in a small marsh. but visible to east and west of the milecastle.

Winshields stands 375 m (1,230 ft) above sea level and is the highest point on the Wall. The prospect is very fine in every direction: on a clear day the Solway is easily seen, with Criffell to the west and the flat top of Burnswark Hill to the north-west forming a noble background.

At first, one course of the south face of the Wall is visible running on from the milecastle, then the core and finally the Wall itself. Beyond the trig point, **T 40a** (Winshields), with narrow walls 1 m (3 ft 3 in) wide, was found in 1946 to have been demolished by the Romans and is no longer visible. Next comes the deep valley of Lodham Slack, where the Wall, standing upon the Broad Foundation, has its ditch again. **T 40b** (Melkridge), on the summit of the next ridge, investigated in the same year, had also been demolished, but it could be recognised as having broad walls 1.22 m (4 ft) wide and an east door. It is rather larger than normal being about 5.79 m (19 ft) square internally. A gentle descent leads onto **MC 41** (Melkridge), a short-axis milecastle with narrow side walls and type I gates, which had undergone extensive reconstruction. The debris from the robbing of its walls is conspicuous. The milecastle lies 212 m (232 yards) to the west of its measured position; it has been pointed out that it is presumably not coincidental that it sits at the lowest point on the ridge visible from Haltwhistle Burn fortlet.

The next gap, a bold one, is named Bogle Hole, and then comes Caw Gap. The Wall bends south on each side of the gap and the ditch appears, together with its counterscarp bank. The ditch ends on the west side of the gap only to reappear

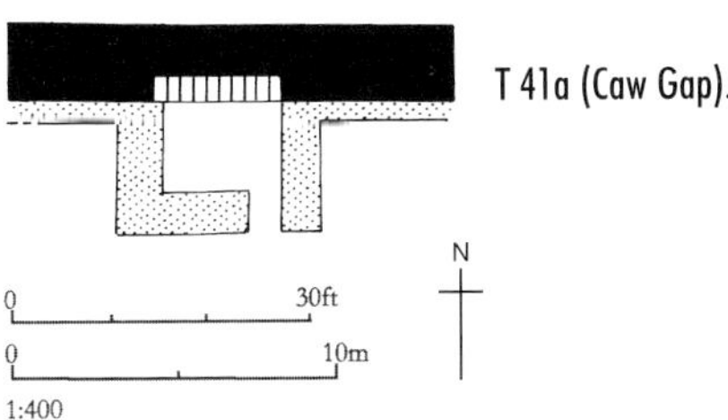

T 41a (Caw Gap).

opposite **T 41a** (Caw Gap). The turret measures only 3.27 by 3.58 m (10 ft 7 in by 11 ft 9 in) internally. Its walls are broad and the door lies to the east. Only one course survived demolition when the recess was built up and the wing-walls were reduced to their foundations. In the north-east corner outside the turret was a hearth.

To the south, two large stones, overlooking the Military Road, called 'the Mare and Foal', are of Bronze Age date. The Stanegate (see page 446) crosses the modern road junction and passes to the south of the stones.

Westwards from the turret the Wall has been consolidated. To the south, in places, the Broad Foundation projects. At two points the Wall is reduced in thickness by 30 cm (1 ft) at a single inset. After Bloody Gap comes Thorny Doors where the Wall, stepped down the slope, stands 13 courses, over 2.44 m (8 ft), high. The ditch is fronted by a small mound. **T 41b** (Thorny Doors) could not be located in 1967, presumably because it had been thoroughly demolished. To the north, fallen from the cliff, two building stones have been found. One is a normal centurial stone, but the other commemorated work by the Durotriges of Dorset. It is matched by a duplicate from the same area and other stones from Thirlwall and Howgill recording work by the cities of Britain. These are not dated, but it has been suggested that they belong to the fourth century when all the provinces of Britain were combined into one diocese. West of here, there are again slight offsets and insets in the south face of the Wall.

On the east side of the next gap, properly named Hole Gap, is **MC 42** (Cawfields). It sits 21 m (23 yards) to the west of its correct position, in order, it has been argued, to allow it to maintain contact with Haltwhistle Burn fortlet. The milecastle was first examined by John Clayton in 1848 and re-excavated in 1935. It is a short-axis milecastle measuring 14.93 by 19.20 m (49 by 63 ft). The walls, 2.44 m (8 ft) thick, stand seven or eight courses high. The gates, of type I, are of massive masonry. Both

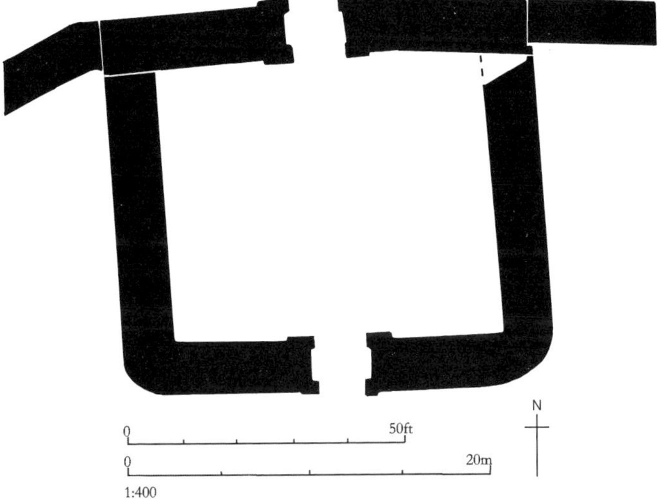

MC 42 (Cawfields).

display marking-out lines on the lowest course. The pivots for the doors survive at the north gate, while at the south is a bar-hole on the east side. The north wall was built to broad gauge before the rest of the milecastle: the butt joints of the side walls meeting the north wall and the points of reduction immediately beyond these walls are clear. The passage of the south gate was reduced in length to fit the narrow south wall, but still had to project into the milecastle. The passage remained too short to accommodate the gates and so the foundation blocks of the inner pier had to be cut away to allow the gates to be fully opened. The stones of the gate are not well dressed; the top stone of the south-east pier is particularly badly cut.

Clayton's clearance produced two inscribed stones. One is a fragmentary inscription of Hadrian recording building of the structure under the governor A. Platorius Nepos. The other is a tombstone, cut down to serve as a hearth-stone, and what

The fragmentary tombstone of Dagvalda found at MC 42. (660 x 610 mm)

remains of the inscription has been translated as: "To the divine shades: Dagvalda, a soldier of a Pannonian Cohort lived … years; Pusinna erected this tablet". It is possible that this regiment was based at Great Chesters 1.6 km (1 mile) to the west; or that the regiment was assigned the duty of providing soldiers to man the milecastles and turrets in this stretch of the Wall. Other artefacts found in the milecastle include a shield boss, some spearheads and part of a hand-mill marked *7 Luci*, the century of Lucius.

North of the milecastle, the rampart, but no ditch, of a camp, **Cawfields**, enclosing an area of 0.6 ha (1.5 acres), survives. One of similar size lies about 350 m (380 yards) north of Great Chesters fort at **Chesters Pike**. In between is a larger camp, **Burnhead**. It covers 3.5 ha (8.6 acres) with a gate still visible in each side.

South of the milecastle lies Haltwhistle Burn fortlet (see pages 446-8) and several camps. On the Military Way, three milestones have been found. One dates to 222-3 during the reign of Severus Alexander (222-35); it records 18 miles, possibly from the Portgate a little over 32 km (20 miles) to the east. The second is of the Emperor Numerian (283-4) while the third, uninscribed, still lies on the spot. South of the Vallum, and close to a vanished spring, was found an altar to Apollo dedicated by a soldier from Upper Germany. All the inscriptions are now in Chesters Museum. In Hole Gap there is a short length of ditch, with a small mound to the north, but from the adjacent summit to Haltwhistle Burn the Wall, including **T 42a** (Burn Head), has been destroyed by the former Cawfields Quarry. The Wall turns before the quarry edge, with a curve to the south and a sharp angle to the north.

The **Vallum** from Twice Brewed to Haltwhistle Burn, is in a state of perfection hardly equalled in any other part of its course. There are gaps in the north mound while the marginal mound is present throughout, often more substantial than almost anywhere else. Gaps in the south mound appear at the farm of Shield-on-the-Wall. Immediately to the west of the modern minor road three complete gaps have been dug; then comes a series of gaps marked out but not completely excavated; next a length where not even that has been done; then, halfway down the hill, the completed gaps begin again. In the low ground between the track to MC 42 and the road to the quarry, excavation in 1939 revealed that the sides of the ditch had been revetted in turf capped with clay and founded upon flagging.

Excavation south of MC 42 in 1958 revealed that there was a gap in the north mound but not in the south: no patrol-track was found on either berm. The causeway is secondary, erected over a considerable accumulation of silt. A lightly-metalled road crossed the causeway from the gap in the north mound as far as a newly-created gap in the south; it was subsequently re-surfaced following subsidence of the causeway. A section excavated just to the west revealed that the marginal mound was composed of similar material to the south mound, with, superimposed on its southern margin, a deposit of silty material, containing a sherd of samian pottery dating to the mid-second century. A fragmentary inscription of the type recording construction of the Vallum was also recovered.

The planning of the **Military Way** is also interesting. Opposite MC 42 it crosses the north mound of the Vallum, travels for 230 m (250 yards) along the north berm and then recrosses the mound. The position of the Vallum in relation to the steep hill left no room for the road; but if the road had been contemplated when the Vallum was laid out, nothing would have been easier than to place the Vallum a little more to the south. The road is thus demonstrably later in the frontier-scheme than either Wall or Vallum.

To the west of the former quarry, on the Haltwhistle Burn, a spoil tip has now buried the site of a Roman **water-mill**, found just below the point where the burn is crossed by the Military Way. An artificial channel had been cut across a bend of the stream, and a weir constructed to direct water into it. Something like 6 m (20 ft) of this channel had been widened and deepened, and partly, at least, lined with timber. Here, on the bank above, a rectangular stone building lay, measuring 6.93 by 4.77 m (22 ft 9 in by 15 ft 8 in) in size. Fallen stone-work, several large millstones (now in Chesters Museum) and pottery were all recovered during the excavation in 1907-8, enabling the excavator, F. G. Simpson, to interpret the building as a water-powered mill with undershot wheel, dating to the third century. A rampart and ditch surrounded the mill on the landward side.

From the modern entrance to Cawfields car-park, the Wall begins its gradual ascent to Great Chesters fort. To the north the ditch is present with the normal, broad upcast mound sitting on its northern lip. In various places stones of both the south and north faces of the Wall are visible. **T 42b** (Great Chesters) is beside the point where the Wall bends westwards towards Great Chesters fort. To the north lies a temporary camp enclosing 3.5 ha (8.6 acres) with its visible entrances protected by traverses.

GREAT CHESTERS (*AESICA*)

Great Chesters fort, like Carrawburgh, lies wholly south of the Wall though attached to it. The fort is nearly 10 km (6 miles) from Housesteads, measures 108.2 by 127.7 m (355 by 419 ft) and covers 1.2 ha (3 acres). Like Housesteads it faces east. The Military Way, still visible, enters by the main east gate, the *porta praetoria*, and leaves by the back gate, the *porta decumana*. A branch of the Stanegate, on the site of the farm-road, comes in by the south gate, the *porta principalis dextra*. The ancient name of the fort was *Aesica*. A relationship with the name of the Celtic god Esus or Hesus has been suggested.

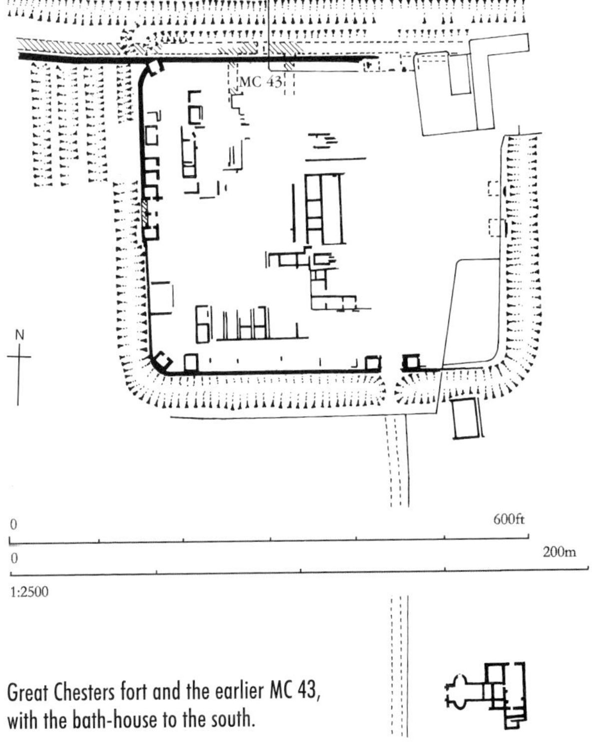

Great Chesters fort and the earlier MC 43, with the bath-house to the south.

Several regiments are recorded here. The unit in the Hadrianic period may have been the Sixth Cohort of Nervians. A cohort of Raetians is recorded building under Marcus Aurelius in 166-9, and a unit of Gauls dedicated an altar to Jupiter, suggesting that they were based at the fort at some time. By 225 the Second Cohort of Asturians were in residence and is probably the unit recorded in the *Notitia Dignitatum* as the First Cohort of Asturians. Coins also support occupation of the fort continuing into the late fourth century.

In the mid-eighteenth century some of the walls of the fort were standing about 3.66 m (12 ft) high. Today only the rampart and ditch systems are clearly defined, there being no less than four ditches on the west side. The fort was selected for excavation in the 1890s and at that time the gates, the south-west and north-west angle towers, the rampart backing along the south and west walls, the headquarters building, the commanding officer's house, the granaries together with several internal buildings, the bath-house and other "suburban" buildings were examined either wholly or in part. Importantly, at the west gate, later walls were not removed, as had too often been the case during earlier excavations at Wall forts. Thus in many ways this work can be seen as the beginning of scientific excavation on Hadrian's Wall.

Subsequent excavations included the examination of the north-west corner of the fort and its defences in 1925, while in 1939 **MC 43** was located below the fort. The milecastle was 200 m (66 ft) to the east of its measured position, in order, it has been argued, to maintain contact with Haltwhistle Burn fortlet. The milecastle had a short axis and narrow side walls laid out from an internal setting-out line; the remains of the north gate conformed to type I. Excavation demonstrated that little survived of the walls apart from their foundations. In 1950 and 1951 the east ditch and the Vallum crossing were examined.

A stile provides access to the fort at the **east gate**. A large building inscription of the Emperor Hadrian, mentioning the

Inscription recording building at Great Chesters under Hadrian. (0.812 x 1.117 m)

title of *Pater Patriae* (father of his country) conferred in 128, was found outside this gate in the middle of the nineteenth century and is now in Chesters Museum. The overgrown remains of the south gate contain an uninscribed altar. During excavations in 1894 finds of greater value were made here, a hoard of jewellery. The hoard included a gilt-bronze brooch which has been described as a masterpiece of Celtic art, a large silver brooch, a silver necklace with carnelian inset, a silver

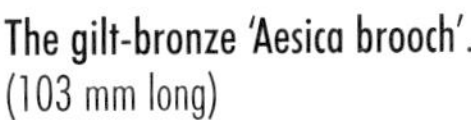

The gilt-bronze 'Aesica brooch'. (103 mm long)

The silver ring. (20 mm across)

The necklace is formed of two lengths of three chains; the stone in the central ornament is a cornelian. (117 mm across)

bracelet and one silver and two gold and rings. The items range in date from about 70-80 to the third century, and it is probable that the hoard was concealed towards the end of that century. Replicas are on display in the Museum of Antiquities, Newcastle.

The **west gate** is the only gate on the Wall which still exhibits, intact though grass-covered, the various blocking walls by which it was first reduced to one portal and then finally closed altogether. Excavation revealed that burnt debris and building material covered the original road surface and clay floors of the towers to a depth of 46 cm (18 in); a new floor of flags was laid on top and the southern outer portal blocked. 15 cm (6 in) above, another floor of flags was laid in the towers and the north portal was blocked. Finally, a new wall was built across the entire front of the blocked portals. None of these changes can be dated.

In the centre of the fort is the arched roof of the underground **strongroom** situated in the headquarters building and consolidated by English Heritage. To the north lay the granary. An inscription, found in 1761 and now in the

Museum of Antiquities, Newcastle, commemorated its rebuilding under the Emperor Severus Alexander in 225 after it had become ruinous through age. To the south, excavation disclosed the commanding officer's house, much rebuilt, and with several heated rooms. Inscribed stones reused in its walls included two tombstones and an ornate altar to Jupiter Dolichenus by a centurion of the Twentieth Legion, Lucius Maximius Gaetulicus, who also saw service at Newstead on the Tweed in the second half of the second century. South-west of this building six rooms of a late **barrack-block** consisting of an officer's block and several separate rooms may be recognised beneath the turf. Lean-to buildings, one a smithy, were found to have been erected against the inside face of the west fort wall: some are visible. The 1895 excavations of the fort defences produced a fragment of a millstone inscribed >A[ ]*to mola* VII[, the seventh (or eighth or ninth) mill of the century of Antonius.

Little survived of the **north gate** which had been badly robbed in the eighteenth century. The **north-west corner tower** was examined in 1894-5. It had been rebuilt some time after 342 as a coin of the Emperor Constans (337-50) was found in its mortar core. A large heap of rounded stones, probably ballista balls, was found at the base of the tower. The tower is not quite centrally placed on the curve and, unusually, its west wall cuts across the re-entrant between fort and Wall: all are contemporary. Excavation has demonstrated that the Broad Foundation, including the north wall of the milecastle, was laid out across the site; the north ends of the four west **ditches** respect this foundation. When the fort came to be built, the Narrow Wall, which also forms the fort's north wall, did not use the Broad Foundation but was erected immediately to its south, crossing the ends of the ditches, into which it later subsided. A small extra ditch was squeezed between the Wall ditch and the north wall of the fort and the western end of this curved south to cut through the Broad Foundation, with an additional short spur ditch added from the Wall ditch. These ditches resulted in Great Chesters being the most heavily protected fort on the Wall. It may not be a coincidence that the view to the north is restricted.

The four ditches to the west did not continue round the whole circuit of the defences. Excavation in 1950 and 1951 revealed that there were two to the east, the outer joined at the south-east angle by two small channels, apparently for drainage. Only one ditch is known to the south. The reason for four ditches to the west is not known. One possibility is that the two outer ditches were provided for a larger fort than that built and the two inner ditches added within the larger framework when plans changed.

Immediately beyond the single south ditch, two buildings were found in the 1890s. The **bath-house** lay 100 m (100 yards) to the south of the fort, east of the road to the Stanegate. Its features are clear from the plan. There are, from east to west: changing room with a latrine beside it; cold room with cold bath to the south and hot dry room to the north; small warm room; large room, which was probably two originally, a second warm room and the hot room next to the furnace. A hoard of over 100 late-third-century coins found in the hot room may indicate the date of abandonment of the building.

The **Vallum** passes south of the fort and was crossed by an original causeway of undisturbed subsoil revetted in stone. Stone robbing had removed evidence for the gate structure while the modern track prevented its width being determined during excavation in 1951. Further south are traces of two groups of **barrows**, indicating the location of the cemetery. One group lies beside the Stanegate and the other by Markham Cottages on the modern Military Road.

Little is known of civilians at Great Chesters, but several tombstones survive. One is to L. Novellius Lanuccus, aged 70, set up by his daughter; a second to Aelius Mercurialis, by his sister Vacia; and a third to Nigrina, erected by Aurelius Casitto, a centurion of the Sixth Legion. There are also two to young

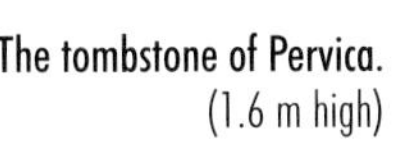

The tombstone of Pervica.
(1.6 m high)

girls; one to Pervica, the other set up by Aurelia "to her very dear sister Aurelia Caula who lived 1 year 4 months".

A remarkable feature of this fort is the **aqueduct** which feeds it from the north. This is a channel or leet, three or four feet deep and the same wide, running along the north margin of the basin of the Caw Burn. In order to cross its northern tributaries, an extremely winding course is taken, but the line is so well planned that only once was it necessary to construct a bridge or embankment. This structure is now gone, but its site is named Benks Bridge. The aqueduct is 10 km (6 miles) long, though the direct line is little more than 3.6 km (2¼ miles). By this means, the water of the Caw Burn was brought to within about 320 m (350 yards) of the fort. The aqueduct is then lost but, owing to a fall in the ground, the water could only have been brought over this part of its course by an embankment or a sealed pipe forming an inverted siphon.

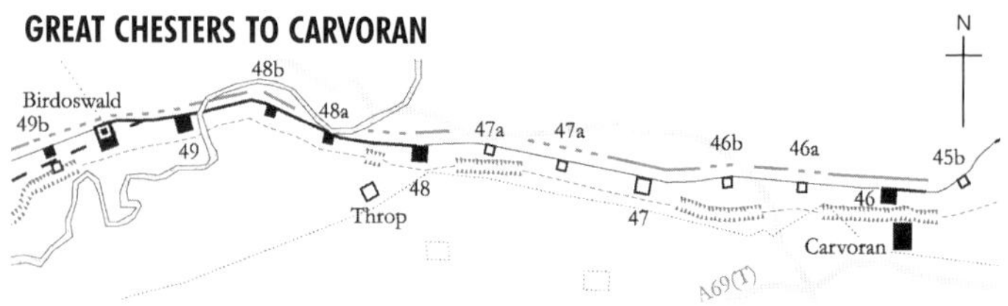

Near Great Chesters the **Vallum** is of great interest. 400 km (440 yards) west of the causeway serving the fort it runs almost straight, into a large field directly south of Cockmount Hill farmhouse. Here are ten successive crossings in the ditch and gaps in both mounds, about 50 m (163 ft) apart, though a modern track has somewhat obscured those in the south mound and the marginal mound is only visible for a short length, while a modern drain in the ditch has slightly disturbed the crossings. Excavation in 1939 showed that the crossings were made when the ditch had been open sufficiently long for the upper half of its very steep sides to have washed down to the bottom. Vegetable matter then grew, to be succeeded by the crossings. These preserved, behind their mass of filling, the steep profile of the original ditch, modified only by the weathering that had occurred before they were constructed. Further west, in the next field, small heaps on the berm probably result from later cleaning out of the Vallum ditch. The Vallum then runs along the north slope of Blake Law, avoiding the marsh at its foot. The ditch is cut into the slope for 230 m (250 yards) and for the western 90 m (100 yards) is stepped to form the south berm, and the south mound is unusually broad. The marginal mound can be seen on both berms, blocking crossings and gaps. Then the Vallum swings north, across the marsh, and turns along its north margin. At Allolee, cultivation has reduced it to poor condition.

The **Narrow Wall**, leaving Great Chesters, runs behind the Broad Foundation up to **T 43a** (Cockmount Hill), which relates to the latter. Broad Foundation and Narrow Wall then run

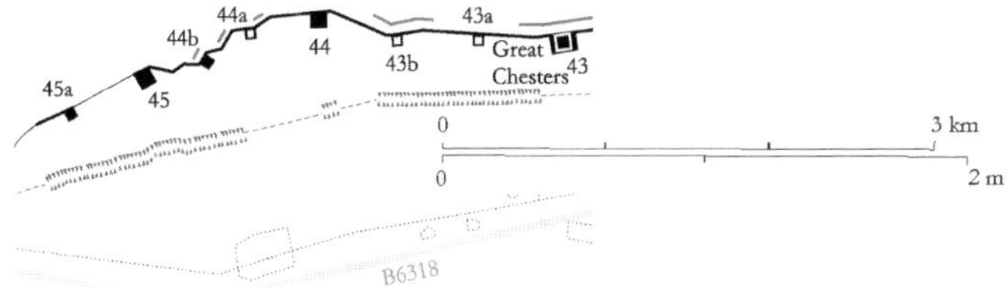

parallel as far as Cockmount Hill Wood, where both are visible, though overgrown. Before leaving the wood the two start to converge, the Narrow Wall gradually running up on to the Broad Foundation. The builders of the Narrow Wall clearly knew of the existence of the earlier foundation for they followed its line closely, but for some reason chose to ignore it for nearly 1 km (about half a mile): perhaps they considered the foundations too shallow. An uninscribed milestone from the Military Way forms the west post of the gate at the west end of Cockmount Hill Wood, on the Wall-line.

The Wall now climbs gradually. **T 43b** (Allolee East) is about 90 m (100 yards) beyond the edge of the wood. The ditch hereabouts is very irregular, now dug fully, now to half width only, or often not at all. Here and there the north face of the Wall is seen for short lengths. **The Military Way** can be traced as far as Walltown as a well-preserved terrace.

East of Allolee farmhouse, the site of the long-axis **MC 44** (Allolee) is very distinct. Beyond it, the rebuilt north face of the Wall stands up to nine courses high for about 180 m (200 yards), while the south face is not exposed at all. Opposite Allolee farmhouse only the core is to be seen. Of two centurial stones recorded in the south wall of the farmhouse, one is lost and the other now very indistinct. Beyond MC 44 the crags are broken by frequent gaps known as the 'Nine Nicks of Thirlwall'. The Wall climbs and descends them unflinchingly, seizing the crest of the rugged cliffs wherever possible.

In the first two nicks the ditch reappears and the Wall makes a re-entrant; **T 44a** (Allolee West) occurs at a turn on the crest between them. Little masonry survived, suggesting that the turret had been obliterated. Beyond the second nick comes Mucklebank Crag, 260 m (860 ft) high. There, in a right-angle of the Wall, **T 44b** (Mucklebank) was found in 1891 and excavated in the following year. Because it lies in an angle, its north and west sides are both recessed into the Wall. The interior is unusually small, measuring only 3 m (10 ft) square. The turret was covered with the stones from its upper courses and several slabs about 60 cm (2 ft) square and 8-10 cm (3-4 in) thick; these were not roofing slates and were presumably from either an upper floor or a wall-walk. The number of large nails found in the debris also led to the suggestion that the upper part of the turret was of timber. The two fragments of an arch, now lying within the turret, are probably from the doorway. A centurial stone was in the wall at the south-east angle.

The original floor was of beaten clay: animal bones and charcoal were found on it. The next floor, 46 cm (18 in) higher, and its successor another 15 cm (6 in) above, were of flags. The hearth was apparently against the south wall. A variety of pottery and part of an *amphora* as well as metal studs and buckles were also found in the turret together with a coin of the Emperor Valens (364-78).

Walltown Nick is a wide gap, with an equally bold re-entrant, the Wall ditch crossing in a straight line with a broad upcast mound to the north. After climbing the west side of the nick, the Wall, of which much core is visible, runs along the crags to **MC 45** (Walltown). This is a long-axis milecastle, and large stones robbed from its gateway can be seen lying behind troughs to the east of Walltown Farm. A splendid section of Wall runs for 140 m (150 yards) to the edge of the former Greenhead Quarry.

T 45a (Walltown) lies on the west side of the quarry, 90 m (100 yards) short of the normal measured position. It was built as a free-standing tower before the Narrow Wall, 2.25 m (7 ft 4 in) wide above the offset, was brought up to its east and west sides. The tower measures about 5.80 by 5.50 m (19 by 18 ft)

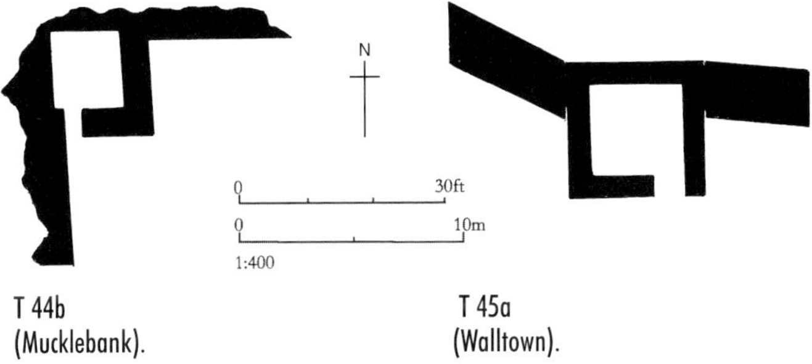

T 44b (Mucklebank).

T 45a (Walltown).

externally, with its foundations resting on bedrock up to four courses deep depending upon the uneven nature of the rock surface. The door was probably in the south-east corner. The foundations, examined in 1959, contained a fragment of a pot of Hadrianic date. It is possible that the structure was built early in Hadrian's reign as a look-out for the troops on the Stanegate, probably at Carvoran, to be subsumed within the Wall built a little later. Pottery indicated occupation in the second century only.

The Wall runs on for about 400 m (440 yards) to the edge of the quarry, stepping down and up nicks and using the dolerite as its foundation in places. The huge bite of the quarry has removed the rest of the Nine Nicks and the Wall with them, including **T 45b** (Walltown West). Before destruction it was recorded that this turret stood up to 11 courses high and had narrow side walls. Pottery and animal bones were found inside, including the lower jaw of a young boar.

The **Vallum** is difficult to follow through the wood to the south, though it survives well, the ditch cut through the rock, and the marginal mound prominent.

West of the modern road, the Wall and Vallum start again. The Wall survives as a mound, but the ditch is pronounced, running on to the site of MC 46. The ditch and north mound of the Vallum are also visible before the earthwork makes a detour round the fort of Carvoran.

CARVORAN (MAGNA)

Carvoran is the *Magna* of the *Notitia Dignitatum*, which records the Second Cohort of Dalmatians at the fort. The name means stone or rock. Under Hadrian, the First Cohort of Hamian Archers, originally raised in Syria, was based here. Their commander, Flavius Secundus, set up an altar for the health of Aelius Caesar in 136-7. The same unit was also attested under the governor Calpurnius Agricola (163-6) when it erected altars mentioning the prefect Licinius Clemens; these are now at Newcastle and Chesters Museums. The Second Cohort of Dalmatians may have been based here, perhaps in the second century, for a standard-bearer (*imaginifer*) of the unit dedicated an altar at Carvoran. A soldier of the Twentieth Legion was buried here, while a *numerus Magn...* is also recorded at the fort. Two building inscriptions of the First Cohort of Batavians have been linked to the construction of the Vallum.

Carvoran lies at the junction of the Stanegate and the Maiden Way, which ran south via Whitley Castle (where the fort retains impressive earthworks) to Kirkby Thore. Aerial photography has been interpreted as revealing evidence for an earlier larger fort below the visible remains and extending to the south. However, geophysical survey in 1999 failed to reveal any trace of this fort. Excavations under the buildings attached to the Roman Army Museum revealed ditches containing early second century (Trajanic) pottery.

The visible **fort** measures 129 by 123 m (440 by 419 ft) and covers 1.65 ha (about 4 acres). Building stones show that it was walled in stone by the Hamians themselves, under Flavius Secundus, at the fort in 136-7. One inscription records the construction (*vallavit*) of 112 feet (34.14 m) of the wall, with two others probably recording the same distance. Part of a further inscription, recovered from a field wall, but possibly originally from the north gate, also records building under Hadrian. Geophysical survey in 2000 revealed that the fort faced south.

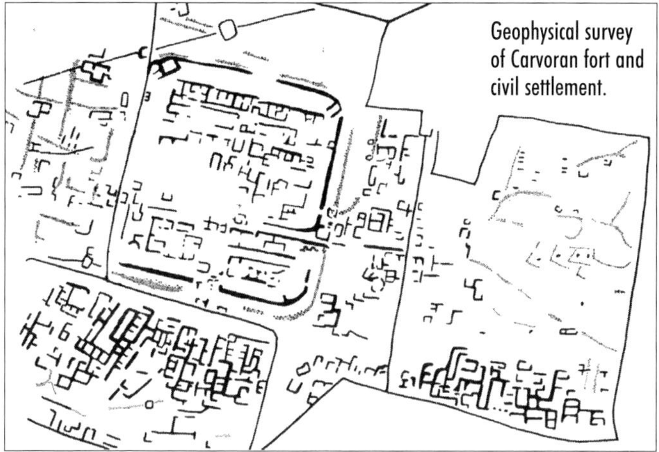
Geophysical survey of Carvoran fort and civil settlement.

Investigation of the east, south and west walls of the fort together with the south gate in 2001-2 revealed that they had been comprehensively robbed. The north gate was located in 1973 and its west portal shown to contain secondary blocking. The north-west angle tower is visible. Little is known of the internal buildings of the fort, but a bath-house was recorded in the south-west corner in 1830.

The Hamians made dedications to the goddesses Hammia and Syria. From the site there is also a very remarkable metrical dedication to the Virgin of the Zodiac, with reference to Julia Domna, wife of the Emperor Septimius Severus, by a prefect honoured with tribune's rank, and a small altar to Jupiter of Heliopolis, that is the great Ituraean god Jupiter-Hadad, whose worship was centred at Baalbek in modern Lebanon. There is a dedication to Epona and also one to Fortuna by a centurion who had served in all three British legions. Carvoran has furnished several dedications to the god Vitiris, whose altars are confined to the Wall and its neighbourhood and centre upon this site, as if the cult had its seat in this vicinity. He is equated with the Roman Hercules and also with the Celtic god Mogons.

A well yielded fine stag's antlers and a double-barbed javelin-head of the type used by German soldiers in the fourth century.

The **Stanegate** passes to the south of the fort, in a hollow. Geophysical survey has revealed the presence of buildings between the road and the fort and to the west of the fort: presumably this is the civil settlement.

The **Vallum** swings north to make a wide and regular diversion around the fort on the north, similar to its normal diversions to the south of other forts, except that this detour excludes the fort from the Wall. One possibility is that it was avoiding a bog; another is that it was avoiding an existing fort, intended to be abandoned when the Wall was built. It has been suggested that the retention of a fort at this location followed a decision to place a smaller unit at Great Chesters, in effect splitting a larger force between the two sites.

In 1951 two crossings of the Vallum within the diversion were examined, both secondary. That opposite the fort's north gate was composed of Vallum-mound material: its surface was lightly metalled. Metalling was also recorded on the south berm. Analysis of the botanical remains from the lower fill of the ditch revealed, not surprisingly, a damp environment.

Several tombstones are known. In the eighteenth century a mound east of the fort yielded a stone sarcophagus containing organic remains and two gold rings. The most remarkable artefact found at Carvoran is the *modius* or measure found in 1915 just north of the north-east angle of the fort. It bears an inscription stating the weight of the contents, 17½ *sextarii*. This unusual sum can be divided by seven to produce a figure of 2½ *sextarii*, close to the amount of grain issued daily to each Roman soldier according to the second-century BC writer Polybius. It would appear that we have evidence for the use of the seven-day week by the Roman army. The measure is now in Chesters Museum.

The **Roman Army Museum** at Carvoran offers interpretation of the fort, Hadrian's Wall and the Roman army.

CARVORAN TO BIRDOSWALD

The platform of **MC 46** (Carvoran) can be faintly discerned at the top of the bank, just west of the northward deviation of the Vallum. The ditch is particularly striking descending the bank to the River Tipalt, and the Vallum only a little less so. **T 46a** lies under Holmhead. Built into a wall is an inscribed stone, upside down, reading *Civitas Dumnon(iorum)*. The Dumnonii occupied the south-west peninsula of England and may have provided help for the repair of the Wall in the fourth century. A centurial stone, also upside down, reads *>Iul Ianal*, the century of Julius Janalis (built this).

A building stone recording work by the *civitas Dumnoniorum* found at Holmhead. (203 x 350 mm)

Further west, even the ditch is indistinct between the railway and the road. Immediately west of the road, a short stretch of Broad Wall is preserved, three courses high and, when found, still retaining patches of mortar on the face of the stones. The ditch here was 10 m (33 ft) wide and 1.83 m (6 ft) deep, with the counterscarp bank distinct. Its course is clear up to the site of **T 46b** (Wallend) which lies below the farm.

From the road, the **Vallum** is also clear running across the golf course. Towards the west end, gaps have been dug in both mounds. However, the material was not used to make crossings over the ditch but has been recorded lying untidily outside the gaps in small heaps as it was dumped from baskets by the diggers, the work never completed.

MC 47 (Chapel House) lies 300 m (330 yards) east of the farm of that name. Investigated in 1935, it was found to be unusually large for the Stone Wall, measuring 21.03 by 18.29 m (69 by 60 ft), with broad side walls. All walls were badly robbed but evidence was found for two long buildings on either side of the central road and an oven in the north-west corner. Limited evidence indicated that the gates were of type III. An inscription first noted at the farm in the mid-nineteenth century records building under Hadrian by the Twentieth Legion. Interestingly, no governor is mentioned which suggests it dates later than Platorius Nepos, that is to 127-38.

Part of a inscription found at MC 47 (Chapel House) recording work by the Twentieth Legion under Hadrian.
(305 mm x 660 mm)

T 47a (Foultown) stood at the normal interval westwards. At the hamlet of Gap, on the watershed between Tyne and Irthing, the Vallum, here very distinct, takes higher ground than the Wall. Just beyond the hamlet is the site of **T 47b** (Gap). Both turrets were located in 1912. The **ditch** between Gap and the railway at Gilsland is again unusually large, measuring 15.20 m (50 ft) wide in several places as it often does between Carvoran and the Irthing, with the outer mound commensurately prominent. In 1971, behind the Station Hotel, it was found to be 1.22 m (4 ft) high and at least 9 m (30 ft) wide. On a knoll called Rose Hill, possibly a medieval motte, later removed to build the railway station, Lingard saw a sculpture of a flying Victory: the stone is now at Castle House, Rockcliffe. On the stone, behind the Victory, is a depiction of a domed shrine similar to Arthur's O'on which formerly stood near Falkirk beside the Antonine Wall.

West of the former railway station, in the field to the south, the ditch survives well, 15.20 m (50 ft) wide. Beyond, the wooded gorge of the Poltross Burn divides Northumberland and Cumbria. The Vallum approached the stream by deep cuttings on each bank, the steep sides of its ditch being revetted with masonry. The Military Way crosses the burn between Wall and Vallum and turns onto the north berm of the

Vallum where it remains for at least 540 m (600 yards). South of MC 48 it was 6.7 m (22 ft) wide.

The investigation of **MC 48** (Poltross Burn) in 1909 was one of the most important excavations along the line of the Wall. Here was first established a chronology for the smaller structures on the Wall. The milecastle was subsequently taken into the care of English Heritage. It lies at the east end of the only mile on the line of the Wall where both milecastles, both turrets and virtually the whole of the Wall is visible.

The milecastle lies at an angle in the Wall. It measures 21.34 by 18.52 m (70 by 60 ft 9 in) internally. All its walls were built to the broad gauge, but beyond the 3.66 m (12 ft) long wing-wall at the north-east corner there is a reduction to 2.13 m (7 ft): the point of reduction at the north-west corner was located in 1929, but unfortunately its exact position is not known. The north face, with three courses below the offset, clearly demonstrates that the Wall here was built to standard B.

The gates, 2.90 m (9 ft 6 in) wide, are of the largest type on the Wall, type III. Built in larger masonry than the rest of the milecastle, the passage at the north gate is 3.96 m (13 ft) long with piers for front and rear arches. Local stone was used, which was difficult to work and therefore poorly dressed. The original pivot stones were not in position and had probably been removed when Hadrian's Wall was abandoned in favour of the Antonine Wall in the 140s. On reoccupation, the pivot

Sculpture of Victory found at Gilsland. (0.58 m high)

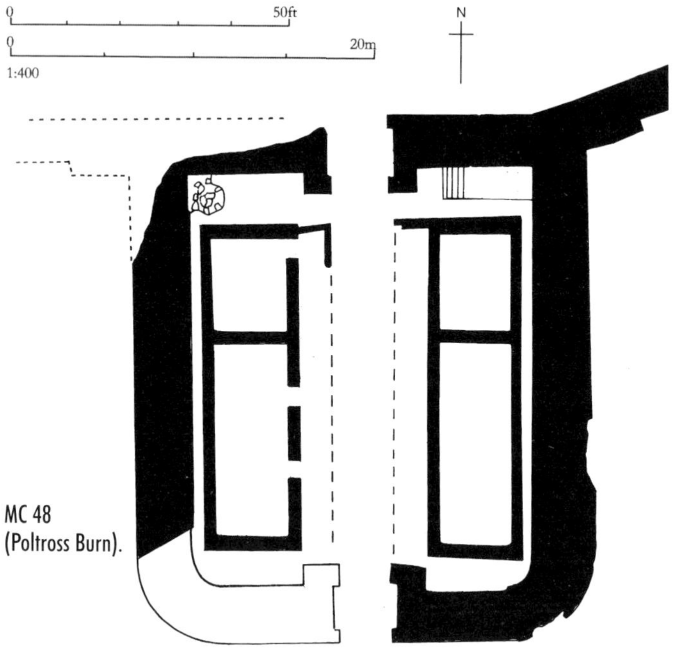

MC 48 (Poltross Burn).

stones were renewed. The gate was subsequently reduced in width with a low platform placed behind the reducing wall. The floor level in the passage was later raised and it seems probable that the western side of the former passage was turned into a room: a small hearth lay here. Only one side of the south gate survived, together with part of a reducing or blocking wall.

Inside the milecastle lie two large stone buildings each fronted by a metalled path and facing onto a central road. The fall of over 2.74 m (9 ft) from south to north necessitated a step between each room. The buildings displayed are divided into three rooms, but their predecessors each contained four. These had floors of beaten clay, each room being entered by a door to the right-hand side of its front wall. Two rooms together roughly equate to the size of a *contubernium* (double barrack-room) in a fort and this suggests that the two buildings might have contained the equivalent of four *contubernia* providing accommodation for 32 soldiers. There were two later floor levels, each of flags: several rooms contained hearths. The discovery of six pieces of thin flags showing nail-holes offers an indication of the roofing.

In the north-east corner of the milecastle survives the base of a flight of steps dating to the earliest period. Projection upwards of the three steps indicates that the top of the staircase was 3.66 m (12 ft) above the ground: owing to the fall of the ground the height on the north side was 4 m (14 Roman feet). This is the best indication of the height of Hadrian's Wall. However, it cannot be certain whether the steps led to a walk-way along the top of the Wall, along the top of the milecastle walls, or merely gave access to the gate tower. An oven, or rather five superimposed ovens, occupied the north-west corner. The 1909 excavations produced a rich harvest of finds including fragments of armour, a sword chape, harness mounting, several spearheads and a clay sling-bullet. The discovery here of four items of equipment associated with horses is particularly interesting; if horses were based here, the amount of space available for soldiers would have been reduced.

Coins, brooches and pottery allowed a framework for the occupation to be advanced. Three burnt coins led to the conclusion that the first main period came to a close with the invasion of 180. Coins indicated that the second period ended after 270 and the third began before 300, while it was argued that the final abandonment took place as early as 330. Re-examination of the pottery allows the occupation to be extended into the later years of the fourth century.

The railway can be crossed beside the milecastle. Beyond, the Narrow Wall sits on the base of the Broad Wall, which stands up to three courses high, with an offset visible at this level in one place. The mortared cores of the Broad and Narrow Walls were found to be homogeneous in 1928 suggesting that work might even have been in progress here when the decision was taken to narrow the Wall. An alternative explanation is that the Wall was later rebuilt with a mortared core. The ditch is visible to the north and the Vallum ditch to the south. Across the modern road, the Wall and Vallum converge until the north mound of the Vallum comes within some 4.57 m (15 ft) of the Wall. The north face of the Wall supports the rear wall of the house named Roman Wall Villa. The Wall continues westward as Narrow Wall on Broad Foundation. Here was found one centurial stone reading *>Coccei Reguli* and another *Coh VI >Lousi Suavis* fallen from the south face; an identical stone of the latter century was also found west of T 48a and of the former to the east of T 48b.

T 48a (Willowford East) was examined in 1923. It is 146 m (160 yards) west of its correct position. Its wing-walls are prominent, 3.66 - 3.96 m (12 - 13 ft) long. The turret was recessed 1.98 m (6 ft 6 in) into the Wall, rather further than usual and resulting in a north wall only 76 cm (2 ft 6 in) thick. Its door lay to the west end of the south wall. Several levels were recorded inside. The earliest floor was of clay with the hearth probably in the centre of the turret. The second floor, 20 cm (8 in) higher, was of flags, with the hearth moved to the south-east corner. The door jambs were rebuilt at this time. Masonry debris 50 cm (1 ft 8 in) thick intervened between this floor and its successor, which was of flags set in clay. A stone-built base now occupied the south-east corner. The final floor lay on a further 60 cm (2 ft) of masonry debris. Two hearths lay on the new flagged floor, one in the centre. Several stones with a bevelled edge were found close to the inside walls of the turret; it was suggested that they had served as a cornice. Flagstones on edge in the masonry debris at this turret and its neighbour were taken to indicate the former existence of a flagged upper room, though possibly only across the recess. Finds included a whetstone, half a quern, two fragments which appear to be from a gaming board, two knives, a brooch, fragments of a pair of tweezers

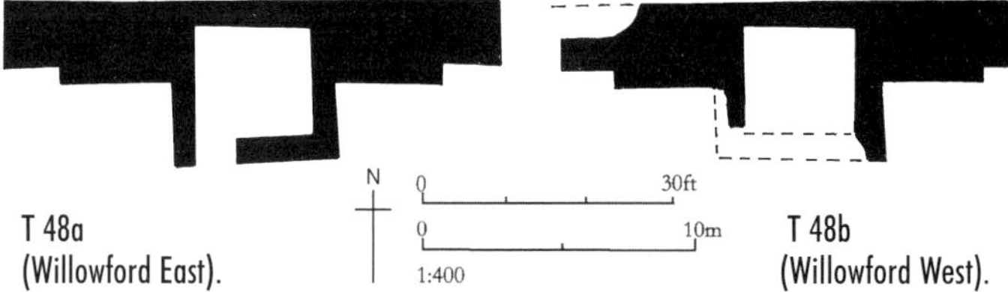

T 48a (Willowford East).

T 48b (Willowford West).

and the normal range of samian ware, mixing bowls, cooking pots, jars, a mug and *amphora* sherds. Occupation continued into the fourth century.

The Wall and ditch have been lost to the river in places, but otherwise the next kilometre (half a mile) to the river is particularly instructive. The Broad Wall is standard B throughout, with the offset above the fourth course. On the south side the abandoned lower courses of the Broad Wall stand up to and above the offset in places with the foundations for the Narrow Wall dug into the earlier core. The ditch survives well with the modern track sitting within it giving a useful indication of scale.

T 48b (Willowford West) was also excavated in 1923, but it was not as well preserved as its neighbour; the south wall is marked out in concrete. The wing-walls are of similar length to T 48a. The turret was recessed 2.13 m (7 ft) into the Broad Wall resulting in a narrow north wall. As at T 48a, four floor levels were found within the turret. The first was of clay with a hearth in the north-west corner. The second was of flags, overlying some masonry debris and ash. The hearth lay in the north-east quadrant. Only 15 cm (6 in) separated this from the third floor, also of flags. The hearth was now returned to the north-west corner. The last floor was composed of large flags, the hearth being retained in the same location. Fallen debris covered this floor. It contained such large pieces of charcoal as to lead the excavator to suggest that the entire upper storey might have been of timber. Finds included a piece of roofing tile, a whetstone, a melon bead, part of a glass bottle, a spearhead, and a similar range of pottery to its neighbour. Some were found in the rubbish tip which lay to the west of the turret.

At the turret, the Wall was 2.95 m (9 ft 8 in) wide above the offsets, but, by 12 m (39 ft) to the west, it had gradually reduced in thickness to 2.31 m (7 ft 7 in). A centurial stone of Gellius Philippus may be seen in the gable of the farm house. In 1993-4, the berm to the north was found to be 5 m (16 ft) wide.

Due south, on **Willowford Hill**, there is a temporary camp 0.5 ha (1.25 acres) in size with entrances to north and east protected by traverses.

The Vallum terminates at the edge of the bank, but the Wall descends from Willowford Farm to the flat ground bordering the river and reaches **Willowford Bridge** by which the River Irthing was crossed. The eastern abutment of the bridge now sits 72 m (240 ft) distant from the river. This reflects movement of the river which started before the Roman period for at one time it lay beside the eastern escarpment of the valley. Although known for centuries, the bridge was not excavated until 1924: it was re-examined in 1940 and again in 1984-5.

Three main periods can be recognised. The earliest remains include a short stretch of Broad Wall erected on substantial foundations, at whose western termination presumably lay the bridge; the end of the Wall is marked by the large stones visible in the north face. The corner of a tower is embedded in this

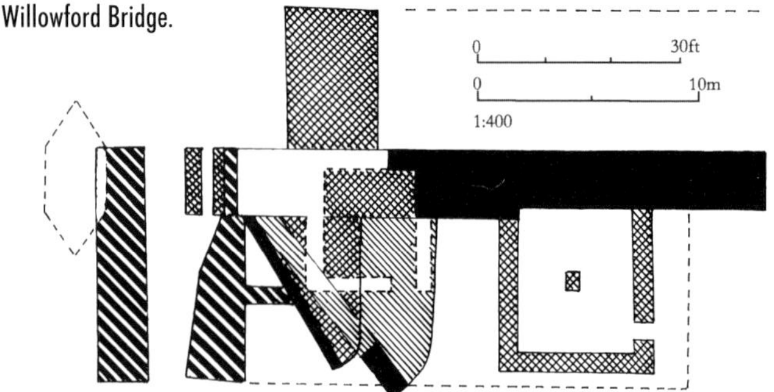

Willowford Bridge.

wall. The bridge was only wide enough to carry a footpath, access to which may have been via the tower. To the north, the ditch became shallower and gradually faded out as it approached the river. This bridge was damaged by flood action and strengthened by the construction of a southern wing wall placed diagonally to the bridge; one fragment of this is visible.

Further flooding sometime in the late second or early third century badly damaged the repaired and strengthened bridge. It was now extended westwards at the same width as the Broad Wall with the berm to the north protected by a block of masonry and the southern, diagonal wing-wall replaced slightly to the west; at the western end of the Wall lay two sluices. A tower, containing much reused material, was built at the angle where the Broad Wall was reduced to Narrow. In the centre of the tower is a stone base, probably to support an upper floor.

Finally, a new pier was constructed, the eastern sluice blocked and a ramp to carry a road across the river erected to the south side of the bridge. This has been removed but the solid masonry base which formerly supported the ramp at this point survives. Stones from the superstructure are laid out beside the bridge.

A modern bridge now carries the walker across the river. At the top of the bank sits **MC 49** (Harrow's Scar). More significantly, this was the beginning of the Turf Wall. The bank down to the river was more gentle in Roman times, but nevertheless it would have been a steep climb for the Turf Wall. No attempt was made to take the **Vallum** down the cliff: the termination of its ditch has been located immediately to the west of the milecastle, which in turn suggests the prior existence of this structure. From here to MC 50 (High House) there is no north mound to the Vallum, all the material from the ditch being placed on the south mound. This was to avoid impinging too closely upon the milecastles and the fort in this sector, where the escarpment of the Irthing leaves little room to the south of the Wall.

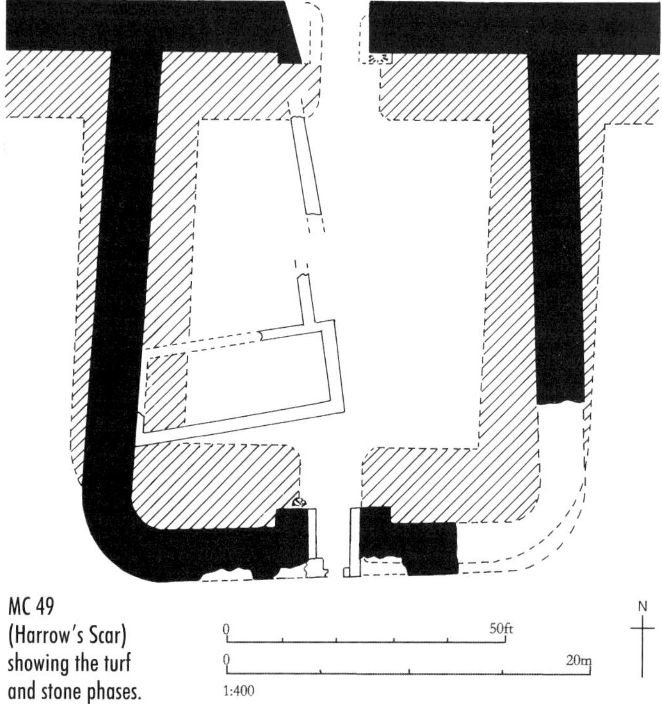

MC 49 (Harrow's Scar) showing the turf and stone phases.

The visible stone milecastle measures 22.86 by 19.81 m (75 by 65 ft) internally. It is crossed by a farm track and contains the remains of a modern cottage. Excavation in 1953 revealed that Roman stratigraphy survived poorly. The south gate of the milecastle was found to be similar to type III gateways on the Stone Wall. The gate was later rebuilt and narrowed using the hard white mortar usually associated with the Severan work. One stone found reused in the gate carried a crude relief of Mars and Victory. The stone walls of the milecastle butt against the Wall; below them lay traces of their turf predecessors 6.10 m (20 ft) wide enclosing an area 16.46 by 15.24 m (54 by 50 ft). Evidence was also found for the timber gates of the milecastle.

The berm to the north of the milecastle is 2.44 m (8 ft) wide. To the right of the modern track leading out of the north gate, the ditch appears to terminate in a butt-end suggesting the existence of an original causeway.

Between MCs 49 and 51 the Wall was realigned when it was rebuilt in stone; today it still stands up to ten courses high. About 46 m (50 yards) west of Harrow's Scar milecastle the Stone Wall makes a northward turn of about 8° and here the berm widens. Excavation has demonstrated, however, that the Turf Wall continued on, aiming for the point where the east gate of Birdoswald fort was later erected. Regular drains through the Stone Wall were provided. On the stretches erected earlier, drains only appear at irregular intervals. It would appear that insufficient attention had been paid to the way in which the Wall would change drainage patterns and perhaps surface water had been collecting against it. Here, the drains are about 6 m (20 ft) apart.

The stretch of Stone Wall from Harrow's Scar to Birdoswald contains several centurial stones and phallic symbols surviving on the south face; a further ten inscribed stones had fallen and are now in museums. Most of the centurial stones are in the topmost surviving course, with the phallic symbols at about half this height. 64 m (69 ft) from the west wall of the milecastle there is an almost illegible stone recording "the century of Marcus Rufus"; at 68 m (74 yards) a clearer stone of "the century of Carus Scipio"; at 190 m (211 yards) a phallic symbol; at 245 m (268 yards) "the century of Julius Primus, cohort VIII"; 9 m (10 yards) further "the century of Secundinus Verullus built 30 paces"; at 275 m (301 yards) there is a stone with a very worn ansate tablet and >*PP*, "the century of the Primus Pilus" (senior centurion of the legion); at 349 m (382 yards) "the century of Tertius"; at 374 m (409 yards) another phallic symbol and after about 397 m (435 yards) the modern road closes this stretch shortly before the north-east corner of the fort at Birdoswald.

BIRDOSWALD (BANNA)

Birdoswald fort is only 5.2 km (3¼ miles) from Carvoran, but it lies 12 km (7⅓ miles) from Great Chesters, the appropriate spacing for the primary forts. Its position is striking. In addition to the bold scarp to the south, at the foot of which winds the River Irthing, a valley to the north takes the overflow of Midgeholm Moss into the Irthing. To the west formerly lay a fairly deep bog. The Hunters of Banna are recorded on an altar found at Birdoswald and presumably reflect the Roman name of the site, which also appears at the correct position on the Rudge Cup and Amiens Skillet. *Banna* means "horn" or "peak", an appropriate name for this fort sitting on its promontory.

The fort measures 176.8 by 122 m (580 by 400 ft) and covers 2.14 ha (5.3 acres). The First Cohort of Dacians, Hadrian's Own, 1000-strong, was based at Birdoswald in the third and fourth centuries, being recorded here in the *Notitia Dignitatum*. The origin of the unit was commemorated by the curved Dacian sword which appears on several items of sculpture. Over 20 altars to Jupiter dedicated by the unit have survived, providing an impressive list of eight tribunes from 205 to 282 (a sculpture of Jupiter with Hercules was also found at the fort). Three stones record that the regiment was temporarily commanded by legionary centurions. The First Cohort of Thracians appears with the Dacians on an inscription recording the building of the granary in the governorship of Alfenus Senecio, 205-8. The regiment was also attested building at Bowes in the Pennines in the same governorship, so unless there were two units of the same number, which is not impossible, the unit may have been sent north to help with the building work at Birdoswald. The *Venatores Bannienses*, who dedicated an altar to Silvanus, were probably a unit based here in the third century. A sherd of samian bearing a graffito *Martini dec* records a decurion named Martinus. This was a cavalry officer, but his unit is not known, though the sherd on which his name appears can be

Birdoswald fort in the third century, but showing early features outside the fort.

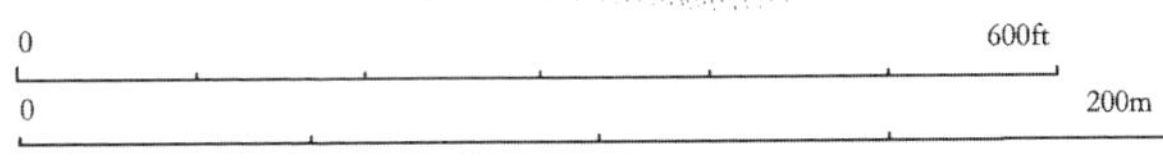

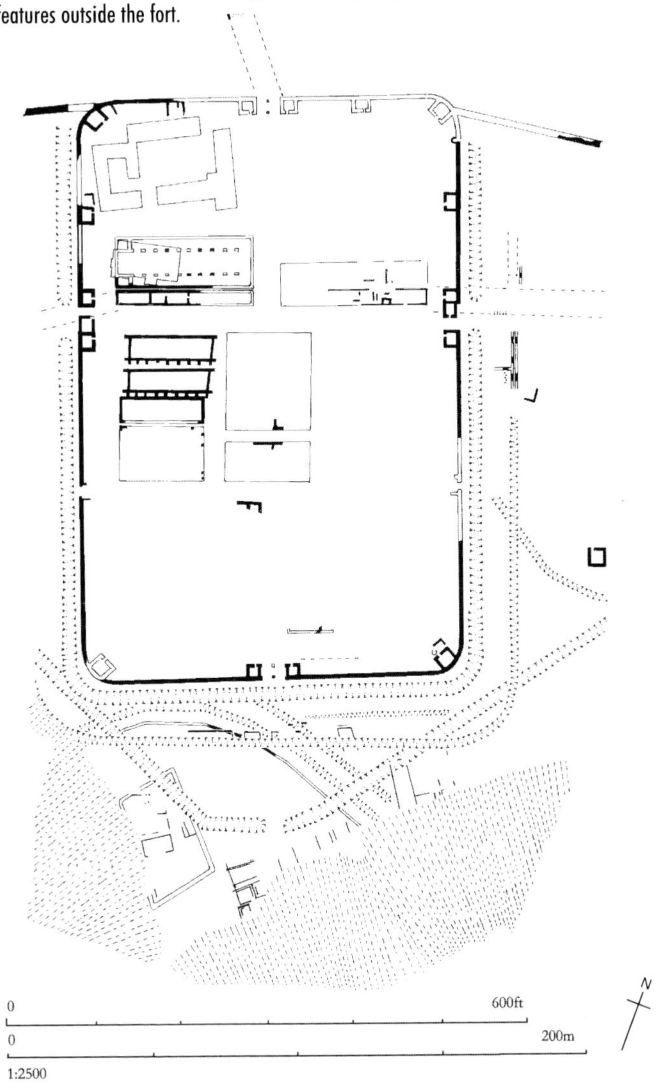

dated to the second century Finally, a stamped tile from the vicinity of Hare Hill, almost 6 km (3½ miles) to the west, is usually read as referring to the First Cohort of Tungrians, but this unit could equally well have been based at Castlesteads.

Birdoswald is in the care of English Heritage. The visitor centre provides an excellent introduction to the site as well as displaying artefacts discovered there.

Altar recording the name Venatores Bannienses. (66 x 46 mm)

The fort has been the subject of excavations in 1833, 1851-2, 1894, 1929-33, 1945, 1949-52 and 1987-99. They have demonstrated that the site had a complex history, of which relatively little is visible today. The earliest discovered structure is a stone tower, east of the fort, found and partly examined in 1930, but no longer visible. Excavation demonstrated that it stood 13 courses high and was 6.10 m (20 ft) square. Geophysical survey has recently indicated that it was surrounded by a ditch. The tower may have formed part of the group represented by Mains Rigg, which also sat within an enclosure, T 45a (Walltown) and Pike Hill, being built early in the second century when the Tyne-Solway isthmus became the northern frontier of the province. If this is the case, it had a different history from the other two, which were incorporated into Hadrian's Wall, whereas this tower appears to have been abandoned.

Immediately south of where the fort came to be built, excavation also located an enclosure on the edge of the escarpment south of the fort. Within it, a shallow ditch defined an area measuring 34.14 by 18.90 m (112 by 62 ft), showing traces of having been levelled down, and presumably created for a special purpose. The enclosure ditch contained pieces of leather from Roman army tents, and it may be that this was the camp of soldiers building the Turf Wall. These soldiers first had to clear the site of alder and birch scrub. The resulting ground would not be able to provide turves for the Wall, which were probably therefore cut on Midgeholm Moss.

The Turf Wall, together with its ditch, crossed the site of the fort. In 1945 the position of **T 49a** was located: nothing survived except the gap in the Turf Wall and a scatter of masons' chippings relating to the construction of the tower, all sealed below the *via principalis* of the fort. The first fort, placed astride the Wall, appears to have been of turf and timber. This is indicated by a variety of discoveries: a section of rampart base; early timber buildings; and pits and artefacts. Its construction led to the demolition of the Turf Wall and the infilling of the Wall ditch. The Vallum ran along behind the Wall, diverging round the fort and leaving a causeway of undug earth revetted in stone opposite the position of the south gate of the fort. However, the Vallum ditch was backfilled very soon after its excavation, the gateway over the Vallum causeway dismantled, and wooden buildings erected across it.

The turf-and-timber fort appears to have been quickly replaced by a stone successor which extended a little further south than its predecessor. The foundations of the fort walls were laid, followed by the lowest courses of the gates, before work ceased. This hiatus was long enough for a thin deposit of soil to collect and scrub to grow in parts of the fort, to be burnt off when the army returned to complete the building of the fort; a few years is indicated rather than a few months. Today this break is represented by the two standards of work still to be seen in the masonry of the gates.

While this fort was being constructed, or shortly afterwards, the Wall was moved northwards, it is presumed in order to provide more space on the escarpment; the Wall now joined the fort at its northern corners. It was probably at the same time that the minor east gate was obliterated. It was after the abandonment of the Antonine Wall in the 160s that the single fort ditch appears to have been supplemented by a second ditch, which cut through the infilled Vallum.

The **stone fort**, that partly visible today, continued in occupation into the fifth century. In 1929 two remarkable inscriptions were found in the barrack-block north-east of the *via principalis*, re-used as paving stones: both are now at Tullie House Museum, Carlisle. They help to date two of the periods of rebuilding. One records the restoration of a granary by the First Cohort of Dacians and the First Cohort of Thracians, under the command of Aurelius Julianus, in 205-8 (see page 31). The second records the restoration by the governor Aurelius Arpagius of the commanding officer's house, which had been covered with earth and had fallen into ruin, the headquarters building and the bath-house, under the

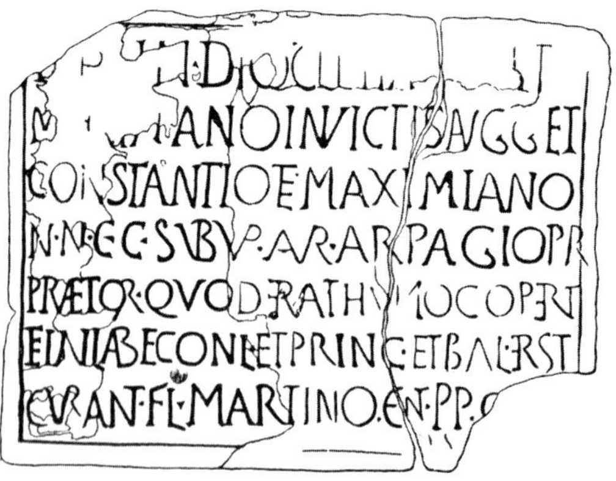

Inscription recording the restoration of the commanding officer's house, which had been covered with earth and fallen into ruin, the headquarters building and the bath-house under the Emperors Diocletian and Maximian and the Caesars Constantius and Maximianus. (624 mm high)

Emperors Diocletian and Maximian, and the Caesars Constantius and Maximianus, that is between 296 and 305, under the command of Flavius Martinus, centurion in charge. These inscriptions indicate two important episodes in the life of Hadrian's Wall: the work under the Emperor Septimius Severus; and the recovery of Britain from the usurpation of Carausius and Allectus, which is believed to have led to restoration work on the northern frontier. However, the reference to a building fallen into ruin and covered with earth suggests a more long-term problem. Indeed, the state of the commanding officer's house has been linked to the different social status of such officers in the later third century, who may not have required such a large dwelling - and we may note that the officer in charge of the rebuilding was a centurion - though a large courtyard house was erected within the fort at South Shields about the same date.

The **entrance** to the fort is through the visitor centre. The fort's **north wall** lies under the modern road, where once the foundations of one of the jambs of the north gate were visible in the road. The remainder of the fort defences are visible, together with the hollow of a ditch around the southern half of the circuit. The fort's curved **north-west angle** stands 12 courses high. Excavation has revealed that the fort once stood independently from the Wall, being cut off by a ditch. Third- and early-fourth-century pottery in its core dates the re-connection of fort and Wall. The well-preserved **angle-tower** was used as a cook-house, its ovens often rebuilt during the second century. The door was then blocked, with facing stones only on the outside. The fort wall continues southward past the interval-tower, standing high except to the west, where the face has been robbed. The **interval tower** along the west wall is poorly preserved. Excavation in 1950 produced evidence for two floors, the earlier of clay and the later flagged. Beyond are two ovens, indicating that the earthen backing to the fort wall had been removed hereabouts.

The main **west gate** was examined during the most recent campaign of excavation. While the gate was of normal plan, in the early third century the outer face of the south tower was rebuilt with stones of a particularly high standard. The stones appear to have been brought here from another building and exhibit a standard of workmanship surpassing anything else on the Wall. Later, the south portal of the gate was built up, with the fort ditch being extended across the face of the blocking wall. The north tower became a smithy. Towards the end of the third century, that is after about 273 according to the coin evidence, the maintenance of this part of the fort apparently ceased. The gate fell into decay but was rebuilt in the early fourth century in such a way that it continued in use well into the medieval period.

The single-portal **minor side gate** has wheel-ruts in its threshold and pivot-holes for a two-leaved door. It was later blocked. The top stone of the south pier, and the upper stones of the south gate, were finished to a markedly less good standard than the lower stones.

The **south gate** was cleared in 1851. The east portal was blocked soon after erection and the passage converted into a room. Late in the Roman period, the west portal was also closed. The blocking walls were removed in 1851. The east tower contained two late-Roman ovens. The east wall of the west tower was rebuilt from the ground in large, irregular masonry probably in the late fourth century. West of the tower there is a corn-drying kiln of post-Roman date. The **south-east angle tower** sits at a higher level and is presumably late in date.

The outer face of the **east wall** exhibits signs of various repairs. The latest repair probably took place in the late fourth century when the wall was rebuilt on the crest of a bank of stone and earth. The rampart backing, between the south-east angle and the minor gate, which had been blocked early in its life but is now open, was cut back to form a flat revetted shelf used for cooking-ovens in the early fourth century, while the new wall had no rampart-backing and no merlons, though the second course from the top was formed by a band of white stone.

The main **east gate** is one of the best-preserved such structures on the line of the Wall: the north-east pier stands to the first arch stone. It was excavated in 1852, when many traces of the alterations which it had undergone were removed. Its north passage and tower are founded in the Turf Wall ditch. Excavation in 1950 showed that the central pier of the gateway was later strengthened and a new roadway and pivot-stones provided. A kiln for the manufacture of tiles was constructed within the tower, probably in the third century. After the collapse of the kiln, the debris burying late-third-century pottery, it was covered by a flagged floor. It was probably early in the fourth century that the whole tower was rebuilt, with a lime floor laid, on which was found some coal. The north portal was now blocked, becoming a room, of which the back wall still stands, the front one having been removed in 1852. The west

Inscription recording building at Birdoswald by the First Dacian Cohort – whose Dacian sword is carved to the right – under the tribune Claudius Menander during the governorship of Modius Julius. (686 x 965 mm)

door of the original tower was also blocked and a new door in its south wall opened. Late in its life, the south tower may have received a hypocaust. Outside the south tower of the gate was found a slab recording building work by the First Cohort of Dacians at the time of Modius Iulius, who is known to have been governor in 219.

Between the gate and the interval tower a bronze arm-purse containing 28 *denarii* current under Hadrian was found in 1949: it appears to have been buried by rampart material during construction of the fort. The interval tower also had a kiln placed within it, and it was later brought back to normal use. Later, its east wall was thickened from 1.5m (5ft) to 3.35m (11ft): it has been suggested that this was in order to support a catapult. By the fence is a medieval kiln.

Statue of the goddess Fortuna. (1.05 m high)

Enough is known of the interior of the fort to appreciate that the plan followed normal conventions. Excavation in 1930 showed that the back wall of the headquarters building stood 15 courses high, being built in a hollow, while the front wall survived only two courses high. To the right a hypocaust was uncovered, indicating the position of the commanding officer's house. Here was found a seated statue of Fortuna, executed by a skilled carver, now in Tullie House

Museum, Carlisle. A gilded bronze statue of Hercules, probably found at Birdoswald in the nineteenth century, is of such quality that it had presumably belonged to a commanding officer.

Gilded bronze statue of Hercules (490 mm high)

To the north of the *via principalis*, lay a long narrow building, commonly interpreted as a storehouse or a stable, because a drain ran along part of its length, and a barrack-block. The buildings had been rebuilt on three occasions, the last dated by coins to after 364-78, its flagged floor including the two inscriptions found in 1929. The third-century building was difficult to interpret, but its successor, probably erected in the early fourth century, included a house containing a hypocausted room; it had a roof of thin sandstone flags. In the later fourth century a long narrow building with a superstructure of wattle and daub resting on low stone walls occupied nearly the same area as its second-century predecessor. The eastern of its three rooms was interpreted as a cook-house and the other two as living-rooms or dormitories.

Barrack-blocks were also traced in the southern part of the fort; a coin-hoard of 30 *denarii*, again those current under Hadrian, was concealed in the primary floor of one room. Later the area was replanned and buildings constructed over the *via quintana*.

To the west of the headquarters building are two large **granaries** excavated in 1987-92. Unusually they are aligned west to east. These were not built until the early third century and it is not known where food was stored before then. However, granaries were planned for this site when the fort was built for their foundations were found, sealed by turf and soil. The existing granaries are substantial buildings, still standing 2.5 m (8 ft 2 in) high. Their plan is unusual in that neither is buttressed on its north wall: presumably this reflected either the lie of the land, which sloped to the south, or the lack of space. The width of their walls has led to the suggestion that each granary contained two storeys. The walls which supported the floor are still visible in the north granary. The internal arrangements of the granaries changed several times during their life, timber supports being replaced by stone, on one occasion, while some of the vents below the floor were blocked. The roof was formed of diamond-shaped slates.

The roof of the north granary collapsed in the second half of the fourth century and the building was not repaired; rather it was used as a stone quarry and a rubbish dump. At about the same time the floor of the south granary was lifted, its basement infilled and a new floor laid: it apparently no longer served its original purpose. The surviving granary appears to have been turned into a large hall, with a hearth at the west

Birdoswald from the air looking north.

end. Among the finds from this level were a gold earring, a finger ring and a worn coin of the Emperor Theodosius I (388-95), the latest from the fort. The site of the north granary was now used for a large timber building. This was later replaced, but in both phases the buildings respected the position of the west gate: the modern posts mark the position of the later timber building. These successive timber buildings have been likened to the post-Roman hall found at Doon Hill near Dunbar in Scotland.

Sculpture of the gods Hercules and Jupiter, found in the fort in 1821. The hole in Jupiter's right hand was intended to hold his thunderbolt, which was probably of metal. (838 mm high)

To the north of the granaries, across the *via principalis*, in the Hadrianic fort was a long narrow building with no internal partitions and a flagged floor. Buildings of this type are presumed to be storehouses, and this one balances that found to the east in 1929. This building underwent modifications at several times, being divided into rooms and finally replaced by a building whose walls were based on large stones. Immediately to the north lay a very unusual building, a *basilica*, equal in size to two barrack-blocks; only its south wall is visible. This was probably a covered training area. Beyond this lay a pair of barrack-blocks,

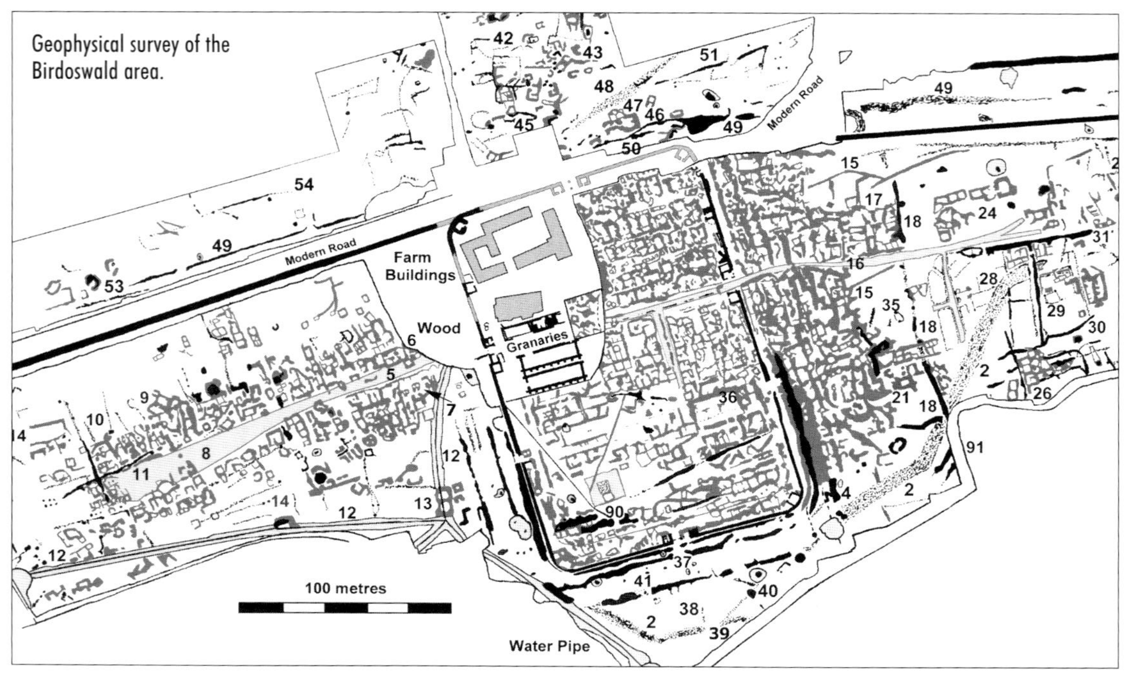

Geophysical survey of the Birdoswald area.

facing each other, and with sufficient space for each to contain eight *contubernia*. These buildings were altered about 200 and again about a century later.

Geophysical survey has indicated that **civilian buildings** were erected both east and west of the fort, covering a greater area than the military establishment. Many had stone foundations and they included both dwellings and workshops. Those to the west lay beyond the ditches, and have been traced for a distance of 200 m (660 ft) along the Military Way; these are mostly strip houses with the short end facing the street. Ditches forming boundary plots have also been recognised. About 100 m (300 ft) from the west gate, the road widened into a long triangular area which may have served as a market place. To the east of the fort, buildings of many different types spread over the fort ditches alongside the whole east wall of the fort as far as a ditch 80 m (260 ft) beyond the fort wall. It has been suggested that this protected a military annexe or the core of the civil settlement. Some buildings lie further east, but the area is mainly occupied by fields. The buildings south of the fort, investigated in the 1930s, were of timber. Interestingly, the survey has provided evidence for buildings and enclosures north of the Wall. South of the escarpment, in the river valley, magnetometry survey has provided evidence for buildings, one being tentatively interpreted as a bath-house.

The **cemetery** appears to have lain to the south-west in the space between the Vallum and the edge of the escarpment. It was discovered in 1961. A complete cremation was uncovered in a third-century cooking pot, together with a small drinking cup. Also found was a tombstone to G. Cossutius Saturninus, a soldier of the Sixth Legion, from Hippo Regius, modern Annaba, in north Africa. The son of the tribune Aurelius Julianus, here in 205-8, died at the age of 1 year and 5 days. One boy buried at Birdoswald bore the name Deciba[lus], the same as the famous king who opposed the conquest of his kingdom by Trajan in the early second century.

BIRDOSWALD TO CASTLESTEADS

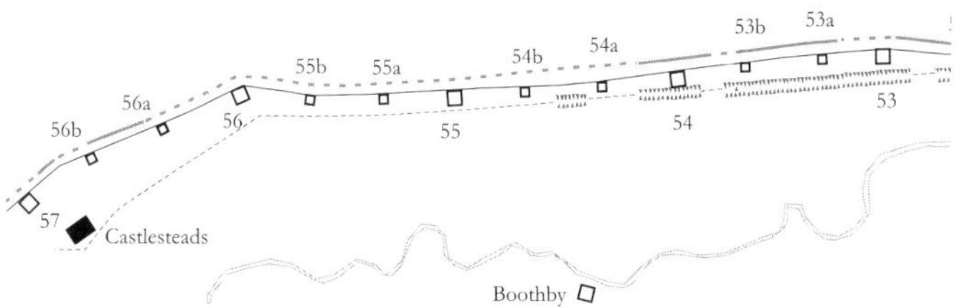

The Narrow Wall with no offset runs westwards from the north-west corner of the fort. In the visible stretches between Birdoswald and T 52a (Banks East) its width varies from 2.29 m (7 ft 6 in) to 2.57 m (8 ft 5 in). It rests on a layer of flags with very little clay and cobble foundations below. Towards the fort, the facing stones are larger than usual. The sector of Stone Wall from here to T 51a was investigated between 1909 and 1912. The Turf Wall, its stone successor and their structures as far as T 57a, unless otherwise stated, were all excavated between 1931 and 1934. The number of stones recording work by the Sixth Legion found in this sector would suggest that this legion was responsible for its construction.

West of Birdoswald, the Turf Wall and its stone successor run separately as far as MC 51 (Wall Bowers). Pottery recovered during the excavations of MC 50, T 49b, T 50a and T 50b on the Stone Wall revealed that these structures were all erected during Hadrian's reign and accordingly that the replacement of the Turf Wall by a new line in stone from MC 49 to MC 51 occurred soon after its construction.

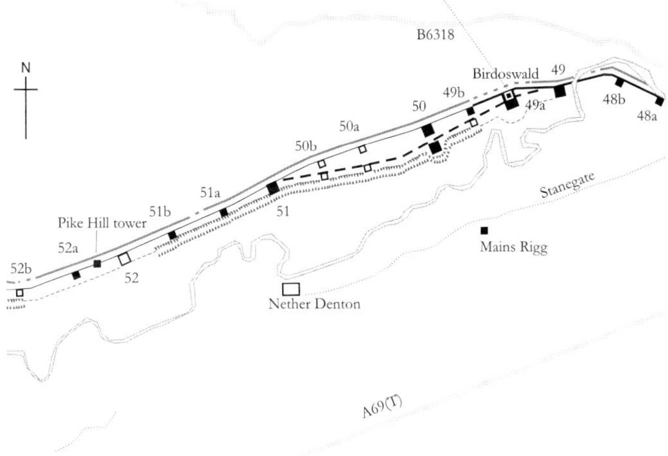

The Turf Wall, running south of the line of the Stone Wall, becomes visible in the second field west of Birdoswald, behind T 49b. Mound and ditch are faint at first, but soon become bold and so continue to MC 51. The Vallum also appears in this field.

T 49b TW was located in 1934, only its side walls, much robbed, being uncovered. **MC 50 TW** (High House) was the only milecastle to have been built on the Turf Wall and not replaced in stone. It measured 20.12 by 16.76 m (66 by 55 ft) within ramparts 6.1 m (20 ft) wide. An interesting distinction between the two gates is that the north had five 23 cm (9 in) square posts on each side of the passage, which had an internal area similar to that of a turret, while the south probably had only three posts to each side and a smaller defined area. On this basis, it has been argued that there was a tower over the one gate but not the other. In fact, six posts are adequate to support a tower so another reason for the difference has to be sought.

A timber building, measuring 9.14 by 3.66 m (30 by 12 ft), lay towards the southern end of the east side of the milecastle. It was divided into two unequal rooms and is presumably a

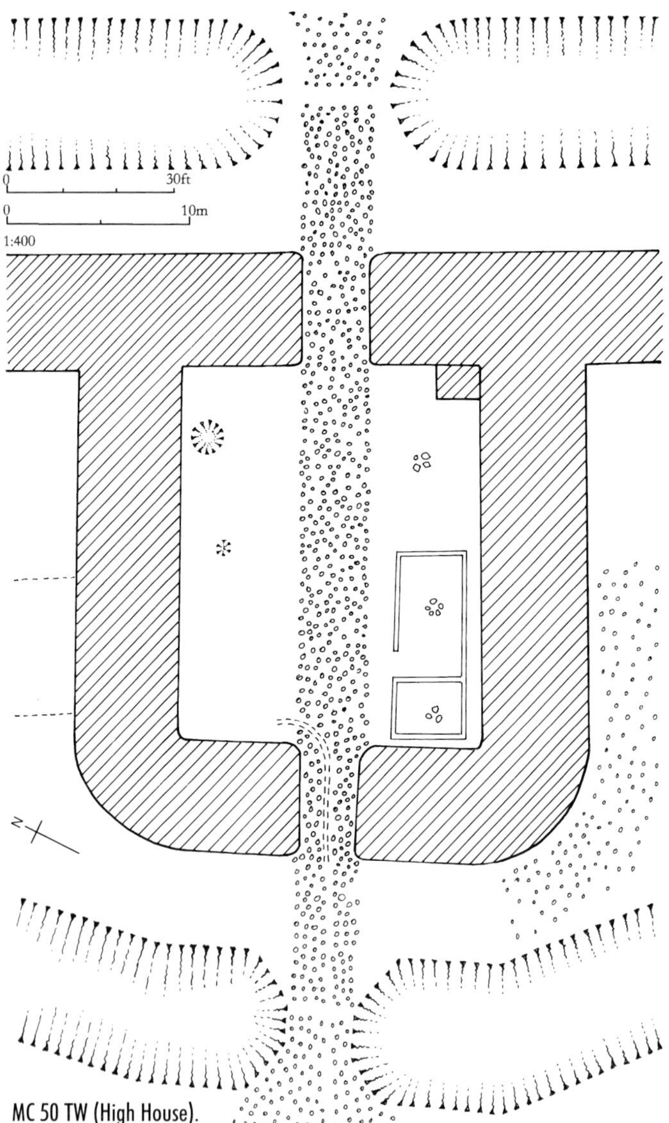

MC 50 TW (High House).

barrack-block. Each room contained a hearth, whose last fires had been extinguished by covering them with a stone. The hearth outside and to the north of the building showed more signs of use, suggesting that the internal fires were for warmth not cooking. A large pot was set into the ground beside the south gate: a drain issuing from it indicated that its purpose was to act as a latrine. The base of a stairway was noted in the north-east corner of the milecastle.

Evidence was found to suggest purposeful dismantling of the milecastle, including both its gates. Pits dug at this time contained the remains of bedding and other rubbish, including a broken leaf of a wooden writing-tablet, a bundle of fragments of leather tents and a broken drinking mug. In one pit was found a fragment of an inscription cut on a wooden panel but otherwise on the same lines as the other milecastle building inscriptions. It has been restored to include part of the names of the Emperor Hadrian and the governor A. Platorius Nepos. This indicates an early date for the construction of the Turf Wall hereabouts.

The road within the milecastle passed through the north gate and crossed the ditch on a causeway of undisturbed earth. A culvert, once lined in wood, lay under the causeway to aid the flow of water. It was replaced in stone and a new road laid.

Fragment of a building inscription in oak found at MC 50 TW (High House) restored as recording the names of the Emperor Hadrian and the governor A. Platorius Nepos. (95 x 260 mm)

The **Vallum** runs close behind the Turf Wall throughout this sector. The north mound, absent from MC 49 westwards, starts again at the west rampart of MC 50 TW. The south mound and the ditch take a southward diversion round the milecastle.

The ground below the Vallum mound had been stripped of turf, presumably for use in the Wall; the kerbs for the mound were then cut from the exposed surface. A track was found on the south berm west of the milecastle, but none to the north of the ditch.

The Vallum ditch was originally interrupted by a causeway revetted in stone, as at the forts. Later, probably at the same time or later than the demolition of the milecastle, the Vallum causeway was replaced by a wide crossing and a new roadway passing through the south mound. Finally, the gap in the mound was blocked by embankments.

West of the milecastle, the Vallum is very well preserved, with gaps visible in the north mound and traces of crossings to be seen in the ditch. In the south mound, as at Shield-on-the Wall and Wallend Common, only slight depressions indicate where the gaps were marked out. The Turf Wall in this sector was also slighted, and there are substantial causeways in its ditch. In 1975 the ditch was found to be 8.53 m (28 ft) wide. The Turf Wall and the Vallum mounds had all been badly damaged by ploughing, but a path, about 2.53 m (8 ft) wide, has been noted on the north berm of the Vallum. The marginal mound becomes increasingly visible as far as Coombe Crag, with, in one section, a mound on the north berm.

Little of **T 50a TW** survived its thorough demolition. The walls were 76 cm (2 ft 6 in) wide, set to the outer edge of the foundation trench. **T 50b TW** had again been demolished. Its hearth lay a little to east of centre suggesting a westerly door. The berm is narrow in front of these two turrets, and at T 51a and T 51b.

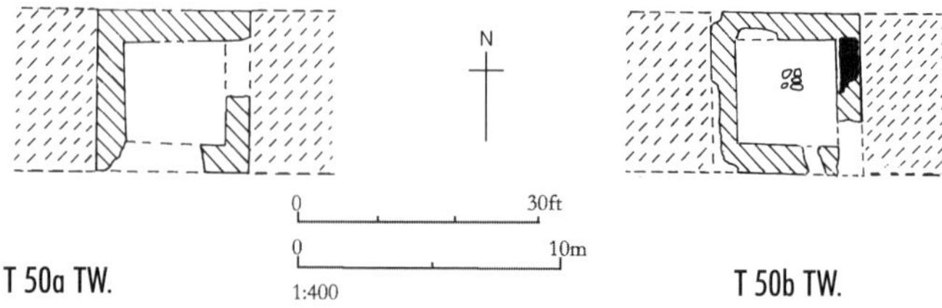

T 50a TW. T 50b TW.

A little beyond the site of T 50b and opposite Appletree barn, a track goes off to the south. Beside this a section across the Turf Wall is traditionally cleaned for the Pilgrimage of Hadrian's Wall. In 1999 the opportunity was taken to cut a section across the Turf Wall and Vallum. It was demonstrated that the turf had been removed from below the counterscarp bank north of the ditch before it was thrown up, presumably to use on the Turf Wall. When the Wall was replaced in stone, the turf rampart was pushed into the ditch leaving but a low mound. The Vallum mounds were constructed as unrevetted clay banks on a denuded ground surface, indicating that vegetation had not had time to regenerate before the construction of the earthwork. The ground below the marginal mound was the same, suggesting an early date for this also. A metalled path ran along the north berm, while a second road between Wall and Vallum may have been the Military Way.

T 49b SW (Birdoswald).

T 49b SW (Birdoswald) is the only visible turret on the re-aligned stretch of Wall from Harrow's Scar to MC 51. Its walls were reduced from a height of six courses to the present level in 1837. The door is placed about 60 cm (2 ft) from the east wall, not immediately beside the corner as is usual on the Stone Wall. A path was found outside the door. Within, there were four floor levels, the first and third were of clay, the other two of flags. The hearth lay in the north-west corner in the first two phases, later being moved to the north-east corner. Part of a base built in the second phase survived by the south wall. The artefacts found here include a brooch in the shape of a long-eared dog and part of a dagger scabbard mounting. The usual range of pottery was recovered at this and next two turrets and indicate occupation continuing into the fourth century. At all three turrets, as well as at T 51b (Lea Hill), fragments of window glass were found.

The Wall disappears under the modern road shortly after the turret. The ditch, however, remains visible to the north for the next 5 km (3 miles) with the broad upcast mound intermittent. At MC 50 a small mound sits on the north lip of the ditch; it may be a marking-out bank or the result of later cleaning of the ditch. Further west, the upcast is roughly spread as a low mound.

The platform of **MC 50 SW** (High House) is visible just beyond the crest of the hill. The milecastle measures 23.16 by 18.29 m (76 by 60 ft) within narrow walls; the gates are of type III. Three phases were noted at both gates. In the third phase, both

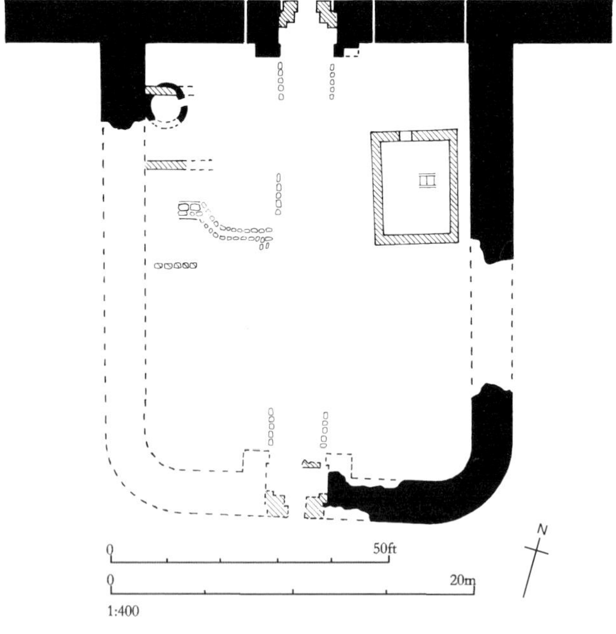

MC 50 SW (High House).

passages were reduced in width, the north to 1 m (3 ft 3 in), by walls constructed on both sides of the passage. The road passing through the north gate expanded into a paved area which extended as far as the ditch. No causeway was found, though there is a modern crossing over the ditch to right of the centre of the milecastle. The original internal buildings were probably of timber; their successors were of stone. The eastern building was clay-bonded and free-standing; the western, probably containing four rooms, was built against the inside wall of the milecastle. Both buildings contained hearths; an oven dating to the first period lay in the north-west corner of the enclosure. The milecastle has produced fragments of three legionary building inscriptions. Two mention the Sixth Legion, and the other refers to a detachment of the Second but is probably later in date. The ten coins included two of the Emperor Constantine I dating to 309-313/4. Four spearheads, an intaglio and a brooch, part of a lamp, of a gaming board and fragments of five millstones were among the finds. The pottery included part of lamp and a strainer.

T 50a SW (High House).

T 50a SW (High House) was found to have been demolished down to the lowest course with the recess blocked up. Two floors survived, the first partly flagged, otherwise of clay, the upper probably originally all flagged. Half a millstone was recovered, but no hearth. Among the debris on the later floor were fragments of two inscriptions of the Sixth Legion. At this turret, and the next, a path was recorded outside the door.

T 50b SW (Appletree) had been damaged by the construction of the road, which possibly removed the final floor. The lowest floor was of clay, its successors of flags. The hearth on the west wall was replaced by two, by the north and the south walls, in the second phase. Finds included brooches in addition to pottery.

At **MC 51** (Wall Bowers) the Stone Wall once more rejoins the line of the Turf Wall and crosses its filled-in ditch. The stone milecastle, which contained a stone building, is surrounded by a ditch, as at MCs 23, 25 and 29, still visible, though here it was only half dug. The side walls butt against the Narrow Wall. The south gate, of type III, had been rebuilt in the fourth century with large monolithic jambs and a massive threshold set in a deep trench. Inside, the wall of an interior building was located, with good evidence for stratigraphy. The Vallum runs some distance behind the milecastle. A primary stone-revetted causeway across the ditch was inferred by the discovery of masonry found in a secondary causeway. A road now crossed the south mound. There is also a causeway over the ditch outside the north gate. Although it is offset by about 4 m (13 ft) from the axis of the milecastle, the existence of the Vallum causeway underlines the possibility that this ditch causeway may also be Roman.

West of Wall Bowers, at a lodge south of the road, a path leads to Coombe Crag, a freestone **quarry** extensively worked by the Romans. On the east face of the crag, soldiers have left inscriptions on the face of the rock, including the names Securus, Iustus, Maternus and, no longer visible, one Daminius, who added "I did not want to do it". An inscription at the foot of the cliff, reading *Faust et Ruf Cos* and purporting to mention Faustinus and Rufus, the consuls of 210, is a forgery.

Immediately west of Coombe Crag Wood the **Vallum** is clear for about 720 m (800 yards) with slight depressions in the mounds, though no crossings are visible in the ditch and no marginal mound.

T 51a (Piper Syke) was excavated in 1970. It was shown to have been of rather poor construction. The north-east corner and the east wall had been repaired before the Turf Wall was rebuilt in stone. The door lay to the east in the badly robbed

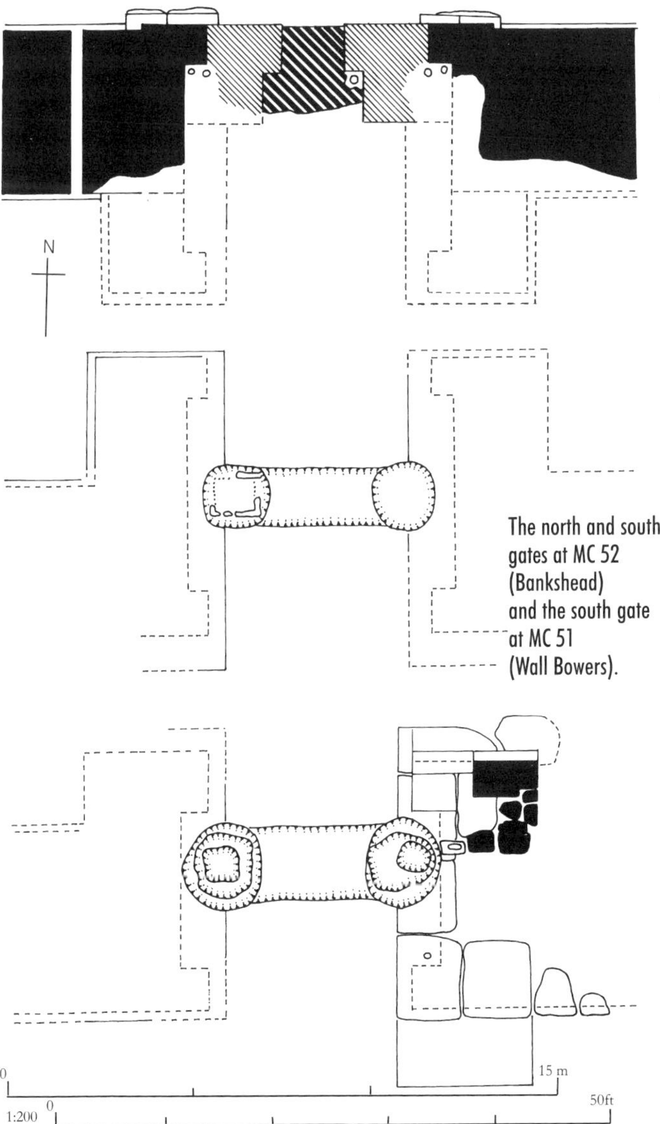

The north and south gates at MC 52 (Bankshead) and the south gate at MC 51 (Wall Bowers).

south wall. There was a central hearth and a second near the north-west corner. Against the north wall there lay a secondary platform only 20 cm (8 in) high: it may have served as a living area where meals could be taken. Pottery indicated occupation in the second century only.

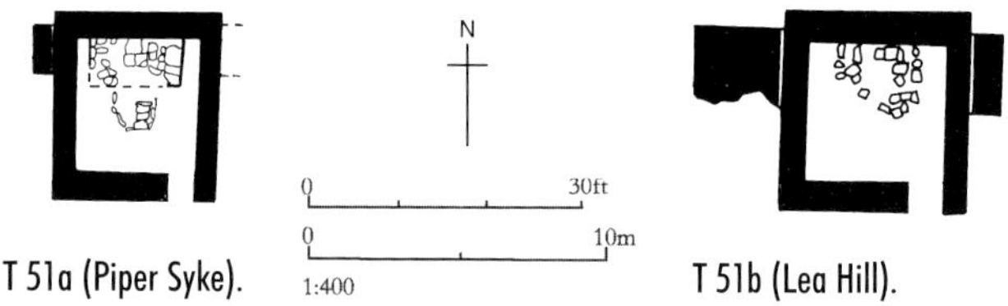

T 51a (Piper Syke). T 51b (Lea Hill).

T 51b (Lea Hill) was excavated in 1958. The north and south walls had a mortar core, but the east and west walls were clay bonded, though the facing stones were mortared. The hearth was placed against the west wall but later moved to the centre, when it was adapted to serve as a small oven. Beside it, set into the ground, was a little stone box. A low platform lay by the north wall. This was not kept clean and gradually broken pottery, bone and other rubbish accumulated upon it; indeed, the standard of cleanliness in the second period was much lower than in the first. The original floor was of clay, and spread over the door threshold, but part of it was later partly cobbled. The second floor was flagged, but strewn with straw as was shown by the marks on corroded metal objects lost in it. Some window glass was found and a possible merlon coping stone. The turret was only occupied in the second century, but there was no evidence that it had then been dismantled or the Wall carried across the recess. The amount and nature of the internal debris suggested gradual collapse. As there was less debris in the northern part of the turret the excavator suggested that this indicated that care had been taken to maintain the Wall. Later, an area was scooped out in the debris and a hearth formed. Finally, a hut was built within the south-west corner of the ruin. There is a record of the discovery of a skeleton outside the north wall of the turret. Immediately to the west of the turret the Stone Wall survives 2.29 m (7 ft 6 in) over foundations 2.44 m (8 ft) wide.

Next comes the site of **MC 52** (Bankhead). Here in 1808 two altars were discovered, dedicated to the local deity Cocidius, one in 262-6 by soldiers of the Twentieth Legion and the other by colleagues in the Second Legion. Excavation showed the milecastle to have been exceptionally large, 23.38 by 27.44 m (76 ft 9 in by 90 ft 3 in) between narrow side walls. Its north gate was of type III. During the second century the level within the gate was raised and new pivot-holes provided. In the second period the gate was reduced to a foot-way 86 cm (2 ft 10 in) wide. At the same time, the inner jambs of the gate were

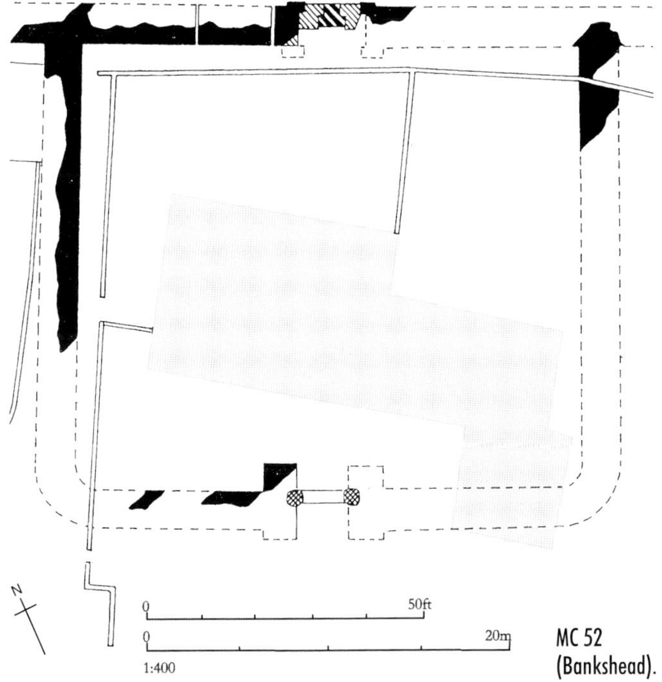

MC 52
(Bankshead).

removed; presumably there was no longer a tower over the gate. The surface of the entrance was later raised and then completely blocked late in the fourth century. The south gate was remodelled in the fourth century by the insertion of large stone jambs and a threshold; some of the iron strapping from the doors was found. Nothing is known of the internal arrangements apart from a short length of wall, though a well-burnt hypocaust pillar was found in the build-up of the final road.

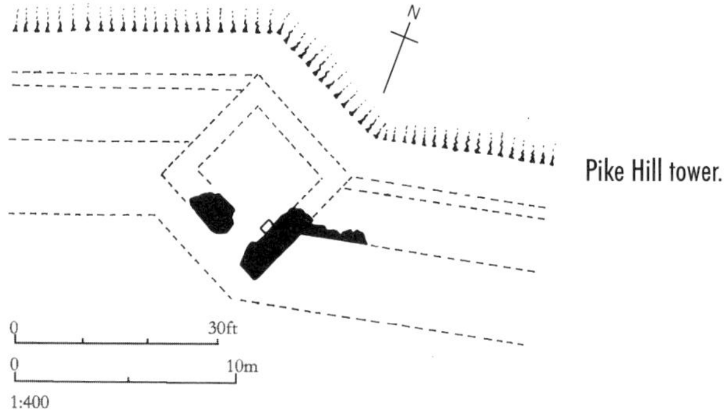

Pike Hill tower.

Between this milecastle and T 52a lies **Pike Hill** and on its summit stand the remains of a tower; only the south corner survives, the rest having been removed by the lowering of the road in 1870. The view is extensive, embracing north Cumbria and beyond. The tower was 6.10 m (20 ft) square and, uniquely on the Wall, stood on a platform of mortared rubble with substantial foundations. The masonry of the tower was dressed to a higher standard than the turrets of the Wall. The tower lies at 45° to the Wall, so that its two eastern sides face Gillalees tower, Nether Denton fort and Walltown turret (45a), and its two western sides Boothby fort on the Stanegate and the outpost fort at Netherby. The ditch to the north follows the line of the Wall and the tower in the same zig-zag pattern. The berm was 1.85 m (6 ft) wide.

Excavation in 1931 revealed the one remaining corner and a ground-floor door, which contrasts with other free-standing towers such as Robin Hood's Butt and Mains Rigg, where access was at first-floor level. The remains of the demolished Turf Wall were recorded below the Stone Wall to the east of the tower. Pottery suggests that the tower had been constructed under Hadrian, or possibly a little earlier. Two floor levels survived inside, and a hearth in the south-east corner. In 1862 a broken slab bearing part of the name and titles of the Emperor Antoninus Pius was found here: it may record repairs to the tower. The tower was still occupied in the late fourth century.

T 52a (Banks East) lies less than 100 m (100 yards) west of Pike Hill and has the distinction of being one of the earliest structures on Hadrian's Wall to be taken into state care, following its excavation in 1933 in advance of road works. The outer faces of the east and west walls of the turret were not as well finished as the north and south walls. The excavators noted that the facing stones were both badly trimmed and irregularly bedded. This was presumably because both walls would be hidden by the construction of the Turf Wall. There is a plinth at the sixth course running along the front of the turret; a single stone on the south wall, bevelled on both edges at the south-east corner by the door, indicates that the south wall was similarly treated. The return on the east side does not run the full length of this stone but is stopped, presumably where it met the Turf Wall. Adding the fallen fragment of wall to that still standing would restore a height of 14 courses. Inside the turret, a platform lay against the north wall, and a hearth by the west wall. Several floor levels were recorded, the second earliest, as has been recorded elsewhere, being covered by

T 52a (Banks East).

fallen stones. The final structural addition consisted of the footings of a rough blocking wall crossing the northern half of the turret in line with the back of the Wall. This was in the correct position for the wall found elsewhere blocking the recess, but it is of a different style though it may reflect the same purpose. The second-century pottery included fragments of two samian vessels and some mixing bowls, while the later levels yielded more jars and cooking pots. The construction of the modern road had damaged the later deposits, but a fragment of late-fourth-century pottery was found immediately below the modern metalling.

The width of the Stone Wall varies from 2.57 m (8 ft 5 in) to the east of the turret to 2.31 m (7 ft 7 in) to the west. The front of the Stone Wall was aligned with the north face of the turret above the level of the plinth. This is unusual as the Stone Wall was normally placed a little further south. In this case, the Stone Wall swung slightly north as it approached the turret from each direction, so the alignment was intentional.

A rectangular structure of stone slabs was found on the berm to the north of the turret. Although described as a tank, it may have been a burial cist. The berm was 2.74 m (9 ft) wide.

The **Vallum** runs in a straight line from the top of the bank (the site of T 52b) to MC 56 (Walton) and is visible for much of this length. The Wall ditch gives out at the bottom of the slope leading down to the hamlet called Banks. The hump of stones in the field beyond indicates the line of the Wall; a large chunk of core lies at a crazy angle having fallen forward. The measured position of **MC 53** (Banks Burn) is just short of the Banks Burn, but it was in fact placed west of the stream at Banks Burn farm-house. Post-Roman activity on the site has removed all trace of internal buildings, leaving only the knowledge that the ground had sloped from west to east and was levelled up within the milecastle walls. These were narrow, the side walls butting onto the north wall, enough surviving to indicate size: 23.21 by 21.95 m (76 ft 6 in by 72 ft). The north gate did not survive, but the south was type III. To the south there is a causeway over the Vallum ditch. Under the northern part of the earlier Turf Wall lay a layer of cobbles about 2.13 m (7 ft) wide.

Ascending **Hare Hill** the Wall stands 3 m (9 ft 10 in) high. The core is original, the facing stones added in the nineteenth century. A centurial stone, recording the century of the *primus pilus* or senior centurion of the first cohort, found at Moneyholes, two fields further west, is placed in the north face. Two hundred years ago William Hutton wrote: "I viewed this relick with admiration; I saw no part higher". Investigations in 2004 revealed the foundations of the Stone Wall 2.88 m (9 ft 6 in) wide sitting on the remains of the Turf Wall. Cracks in the foundations allowed the width of the Wall to be estimated at 2.32 m (7 ft 7 in).

The road downhill leads to Lanercost Priory, where three Roman inscriptions are built into the fabric. One centurial stone on the west side of the cloisters records *Prisc(us)*, while a second on the inside east wall of the undercroft reads *Coh X Pi*. The stones in the undercroft are replicas of the stones formerly displayed here but now at Birdoswald.

About 200 m (200 yards) west of Hare Hill lies **T 53a** (Hare Hill). It was discovered in 1854 or 1855 and recorded by MacLauchlan. Excavation shortly after revealed that it was full of black ashes; the discoverers took it to be a smithy. Re-examination in 1932 revealed this to be a normal Turf Wall turret, built free-standing but with the later Narrow Wall abutting on each side, 2.61 m (8 ft 7 in) to the east and 2.71 m (8 ft 11 in) to the west. It had an eastern door, while the plinth on the north wall lay at the third course. A coin of the Emperor Constantine I (306-37) was found within the turret. The turret lay on the boundary of Lanercost Priory, which is less than a mile (1.5 km) to the south-west, and may have been reused in the medieval period as a watch-tower and beacon.

The Wall now runs along the ridge known as Craggle Hill, with its ditch very bold. The views to north and south are wide,

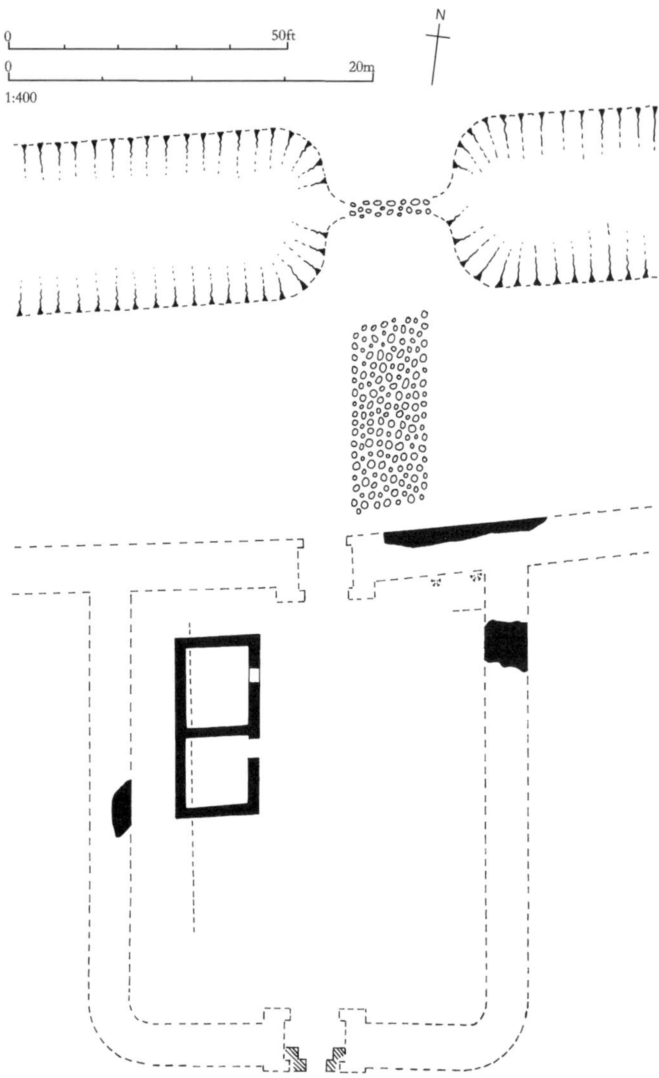

MC 54 (Randylands) showing the turf and stone phases.

and, as the crest of the ridge is reached, to the west. To the south, the **Vallum** follows the lower ground. Breaks occur in the north mound which appear to be purposeful, while the marginal mound is also visible in places. **T 53b** (Craggle Hill) is the most easterly structure built in the red sandstone used for the Wall from here to Bowness. The Wall here, however, was built of yellow freestone.

At Hayton Gate, a track, once a drove road, crosses the Wall, approximately on the line of the **Red Rock Fault**, the great geological cleavage between limestone and red sandstone. West of this point no limestone is obtainable anywhere near the Wall. It has been argued that this led to the use of turf rather than stone for the western 50 km (30 miles) of the Wall. However, this explanation was based on the premise that mortar was used in the core of the Stone Wall. We can now see that the core was usually of clay or earth and mortar was only used to bed the facing stones.

Just west of Randylands Farm comes **MC 54** (Randylands). The central axis of the turf and timber milecastle lay 3.66 m (12 ft) to the east of its stone successor. In front of its north gate lay a thin layer of cobbling, presumably a path leading to a causeway across the ditch. The only evidence for this crossing, which had been removed, was a strip of stone bottoming, interpreted as the base of a culvert through the causeway. The 12 m (40 ft) wide berm here is probable due to the sandy nature of the subsoil. Clay was used instead of turf in the milecastle ramparts and in the Wall for the 0.8 km (half mile) to the west. Pollen analysis suggested that no suitable turf would have been available here owing to the presence of scrub on the localised sands and gravel.

This turf and timber milecastle appears to have been soon replaced for pottery from the lowest level of the stone milecastle does not differ from that found at MC 50 TW (High House). This conclusion is supported by the small group of pottery found in the lowest level of the stone building, which does not need to be later than the reign of Hadrian, and by the structural sequence at the south gate.

The stone milecastle measured 23.62 by 19.66 m (77 ft 6 in by 64 ft 6 in) within narrow side walls. The foundations of the side and north walls of the milecastle were homogeneous demonstrating contemporaneity. Both gates were type III. At the south gate there were two second-century road levels (interpreted as IA and IB), with the earlier pivots being replaced, before the gate was narrowed by masonry added to each side of the passage. Within the enclosure, in the northern half of the west side, lay a two-roomed stone building measuring 6.55 by 3.20 m (21 ft 6 in by 10 ft 6 in). The larger northern room was partly paved and fitted with stone benches; it also containing a hearth and two millstones set into the ground. On the road immediately outside the gate was found a coin of the Emperor Claudius II (268-70). Much of the pottery from the site dates to the mid- to late fourth century.

This milecastle appears to have been the most westerly structure on the Turf Wall to have been rebuilt under Hadrian. When the remainder of the Turf Wall was replaced, it was to an 'intermediate gauge' about 2.59 m (8 ft 6 in) wide. The core of this Intermediate Stone Wall up to 1.5 m (5 ft) high, with hard white mortar, may be seen in the field immediately to the west of the Burtholme Beck. This sector is interesting because the Wall was here realigned, in this case owing to a local structural problem. As the Wall ditch climbed the slope from the Burtholme Beck, it will be observed swinging northwards and taking the bottom of the northward slope. This arrangement is secondary. The older ditch, infilled but still marked by reeds, followed the Wall to the turret, **T 54a** (Garthside).

Excavation of this turret in 1933 produced a complex and unique sequence. A normal Turf Wall turret had been first erected within the line of the Turf Wall. Its door lay to the west. The threshold was well worn and the floor showed evidence for repair. The pottery associated with this turret is Hadrianic in

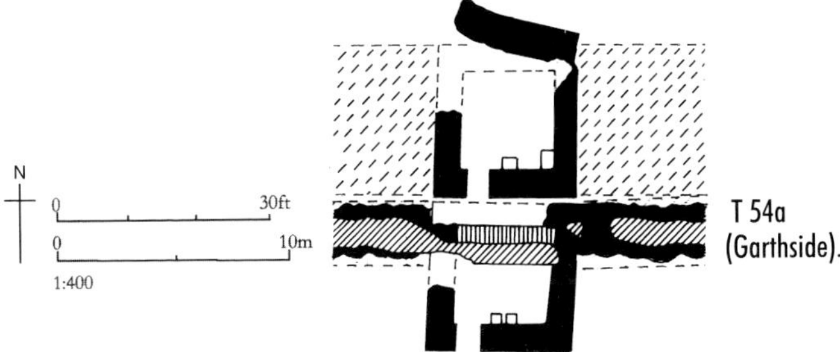

T 54a (Garthside).

date. The north wall then peeled away following the collapse of the south lip of the ditch owing to the sandy subsoil: the berm here was about 2.44 m (8 ft) wide. Replacement of Wall and turret led to two changes. The Turf Wall and ditch were realigned a little to the north, while the replacement turret was erected immediately to the south of its predecessor. The turret was thus free-standing. This unique position for a Wall turret may be used to argue against the existence of a wall-walk along the Wall top. The new turret also had a western doorway. Its facing stones used hard white mortar, but the core was clay-bonded. It contained two hearths set against the centre of the south wall, but only one level of occupation. The pottery dates from the Hadrianic to the late second century, suggesting construction late in Hadrian's reign at the earliest and abandonment before the end of the second century. The Stone Wall did not follow the line of the secondary Turf Wall but incorporated the tower back into the linear barrier. Its north face was set flush with the lower courses of the tower, indicating that this structure had no plinth. The turret was later demolished and the Wall built across its site, part of the structure being incorporated into the rebuild.

The Vallum is still visible south of T 54a but not west of the modern road. This road swings north of Howgill heading for Walton. At **T 54b** (Howgill) four courses of red sandstone were recorded, the turret projecting 76 cm (2 ft 6 in) in front of the Stone Wall. In the wall of an outhouse at Howgill Farm there is a rough inscription recording work by the Catuvellauni of southern Britain: this probably dates to the fourth century. Nearly due north of Low Wall, at the sharp bend in the road, is the low platform representing **MC 55** (Low Wall), partly excavated in 1900. The junction of the west wall of the stone milecastle with the Stone Wall was located. While it was determined that, unlike in the previous easterly 8 km (5 miles), the Wall was not built first, it was not possible to decide whether the two walls were bonded. Later-fourth-century pottery was found.

T 55a (Dovecote) has been located. Its north wall projects beyond the Stone Wall and is in a fair state of preservation, though the others are much robbed. **T 55b** (Townhead Croft), which ought to lie beside the King Water, has not been found, but at the appropriate position the berm narrows to about 1.83 m (6 ft), indicative of the position of the turret. Immediately to the west of the Water a short length of Intermediate Stone Wall in red sandstone is now covered for its own protection against the weather. Beyond, the ditch is seen climbing the hill to Walton, and the berm widens to 6.10 m (20 ft).

MC 56 (Walton) has been sought but not found. It is possible that it was not built in its calculated position but moved to take advantage of the topography, though it may have been destroyed by the village. Through Walton the general course of the Wall lies below the Centurion Inn. At the west end of the village, Wall foundations were located in 1901, one of the stones being identified as coming from the Coombe Crag quarry. The Wall was next located at Sandysike in 1933, on deep masonry foundations 2.90 m (9 ft 6 in) wide near the stream, though **T 56a** (Sandyside) was not found. From the farm the ditch runs down to the Cambeck. Just short of the Beck **T 56b** (Cambeck), projecting 84 cm (2 ft 9 in) to the north of the Stone Wall, survived badly behind a berm 5.18 m (17 ft) across. A modern bridge carries the footpath over the Cambeck. An account of the destruction of the Wall hereabouts in 1791 shows unmistakably that it was the Intermediate Wall, being 2.44 m (8 ft) wide and faced with large stones, the space between them filled with alternate layers of rubble 30 cm (1 ft) thick and mortar 10 cm (4 in) thick.

The **Vallum**, of which no sign appears on the surface, was traced by excavation in 1900 in a straight line from MC 55 to a point about 300 m (300 yards) south-east of the Centurion Inn, on the north end of Crowhall Wood, where it turns rather sharply to the south. Another southward turn, nearly 1 km (half a mile) farther on, brought it to the south side of the fort at Castlesteads. Having skirted round the fort, it turned west again to converge with the Wall beyond the Cambeck, on whose west bank its ditch is visible.

The Roman **quarries** on the River Gelt, with their inscriptions, lie about 6 km (4 miles) to the south of this point. The most famous of the inscriptions are on the 'Written Rock of Gelt', which stands 10 m (30 ft) above the river and can now only be viewed from the riverside path. One inscription records the work by "a detachment of the Second Legion under the junior officer (*optio*) Agricola". Beside the inscription is a drawing of a human face. To the right, a second inscription was cut "in the consulate of Aper and Maximus", that is in 207. Less than 1 km (about half a mile) higher up the river, on the opposite side, is the quarry face of Pigeon Crag, with the names of men from the Sixth Legion. Beside it and just above the ground surface is a small altar carved in low relief and set in a niche. Above it are two vertical lines surmounted by a horizontal line, the whole possibly forming a partially carved second altar. 7.5 km (nearly 5 miles) south-west, and the same distance south of MC 60, another quarry inscription beside the River Eden at Wetherall, but now nearly inaccessible, records work by the Twentieth Legion.

One of the quarry inscriptions on the Written Rock of Gelt. (1.656 m wide)

VEX·L·LEG·II AVG·OF·APR·
SVB·AGRICOLA·OPTIONE

CASTLESTEADS (*CAMBOGLANNA*)

Castlesteads fort is almost 11.2 km (7 miles) from Birdoswald. It sits on a high bluff overlooking the Cambeck valley and the break in the mosses to the north-west which carries the modern road from Brampton to Longtown. The site was drastically levelled in 1791, when the gardens of Castlesteads House were laid out and today nothing is visible of the fort apart from the southern edge of the fort platform, while the view described above is obscured by trees.

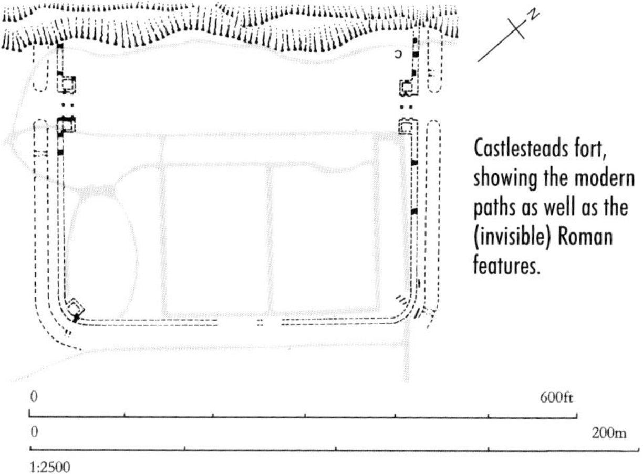

Castlesteads fort, showing the modern paths as well as the (invisible) Roman features.

The fort is named as *Camboglanna* on the Rudge Cup, Amiens Skillet and Ilam Pan. Its meaning is perhaps best rendered as "the bank at the bend", and indeed it is at the bend of the Cam Beck. This stream has so far eroded the north-west front of the fort that the side gates now lie only 15 m (50 ft) from the edge of the gorge. From east to west the fort measures 120 m (394 ft) and it is thought to have been originally about 122 m (400 ft) square, covering some 1.5 ha (3.75 acres), though it is not impossible that the fort faced south rather than north and was therefore somewhat larger.

Inscriptions at Castlesteads show that the Fourth Cohort of Gauls, a part-mounted unit, was here, presumably in the second century as it was later at Vindolanda, while the Second Cohort of Tungrians, also part-mounted, is attested in 241. Although this unit contained a thousand men, the size of the fort would suggest that not all were based here. Owing to an error, the unit at Castlesteads is not listed in the *Notitia Dignitatum*.

Excavations in 1934 revealed the east, west and south walls of the **fort**, the east and west double-portal gates and south-west angle tower. The gate towers were built one course deeper than the fort wall, whose foundations were the normal 1.85 m (6 ft) wide. All walls had been heavily robbed, but roof-tiles occurred in a number of the towers at ground-floor level, suggesting the possibility of oven-bases, as at Birdoswald, rather than collapsed roofs. Space allowed only for the identification of one ditch, 4.88 m (16 ft) wide. No contact has been made with any internal building, but an external bath-house was located and partly dug in 1741.

This was not the first fort on the site for under the south-east angle were found the remains of a turf rampart not less than 3 m (10 ft) wide resting on flagging and stones set in clay. A ditch lay beyond this rampart, infilled presumably when the stone fort was erected. It would appear, however, that the two forts were not quite on the same alignment, which might account for the asymmetrical placement of the stone fort within the Vallum diversion. Castlesteads is unique along the whole Wall for sitting between the Wall and Vallum but not being attached to the former; presumably either its pre-existence or the lie of the land dictated its location.

Geophysical survey south of the fort between 1999 and 2001 revealed the line of the **Vallum**, together with its causeway, and, beyond, the buildings of a civil settlement with its attendant roads and field boundaries. A water-course, now long filled in, separated the settlement from a group of fields to the east; two phases could be recognised in this field system. Less than fifty buildings have been identified in the civil settlement, but it may have spread further west outside the area surveyed.

Altar to Jupiter erected by the Second Cohort of Tungrians.
(635 mm high)

The goddess Victory standing on a globe and holding a laurel wreath.
(457 mm high)

Several altars and items of sculpture are preserved in the summer-house in the garden of Castlesteads House. The finest is an altar to Jupiter by the Second Thousand-strong Cohort of Tungrians, part-mounted, c. L. The letters c. L. have been expanded as *civium Latinorum*, which would indicate that the entire body of soldiers had been given the rights of Latin citizens. Such a designation would be unique, and so *coram laudata* (publicly praised) has also been offered as an interpretation of the letters. There are a further seven dedications to Jupiter known from the site by this regiment and the Fourth Cohort of Gauls together with other dedications to and statues of the state gods.

An altar to *Discipulina Auggg* is a reference to the Emperor Septimius Severus and his two sons, Caracalla and Geta who were joint *Augusti* from 209 to 211. The site has also yielded three altars to Mithras, although the temple from which they come remains unlocated, and altars to Belatucadrus and the Mother Goddesses, whose temple, also unlocated, according to an inscription was restored because it had collapsed through age. The summer-house also contains a statue of a headless Fortuna, the gravestone of a soldier holding a writing-tablet case, probably symbolic of his office, and part of the gravestone of a woman; other inscriptions and sculpture are in Tullie House Museum, Carlisle. An altar found about 1690 is to the local god Maponus by four Germans, presumably soldiers, Durio, Ramio, Trupo and Lurio. Finally, the site has yielded an inscription Bedaltoedbos, possibly dating to the late fifth or sixth century, the name being allied to Belatucadros.

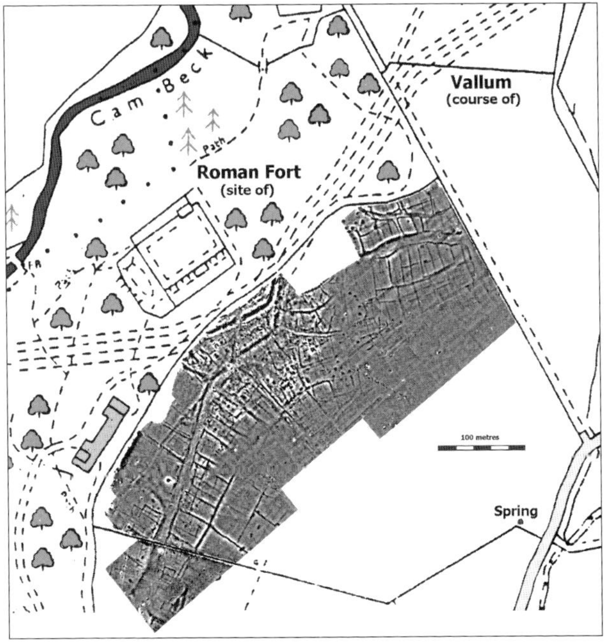

Geophysical survey of the Castlesteads area.

CASTLESTEADS TO STANWIX

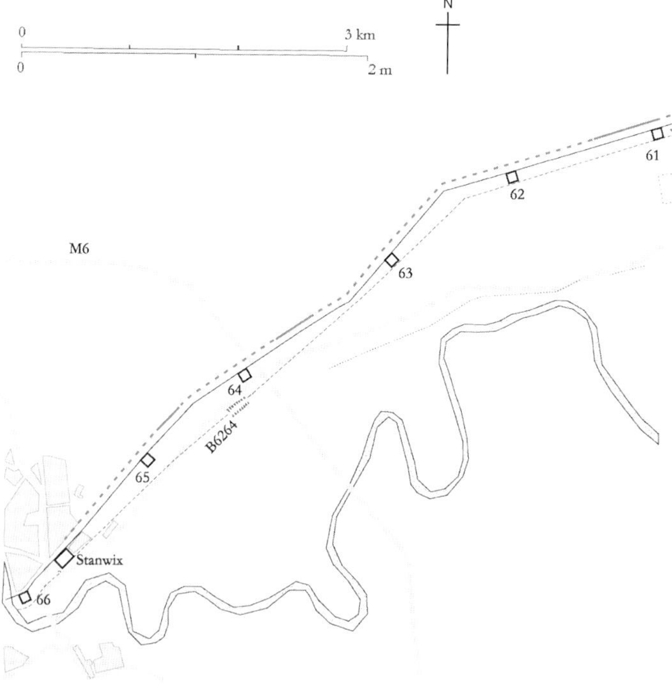

Returning to the Wall at the Cam Beck, the ditch is seen cutting deep into the red sandstone of the west bank. The ditch can be followed almost to Newtown. Cambeckhill farmhouse lies beside

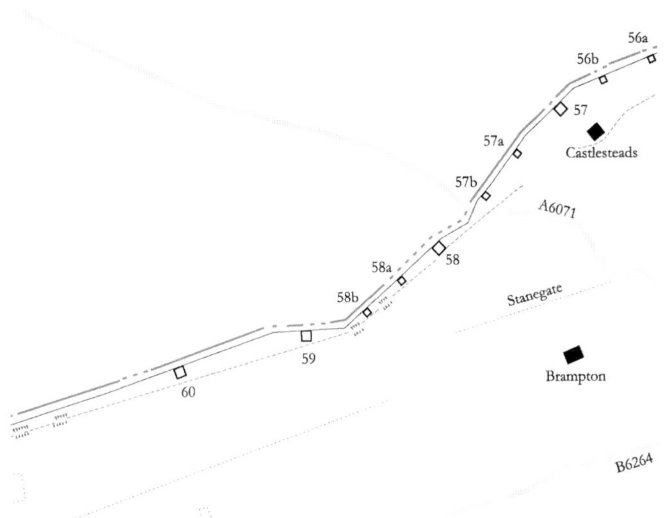

the site of **MC 57** (Cambeckhill). **T 57a** (Beck), beyond the farm of that name, was built of red sandstone. Finds included part of a samian bowl and a coin of Hadrian. The berm was narrow here but widened to the west. Headswood occupies a commanding situation above the valley. The course of the Vallum is not known from the Cam Beck, but it has been located south of Headswood.

About 200 m (200 yards) west of Newtown lies the site of **MC 58** (Newtown) just beyond the last house on the left. The Wall now follows a field-path south-west of White Flat, where the mound of the Wall intermittently helps to form the field boundary. Opposite Cumrenton the Vallum is visible with the marginal mound. An inscription of the Fourth Cohort of Lingones found in this Wall mile is on a thin slab and therefore may record work on the Vallum. Where the Wall bends northwards the ditches of both Wall and Vallum are visible, about 35 m (110 ft) apart. From a little beyond here an ancient

A stone recording work by the century of Iulius Tertullianus of the Second Legion found near MC 59. (203 x 254 mm)

drove road follows the line of the Wall, at the end of which tall hedges and cultivated fields make the work difficult to trace. 400 m (440 yards) beyond the bend is the site of **MC 59** (Old Wall). Old Wall farm contains many Roman stones. Beyond the farm the ditch is visible. High Strand, the traditional site of **MC 60**, in 1851 yielded an altar to Cocidius, erected by the Sixth Legion and now at Castlesteads.

At Bleatarn, the Wall runs a little north of the farmhouse, the Vallum immediately south of it. It has been recorded that the tarn contained many piles of wood in the early nineteenth century, and it is not impossible that the Wall was here carried over soft ground on pile foundations. The Vallum with both mounds and a south and north marginal mound, are visible. Excavations in 1895, 270 m (300 yards) east of the Baron's Dyke, located the site of a quarry used for building the Wall; it encroached slightly on the north mound of the Vallum. Wedge holes for working the stone were still visible.

On White Moss, a little further west, the Vallum ditch was found in 1894 to be defined by a mound on both sides of the ditch. In the marsh its steep sides would have been in danger of collapsing, and were therefore constructed by building up a mound on each side, above ground, instead of digging into the marsh, thus creating four parallel mounds. A section across the Military Way cut in the same year, revealed a gravelled road 6.7 m (22 ft) wide, with kerbs, axial rib and lateral ditches.

The measured position of **MC 61** (Wallhead) is a little east of Wallhead farm, west of which the Wall ditch is again in good condition. North of the farm, the substantial bank on the north side of the road includes the Wall, here about 2.44 m (8 ft) wide with both faces visible. Further west, in 1980 and 1981, only the north-facing stones of the Stone Wall, together with remains of a culvert, were found to survive on top of the demolished Turf Wall. The ditch was V-shaped, 6 m (20 ft) wide and at least 2.44 m (8 ft) deep. Turf had been stripped from below the counter-scarp bank, presumably for use in the Turf Wall. The Vallum mounds had been revetted in turf, and the area below again earlier stripped of turf. The Vallum ditch, 7.6 m (25 ft) wide at the top, 5.5 m (18 ft) at the bottom and 1.6m (5ft) deep, had been deliberately filled after only a little silt had accumulated.

About 540m (600 yards) east of Walby, where the modern road turns sharply north, traces of **MC 62** (Walby East) were once visible. Limited investigation in 1999 suggested the existence of a long-axis milecastle with an internal width of 16.54 m (54 ft 3 in).

In 1975 the Wall ditch and Vallum were located, 16.4 m (54 ft) and 36 m (110 ft) respectively north of their predicted lines. The ditch was found to be 10.5 m (34 ft 6 in) wide and 3.7 m (12 ft 2 in) deep, including a basal slot 1.4 m (4 ft 7 in) wide and 60 cm (2 ft) deep; the ditch appeared to have been deliberately infilled. The Vallum ditch was 5.6 m (18 ft 5 in) wide at the top, 3.8 m (12 ft 6 in) at the base and 1.80 m (6 ft) deep. After some

An altar to Cocidius by soldiers of the Sixth Legion found near MC 60. (457 x 305 mm)

silting, a 30-cm (1 ft) layer of whole turves on edge covered by 60 cm (2 ft) of clay was deposited. There was no evidence of recutting. Neither Vallum mounds nor Military Way were located.

At Walby an old track flanked by hedges follows the line of the Wall for over a mile with the northern hedge bank usually on the line of the Wall itself. A little west of the presumed site of **MC 63** (Walby West), the Vallum almost shaves the Wall without changing course. In 2000, the north face of the flagstones forming the foundations of the Stone Wall was located. A crack in the flagstones 24 cm (9½ in) behind the edge indicates the location of the north face of the Wall. Excavations in Brunstock Park in 1894 confirmed the flat-bottomed section of the Vallum ditch and located the Military Way. The ditch, bounded by fences, crosses the park. Just beyond the park, the M6 cuts across the Wall.

MC 64 (Drawdykes) was located in 1962, 110 m (360 ft) west of the motorway. It measured 14.63-15.24 by 17.83 m (48-50 by 58 ft 6 in), and is thus a short-axis milecastle. The walls were extensively robbed and their edges could not be defined. Beside the north gate were found traces of mortar adhering to the external wall of the milecastle. The gate, 3 m (9 ft 10 in) wide, had been completely blocked. A cobbled road passed through the milecastle and a similar surface was located west of the enclosure. Rubble on the west side of the interior may indicate the former existence of a building. Two fragments of samian were recovered. 19 m (63 ft) west of the milecastle, the Wall was crossed by a culvert. Here the flagged footings of the Stone Wall survived above the remains of the Turf Wall. The core of the Wall was mortared rubble. Immediately to the south of the Wall was an area of metalling extending at least 9 m (30 ft) to the south. In 1964 a fragment of a milestone inscribed *MP* was found about 25 m (80 ft) west of the milecastle.

To the south of the milecastle sits Drawdykes Castle. A tombstone from Stanwix, built into the south face of the castle, is

A tombstone from Stanwix reused at Drawdykes Castle. (965 mm square)

crowned by lions devouring human heads, a motif symbolic of death. Its inscription may be translated: "To the spirits of the departed (and) of Marcus Troianus Augustinus; his dearest wife, Aelia Ammillusima, saw to the making (of this tomb)". The Vallum is faintly visible west of Drawdykes Castle. It runs just south of the main road from Drawdykes to Whiteclosegate, where it crosses the road and bends slightly south.

The line of the Wall passes between the caravan park and the former army base, Hadrian's Camp. Traces of foundations, and some standing stonework, were uncovered here during the Second World War. In 1972 the opportunity was taken to examine a drainage trench immediately west of Centurion's Walk. The core of the Stone Wall, formed of clay and cobbles, survived, while the berm measured 7.31 m (24ft) wide and the ditch 8.53 m (28 ft). 4.88 m (16 ft) to the south, a spread of broken stone, about 4.27 m (14 ft) wide, was tentatively identified as the Military Way.

The line of the Wall, having run straight for 2 km (over a mile) from Wallfoot, turns on the crest within the former army camp and aims for Stanwix. The ditch is still visible. **MC 65** (Tarraby) was located by resistivity survey in 1976 130 m (133 yards) west of the hamlet of Tarraby and slightly west of its measured position. Trial excavation revealed the survival of two courses of footings. Nearby, an altar to Cocidius by the Second Legion was discovered covering a culvert through the Wall. Fragments of an ornate dedication to Mercury have also been found here.

From Tarraby, a footpath follows a hedge, on the Wall line, along Tarraby Lane which takes the crest of a low ridge; the Vallum lies to the south, at the bottom of the slope immediately to the north of the gardens of Whiteclosegate Road. Excavation in 1976, in advance of building, showed that the area between Wall and Vallum had been cultivated prior to the construction of the Wall, and the boundary ditches of fields were found. One ditch had been culverted under the Wall. In one area south of the Vallum, cultivation appeared to have continued through the second century. An unmetalled track or hollow-way was associated with the Turf Wall. The footings of the Stone Wall, two flags deep and 3.20 m (10 ft 6 in) wide, were of red sandstone with a core of sandstone rubble and sandy mortar. The berm was 11.5 m (37 ft 9 in) wide and the ditch 6.5 m (21 ft 3 in). Two phases of construction were identified in the upcast mound in 1993, though neither was dated. Investigation in 1975 failed to locate **T 65a** at its presumed site on the summit of Wall Knowe Hill. A cobbled road surface south of the Vallum could not be positively identified as Roman.

STANWIX (*UXELODUNUM/PETRIANA*)

The fort lay on a fine natural platform today occupied by Stanwix Church and Stanwix House, a little over 12.8 km (8 miles) from Castlesteads. To the south lies the steep bank falling to the River Eden, while the land falls somewhat more gently to the north. This position is reflected in its Roman name, *Uxelodunum*, "high fort". The name is given on the Rudge Cup, the Amiens Skillet and the Ilam Pan. However, the *Notitia*

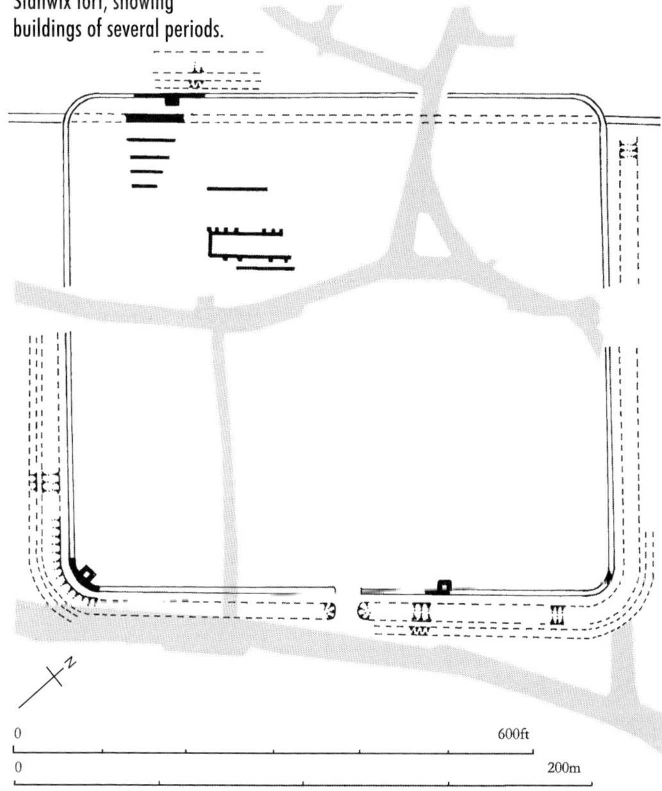

Stanwix fort, showing buildings of several periods.

Dignitatum offers the following entry: "Prefect of the *ala Petriana, Petriana*". This is probably a scribal error, the name of the unit being repeated as the fort name, though it is not impossible that the name of the fort changed, as is attested elsewhere.

The *ala Augusta Gallorum Petriana milliaria civium Romanorum bis torquata*, was named after one of its prefects, T Pomponius Petra. It probably came to Britain with the governor Petillius Cerialis in 70/1. The tombstone of a standard bearer of the regiment now in Hexham Abbey suggests that it was based at Corbridge. By 98 its soldiers had won a block grant of Roman citizenship for gallantry in action. It later acquired other military decorations, being awarded two *torques* (ornamental necklaces). A building inscription found at Carlisle records only one *torque* so there were presumably two separate awards made. Also in Trajan's reign it was raised in size from 500 to 1000 (actually probably either 720 or 768) men. It presumably gained its decorations under Domitian or Trajan, probably during the wars against Dacia (modern Romania). The regiment may have been based at Old Penrith, perhaps during Hadrian's reign.

The size of the fort at Stanwix reflects the strength of the unit. It measured 185 by 215 m (609 by 700 ft) and covered 3.96 ha (9.79 acres). Little is known about the fort apart from its defences. The south-west angle tower, south wall and east wall were traced in 1940, with the north wall being located in 1984. This was uncovered in the grounds of the Cumbria Park Hotel. A length of wall was subsequently left exposed for public viewing and the line of the wall marked out by setts; the exposed portion of wall lies close to the north-west corner of the fort. This and the south-west corner, a low rise in the churchyard, are the only remains visible today. Brampton Road lies more-or-less on the line of the south defences, with Well Lane marking the east defences. The northern end of Romanby Close lies approximately at the north-east corner of the fort.

The northern defences consisted of a stone wall with a clay rampart backing, fronted by two ditches; an interval tower was also found. The north wall was 1.73 m (5 ft 8 in) wide with a chamfered base course above the footings on the north side; the rampart backing was at least 3.5 m (11 ft 6 in) wide. To the south of the tower lay a feature tentatively identified as an oven. The fort appears to be an addition to the Wall which was located in 1932-4 a little to the south of the north fort wall, with the north lip of its ditch found in 1984 to lie under the interval tower. A few metres further south, a turf deposit, probably a rampart, was recorded in 1997. No other trace has been discovered at Stanwix of a turf-and-timber fort, but the known fort is clearly later than the replacement of the Turf Wall in stone. The sequence is therefore: Turf Wall with presumed turf-and-timber fort; replacement of Turf Wall by Stone Wall; stone fort projecting beyond the Stone Wall. The small amount of pottery recovered from the rampart backing of the stone fort dates to the second century. It may be surmised that the *ala Petriana* was not the first unit to be based

Part of a cavalryman's tombstone from Stanwix. (889 x 482 mm)

here, but took up residence, perhaps in the later second century, when a new, and larger, fort was erected for it. The tombstone of a cavalryman, now in Tullie House Museum, suggests that the unit here in the Hadrianic period may have been a 500-strong cavalry regiment.

The causeway over the south ditch was located beside Brampton Road in 1933. This was placed centrally in the southern defences, but this in itself gives little indication of the internal arrangements, which might have been unusual in such a large fort. Little is known of the interior buildings. A series of four parallel walls, possibly representing two barrack-blocks and lying towards the north fort wall, were examined in the school yard in 1934: they were associated with fourth-century pottery. A large granary was located further south in 1940.

Finds of the early to mid-Antonine period are scarce, suggesting abandonment of the fort during the occupation of the Antonine Wall. Coins found on the site of the former Miles Macinnes Hall on Scotland Road during work there in 1986 indicate reoccupation later in the second century and probably relate to the presence of the *ala Petriana*. The fort has yielded little material dating to the third and fourth centuries, though a layer containing late-fourth-century pottery was overlain by timber buildings. An altar bears the consular date of 167 while a building inscription of the Sixth Legion dates to the reign of the Emperor Gordian III (238-44). There are two different sculptures of Victory.

The elucidation of the succession of forts helps understanding of the line of the **Vallum**. In 1932-34 the Vallum was traced from the east heading for the south-east corner of the fort. Beyond the fort's south-west corner, immediately south of the junction of Brampton Road and Scotland Road, the Vallum turned sharply north as if it was returning to its normal line after diverging round the fort. The proximity of the Vallum to the southern defences of the fort, which barely left room for the north mound, can be explained if it related to the earlier,

Medallion, found about 1850, bearing a portrait of Agrippina, mother of the Emperor Caligula, probably made in 39, and presumably the heirloom of an officer based at Stanwix. (46 mm diameter)

smaller fort. A causeway, located in Rickerby Park and at least 12 m (40 ft) wide, may be an original crossing relating to this fort.

A **civil settlement** lay to the west of the fort where deep deposits and the remains of buildings have been recorded. East of the fort, at Tarraby Lane and on the north side of Brampton Road, some evidence was found in 1984 and 1998 for timber buildings. It may be expected that the presence of a large unit in the fort would have led to the existence of an extensive civil settlement. More unusually, an extensive clay platform up to 50 cm (1 ft 8 in) thick and covering perhaps 3.15 ha (7.5 acres) was recorded east of the fort in 1996: it was interpreted as an exercise ground.

At King's Meadow, south of the fort, a quantity of Roman objects was found in 1930, including brooches and other personal ornaments, mountings for cavalrymen's uniform and horses, and odds and ends of metal, probably of mid-second-century date. Once interpreted as the contents of a bronze-founder's workshop, it has since been suggested that they may have formed a votive deposit. Two items are marked with their owner's name and the troop to which he belonged.

Cremation burials were found north-east of the fort, and south of the Vallum at Whiteclosegate in 1936, where urns were discovered in 1872, indicating the location of a cemetery.

STANWIX TO BURGH-BY-SANDS

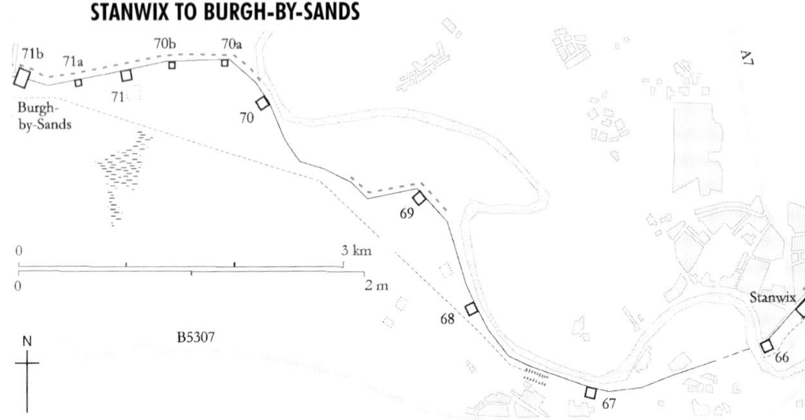

Just beyond the north-west angle of the fort the modern road follows the line of the Roman road north. Road metalling up to 1 m (3 ft) deep was found in 1986 beside Scotland Road indicating that the line had shifted slightly to the west since Roman times. At the point where the road passed through the Wall there was probably a gateway, as at Portgate on Dere Street, though no trace has been recorded. To the south, the road crossed the River Eden into Carlisle. Here some stones, including part of a column base, have been found.

The Wall continued in a straight line, with its line marked by plaques on the front of 1 Church Terrace and 19/21 Scotland Road stating "Roman Wall; beneath this spot lie the foundations of Hadrian's Wall. Built 126 A.D.", to the edge of the bluffs above the River Eden where a stone pillar beside the path opposite Aughton House on Cavendish Terrace records "Roman Wall. Site of 1886"; the Vallum lies parallel to the south. The scarp above Hyssop Holme Well has been eroded since Roman times. On its summit is the measured position of **MC 66** (Stanwix Bank). Pennant in 1772 noted here the "vestiges of some dykes describing a small square, the site of a fort to defend the pass".

The Wall crossed the Eden by a bridge. Camden recorded "within the chanell of the river, mighty stones, the remaines thereof", but whether this was the Wall bridge is another matter. When the river at the junction of the Eden and the Cardew was dredged in 1951, some 80-90 sandstone blocks were recorded, including cut-water pieces, stones with sockets for butterfly cramps, and a slab inscribed by "the century of Vesnius Victor". About 100 stones are displayed amongst the trees in an enclosure 100 m (100 yards) east of the confluence of the Cardew and Eden.

The Wall then ran west-south-westwards across the sewage works, where it was found in 1854, excavated in 1886 and marked with stone pillars, and finally exposed again in 1931, when a considerable stretch of its foundation was removed to the grounds of Tullie House. 2.69 m (8 ft 10 in) wide, the foundation consisted of a layer of rough flags bedded in clay laid on the gravel subsoil. Only two facing stones survived. At the south end of the abandoned railway bridge Roman coins have been found, near the presumed site of **MC 67** (Stainton).

Wall and Vallum draw together again on the high ground called Davidson's Banks and run along the south bank of the river. The Wall was so close to the cliff edge that the ditch may not have been provided. A length of **Vallum** survives between the pylons and four or five gaps, spaced at the usual intervals of 41 m (45 yards), have been recorded in its north mound. Just beyond the stream and east of the measured position of **MC 68** (Boomby Gill) the two works diverge and the Wall keeps to the riverbank as far as Grinsdale, while the Vallum aims straight for Kirkandrews. Between Wall and Vallum, at **Boomby Lane**, aerial photography has revealed two overlapping marching camps. South of the Vallum are two more camps, also no longer visible on the ground, at **Nowtler Hill**, the larger 0.5 ha (1.2 acres), and the other about half the size.

At Grinsdale the Wall leaves the river and occupies the bluffs that overlook the river flats. The hollow on the line of the Wall ditch between the stream and the new houses on the south-east edge of the village of Grinsdale is the result of modern activity. The ditch is visible to the west of the village, on top of the ridge beyond the trees and immediately beyond the presumed site of **MC 69** (Sourmilk Bridge), which limited geophysical survey and trenching in 2000 failed to locate. At Doodle Beck, MacLauchlan noted a greater quantity of foundation stones than usual, although what structure they might have related to is uncertain: a bridge or a turret perhaps.

At Kirkandrews the Wall swings back towards the river and at Kirksteads, almost 2 km (1 mile) to the south, an altar was found in 1803 dedicated by "Lucius Iunius Victorinus Flavius Caelianus, commander of the Victorious, Dutiful and Loyal Sixth Legion, on account of the successful operations beyond the Wall (*ob res trans vallum prospere gestas*)". It is now in Tullie House Museum, Carlisle.

From Kirkandrews the Vallum runs straight, by Monkhill and Wormanby, to Burgh-by-Sands, lying south of the modern road as far as Monkhill and then north of it, until the point where the road crosses the disused railway beyond Wormanby.

The measured position of **MC 70** (Braelees) lies where the Wall meets the river north-west of Kirkandrews; investigations in 2000 failed to locate it. The ditch, absent since Doodle Beck, reappears at Monkhill Beck, where the Wall, also visible, swings

Altar found at Kirksteads
(1.137 m high)

away from the river. In a wall at Beaumont, at the road junction and diagonally opposite the church, is part of a building-stone of the fifth cohort of the Twentieth Legion, fished out of the Eden in a salmon net in the nineteenth century. In 1934, an altar was found during demolition work dedicated to Jupiter and the Genius of the unit of Aurelian Moors; it probably originated in Burgh. In the churchyard at Beaumont the Wall was found in 1928 to be about 2.44 m (8 ft) wide, its flag footing set upon a foundation of clay and cobbles a foot deep which was probably the base of the Turf Wall. The stones used for the core came from Stonepot Scar, north of the Solway.

The track starting just north of the church follows the line of the ditch. At the gate into the second field to the south a hollow lies on the line of the ditch. **MC 71** (Wormanby) was located in 1960, close to the north-east corner of the large field where the track ends and the line of trees start. Its west and south walls were found and the road running through it. In 2000, the east wall was located. Almost nothing of the stone milecastle survived, but the bottom courses of the turf milecastle were identified. Immediately south of the milecastle part of a camp, **Beaumont**, has been revealed by aerial photography.

In 1922 the ditch could still be seen on the eastern slope of the valley of the Powburgh Beck. The Military Way lies 60 m (65 yards) behind the Wall and traces of a culvert were seen here on the right bank of the beck in 1922. To the west of the stream, in the area formerly known as Speer-garth-holes, it was reported in 1886 that the foundations of the Wall lay upon great beams of black oak. Here, in 1950, the site of the fortified manor-house of Burgh-by-Sands was examined. Both ditch, packed with large boulders to support the tower, and the foundations of the Wall at Intermediate gauge, were found to lie below the medieval building. The Wall was noted in the modern road in 1877 by the artist D. Mossman as making a sharp turn just before reaching the fort at Burgh, so as to meet the east wall at close to a right-angle.

BURGH-BY-SANDS (*ABALLAVA*)

Topography dictated the position of this fort. It sits on a low hill, which ought to lie on the site of **T 71b**, only 9.2 km (5¾ miles) from Stanwix. There was an important crossing of the Solway at Burgh; this is where Edward I hoped to cross in 1307 though he died before being able to invade Scotland again. The existence of this crossing may have influenced the siting of the Roman fort here.

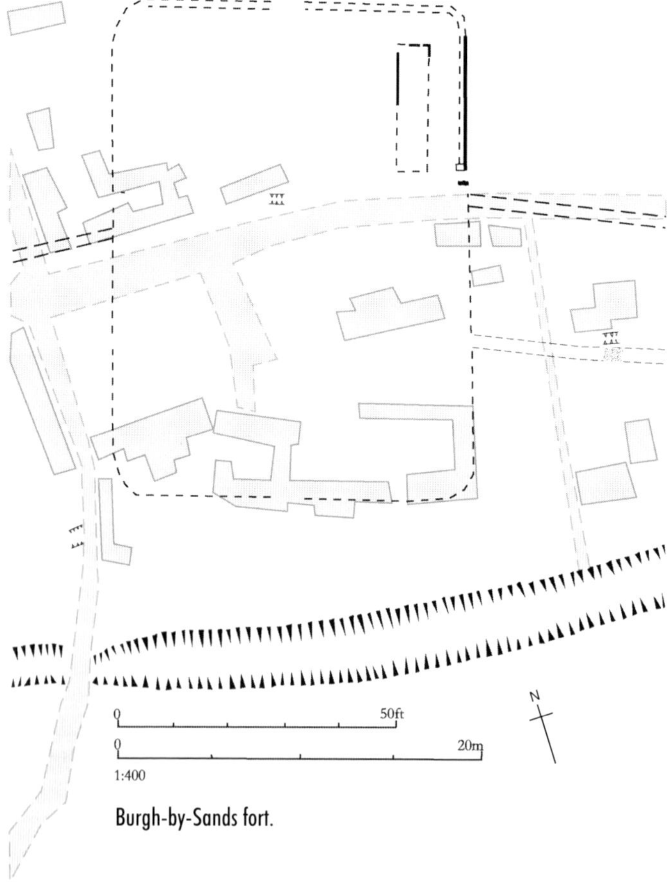

Burgh-by-Sands fort.

The fort is named on both the Rudge Cup and the Amiens Skillet, but, rather surprisingly, does not appear on the Ilam Pan. The significance of this is not clear; the name may have been omitted in error or because the fort was not occupied. *Aballava*, means "apple" but perhaps rather than referring to one, possibly sacred, tree, it meant "orchard". The First Nervan Cohort of Germans dedicated an altar to Jupiter, probably in the second century. An altar found at Beaumont in 1934 and dedicated to Jupiter and the Genius of the unit of Aurelian Moors, Valerianus' and Gallienus' Own, dated from 253 to 258. This is the regiment recorded here in the *Notitia Dignitatum*. The altar was dedicated by Caelius Vibianus, who is described as being tribune of a cohort - perhaps the Nervan Cohort - and commander of the unit of Moors. In 241 a cavalry unit of Frisians of Aballava was recorded on an altar at Papcastle. The unit may have been based earlier at Burgh, incorporating the fort name into its title; more likely an officer, however, is recording his transfer from the unit at Papcastle to that at Burgh.

The **fort** lies on the highest ground, at the east end of the village, its approximate location being readily discernible in the rise and fall of the modern road over the east rampart and ditch and the west rampart and ditch. The church sits within the south-east corner of the fort and is partly built of Roman stones, some of which are readily identifiable from their distinctive diamond-shaped tooling. The modern road lies on the line of the Wall.

Burgh is one of the least explored and understood of all the forts on the Wall. Although earlier visitors presumed a fort here, no remains were visible. Excavations north of the church in 1922, when a new burial ground was formed, resulted in the location of the east wall, 1.83 - 2.13 m (6 - 7 ft) thick, with an earth backing, and the east gate of the fort, with a road leading out. Within the fort, stone buildings running north-south were interpreted as barrack-blocks. The Roman levels and buildings

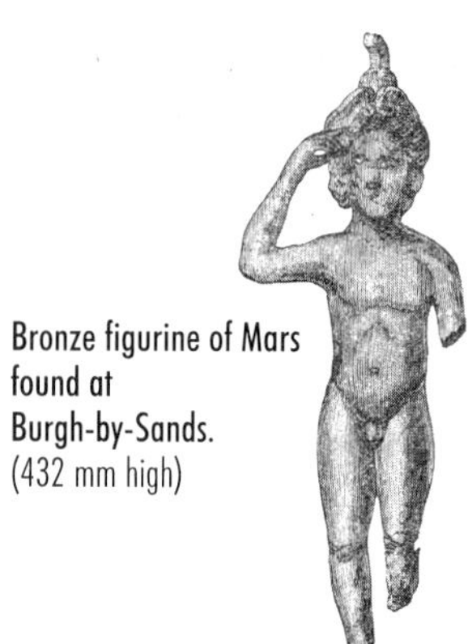

Bronze figurine of Mars found at Burgh-by-Sands. (432 mm high)

were all badly preserved, though pottery of the second to fourth centuries was recovered. The sketch plan of the site prepared on the basis of these discoveries suggests a fort measuring 156 m (520 ft) north-south by 125 m (410 ft) east-west, giving an area of about 2.04 ha (nearly 5 acres).

In 1993, an excavation to the east of Demesne Farm, in the centre of the fort, revealed that a ditch, 6 m (20 ft) wide and 2.20 m (7 ft) deep and running west-east, passed under the fort; it was presumably the Wall ditch. It had been filled in and recut apparently leaving a 4 m (13 ft) causeway across it. Following further backfilling, which included turves, a stone building was erected on the site.

Geophysical survey north of the Wall and east of the graveyard extension has revealed a linear feature running from the Wall to the north-east corner of the fort, possibly representing a realignment of Hadrian's Wall as at Birdoswald. Within the triangle formed by this ditch and the Wall, a road approached the east gate of the fort, with a side road leading north. Hearths have also been located in this area, together with second- and third-century pottery. In 1976 a fragmentary sculpture of a *genius* pouring a libation onto an altar was found in this area.

Excavations on several occasions between 1978 and 2002 south and east of the fort has led to the discovery of buildings, presumably of the **civil settlement**. Trenching in the back garden of the vicarage south of the Wall and east of the fort in 1980 and 1982 led to the discovery of several superimposed timber and stone buildings dating from the mid-third to the early fourth century and fronting onto a major east-west road, perhaps the Military Way. Quantities of slag and charcoal indicated metal-working activities. Pottery included a few fragments of Frisian ware of the type found at Housesteads and Birdoswald: a unit of Frisians may have been at Burgh in the third century. South of the former canal and, we may presume, the Vallum, timber buildings, probably divided by gullies forming property boundaries, have been excavated. In one area, occupation was confined to the second century, though close by it continued into the fourth century.

The **bath-house**, south of the fort, was destroyed in making the canal, itself replaced by the railway line, now also abandoned. Further south, the tombstone of a Dacian tribesman may indicate the location of the cemetery. Three altars to the god Belatucadrus are known from the fort, and one to the goddess Latis.

The line of the **Vallum** is not securely known. In 1978, a ditch about 6 m (20 ft) wide with steep sides was located on the presumed line of the Vallum about 100 m south of the cross-roads immediately west of the fort. In 1980, in the rear garden of the former vicarage, a 5.50 m (18 ft) wide ditch was located, aligned on the Wall ditch to the east of the fort; this cannot be fitted into any known interpretation of the remains.

About 1 km (⅔ mile) south of the village, on a low ridge, and astride the modern road to Moorhouse, sits a rectangular enclosure with a single ditch initially recognised through aerial photography. It is divided into two parts by a cross-ditch, though whether the site was reduced or extended is not clear. The large enclosure covers 2.83 ha (7 acres), the smaller about

1.49 ha (3.7 acres). Excavation has revealed the post-pits of a timber tower with early-second-century pottery and timber buildings; aerial photography also suggests the existence of a stone headquarters building and a granary. A fragment of a stone building was also found in the eastern part of the large enclosure. It has been argued that the remains represent a fort of the early Hadrianic period.

To its north-west lay another rectangular enclosure, also found from the air in 1977. It lay immediately to the south-west of Hill Farm at the west end of Burgh-by-Sands. Measuring 184 by 113 m (600 by 370 ft), it covered 2.07 ha (5.13 acres), but was enlarged to 3.35 ha (8.4 acres) by increasing its length to 290 m (880 ft). Pottery again indicated occupation in the first half of the second century.

The recent excavations have failed to clarify the location, size and date of the Wall fort at Burgh. Hadrianic pottery from the area south of the fort suggests the existence of a contemporary military installation, but this has not been found. The stone fort lay astride the Wall, but the Wall ditch was infilled and re-cut before it was constructed. It is possible that the fort to the south of the Wall at Moorhouse was retained for some time before being succeeded by a replacement astride the Wall. This might account for the absence of the name *Aballava* on the Ilam Pan and the fact that the Vallum appears to run underneath the fort.

Altar to the local god Belatucadrus, found in 1702 to the south-west of Burgh-by-Sands.
(152 x 101 mm)

BURGH-BY-SANDS TO DRUMBURGH

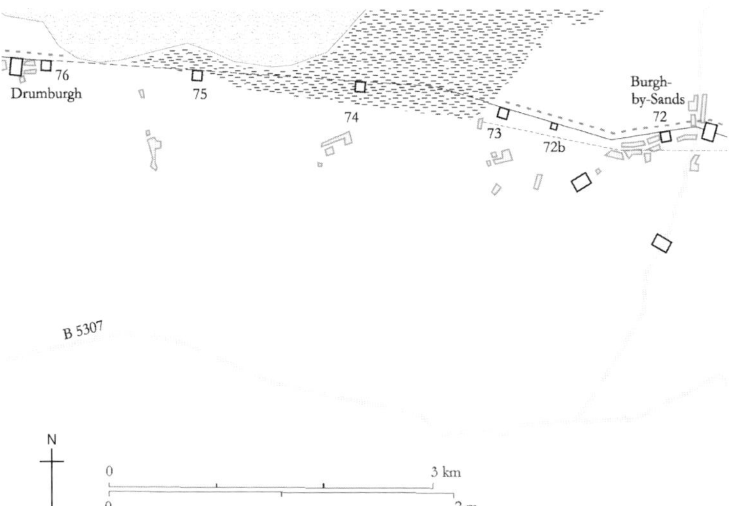

The line of the Wall changed direction at the fort. Approaching from a little south of east, it crossed the fort site, where the ditch has been located and then turned to run slightly south of west for a quarter of a mile to the site of **MC 72** (Fauld Farm), which is crossed by the access road immediately west of Fullwood House. The north and west walls of the stone milecastle were located in 1960, robbed to their foundations. Further work took place in 1989. This resulted in the discovery that the walls of the turf milecastle had wide cobble cheeks creating a base 6 m (19 ft 8 in) wide. The east wall of the stone milecastle was found, allowing the width to be determined as 18.94 m (62 ft 2 in). The rebuilding of the milecastle in stone was undated. The north wall lay only 36 cm (1 ft 2 in) behind the north side of the base of the turf rampart, while the east and west walls were placed in the centre of the demolished turf work. The footings of the north wall were 2.80 m (9 ft 2 in) wide, with the wall itself 2.50 m (8 ft 2 in) across, while the footings of the east wall were 2.68 m (8 ft 9 in) wide and the wall 2.20 m (7 ft 3 in). The east wall appeared to butt against the north wall, indicating the building sequence.

At the west end of the village, shortly before the road bends to the left, a lane leads north to the Sewage Works. Beside the ditch, a cobble foundation 5.65 - 5.8 m (18 ft 6 in - 19 ft) wide, was found under the Turf Wall in 1986, but not in an excavation trench 22 m (70 ft) to the west. The measured position of **T 72a** (West End) lies between the two trenches excavated in 1986. At this location two sherds of pottery of Hadrianic or later date were found in 1960. There was no trace of an underlying buried soil below the Turf Wall, indicating that the turf had been first stripped. The uncohesive nature of the turf blocks used in the rampart suggests that they had been cut from land which had been ploughed but then reverted to grassland. The Stone Wall was 2.60 m (8 ft 6 in) across the footings and narrowed to 2.44 m (8 ft) above the offset. The facing stones were sandstone, both red and yellow, while broken stones, glacial erratics and stone from the shore, were used in the core. Two culverts, 6.90 m (22 ft 7 in) apart, passed through the Stone Wall. The north face of the Stone Wall lay 1.22 m (4 ft) behind the front of the Turf Wall. The berm here was 11 m (36 ft) wide. The Vallum ditch was 6 m (19 ft 8 in) wide, while a layer of sand and cobbles on the north berm may have been a path.

At the lane, the Wall turns and runs west-north-westward. **T 72b** (Rindle Hill) was identified in 1948 at the north-east corner of the field north of Vallum House. It was a Turf Wall turret, with the front and back walls thicker than the side walls. The walls, of whitish-grey sandstone, were erected on two courses of clay and cobble foundations. The turret projected 1.22 m (3 ft 11 in) north of the Stone Wall, which was of red sandstone placed directly on the demolished Turf Wall. In the same year, the south face of the Wall was traced almost to **MC 73** (Dykesfield). On Watch Hill, about halfway between the turret and the milecastle, in 1934 the Stone Wall, 2.65 m (8 ft 8½ in) wide, was

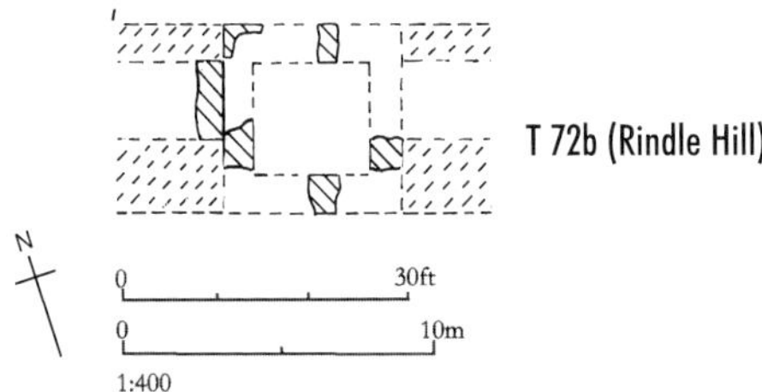

T 72b (Rindle Hill).

found to retain only one course of the south face standing on a flag footing. The berm was abnormally wide because the Stone Wall had been erected just behind the levelled Turf Wall and not on top of it; the original berm of 1.83 - 2.44 m (6 - 8 ft) had been widened to 9 m (30 ft). Geophysical survey at the milecastle in 2002 suggested this arrangement continued at least to this point.

MC 73 was located in 1948. It measured 19.05 by 18.53 m (62 ft 6 in by 60 ft 8 in) within walls 2.03 m (6 ft 8 in) thick. The geophysical survey confirmed the location of the milecastle and offered internal dimensions of 19.25 m (63 ft) by 18 m (59 ft). The existence of both stone and timber internal buildings and a hearth(s) were indicated, and a possible causeway over the Wall ditch. Anomalies outside the milecastle suggest the existence of an enclosure lying to the east of the milecastle abutting the south face of the Wall, with two further enclosures to the west, one possibly containing stone buildings.

The **Vallum** has been traced from the low ground behind the Greyhound Inn at Burgh-by-Sands to the west end of the village, and it then runs, faintly visible, through the fields to Dykesfield, about 50 m (160 ft) north of the modern road. Geophysical survey in 2002 placed the Vallum 45 m (147 ft) south of its course on the OS maps.

At Dykesfield the modern road descends into the marshes. Here the Wall now ends and it has been assumed that it crossed the marsh and has since been lost, presumably owing to post-Roman coastal erosion. However, a strong anomaly on the headland at the end of the Wall led the geophysical surveyors to propose that the Wall ended here and had never been constructed across the marsh. If the Wall did continue across the marsh, it will have turned slightly south, probably at the site of **T 73a**, to head for Drumburgh. **MC 74** (Burgh Marsh) and **MC 75** (Easton) are now lost without trace.

The Wall emerges east of Drumburgh village. The disused railway swings north and just beyond, in the corner of the field, is the site of **MC 76** (Drumburgh). Here the Wall is running almost due west, and excavation in 1899 traced it up the hill to the fort. It measured 2.95 m (9 ft 7 in) across the footings. Further investigation in 1947 revealed poor foundations and cracking of the footing-flags along the line of the face of the Wall. The lowest courses of the Turf Wall had been left to act as a base for the Stone Wall which was placed 1.02 m (3 ft 4 in) behind the front of the rampart. The berm and ditch were here found to be some 7.31 m (24 ft) wide and 8.84 m (29 ft) wide respectively.

The Ilam Pan, also known as the Staffordshire Moorlands Pan, was found in 2003. It names four forts in the western sector of the Wall: *Mais*, *Coggabata*, *Uxelodunum* and *Cammoglanna*, that is Bowness-on-Solway, Drumburgh, Stanwix and Castlesteads. The first two names are visible on this view of the pan. (actual size)

DRUMBURGH (*CONGABATA*)

Drumburgh occupies a bold knoll with excellent outlook over the flatter lands to east and west and the Solway shore to the north. A ford crosses the Solway at this point. The *Notitia Dignitatum* placed the Second Cohort of Lingones here at *Congavata*. The Ilam Pan gives the name as *Coggabata*. Perhaps the correct rendition is neither, but *Congabata*. This may mean "dish-like" and is perhaps a reference to the bold knoll on which the fort sits, which might be seen as an upturned dish.

The fort lies towards the north-west corner of the modern village, its location largely occupied by Drumburgh House,

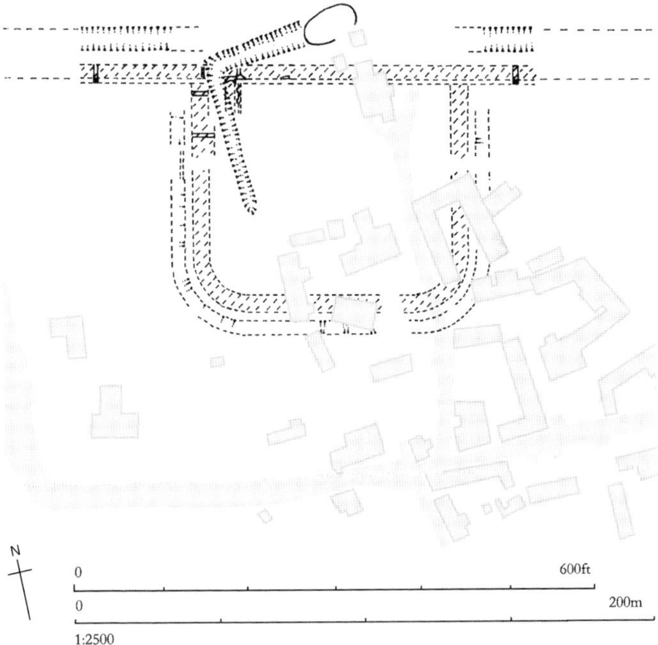

Drumburgh fort showing the turf and stone phases.

Sculpture of the godess Victory found near Drumburgh in the nineteenth century. (425 mm high)

Grange Farm and their attendant grounds. It was examined in 1899 and again in 1947, but, largely owing to the modern buildings, the work was small-scale.

The **first fort** on the site related to the Turf Wall. It measured 82.3 by 96.3 m (270 by 316 ft) and covered 0.8 ha (1.96 acres). It was thus the smallest fort on the Wall. The west rampart was located in 1947, 5.79 m (19 ft) thick, and formed of grey clay; similar grey clay was found in the appropriate position for the east rampart. Such material is available on the foreshore and from the adjacent marshland. The Turf Wall immediately to east and west of the fort was of normal turf construction. Beyond the rampart lay a single ditch, 4.57 m (15 ft) wide, broken for causeways outside the west and south gates. The road leaving the former was crossed by a palisade trench 76 cm (2 ft 6 in) wide and over 60 cm (2 ft) deep. In the centre of the south defences, the ditch had been filled with tightly-packed whitish-grey clay before much silt had been allowed to accumulate in the bottom. Immediately north of the west gate, a thickening of the rampart may indicate the position of an *ascensus* or stairway-ramp.

Little is known of the **stone fort**. In 1899 the north and west walls were located at the north-west corner. The west wall lay inside the turf rampart and was bonded with the Stone Wall. Inside the north-west angle, and leaving no room for an earthen backing nor an *intervallum* space, lay a granary. The Roman remains here were damaged by the ditch bounding the north side of the medieval grange of Drumburgh, while robbing from medieval times onward has removed buildings and foundations. The latest coin from the fort dates to 350-360, while pottery indicates continuing occupation into the last decades of the fourth century. An undated inscription found at Drumburgh in 1859 records work by Vindomorucus.

The size of the fort as known precludes it being occupied by a complete unit. The position of the south gate suggests that the fort faced east, and, not surprisingly, the internal layout, in so far as we know anything, was unusual. It has been suggested that the plan recovered through excavations reflects only part of an original fort which lay astride the Wall. While only further excavation can test this hypothesis, it is worth noting that topography would allow such a proposal.

Small red sandstone blocks bearing evidence of Roman tooling were found on the foreshore, suggesting that a harbour may have lain here.

Drumburgh Castle, south of the village street, is a fine old Cumbrian manor-house. It was fortified in 1307 by Robert le Brun, but the present house was built by Thomas, Lord Dacre, under Henry VIII. Leland noted that at "Drumbuygh the lord Dakers father builded upon old ruines a prey pyle for defens on the contery ... The stones of the Pict Wal were pulled down to build Drumuygh. For the Wal ys very nere yt." The house is in fact almost entirely built of Roman stones.

A building stone recording work by Vindomorucus at Drumburgh.
(330 x 432 mm)

DRUMBURGH TO BOWNESS-ON-SOLWAY

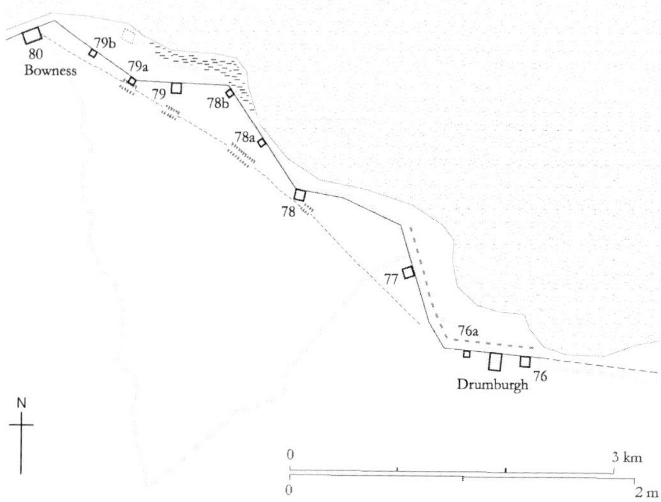

A slight rise betrays the line of the Wall in the field to the west of Sea View on the western boundary of the village. In 1945 the Vallum was located to the south. **T 76a** (Drumburgh) was located 11.89 m (39 ft) east of the garden gate south of the former Drumburgh school-house in 1948. At the school the road turns north-west, while the Wall goes straight on across the field, and then itself turns sharply north, to meet the road again at the next bend. Beyond the disused railway the road broadly follows the Wall as far as Port Carlisle. From the point that the Wall reaches the Solway coast, its ditch is omitted.

MC 77 (Raven Bank) was sought in 1973 just south of the Glasson road-junction, but not found. The Stone Wall was sectioned and the rubble and clay foundations recorded as 2.55 m (8 ft 4 in) wide, with one course of red sandstone surviving. Almost 4.88 m (16 ft) to the north a patch of turf was found, about 3 m (10 ft) wide and 25 cm (10 in) thick, laid directly on the red clay subsoil.

When the canal was dug, in whose bed the Port Carlisle railway later ran, the foundations of the Wall were found to lie on piles. Some of the piling was used for the jetty at Port Carlisle and the chair of the president of the Society of Antiquaries of Newcastle upon Tyne was also made of it.

The line of the **Vallum** is taken by a deep drain from the sharp bend in the road west of Drumburgh to Glasson. From Glasson, the Vallum runs just east of the track as far as the entrance to the Glendale Caravan Park, in the field to the south of which the Vallum ditch is visible. The Vallum is also visible running along the west side of the field to the north of Kirkland Farm. Excavation in 1934 demonstrated that it had the normal proportions with the south mound retained by a pair of turf-built kerbs.

MC 78 (Kirkland) was identified in 1934 and re-examined in 2000. Its size can only be determined approximately at 25 by 20 m (80 by 66 ft) externally as no wall faces survived. The corners were square on the inside. The west wall measured 2.79 m (9 ft 2 in) across the foundations, with some of the internal facing stones surviving beyond the sandstone and clay core. A layer of clay about 30 cm (1 ft) thick was laid across the interior of the milecastle, overlapping the lowest course of its walls. The foundations of the Wall are 2.86 m (9 ft 4½ in) wide but the flags do not extend across the whole width, leaving a gap of about 90 cm (3 ft) in the centre. The lack of foundations caused the core to sink and tip up the external flags. The 1934 excavations also demonstrated that there was no ditch here.

T 78a (Kirkland) was located in 1948, 30 m (100 ft) north-west of the west corner of Kirkland Farm in the south hedge of the road. At the beck south-east of Port Carlisle traces of the Military Way have been seen. Over the door of Hesket House at the west end of Port Carlisle is a fragmentary altar retaining the words *Matribus suis milite(s)*, dedicated to the Mother Goddesses by a contingent of soldiers. A little to the east, beside the shore, there was formerly a mound called Fisher's

Altar to the Mother Goddesses.
(254 mm high)

Cross, in which Roman coins have been found. Here the Wall reached the coast and turned sharply westwards. From Port Carlisle to Bowness, Wall and modern road separate, the former lying south of the road. Field boundaries mark the line of the Wall most of the way to Bowness. Excavation in 1930 revealed the foundations 2.82 m (9 ft 3 in) wide. Here the Wall had been built upon a substantial sea-bank with no ditch in front. A section of the Wall was obtained 33.50 m (110 ft) east of MC 79. It was 2.62 m (8 ft 7 in) wide on foundations 2.79 m (9 ft 2 in) in width. The lowest course was pointed with inferior mortar, but the core above this course was set in hard white mortar, generally associated with the Severan period.

MC 79 (Solway House) sits on slightly elevated ground immediately to the east of the red barn. It was excavated in 1949, and found to have been erected on a platform of alternate layers of gravel and turf, perhaps up to 1.8 m (6 ft) thick. In its Turf Wall phase the milecastle had been a short-axis type, measuring 12.34 by 14.71 m (40 ft 6 in by 48 ft 3 in), with square interior corners like MC 78. A staircase-ramp sat in the south-eastern corner. Two posts of the south gateway survived, giving a width of just under 3 m (10 ft). No building was found in the eastern portion of the interior, just cooking hearths, four in number. The Turf Wall milecastle was found to have been thoroughly demolished when replaced in stone. The stone replacement measured 17.53 m (57 ft 6 in) square, and was thus unique in plan. The gateways would have been of type II or III on the Hadrianic Stone Wall, but only the solid cobble foundations of the piers remained. The north wall was 2.59 m (8 ft 6 in) wide and the other walls 2.46 m (8 ft 1 in). A pit beside the north gate yielded over 100 dressed stones, including 10 fragments of chamfered plinth, associated with a third-century cooking pot. Perhaps at this time the gate was reduced to a postern, and the tower demolished. A timber building, 12.80 by 3.35 m (42 by 11 ft), had stood in the eastern area in this period. In the north-east corner lay a hearth, which used a former stone gaming board as its floor in one phase. A more unusual find was the lead casing of a plumb-bob.

Evidence relating to the date of the replacement of the original milecastle was recovered. Hadrianic-Antonine pottery types were found in the earliest level, showing that the early structure had continued throughout the reign of Hadrian.

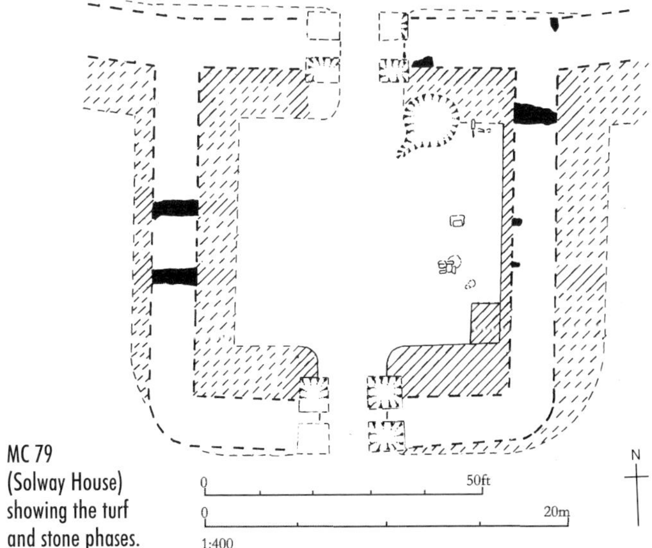

MC 79 (Solway House) showing the turf and stone phases.

Pottery contemporary with the construction of the Antonine Wall was absent, suggesting rebuilding after the re-occupation of Hadrian's Wall about 160. This is still the best dating evidence for the rebuilding of the western part of the Turf Wall in stone. Third-century pottery, a single sherd from an early-fourth-century vessel and a coin of the Emperor Constantius I (305-6) were also found. Artefacts included a spearhead.

On leaving the milecastle, the Wall bends slightly north. When first seen here by Bruce, it was several feet high and gunpowder had to be used to bring it down. Horsley reported it hereabouts ten feet (3 m) high. A stump of Wall core survives 223 m (245 yards) west of the milecastle in the hedge. At the site of T 79a, the Wall turns sharply northwards. To the south, on the slightly elevated ground of **Brackenrigg**, two overlapping camps have been discovered through aerial photography.

T 79b (Jeffrey Croft) was located in 1934. The footings of its west wall, 96 cm (3 ft 2 in) wide, were set on foundations of two layers of cobbles and supported a wall formed of well-cut small red sandstone blocks. The south wall was 1.12 m (3 ft 8 in) thick while its north wall together with the Wall itself had been robbed. The dimensions are those of a normal Turf Wall turret, the discovery demonstrating that the normal pattern of milecastles and turrets had extended along the whole length of the Wall. The ditch is also known in this area. North-east of T 79b beside the coast, sits a small marching camp, **Knockcross**, at Grey Havens, probably originally enclosing 0.6 ha (1.5 acres), but no longer visible.

After a southward turn, due south to Port Carlisle, the **Vallum** runs north of Acremire Lane straight for Bowness. It is visible crossing two fields (the first immediately to the south-west of MC 79) and in the hedge lines running over it. Just short of Bowness, the Vallum turned slightly west, but its line south of the fort is not known. Local tradition places the Military Way just behind the Wall as it approaches Bowness.

BOWNESS-ON-SOLWAY (*MAIA*)

Bowness, the western terminal fort of the Wall, sits on a low, flat promontory formed of clay and rising a little over 15 m (50 feet) high, at the southern end of a ford across the estuary. The fort names on the Rudge Cup, Amiens Skillet and Ilam Pan start with *Maia*. The name meant "larger", perhaps in comparison to the hill on which sits Drumburgh. The fort does not appear in the *Notitia Dignitatum*, but one interpretation of the document would place the First Cohort of Spaniards here. The unit at Bowness in the third century was commanded by a

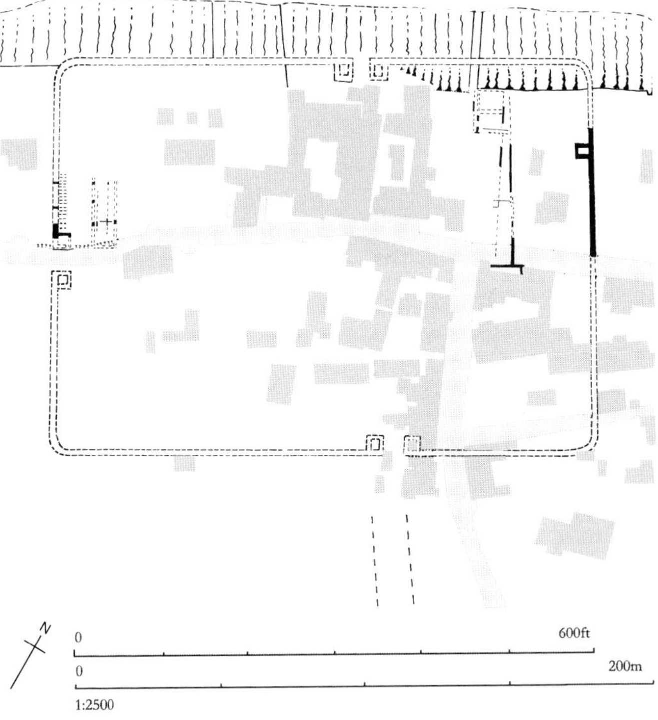

Bowness fort, showing Roman buildings of various periods.

Altar to Jupiter dedicated by a tribune in 251-3, sitting over a door at Bowness House Farm, but now almost illegible. (406 mm high)

tribune; Sulpicius Secundianus was recorded on two inscriptions of 251-3, but not, unfortunately, his unit. A building inscription, probably second century in date, indicates work by the Sixth Legion.

The modern village has obscured the fort and thus information about its dimensions has been accumulated gradually and with great difficulty. It sits on the slightly raised ground at the west end of the village. Today only the south-west corner of the fort platform is visible. The south and west walls were located in 1930, when it was also discovered that the north wall had been destroyed by coastal erosion. In that year part of the north tower of the west gate was examined, immediately north of the modern road; it was examined again in 1967 and excavated more fully in 1973. The position of the east wall was established in 1988. It could then be determined that the fort measured 128 by 188 m (420 by 616 ft) and covered 2.31 ha (5.78 acres), thus being the second largest on the Wall. A thousand-strong unit would be an appropriate regiment to be based in such a fort and this is supported by the title of the commanding officer being tribune. The mound of the road leading south from the fort to Kirkbride, which is still clearly visible, provides the position of the south gate, and demonstrates that the fort faced east.

Beyond the rampart lay two ditches. To the east, the inner was 4.50 m (14 ft 9 in) wide and 2 m (6 ft) deep and the outer only 2 m (6 ft) wide and 1 m (3 ft) deep, terminating opposite the northern interval-tower. A considerable depth of silt had accumulated in the inner ditch before being covered by tumble from the fort wall. After recutting, the outer ditch was backfilled and sealed by cobbles, to be replaced by a ditch of similar dimensions. At some time the berm, 3.5 m (11 ft 6 in) wide, was also surfaced with cobbles. An unusual discovery was a line of three post-holes 1 m (3 ft 4 in) outside the internal tower on the east wall: these may have supported scaffolding. Two ditches lay to the west, the inner 6 m (20 ft) wide. Facing stones were found in the bottom of the ditch, with medieval filling above. The outer ditch was 16 m (50 ft) wide and 1.5 m (5 ft) deep; it had clearly been reshaped in the medieval period. Only one ditch has been located at the south-east corner.

The earliest fort on the site was of turf and timber. The rampart was of clay, only 4 m (13 ft) wide. At the west gate, a group of four post-holes possibly formed part of an original timber gate. The front of the rampart was cut away for a stone wall, whose clay-and-cobble foundations varied in width from 1.32 to 1.70 m (4 ft 4 in to 5 ft 7 in); the wall itself has a recorded width of 1.40 m (4 ft 7 in) with a core of rubble and clay. That part of the east fort wall beside the northern interval tower was replaced at an unknown date, probably owing to its destabilisation from water action.

The modern road passes through the middle of the fort, using the sites of the Roman east and west gates. As a result, at the latter only part of the north tower survives. To its north, at some stage the rampart backing was cut away to allow a hearth to be placed here. Inside the intervallum road lay a long stone building, only 3.45 m (11 ft 4 in) wide. Its foundations cut through a spread of charcoal sealing a post-hole, presumably relating to the earliest fort. The stone building was replaced, probably in the first half of the third century, by a substantially larger structure of similar plan, but 6.90 m (22 ft 8 in) wide. A timber partition may indicate that the building was a barrack-block. A timber sill-beam hints at later rebuilding here.

In 1976 excavations were undertaken in the north-east quadrant of the fort. The first Roman activity in the area was the digging of a large rubbish pit and its subsequent infilling with a miscellaneous collection of material including samian and black-burnished pottery, glass, iron, slag, tile, bone, lead and two small pieces of leather as well as stones and clay. This was sealed by red clay which formed the basis for the first buildings. These were constructed of timber, the uprights being set into sleeper walls. The ground sloped gently towards the south-east and thus each room was levelled up by a fill of heavy stones and turf. The building was at least 57 m (187 ft) long, its northern end being destroyed by coastal erosion, and it exhibited three phases of use, all of which appeared to date to the second century. While internal partitions and the presence of a veranda to the west suggest that this was a barrack-block, it was unusually arranged. In the fourth century another building was erected in this area.

Late fourth-century material from the fort is sparse, though a coin of the Emperor Gratian (367-75) has been recovered: it may not be coincidental that the fort does not appear in the *Notitia Dignitatum*. No evidence has been found for the destruction of the fort at any time by fire.

The **civil settlement** lay south of the fort. A fragment of a gold object was found here in 1938. Buildings are known to have lined the road leading from the south gate to Kirkbride; one may have been the regimental bath-house. In 1999 and 2000, in deep deposits, traces of buildings, metalled surfaces and leather and pottery of second-century date were discovered immediately south of the fort. Examination in 1960 of the area north-west of the west gate failed to reveal any evidence for Roman buildings.

Bowness has produced an unusual inscription, a trader's vow made as he set out upon a venture: "...grant that a profitable return may add surety to my vows, I will presently hallow my poem one by one with letters of gold". The final sentiment is inspired by Virgil (*Eclogues* 7, 35-6). No trace of gold is today, however, visible on the stone, which is in Tullie House Museum, Carlisle.

THE WEST END OF THE WALL

Reginald Bainbrigg wrote in 1601, "the fundacions of the picts wall may be sene, upon the west shor at a lowe water, covered with sand, a mile and more within the sea". One hundred years later, Bishop Nicholson recorded in his diary for Friday 29 August 1707, "the conclusion of the picts wall very discernible at a Quarter of a mile west of Bowness". MacLauchlan in the middle of the nineteenth century observed that "the old inhabitants point out, at about 228 m (250 yards) from the north-west angle of the station, a spot where a quantity of stone was dug out from the beach many years since, for building purposes, and the line of it was followed for some distance under the sand, without arriving at the end of it. The direction of these remains, as printed out by the old people, would fall in with a continuation of the north front for about 100 yards, thence down a natural ridge, well suited to a line of defence...".

These three accounts appear to carry the Wall on from the fort at Bowness for some distance, perhaps as much as a mile. This stretch may have contained Ts 80a and 80b, but we cannot be certain; nor in truth can we definitely identify what was described 150 years and more ago.

A figure wearing a heavy cloak known as the *cucullatus*, often worn by those who had to go out of doors in bad weather. Found at Birdoswald in the nineteenth century. (178 x 127 mm)

Maryport from the air looking south-east. The Senhouse Roman Museum is housed in the former battery overlooking the cliffs.

CHAPTER 4

THE CUMBRIAN COAST

INTRODUCTION

At Bowness the Solway Estuary begins to open out and the south shore turns away markedly from the north: this could be the reason why the Wall ends here. Even so, Criffel and the far side look remarkably close, while beyond the flat-topped summit of Burnswark can be seen on a clear day. A series of milefortlets and towers continued observation beyond Bowness. They are even more regularly spaced than the milecastles and turrets on the Wall itself, the intervening distances varying between 495 and 501 m (540 and 546 yards), no doubt a reflection of the topography which favoured such accuracy. The milefortlets and towers can be traced for about 40 km (25 miles) to Rise How, just south of Maryport. It has been long assumed that they continued to St Bees' Head, 64 km (40 miles) south-west of Bowness, but careful field work has failed to locate any sites so far south. Part of an enclosure discovered under the fort at Ravenglass has been tentatively identified as a milefortlet, but this is unlikely for it differs in significant details from the milefortlets of the Cumbrian Coast. Furthermore, Ravenglass lies 48 km (30 miles) from the last known site on the Cumbrian Coast.

The numbering of the milefortlets and towers starts from Bowness, technically 0. It was formerly thought that the structures continued round the edge of Moricambe Estuary, but it is now known that they do not. MF 5 (Cardurnock) lies on the north side of the estuary, with MF 9 (Skinburness) 5 km (3 miles) distant across the water to the south-west. However, rather than renumber the subsequent sites, the traditional numbering has been retained here. Possibly the movement of

Bowness
1
1a
2b
3
3a
3b
4
Cardurnock
4b
5
Kirkbride
0
3 km
0
2 m
N

the coast has resulted in the loss of some installations. Sand blow, sand extraction and agricultural activities have led to the disappearance of other structures. MF 21 (Swarthy Hill) has been laid out for public inspection; otherwise only the platforms of MF 1 (Biglands) and MF 3 (Pasture House) are faintly visible.

The fortlets and towers were supplemented by forts. The spacing of these is different from that on the Wall, the original plan probably being for three forts, each pair about 16 km (10 miles) apart. The earthworks of both Maryport and Moresby are visible.

Various antiquarians recorded a paved road along the coast, Ferguson as late as 1880 on the Cardurnock peninsula. Such substantial remains have not been recorded archaeologically, though a metalled road has been found at various places in the vicinity of MF 4 (Herd Hill) and MF 5 (Cardurnock). Ditches, possibly flanking a road, show on aerial photographs of Silloth and Beckfoot: presumably the road along the coast has been mostly ploughed out.

BOWNESS TO BECKFOOT

Beyond Bowness, a pronounced raised beach runs south of the modern road for some distance. If **Ts 0a** and **0b** do not lie on Bainbrigg's "wall", they may lie on this raised beach. The measured position of T 0a lies in the next field beyond Pottery House, and of T 0b on Herd Hill, partly eroded since Roman times. After almost a Roman mile the raised beach begins to flatten and **MF 1** (Biglands House) lies on what is no more than a low rise. The fortlet's ditch is faintly visible from the road, encircling slightly raised ground in front of the farm and bungalow. Excavation in 1974-5 showed the fortlet to have measured 22.86 by 16.76 m (75 by 55 ft) within a 6 m (20 ft) wide rampart of turf which had been cut from the adjacent salt marsh. Beyond, lay a ditch 4.27 m (14 ft) wide and 1.37 m (4 ft 6 in) deep. The gate was 3.66 m (12 ft) wide and formed of six posts

MF 1 (Biglands).

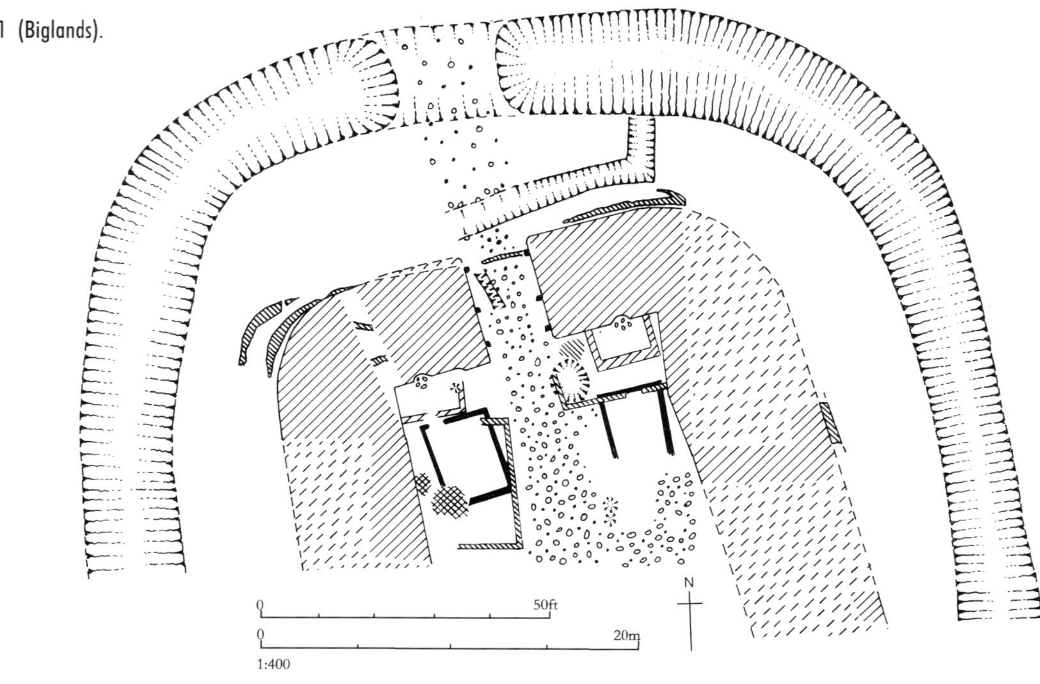

presumably surmounted by a tower. Within, two small timber buildings were separated by a road, which led north through the gate and across the ditch by a causeway. Two areas of cooking fires lay immediately inside the north rampart, each within its own small enclosure defined by a turf bank.

This fortlet was demolished, apparently about 140. It was rebuilt when Hadrian's Wall was reoccupied. The rampart was widened to 9 m (30 ft) and provided with a timber revetment, the gate rebuilt, and the internal buildings replaced, to the west, by a single building measuring 7 m (23 ft) by a little over 3 m (10 ft). This fortlet was in turn demolished and again rebuilt. The gate was reduced to a passage and the causeway removed; no trace was found of an internal building. A coin indicates that this third phase started after 171, but it did not continue beyond the end of the second century. The small number of finds includes brooches, a gaming board and some iron strapping probably from the gate, and the pottery includes cooking vessels, flagons, mixing bowls and *amphorae*.

In 1975 aerial photography revealed two parallel ditches 46 m (150 ft) apart to the north-east of the milefortlet and directed towards its external corners. Excavation demonstrated that the northerly (forward) ditch, about 1.5 m (5 ft) wide and 80 cm (2 ft 7 in) deep, had been recut at least twice. The southerly ditch, 2 m (6 ft 6 in) wide and 60 cm (2 ft) deep, on the other hand had been allowed to silt naturally; the fine silt at the bottom contained a sherd of pottery probably of early-to mid-second-century date.

No structure is known between MF 1 and T 2b (Campfield). Quarrying in the 1960s of a distinct green mound at the measured site of **T 1a** has perhaps destroyed this tower. Coastal erosion has probably removed a promontory, now represented by High West Scar, visible at low tide, and indicated by the northern diversion in the modern road. Here may have lain **MF 2** (North Plain).

A tower was tentatively identified 400 m (440 yards) south-west of Campfield Farm in 1928 on the basis of the removal of several cart-loads of stone from an old building. The outline of a square tower sitting on the raised beach was photographed from the air in 1949: this is **T 2b** (Campfield). Excavation in 1993 revealed the foundations of a tower measuring 6.3 by 6 m (20 ft 8 in by 19 ft 8 in) externally and 3.5 m (11 ft 6 in) internally; the walls had been robbed out. External paving indicated that the door lay on the east side of the south wall. The tower appeared to have been demolished in antiquity. Two late-third-century coins dating to 259-68 and to 271-3 were found unstratified beside the robber trench while pottery indicated occupation perhaps extending well into the third century. The excavator argued that this tower was preceded by two timber towers. The evidence for the first consisted of two post-holes and a possible third defining an area measuring 2.25 by 2.75 m (7 ft 4 in by 9 ft). The second tower, also small at 4.5 m (11 ft 6 in) square externally and 3.25 m (10 ft 8 in) internally, was formed of nine posts resting on, but penetrating through, dwarf walls, a unique form of construction on the Cumbrian coast. A road, resurfaced once, lay to the south of the structures, while the ditch, recorded at MF 1, was found to run in front of the tower, and beside it, on an aerial photograph taken in 1975, is a second possible stone tower.

MF 3 (Pasture House) lies immediately east of the farm of that name, on a slight rise. It was recognised in 1945 by the discovery of turf-work: Robinson had found dressed stones and pottery here in 1880. The ditch is still faintly visible. Aerial photographs indicate that the enclosure measures 48 m (52 yards) square over the ditch centres.

T 3a (Pasture House West) is in the second field to the west of the farm. It was discovered in 1880, when it survived as a mound. Ploughing had damaged the site and quantities of stone blocks had been removed. Excavation produced dressed stones, mortar and some Roman pottery including a sherd of samian.

T 3b (Herd Hill North), also located in 1880, lay towards the shore, two fields on. It measured 5.79 m (19 ft) externally and 3.96 m (13 ft) internally. The walls survived differentially, that to the south up to four courses high. All walls were found fallen outwards, some stones lying face downwards for a distance of about 2.74 m (9 ft) from the foundations, which were of cobbles set in "cement". The facing stones appear to have been bedded in mortar. On the flagged floor lay mussel shells, a spearhead or knife, and much pottery - coarse ware, mixing bowls, a fragment of figured samian, the neck of an *ampula*, and an *amphora* handle bearing the name *Romani RR*. The bones included part of a human skull. The stones from the two towers were used to build a gable to an outhouse at Pasture House.

It was turf-work again which allowed **MF 4** (Herd Hill) to be identified in 1945, sitting on a low, spread sand dune. Several cremations associated with Hadrianic pottery were noted in 1954 about 100 m (300 ft) north of the milefortlet. The pair of ditches, here 30.50 m (100 ft) apart, were recorded between MF 4 and the site of T 4a from the air and sectioned on the ground. Both showed evidence of recutting. A lightly-metalled track was also postulated here. It has been suggested that **T 4a** (Pow Drain) lies on the ridge north of Cardurnock village, though this has not been confirmed.

To the west of Cardurnock village, **T 4b** (Cardurnock) sits on the crest of the slope looking straight across the Solway at Criffel. In 1977 remains were found here which were interpreted as evidence for separate timber and stone towers. The latter consisted of the robbed remains of a foundation trench, which, it was argued, formed one side of the tower: this itself is unusual as the cobbles were not normally robbed from the towers. Further, the foundation trench was only about half the normal width and the internal area of the 'tower' smaller than usual; no Roman pottery was found. The other site lay beside a narrow trench interpreted as the construction trench for a palisade. The 'tower' consisted of a layer of red clay, 4 by 3 m (13 ft 2 in by 10 ft), set on large pebbles and containing one fragment of a Roman tile. This was interpreted as the base of a platform "a metre or so high", from which sentries could overlook the adjacent palisade. This would be a unique structure. The existence of a tower here remains unproven, while elsewhere the "palisade" has been interpreted as a deep field drain.

MF 5 (Cardurnock) was examined in 1944 in advance of an extension of Anthorn airfield. The post lay on a slightly elevated ridge with excellent views over the north coast of the Solway as well as to the south. It was found to be larger than normal, measuring 38.40 by 30.48-26.52 m (126 by 100-87 ft) internally. Turf-built, its ramparts measured 6.40-8.84 m (21-29 ft) across and were surrounded by a ditch 5.49 m (18 ft) wide and 1.90 m (6 ft 3 in) deep. The ditch was broken for a causeway towards the west end of the north side, almost opposite a narrow entrance. Inside, two timber barrack-blocks, measuring 33.53 by 8.53 m (110 by 28 ft), were carefully constructed on raised timber floors each surrounded by a drain. The remaining surface of the milefortlet was gravelled. A latrine lay in the south-west corner, and beside it, embedded in the rampart, a timber tower, about 4.30 m (14 ft) square. Pottery indicated construction under Hadrian.

In its second phase, the milefortlet was reduced in size to 31.09 by 23.77-21.95 m (102 by 78-72 ft), with the north and west ramparts built within their predecessors. The internal area was thus reduced from 1130 m^2 to 710 m^2. A trench on the berm round the south and east sides was interpreted as holding a palisade offering additional protection here. The gate lay more towards the centre of the north side. Within, no buildings were found, ploughing having been severe, but three hearths were noted. The rampart was subsequently repaired, and amendments made within. The pottery indicates that occupation fell within the second century, perhaps tipping over

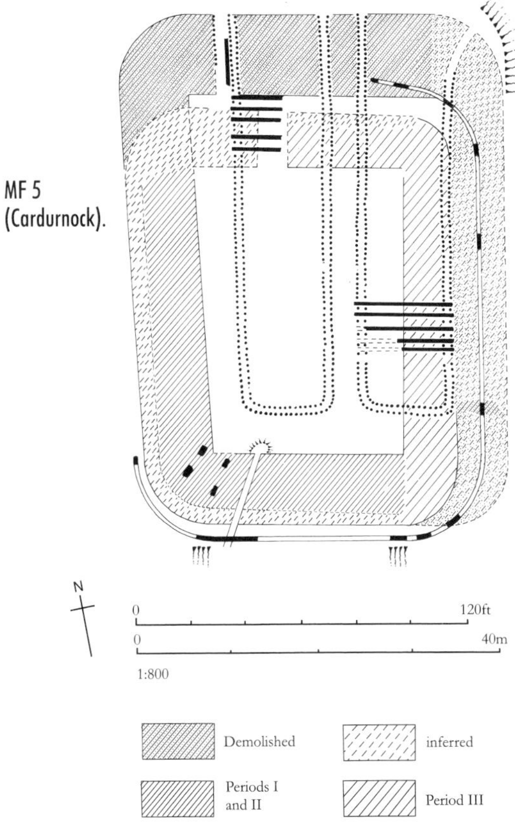

MF 5 (Cardurnock).

into the early years of the next century. The site also produced a small but significant quantity of late-fourth-century material, though no structures could be associated with this pottery: there may have been a hiatus in use in the third century, occupation being later resumed and continuing after 368. The other finds included parts of three knives, two spearheads, part of a key and two gaming counters; pottery included samian as well as cooking pots, jars and mixing bowls.

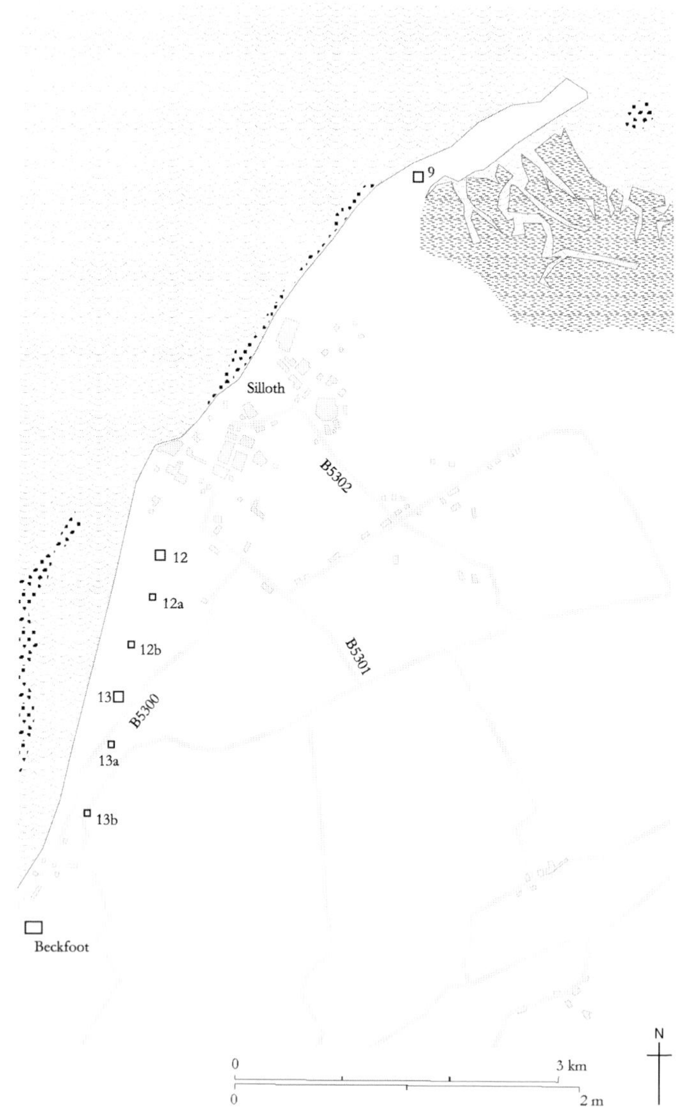
9
Silloth
B5302
12
12a
12b
B5301
13
B5300
13a
13b
Beckfoot
0
3 km
0
2 m
N

MF 5 sits on the north side of Moricambe Bay into which flow the Rivers Wampool and Waver. On the opposite side is **MF 9** (Skinburness). This site was discovered through aerial photography in 1949 and appears to be larger than the normal milefortlets, measuring about 45.72 by 36.68 m (150 by 120 ft) over the rampart, almost exactly the same size as the later periods at MF 5. These two fortlets would appear to be serving a special purpose on each side of the bay. Study of coastal change suggests that the Grune has extended to the north-east since the second century. Today the milefortlet sits on a low sand hill with wide views in the field beyond the last cottage on the track running along the Grune Point.

A pair of slight ditches crossing Silloth school playing fields may delineate a road, presumably Roman in date. Features originally interpreted as palisades have now been shown to be deep field drains. An altar dedicated "To the Mothers of the Fates" was found on the coast at Skinburness in 1866: it may have originated at **MF 10** (East Cote). A watching brief was held in 1992 when one possible site for the milecastle was built over, but nothing was found. It remains possible that the milefortlet was lost due to the coastal erosion which occurred following the construction of the pier at Silloth in 1855.

From MF 9 to Silloth the coast is covered by ribbon development and no sites are known for 5 km (3 miles): they may lie under or beside the houses or have been lost to coastal erosion. MF 12 and the next two towers lie on Silloth golf course, and are inaccessible, though their general locations may be observed from the path running along the east edge of the golf course. **MF 12** (Blitterlees) was located in 1963 and examined in 1967. The site had been levelled prior to construction work commencing. The milefortlet had a rampart of turf 8.5 m (28 ft) wide placed on a clay base 1.07 m (3 ft 6 in) thick. Inside the south rampart an area of red clay may have formed the base for a cooking area. A drain further west may indicate the position of a latrine. Two sherds of pottery of second-century date and another dating to about 290-370, together with a piece of Skiddaw slate, were found. The fortlet was reduced in size and the outer face of the south rampart refaced at unknown dates.

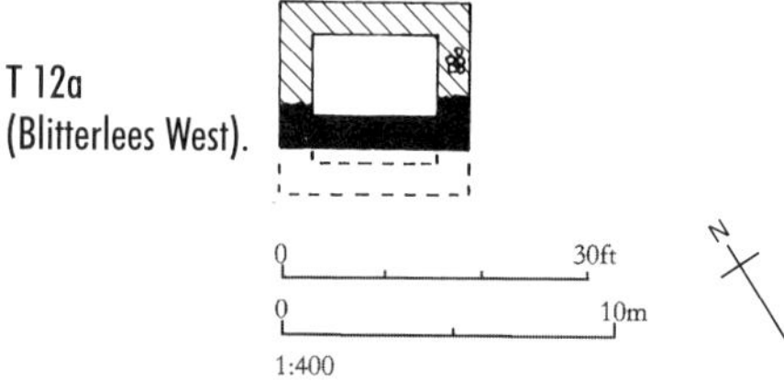

T 12a (Blitterlees West).

T 12a (Blitterlees West) was found in 1963 and excavated in 1966. It sits on an isolated hillock of sand rising to a height of 3 m (10 ft). It had been built to the usual specifications, 5.79 m (19 ft) square, but when the south wall collapsed its successor was erected a little further north, thus reducing the internal width from 3.96 to 2.44 m (13 to 8 ft). The floor was of sand and the door probably lay to the east. No pottery later than Hadrian's reign was found.

T 12b (Blitterlees South), at the southern end of the golf course, was excavated in 1955: it stood on a hillock. Measuring internally 3.50 m (11 ft 6 in), up to four courses of masonry survived, with no offsets. The door lay in the east wall. Beside it, and against the north wall, lay five superimposed hearths. The door had been subsequently blocked and another structure erected on the site with walls 66 cm (2 ft 2 in) wide, but still standing three courses high, just 2.59 m (8 ft 6 in) apart. A cooking pot repaired with a lead rivet was found and other Hadrianic pottery. The excavation trench is still visible.

Excavations in 1954 and 1980 followed by geophysical survey in 1994 failed to find **MF 13** (Wolsty), though three parallel lines were recorded: these may be of Roman date or the result of modern ploughing. Beyond Heather Bank a low dune ridge begins, to the east of the road. **T 13a** (Wolsty North) was located in 1954 just south of Cunning Hill: the site is crossed by a field boundary. 6.10 m (20 ft) square, the tower measured 4.09 m (13 ft 5 in) by 3.81 m (12 ft 6 in) internally: its stones are still disturbed by the plough. Hadrianic pottery and a coin of the same date in almost mint condition were found, the latter apparently wrapped in moss or chaff. Beyond the north wall lay a thin clay spread, burnt in patches. The remains were covered by demolition material.

T 13b (Wolsty South), also on the sand dune, is in the field to the north of Robin Hill. It was examined on Christmas Day 1880! The foundations were 1 m (3 ft 3 in) deep, formed of four courses of cobbles separated from each other by a layer of clay. They defined a structure measuring 6.25 m (20 ft 6 in) externally and 3.81 m (12 ft 6 in) internally, but with the walls entirely robbed. A few lumps of mortar were found outside the north-east wall, and may indicate that the facing stones were bedded in mortar. The entrance lay to the south-east and a rough pavement, 1.83 by 1.22 m (6 by 4 ft), lay opposite the centre of that wall. A layer of rubble and a streak of clay indicated the floor level, and burning represented a hearth. Pieces of coal and iron, coarse and samian pottery were recovered. In 1963 pottery of second-century date was found at the site. **MF 14** (Beckfoot) and **T 14a** (Beckfoot North) have not been located.

BECKFOOT (? *BIBRA*)

The fort ought to sit on the site of T 14b. Marked by a trig point, it lies to the east of the modern road, its north-west corner overlain by a bungalow. It occupies a slight rise with an outlook to the north as far as Silloth and Maryport to the south. The fort platform may be discerned and in particular its western rampart and south-west angle. The name of the fort may be *Bibra*, if interpretations of the *Ravenna Cosmography* are correct: this may mean "Brown or Beaver River". An inscription from the site (now in the Senhouse Museum at Maryport)

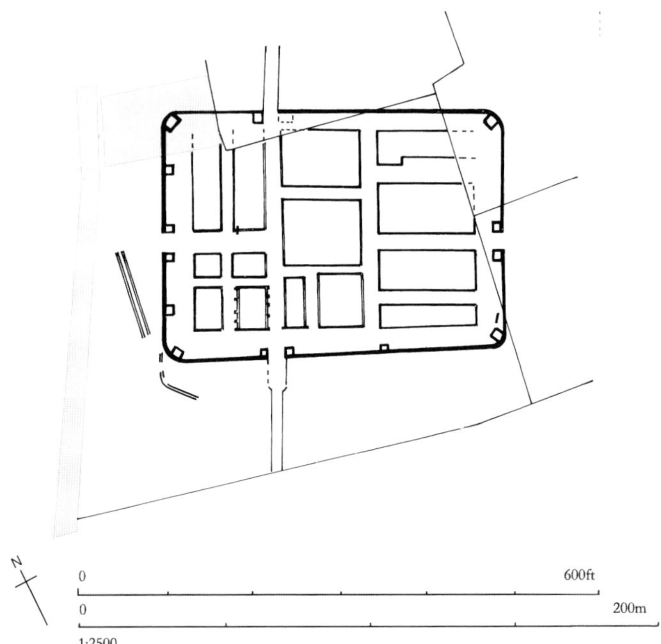

Beckfoot fort based on the 1880 excavations and aerial photographs.

records the only unit known here: the Second Cohort of Pannonians.

The **fort** measures 86.26 by 123.44 m (283 by 405 ft), giving an area of 1.35 ha (3.25 acres). It was examined by Joseph Robinson in 1879-80, who traced its outline and located several buildings inside and out. The fort wall is 1.83 m (6 ft) wide with an earthen bank 4.57 m (15 ft) wide behind. Inside and towards the northern end of the west wall was a solid block of masonry, measuring 3.35 by 2.13 m (11 by 7 ft). Three gates were located – the fourth, the west gate, may have been blocked in antiquity thus hindering its rediscovery – the four angle towers and an internal building beside the south gate in the central range. The site was particularly receptive to aerial photography in 1949 when the internal layout was revealed, including the headquarters, commanding officer's house, granaries (unusually in the forward part of the fort), and several barrack-blocks. Subsequent aerial photographs have revealed three ditches, and a road leading to the fort from the north and continuing south. Pottery from the fort ranges from Hadrian to the late fourth century. A coin of the Emperor Constantius II (337-61) has also been found.

Robinson recorded buildings beyond the west, south and east ramparts, including part of a large structure to the north-east which may have been a bath-house, and a raised water channel by the south-west corner. Aerial photography south of the fort has revealed three sides of an enclosure covering 0.81 ha (2 acres), and possibly a temporary camp, and also part of a field system.

A cremation **cemetery** is known 500 m (500 yards) south-west of the fort: burials are regularly exposed in the dune face above the beach. The cremated bones were placed, sometimes in pots, within pits and stone cists. In 1948, the remains of a funeral pyre were recorded. Included in the debris were part of a sword, shield-boss, spearhead and arrowhead, together with 31 nails, some with specks of gold still adhering, presumably from gold leaf and indicating cremation on a funeral couch. In 1954, a cremation pyre was excavated. It contained fragments of a cooking pot, nails and calcined bones. The range of finds from the cemetery also includes brooches, knives, hobnails and metal strips possibly from a wooden box. Artefacts indicate that the cemetery was in use from the second to the fourth century.

BECKFOOT TO MARYPORT

After Beckfoot fort the modern road runs due south for a short distance, passing to the east of the measured position of **MF 15** (Beckfoot Beach). In 1956 mixed sand and gravel overlying a

Beckfoot
15
15a
16
16a
16b
17
B5300
Allonby
20
20a
20b
21
0
3 km
0
2 m
N

line of 'fossil' turf noted in the cliff was interpreted as evidence for the upcast mound beyond the fortlet ditch; slight traces of turf-work and grey clay supported the interpretation. Later observations revealed gravel, at the correct position for a back gate, with dark sandy turf above it. The material had been eroded away by 1981.

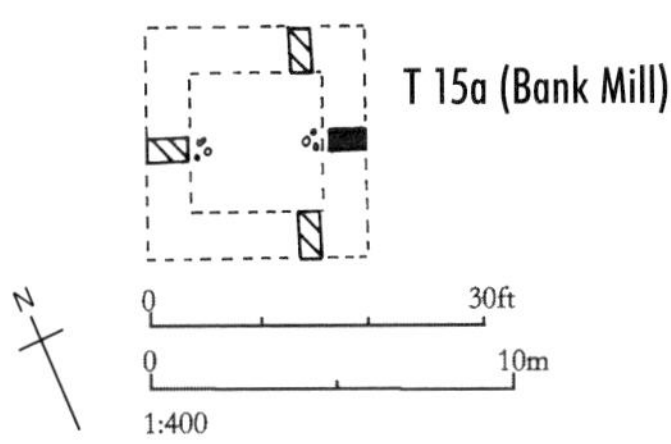

T 15a (Bank Mill).

T 15a (Bank Mill) sits on a dune-shaped hillock some 6 m (20 ft) high, nearly due west of the Newtown road junction. The site is within 74 m (80 yards) of the shore and is accessible from the track to the beach. The tower was excavated in 1954 and 1956. The walls, of red sandstone, stood up to four courses high upon their clay and cobble foundations; the core of the wall was bedded in earthy, sandy gravel. The floor was at the level of the lower offset, which occurred at the top of the second course. The door, 90 cm (3 ft) wide, was located in the north-east corner, its original sill showing signs of wear; it had been raised, apparently to block drifting sand. Demolition, however, appears to have followed soon afterwards. Outside the door lay a lightly gravelled path, while beyond the north-east corner patches of clay were recorded. Within, the floor was of sand, with two superimposed hearths against the west wall. Hadrianic pottery was found. The remains were sealed by a layer of earthy gravel, masonry debris and cobbles, presumably from the demolition of the structure.

T 15b (Mawbray Bank) has not been found: it may lie beneath the sand dunes. **MF 16** (Mawbray), on a hillock, was located in 1969 and examined further in 1972 when the rear entrance was recorded. A cambered road 1.83 m (6 ft) wide was flanked by posts. No signs remained of the voids in which the timbers would have sat, which led to the suggestion that they had been removed from their sockets, indicating dismantlement. The gravel of the road, 25 cm (10 in) thick and resting on grey clay, had vertical edges as if retained by timber fences. Finds included samian pottery, *amphorae*, and Hadrianic-early Antonine coarse pottery. The ditch was marked out but appeared not to have been excavated.

Immediately south comes a scatter of farms and cottages, marking Old Mawbray road end. Beyond this lies the Jordan Beck and a large abandoned sandpit, which has claimed **Ts 16a** (Cote How) and **16b** (Mawbray Sandpit). The former sat on a small dune, beside the massive dune of Cote How, at 15 m (50 ft) high, the largest point beyond Bowness. Its north side was noted in 1934 and the tower was excavated in 1937. The foundations consisted of four layers of cobbles interleaved with clay. A thin slab, chamfered on three sides, may have been one end of a merlon-cap from battlements, suggesting a flat roof. To the north lay a hearth and occupation material which yielded a sherd of Hadrianic pottery and another of the third or fourth century. In 1954 a black occupation layer, together with fragments of red sandstone and part of a second-century cooking pot were recorded. Beside the tower, in a modern dump, two spearheads were found in 1934.

T 16b was excavated in 1954. The walls were of red sandstone. A stone chamfered on one side may have been a

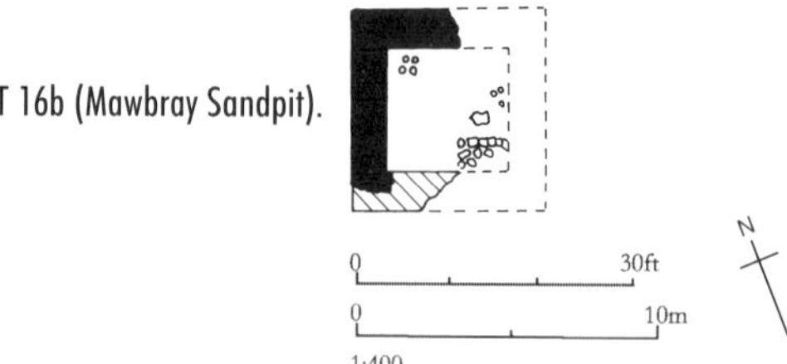

T 16b (Mawbray Sandpit).

merlon-cap. A gravel path led to the door. Inside a rough stone platform lay in the south-east corner. It was set on a thin spread of grey clay, which rested on clean sand. Fibrous material adhering to a spearhead resembled rushes, presumably from the floor. A hearth lay in the north-west corner and several superimposed hearths beside the east wall, resting upon a black occupation layer. Bones of pig and sheep and the shells of oysters, mussels, whelks, winkles and cockles lay in the rubbish round the hearths. The haul of finds was completed by three spearheads, some pieces of sheet lead trimmings, pottery, two fragments of a glass vessel and part of an *amphora*. This last, of Spanish type, bore a graffito formerly thought to record the capacity of the vessel but is now believed to give a date, 26 August. The remains of the tower were sealed by a layer of grey, sandy clay containing broken sandstone and shingle: it is presumably the debris of demolition consisting of the clay and rubble core of the walls. Above this stood a roughly built wall of sandstone and clay.

A little further on, the modern road turns south-east at Dubmill Point. At the bend **MF 17** (Dubmill Point) was discovered from the air in 1976 and investigated in 1983. The milefortlet lies mostly east of the road and measures about 50 m (160 ft) across the ditch, which survives as a slight depression; the berm is unusually wide at 6 m (20 ft). A causeway over the ditch indicates an eastern entrance. There was a hint of up to three phases in the east rampart.

The broad sweep of Allonby Bay, over 10 km (6 miles) wide, is now reached, with Allonby village in the foreground. Beyond, the dark scarp of Swarthy Hill rises to over 30 m (100 ft), to fall and rise again as the less conspicuous ridge of Brown Rigg, the vista closed by the plateau crowned by Maryport. The first 5 km (3 miles) of the bay are devoid of known posts, either the result of coastal erosion or of modern developments.

The site of **T 19b** (Mealo House) was tested in 1969 but nothing was found; a bungalow now occupies the site. **MF 20**

20
20a
20b
21
21a
21b
22
22a
23
Maryport
A594
25
25a
25b
0
3 km
0
2 m
N

MF 20 (Low Mire).

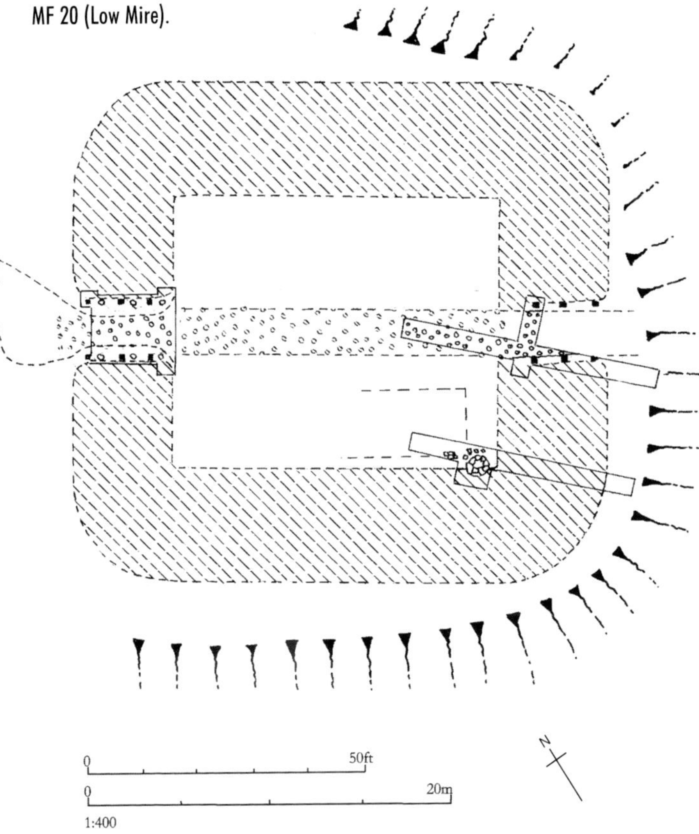

(Low Mire) is on the hillock just north of the farm entrance. It was excavated in 1969 and 1980. It measured 18.29 by 14.63 m (60 by 48 ft) within turf ramparts about 6.40 m (21 ft) wide, which had been twice repaired. There were gates to front and rear. Three periods were identified at the front entrance. The original passage was 3 m (10 ft) long and 2.50 m (8 ft) wide, the gate structure being formed of six posts. This was replaced by a similar structure set slightly towards the interior of the milefortlet. In the third period the passage was narrowed to 1.5 m (5 ft). There was only one period at the back entrance. The internal road, 3 m (10 ft) wide, exhibited three periods. To the north of the road evidence for a wooden building was found. A hearth lay in the north corner of the fortlet and an oven at the south. The latter had been dismantled; its base was covered with blown sand. Finds included fragments of Hadrianic-Antonine cooking pots, a dish, flagon, *amphorae*, a cooking pot dating to about 290-370, a square glass bottle, an iron knife and nails. Walling seen by the farmer during the 1960s may indicate the location of **T 20a** (Blue Dial) at the farm of that name on the ridge.

Rigidity of planning resulted in **T 20b** (Swarthy Hill North) lying on the north shoulder of Swarthy Hill and **MF 21** on the south. The tower was examined in 1962. Built on boulder clay, its foundations were 1.52 m (5 ft) wide, but only about 30 cm (1 ft) deep. The lowest layer of foundations was formed of large cobbles, over which lay grey clay and smaller cobbles and then two courses of thin sandstone flags.

MF 21 (Swarthy Hill) sits on top of the low cliff. It was completely excavated in 1990 and 1991, the only milefortlet to have been so examined. A single ditch surrounded the rampart on all but the west side: it was broken to the east by a causeway. The rampart, about 6 m (20 ft) wide, had internal and external turf cheeks of clay revetting a sand core. The milefortlet measured internally 14.5 by 18 m (47 ft 6 in by 59 ft). The west gate was formed of four posts providing a structure 3 m (10 ft) square. The east gate was based on sleeper beams of timber resting on the surface between the rampart and the road. The road passed through the fortlet, but was not found beyond the gates.

Within the fortlet and south of the road lay three buildings, not uniform in layout. The two westerly shared a common wall and rested against the rampart; the easterly building was free-standing. All appeared to have been erected on sleeper walls.

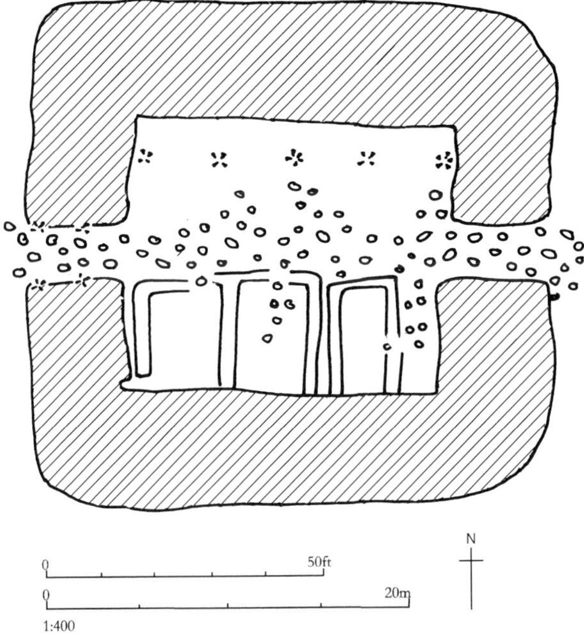

MF 21 (Swarthy Hill).

The western contained a hearth and the central building an oven or furnace. The area north of the road was apparently occupied by a single building, about 18 by 5 m (59 by 16 ft 6 in), resting upon a central row of posts. Entrance ways suggest that it was divided into four cubicles. Both central bays contained a hearth and each outer bay an oven. It is possible that the soldiers slept in the buildings to the south and lived in that to the north. The pottery from the site, which included samian as well as cooking vessels, indicates that the single period of occupation was Hadrianic. Other finds included part of a bead, a gaming board, a knife and a probable adze.

The fortlet has been laid open for display. The ditch has

been excavated, the rampart marked by a bank, the north gate by four posts and the west barracks picked out in concrete.

T 21a (Saltpans) was noted by a sandpit worker just south of Crosscanonby road end as it was being destroyed shortly before 1939. The foundations of **T 21b** (Brownrigg North) were observed in 1962 on the north, seaward slope of the low hill known as Brown Rigg. It was further examined in 1966 when it was found to conform to normal standards; up to two courses of wall survived. Pink clay was used in the foundations rather than the grey found to the north.

MF 22 (Brownrigg), a little to the south of the summit of the hill, was investigated in 1962, 1966 and 1968. The ditch, about 1.5 m (5 ft) deep, ran round three sides, ending at the cliff edge. The rampart, 9.45 m (31 ft) wide to north and 6.40 m (21 ft) to east and west, defined an area 20.73 by 17.69 m (68 by 58 ft). The front gate, 1.83 m (6 ft) wide, led onto a road running along the cliff edge; two surfaces were noted. Internally, two hearths were found, one in the north corner and the other against the south rampart. The pottery, Hadrianic in date, included fragments of a cooking pot, mixing bowl, rough-cast beaker, flagon, *amphorae* as well as a stone cooking pot lid, part of a quern stone and the sole of a military sandal.

T 22a (Maryport Golf Course) was recognised in 1962 as a rectangular stony mound. **T 22b** (Club House) has not been located, though pottery was found in a sandpit here. Fragments of a tombstone recording the death of a child apparently aged between 5 and 9 were discovered when the club house was extended in the early 1950s. Aerial photography has revealed the site of **MF 23** (Sea Brows) on the edge of the cliff. It appears to have a ditch broken for a causeway on the landward side, the defences on the opposite front having been lost to coastal erosion. The enclosure measures about 45 by 40 m (150 by 130 ft). **T 23a** (Bank End Quarry) has not been found and may have been lost to quarrying of the cliffs. **T 23b** (Maryport) probably lies under the fort.

MARYPORT (*ALAUNA*)

The fort occupies a prominent position on the slightly hog-backed, cliff-girt plateau north of the modern town, with an excellent outlook on all sides, including, under good conditions, the Isle of Man. To the south lies the River Ellen, whose name probably relates to the Roman name for the fort,

Plan of Maryport fort and civil settlement based on geophysical and magnetometer survey by Timescape.

Alauna in the *Ravenna Cosmography*. The meaning of the name *Alauna* is not certain, but it may mean "shining" or "brilliant", which would be suitable for a name relating to a river. The visible fort appears to have been established under Hadrian, from whose reign there is a fragmentary building inscription. However, coins and pottery, and possibly a tombstone, indicate the existence of an earlier military installation in the immediate vicinity. The Roman road leading to Maryport from Papcastle is not aligned on the fort but a little to the north and may therefore point to the location of an earlier military installation.

From the sixteenth century, ownership of the fort and the adjacent ground which includes the civil settlement, has passed through successive generations of the Senhouse family, now represented by Joe Scott-Plummer, who has generously placed the inscriptions, sculpture and other artefacts in the care of the Senhouse Museum Trust. They are now housed in the **Senhouse Roman Museum** in the Victorian Battery. The investigations of members of the family have produced one of the most important collections of altars and sculpture in Britain, and certainly the most important still in private hands. The altars in particular provide valuable evidence about the regiments based at Maryport and their commanders, which is of wider relevance to our understanding of the Roman army.

On 18 April 1870 a group of pits about 300 m (300 yards) north-east of the fort yielded 17 altars, most dedicated to Jupiter: these form the core of the 22 altars dedicated to this god which have been found at Maryport. It has been suggested that they were erected beside a parade ground, but it now seems more probable that they had formerly stood in a shrine: a dedication slab to Jupiter may be from that building. At an unknown time, and for an unknown reason, many altars were removed from the shrine and buried in the pits.

Most of the altars are dedicated simply to I.O.M., the standard abbreviation for *Iovius Optimus Maximus*, Jupiter

Best and Greatest. They appear to form part of an annual series dedicated either on 3 January, when vows were paid and undertaken for the welfare of the emperor and for the eternity of the empire two days after every unit in the Roman army had renewed its oath of loyalty to the emperor, or on the anniversary of the emperor's succession, 11 August in the case of Hadrian. On his first occasion, the commander usually dedicated the altar on behalf of himself and the unit; later he himself only dedicated, presumably with the unit's involvement understood. The formula is simple on most altars, but some are more detailed and relate to a specific event such as a promotion or transfer. The careers of these commanders indicate the integrated and cosmopolitan nature of the officer class of the Roman army. The officers at Maryport came from Italy, Provence (southern France), Noricum (modern Austria), north Africa and possibly Spain. They moved between posts in Britain and the provinces of Upper Pannonia (modern Austria), Lower Pannonia (Hungary), Lower Moesia (Bulgaria and Romania), Dacia (Romania) and Judaea (Israel), travelling on occasions from one end of the empire to the other to take up their next appointment. It is not impossible that a detachment of one regiment based at Maryport, the First Cohort of Spaniards, was dispatched to the east to

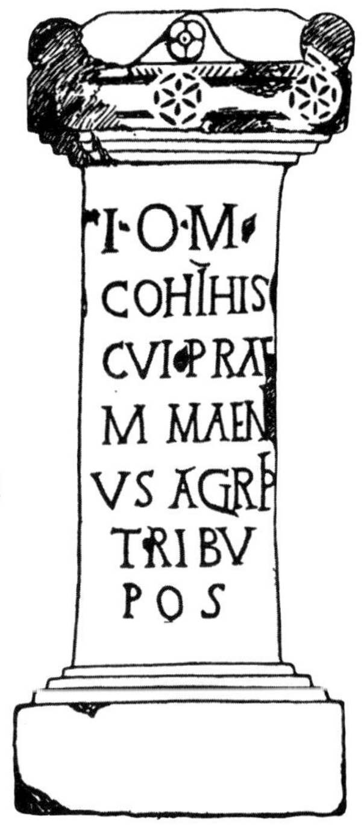

An altar to Jupiter erected by M. Maenius Agrippa on behalf of the First Cohort of Spaniards. (1109 x 452 mm)

participate in the Jewish War of 132-5.

Several regiments are attested at the fort. The earliest was the First Cohort of Spaniards, a thousand strong and containing both infantry and cavalry. No less than six commanders of this unit are recorded at Maryport on the series of dedications to Jupiter. One, Maenius Agrippa, was recorded at his home town of Camerinum in Italy, as being a host to Hadrian. It is often assumed that this was at Maryport, but it is perhaps more likely that the occasion was in Italy. Agrippa and C. Caballius Priscus are recorded as tribunes whereas the title of the other four commanders was prefect. The commanders of different types of unit had specific titles: a tribune normally commanded a thousand infantry and a prefect five hundred. It would therefore appear that the unit changed its size while at Maryport, but whether it was increased or decreased is debatable. The number of altars, assuming they were erected annually, suggests that we have an almost complete series for this unit and that therefore each commander served an average of three years. The altars erected by this unit are decorated in a distinctive style with wheels, dot-and-circle and concentric circle motifs, half-moons, triangles and zigzags.

A dedication slab to Jupiter, also found in one of the pits, was erected under Antoninus Pius by Postumius Acilianus, prefect of the First Cohort of Dalmatians. The emperor does not bear the title *pater patriae* which he accepted in 139. Accordingly, if this is not an accidental omission, the unit should have arrived at Maryport in that or the preceding year. Perhaps the shake-up caused by the impending invasion of Scotland prompted the change of unit. Coin evidence suggests that the fort may have been abandoned during the occupation of the Antonine Wall, so the stay of the First Cohort of Dalmatians at Maryport may have been brief.

The First Cohort of Baetasians was stationed at Bar Hill on the Antonine Wall at this time, but later came to Maryport. It had a distinguished war record, its soldiers having been

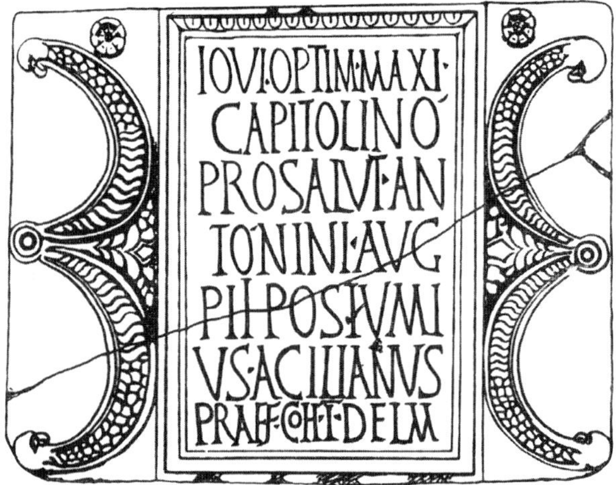

A dedication to Jupiter for the safety of the Emperor Antoninus Pius erected at Maryport by Postumius Acilianus, prefect of the First Cohort of Dalmatians. (610 x 762 mm)

awarded Roman citizenship for meritorious conduct: this may have been during the Antonine re-conquest of Scotland in 139-42. The date of its service at Maryport is not known, but as some of its altars were found in the pits together with those of the other second-century garrisons, a date in that century is probable. Other inscriptions record a tribune, possibly in the third century and suggesting that a thousand-strong cohort was based here, while EQ appears on one stone, indicative of cavalry. In the *Notitia Dignitatum* the Third Cohort of Nervians is listed as being at *Alione*, which has been equated with the *Alauna* of the *Ravenna Cosmography*, though this is uncertain.

The **fort** survives as a well-defined earthwork: no stonework is visible today. It measures about 142 by 146 m (466 by 479 ft) and covers 2.07 ha (5.12 acres); it is unusual in being square in shape. Today the crest of the rampart lies within the fort wall, which has been largely robbed and survives as a terrace between the rampart and the inner ditch. This crest stands 3.10 m (10 ft 2 in) above the bottom of the ditch to the west and 1.60 m (5 ft 3 in) to the east. Beyond the rampart, two shallow ditches separated by a broad, flat-topped bank are visible round the west half of the defences. To the east, excavation in 1966 located a third ditch, no longer visible, which in turn had cut an earlier slot. There was also a suggestion of a fourth ditch, now lying under Camp Road. Breaks in the earthworks indicate the location of the gates.

The fort wall was about 2 m (6 ft 6 in) wide, with a clay rampart-backing nearly 6m (20 ft) wide. The locations of the north, west and east angle towers of the fort are revealed by robber trenches. The north gate was excavated in 1787. Its tower was furnished with a plinth at the lowest course, while the gate threshold was rutted. The arch stones still lay in front of the gate but were subsequently removed. Although the plan indicates a single portal, recent survey has provided evidence for a second passage-way. A representation of a fort gate found at Maryport is of a double-portal gate surmounted by a second storey lit by five windows; to the side stands the goddess Venus.

A depiction of a gate, with a relief of Venus to one side, found at Maryport.
(330 x 457 mm)

The **headquarters building** was cleared by the Senhouses, when the strongroom vault and the well were located. The strongroom was first examined about 1686 and it was reopened in 1766. It measured 3.20 by 3.65 m (10 ft 6 in by 12 ft) making it the second largest known in Britain, after South Shields. The headquarters faced north-west, that is towards the coast. It is not exactly in the centre of the fort but lies 5 m (16 ft 6 in) to one side of the main axis, which may indicate rebuilding within the fort. To its north-east, an internal bath-house, found in 1788, is presumed to be part of the commanding officer's house. Geophysical survey suggests the presence of two granaries on the other side of the headquarters building and up to 12 barrack-blocks, though two at least are likely to be stores or stables.

The only modern excavation within the fort, in 1966, examined a small area in the north-east corner. In the first period, two **barrack-blocks** ran south-west to north-east. The soldiers' quarters were 7.70 and 7.80 m (25 ft 3/7 in) wide, with, in one case, a detached building for the officer to the north. These were replaced by buildings of exactly the same plan not before the later second century, to be in turn demolished and replaced by two narrow buildings, possible storehouses. A fourth and final period was represented by a repair to the intervallum road, which partly overlay a building of the previous period. Some post-holes may relate to this period too. Pottery indicates a date after about 360 for this phase of activity. Coins, including one of the Emperor Honorius (398-402), supported by pottery, inscriptions and the *Notitia Dignitatum*, indicate occupation of the fort continuing into the late fourth century.

To the north-east of the fort lay an extensive **civil settlement**. Stukeley recorded paved streets and in 1880-1 Joseph Robinson conducted the most extensive excavations there to date. One building lay immediately north of the fort, on the edge of the cliff; others were 'strip-houses' measuring 12-15 m by 6 m (40-50 by 20 ft), and facing onto the main road, 6.4 m (21 ft) wide, leading north-east from the fort. Some contained amounts of iron slag and much coal, indicating industrial activity. Two buildings appear to have been temples. One was round, 10.36 m (34 ft) in diameter, with buttresses, and an entrance to the east. To one side lay a "funeral pyre", one layer of charcoal being 36 cm (1 ft 2 in) thick; a large number of burials were also recorded. The other building measured 14 by 7.60 m (46 by 25 ft); its interior was flagged. It had a porch or narthex at the front and a square apse at the rear. The end wall of the apse had fallen flat and indicated an original height for the building of 4.57 m (15 ft). This building has been interpreted as a *mithraeum*. Two altars were found to the east, one, dedicated to Jupiter, lying on a pavement of freestone blocks. This may have been the location of the shrine to Jupiter whose altars were buried 80 m (260 ft) to the east.

Aerial photography and geophysical survey have revolutionised our knowledge of the civil settlement. Some 40-50 houses have been identified occupying a broad band beyond the north-east defences, where they are densely packed, and also lining the road running north-eastward along the ridge for a distance of over 300 m (330 yards) from the gate of the fort. The dominant form of building was the strip-house, which is especially represented on each side of the road. Several larger houses fronting onto the road had smaller buildings behind. At least 12 buildings had a span wider than the norm of 7 m (23 ft) while some were as long as 26-30 m (80-100 ft). One building by the north corner of the fort appears to have been of courtyard type. Geophysical survey has also revealed that the temples sat within an irregular enclosure.

Ditches have also been recognised. They appear to have served a variety of purposes, defining different areas of land use, acting as boundaries to properties, or to the fields beyond the settlement. Ditches along the rear of the 'back-lands' of the strip houses lining the road appear to define the urban area. They also indicate that an initial core grew in size to be redefined by further ditches. J. B. Bailey recorded a bank with an outer ditch, running from the south-western corner of the fort north along the cliff edge for some 420 m (450 yards), before turning south-east, and then south-west to head again towards the fort. In all it enclosed some 12 ha (30 acres) but excluded the more northerly parts of the civil settlement. Excavation led to the discovery of a Roman building and probable third-century pottery below this bank. No certain vestiges of this bank remain today: it may be post-Roman, or perhaps have protected a small, late civil settlement.

A **road** led directly from the north-west gate, the *porta praetoria*, towards the coast, possibly linking to a coastal route. The road to Papcastle left from the south-east gate of the fort, but no buildings have been recorded here. A second road appears to have branched southwards, on the line of the modern Camp Road. Wooden piles in the river, in the loop of the Ellen, Bailey suggested, may be part of a bridge, while across the river foundations and remains are known, including the possible line of the road. Here also Camden recorded a cobbled area 110 m (125 yards) square defended to west and south by a "massive wall". The purpose and date of this is unknown, but it may relate to harbour installations or a late fort or even be natural. Modern investigations have failed to locate any Roman remains in the area of the modern harbour, whose construction altered the earlier topography and may have swept away earlier remains.

Also, south of the fort, until its destruction shortly before 1922, lay a mound known as Pudding Pie Hill. Formerly interpreted as a tribunal beside an exercise ground, this is more likely to have been a prehistoric burial mound. Geophysical survey has revealed other evidence for pre-Roman settlement, including a rectilinear ditched enclosure, best interpreted as an Iron Age farmstead, to the south-east of the fort.

Tombstones suggest that the **cemeteries** lay well outside the built-up area. Four tombstones have been found at the Ellen crossing 900 m (900 yards) to the east and at the Barney Gill 1,500 m (1,500 yards) north of the fort. They include monuments to Ingenuus, son of Iulius Simplex, aged 10, and Iulia Martina, aged 12, to Iulius Marinus, a centurion aged 40, and Morirex who lived to the age of 70. The tombstones of

The Serpent Stone. (1.24 m high)

Spurcio who was 61 and Rianorix are of a different style and may be post-Roman in date. An uninscribed tombstone of a cavalryman probably dates to the second century. There are also two or three full-length figures of females.

Robinson excavated two groups of burials. One lay in the second field to the north of the fort, beside the two buildings he examined within the civil settlement, which suggests that the settlement had grown in extent during its occupation: subsidence of buildings was probably due to the burials. Some burials here were in stone cists. The other group lay in the fourth field north of the fort, that is beyond the known Roman buildings. A spectacular discovery here was a stone shaft and base, phallic in shape, 1.27 m (4 ft 2 in) high with a human face carved on one side and a serpent on the other. This would appear to have originally been a large altar, recut in this form. The Serpent Stone combines elements of Celtic and Roman symbolism, in a funerary function, and presumably was intended to protect the graves associated with it. In front of the stone lay a pavement measuring 4 by 1.83 m (13 by 6 ft), covering four burials. All around were found other burials, three stone cists, the remains of funeral pyres and calcined bones. Many of the cremations were in urns. Other items found in the area included a second sculpture of a serpent and a fir cone, now on display in the Senhouse Roman Museum. A short distance to the west, immediately north of the civil settlement, high magnetic anomalies may represent further cremation burials.

MARYPORT TO BURROW WALLS

Much is lost below the modern town of Maryport. **MF 24** (Maryport) ought to lie at the junction of Fleming Place and Eaglesfield Street and **T 24a** (Castle Hill) beside a loop in the River Ellen where Roman coins have been found. **T 24b** (Mandle Street) is also lost. At the position of **MF 25** (Risehow Bank) the south ditch, a gravel road and drain, and pottery were found in 1969.

T 25a (Risehow) was excavated in 1981 and 1982: it lies on the summit of the low hill a few metres north of the four houses of Risehow. The tower was of the normal size, 6 m (19 ft 8 in) square, with walls 96 cm (3 ft 2 in) wide and set on the outer edge of the foundations which jutted 44 cm (1 ft 5 in) into the interior. The walls were of red sandstone; lumps of mortar were probably from the pointing of the facing stones rather than the wall core. The door appears to have been towards the north end of the east wall: a paved surface lay outside it. Beyond this was a quarry pit for the clay used in the construction of the foundations. The occupation layer rested on the builders' debris. There were two hearths, against the north-east and

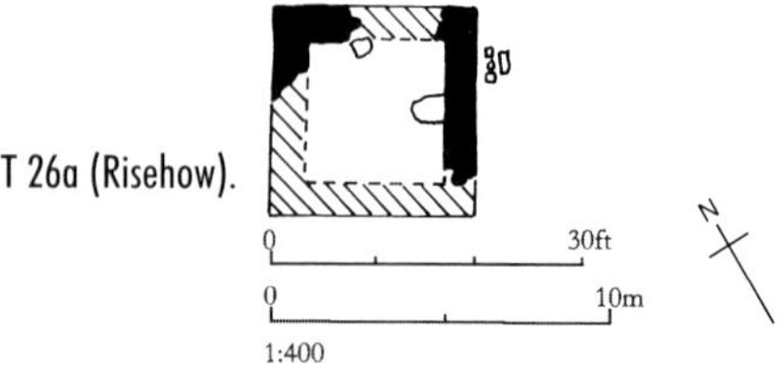

T 26a (Risehow).

south-east walls. Only Hadrianic pottery was found, together with two parts of a quern stone, a whetstone and a fragment of a gaming board. The bones include cattle and shells of periwinkle, limpet, whelk, mussels and an oyster. A corn-drying kiln had later been built within the tower. The tower had been erected on a burial: the leg bones of an extended human burial were discovered in a shallow grave. They were of an adult about 1.65 m (5 ft 5 in) tall. Three sherds of an Iron Age pot in a calcite gritted ware lay nearby.

T 25b (Fothergill, formerly Risehow Tower) was found and recorded in 1880 by Joseph Robinson of Maryport. It lies almost exactly 495 m (540 yards) beyond T 25a, on the south flank of the low hill between Risehow and Fothergill. The plan, drawn by Lloyd Wilson, is schematic, but it reveals a tower of stone, 4.14 m (13 ft 7 in) internally within walls 91 cm (3 ft) wide, a size we can now see is normal (see page 94). He recorded that the floor was of cobble covered with clay. A water bottle with a handle was also found, together with burials, regarded as later. The first tower to be located, it is still the most southerly known. It now lies beneath a reclaimed coal heap on the east side of the road from the Miners Arms.

The summit of Rise How was not used for a tower as the rigid spacing did not place one here. It is not impossible that T 25b was the final tower. It has wide views to the south, towards St Bees' Head where the cliffs commence and access by raiding parties was made difficult. To the south, neither Burrow Walls nor Moresby occupies a prominent position – unlike Maryport and to a lesser extent Beckfoot – which may suggest that their communication with milefortlets and towers was not an issue. Sites have been suggested further south but none proved. A quern found in 1929 on the south bank of the Totter Gill has been taken to indicate the site of a milefortlet or tower. On the bluff known as Oyster Bank, immediately north of Burrow Walls, a wall was located in 1928 with "charcoal and burnt earth, indicating occupation": a Viking sword has also been found here. Beyond Burrow Walls, aerial reconnaissance in 1981 led to the tentative identification of a milefortlet south of the farm at Harrington Parks, south of Harrington, but the crop-mark was reinterpreted as resulting from the application of fertilisers.

BURROW WALLS

Only five miles south of Maryport and nearly halfway to Moresby lies Burrow Walls. It sits on an old cliff top overlooking the Siddick marshes, partly lost to industrialisation: the cliff edge is concealed by the former railway embankment. Both the

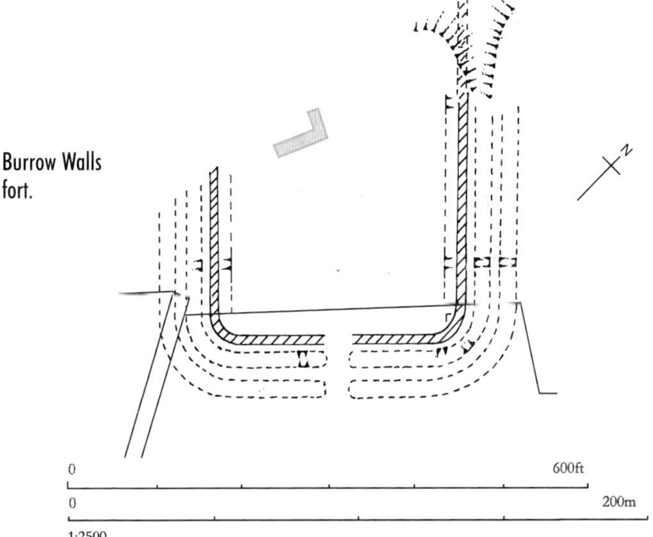

Burrow Walls fort.

Roman name of the site and that of the regiment based here are unknown; nor is the fort visible today. Excavations in 1955 demonstrated that it measures 89 m by an estimated 137 m (292 by 450 ft), and therefore covering a little over 1.2 ha (3 acres). Perhaps a third of the fort has been lost to erosion, probably by the River Derwent. The ruin within the fort, Burrow Walls, is medieval in date, though reusing Roman stones: it stands approximately on the site of the headquarters building.

Only the clay and cobble foundations of the fort wall were found to survive, 2.44-3.05 m (8-10 ft) wide, fronted by two ditches, 4.88 and 5.48 m (16 and 18 ft) wide. Immediately within the north and south fort walls, a third ditch was found, 4.57 m (15 ft) wide. The road leading out of the north gate was located, close to the cliff edge.

All the pottery found at the fort dated to the late fourth century, with the exception of fragments of a second-century cooking-pot and a late third- to early-fourth-century vessel. This, coupled with the unusually short distance to the forts to each side, suggests that this may be a late foundation. The discovery of late fourth-century pottery in both the external and internal ditches does not help to elucidate the history of the site. In 1852 some quern stones and five altars were found at Burrow Walls, of which one survives.

MORESBY (? *GABROSENTUM*)

The fort at Moresby occupies a classic fort site, a low, flat hill, or rather in this case a spur overlooking the sea to the west and the Lowca Burn to the north. Beyond, the land rises on three sides, Lowca Hill restricting the outlook to the north, though St Bees' is visible 8 km (5 miles) to the south. Clearly communication to the north was not a concern for the officers who chose this site. Today, the churchyard of St Bridget covers almost half the fort platform, with the church sitting immediately outside the east gate. The ramparts of the fort south and west of the churchyard are still visible.

Aerial view of Moresby looking north. The church sits beside the fort's east gate.

Inscriptions have been recorded here since the late sixteenth century. One, found during the erection of the church in 1822, attests building by the Twentieth Legion under Hadrian, which, since it gives him the title "Father of his Country", ought to date to between 128 and 138. From its location, it may have fallen from the fort's east gate, though it had possibly been reused as a paving slab. Two stones record the Second Cohort of Lingones and a further three the Second Cohort of Thracians, one tombstone usefully providing corroboration that the latter contained both infantry and cavalry. This soldier had the unusual name Smert(ri)us, and died at the age of 40 after 20 years' service. It seems probable that this tombstone dates to the second century. An altar by the prefect of the cohort, Manilius Nepos, probably dates to the third century. The Second Cohort of Thracians was recorded at *Gabrosentum* in the *Notitia Dignitatum*. The name of the fort means "goat-path" and presumably refers to a steep path up the sea cliffs.

The **fort** measures 109 by 134 m (358 by 440 ft), an area of

An inscription recording building work by the Twentieth Legion at Moresby under the Emperor Hadrian.

1.42 ha (3.5 acres), rather tight for a mixed infantry and cavalry cohort. Its long axis runs east-west, and it has been calculated from the positions of the north and south gates that it faced the sea. Nineteenth-century excavators recorded walls still standing 1 and 1.22 m (3 and 4 ft) high. In 1860, the north wall and gate, the north-west angle and parts of the south gate were found, and in 1951 a single ditch, no more than 3.35 m (11 ft) wide, was located to the north. The fort wall measured 1.80 m (5 ft 11 in) across the foundations, with the wall itself 1.60 m (5 ft 3 in), reduced by an offset to 1.49 m (4 ft 9 in). From the location of small hypocaust pillars recorded during grave-digging, it has been suggested that the commanding officer's house lay on the north side of the fort. Hadrianic pottery has been found as well as a fourth-century Constantinian coin.

A **civil settlement** lay to the south, where conspicuous remains were once visible, and here a building with cement floors has been recorded together with roofing tiles, possibly a bath-house; rescue excavations in 1951 revealed nothing to the north of the fort. A tombstone found in 1962 540 m (600 yards) east-south-east of the fort may indicate the location of the **cemetery**. Inhumations in stone cists were also found underneath Moresby Hall, rather closer to the fort, but are undated. A sculptured tombstone of a young man in a toga was found reused in a stile. A small statue of a horned god is in Tullie House Museum, Carlisle. At the foot of the cliff a natural harbour was destroyed in the nineteenth century: this may have been used by the Romans.

MORESBY TO RAVENGLASS

Beyond Moresby is St Bees' Head. This has been considered a natural end of the frontier installations, though no fort has been located on the headland nor have stray finds been recovered here. Ten km (6 miles) beyond, some Roman pottery has been found on the bluff overlooking the mouth of the river Ehen, and three separate finds of coins have been made in the area, but all could relate to a civilian settlement rather than a military installation. Further south lies the fort at Ravenglass. This sits on the southern end of the plateau south of the modern village. The platform of the fort is visible between the track and the railway line while part of the regimental bath-house stands over 3 m (10 ft) high. An earlier structure has been claimed as a possible milefortlet, but too little survived to warrant certainty. Ravenglass is linked east-wards via Hardknott, also a Hadrianic foundation, to the provincial road network and is clearly part of the contemporary infra-structure.

About 2 km (1 mile) south of Ravenglass on the south side of the River Esk, two sites have produced Roman material including coins, pottery and broken altars, but no evidence has been found to confirm a military context.

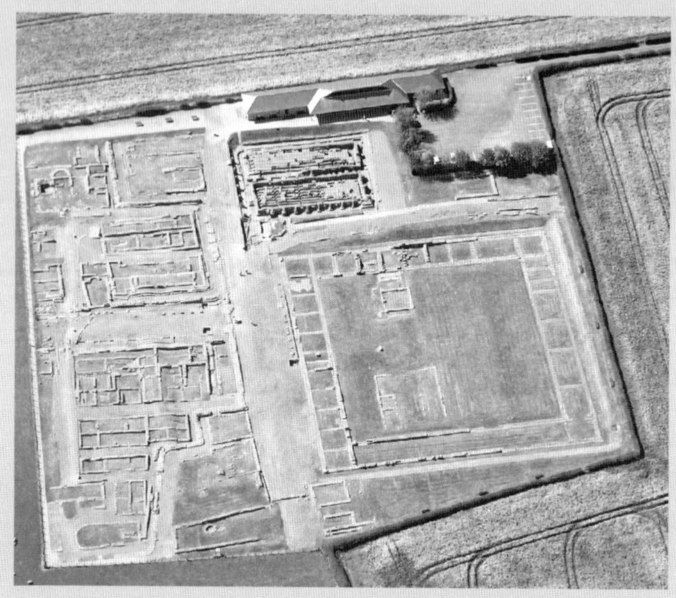

Corbridge from the air looking west. The great unfinished building (Site XI) occupies the bottom right quadrant, with the aqueduct and granaries beyond. To the left sit the military compounds, with the headquarters building of the west compound visible top left.

CHAPTER 5

THE STANEGATE

INTRODUCTION

Stanegate is the medieval name for the Roman road between Corbridge and Carlisle linking the forts across the isthmus. It has been suggested that it was the spine of a frontier system operating through the reign of Trajan until the construction of the Wall (see pages 49-50). Over the last 30 years, the term 'Stanegate frontier' has been extended to encompass the fort at Washingwells, Whickham, on the western outskirts of Gateshead south of the Tyne, as well as sites west of Carlisle, though no road is known connecting any of these sites to the Stanegate or to the main Roman road network. Analysis of the road line has led to the proposal that it was constructed after the forts it connects. This would be in accord with normal Roman military practice.

The road itself was well built, varying in width from 5 to 6.71 m (16 ft 6 in to 22 ft), resting on a solid foundation formed of cobbles or other stones up to 30 cm (1 ft) thick surmounted by gravel up to 25 cm (10 in) deep, and sometimes edged with kerbstones. Today, no metalling is to be seen, though the road survives as a visible earthwork in places and is occasionally used by modern roads and tracks.

A number of milestones are known from the Stanegate, dating to the third and fourth centuries. Remarkably, a complete milestone and the stump of a second are still standing in their original positions, to west and east of Vindolanda. One mile further east a group of seven milestones was found at Crindledykes in 1885. One recorded a distance of 22 km (14 miles), the location of Corbridge to the east, demonstrating that milestones on the Stanegate as well as the Military Way were measured from Dere Street.

WASHINGWELLS

On the southern flank of Whickham Hill, to the south of the Tyne, sits an enclosure. Discovered from the air in 1971, it covers about 1.86 ha (4.6 acres) inside the ditches, which are of two phases. The site has not been excavated and nothing is known of its date: even geophysical survey has failed to reveal any traces of internal buildings, though the post-pits of the south-east gate are visible on aerial photographs. It is only a presumption that the fort was occupied earlier than Hadrian's Wall. The view to the north and west is restricted, though the fort commands the Team Valley between the hill and the ridge occupied by the modern city of Gateshead.

CORBRIDGE

Corbridge lies on Dere Street, the road running north from the Roman province into what is now Scotland, at its junction with the Stanegate. The complex of sites stretches from the western outskirts of the modern village of Corbridge for nearly 2 km (1 mile) westwards along the river terrace. It includes a fort, town, military base, bath-house, mausoleum and bridge, investigated at various times from 1906 onwards. Today the only visible element is the English Heritage site, *Corstopitum*. Here is displayed the core of the town including several military buildings. The museum houses material discovered during the excavations and offers interpretation of the site.

Corstopitum appears in the *Antonine Itinerary* and *Corielopocarium* in the *Ravenna Cosmography*, both probably corrupt. *Corsobetum* has been proposed as the correct version of the former: it would mean "the place of small birch-trees". The Vindolanda writing tablets refer to a place named *Coris*, the nominative form of which should be *Coria*. It has been suggested that this is likely to be Corbridge. 337 men are recorded as being outposted from Vindolanda to *Coria* according to a strength report of about 92-7.

The earliest known site lies on the farm of **Red House** and is now bisected by the A69. It is a military enclosure, defended by a single ditch, measuring 254 m (850 ft) across; its southern end is controlled by the edge of the terrace, but its northern limit is not known. The base may have covered 10 ha (25 acres). Within were timber buildings, including a possible double legionary barrack and at least 13 open-ended buildings, interpreted as storehouses or workshops. To the east sat a large stone bath-house, excavated in 1955-7, and indicating that

Corbridge town, based on the 1906-14 excavations and subsequent work.

occupation of the military base was not intended to be fleeting. However, it did prove to be brief. Artefacts indicate an occupation probably no longer than 10 years, certainly no longer than 20, with the focus on the 80s. It is likely that the base was founded under the governor Julius Agricola in the late 70s, but the existence of two phases in some of the buildings may point to an earlier foundation under Petillius Cerialis in the early 70s. The abandonment of the base may be linked to the withdrawal of most regiments from their forts north of the Cheviots in 87/88. Red House was replaced by a new fort site to the east.

The English Heritage site covers most of the area of this new fort. Excavations have demonstrated the existence of five superimposed forts. A samian bowl discovered in a construction trench indicates that the first was not erected earlier than 85, a date which sits well with the evidence for the abandonment of the Red House base. Built of turf and timber, parts of several buildings have been examined including its headquarters, granary, a possible barrack-block and a corridor building, variously interpreted as a hospital, workshop or store-house. On the basis of the existence in Hexham Abbey of the late-first-century tombstone of Flavinus, a standard bearer of the *ala Petriana*, it has been argued that this regiment was the first occupant of the new fort, but this is uncertain. Indeed, there is some evidence to suggest that the fort was larger than even a cavalry regiment would require, as it may have covered at least 5.3 ha (13 acres).

The bath-house of this fort has been tentatively identified some distance to the north, within the later Roman town. It originally contained three rooms, cold, warm and hot, but was subsequently modified. Beside it stood a separate *laconicum* (hot dry room). Military bath-houses of this type, which consisted of a single row of rooms with a separate hot dry room, generally date to the late first and early second centuries. This building appears to have continued in use as the aqueduct was later routed round it while third- and fourth-century coins were found within it. Voussoirs from an arch with a radius of 4.1 m (13 ft 6 in) found on Site XI in 1909 may have derived from the bath-house indicating that it was eventually demolished.

After some modifications, this fort was dismantled and burnt. A coin of 103 found under the east rampart is the only dating evidence for its successor. The destruction and rebuilding has been linked to other possible changes in troop dispositions in north Britain about this time. The new fort may have covered 2.8 ha (7 acres) and, like its successors, faced south towards the bridge over the Tyne. It was built of turf and timber and, remarkably, the timbers of the headquarters building's shrine are preserved as voids in its stone successor.

The tombstone of the standard-bearer Flavinus, now in Hexham Abbey. (2.64 m high)
Drawn by Miriam Daniels

The remains of a wooden chest discovered in 1964 sealed below the road beside a small corridor building, possibly

An inscription recording building work by the Second Legion at Corbridge in 139, during the reign of the Emperor Antoninus Pius and under the governor Q. Lollius Urbicus. (0.57 m high)

a storehouse, contained three almost complete segmented legionary cuirasses (*lorica segmentata*), fragments of leather, cushions and writing-tablets, scraps of lead and bronze, iron nails, bars and struts, bundles and horse spearheads, knives, saws, a pick-axe, shears, gouges, a jemmy, two block and tackles, a scabbard, pieces of furniture fittings and a set of gaming counters. The armour suggests that some legionaries may have been stationed in this fort. A tile-stamp of the Ninth Legion has been dated to this period and may indicate the builder of the fort if not its occupants.

A change in unit brought changes to this fort. Although the defences and the headquarters remained standing, all other buildings were demolished and replaced. This event is generally associated with the building of Hadrian's Wall, though the evidence is only circumstantial. The abandonment of Hadrian's Wall under his successor, Antoninus Pius, signalled another change. Rebuilding is dated by two inscriptions (in the site museum) to the governorship of Lollius Urbicus (139-42) and specifically 139/40 and shortly after, the work being undertaken by the Second Legion (traces of paint surviving on the stones when they were found indicates that they were gaudily coloured). The main buildings were now either of stone, or timber placed on stone sill walls, while the barrack-blocks were of timber. Much of the visible, but fragmentary, headquarters building is of this fort, while a corner of a corridor building obtrudes from below the fountain house. The granaries of this fort lay below those now visible. The repeated rebuilding of the fort produced the interesting phenomenon of the granaries switching each time from one side to the other of the headquarters building. Perhaps they were always the first buildings to be replaced so that the food could always be kept under cover.

In a subsequent modification, the defences and most principal buildings were retained, but the barrack-blocks were demolished and replaced in stone. To the east of the headquarters a stone building was erected; it is generally interpreted as the commanding officer's house though this identification is uncertain. These changes have been related to the withdrawal from Antonine Wall and its attendant forts in about 160.

Inscriptions demonstrate the presence of legionaries at the fort during the second half of the second century. A detachment of the Sixth Legion was present under Iulius Verus (governor about 158) and Calpurnius Agricola (governor 162 to about 166) when it made a dedication to the Invincible Sun-god. A dedication slab erected under Calpurnius Agricola in 163 attests the presence of a detachment of the Twentieth Legion. Soldiers of the Sixth and the Twentieth Legions were specifically recorded as being on garrison duty at an unknown date. To provide even more complication, a dedication to the Discipline of the Emperors by soldiers of the First Loyal Cohort of Vardullians, one thousand strong, may date to the governorship of Calpurnius Agricola, or later when two or three emperors ruled at the same time. An undated, but probably second-century, altar records a cavalry prefect, Q. Calpurnius Concessinius, who "fulfilled his vow to the god of most efficacious power" after he had slaughtered a band of Corionotatae, a name otherwise unattested.

Considerable doubt surrounds the date of abandonment of the last fort and the construction of subsequent structures on its site. Some military buildings, such as the headquarters, survived to be used for industrial purposes, but parts at least of the rampart were levelled, the space to be utilised for further industrial activities. Later, all was swept away in order to create the large building known since 1907 as **Site XI**, the construction of which heralded major changes at the site. Measuring 67.10 by 65.60 m (220 by 215 ft), it had great foundations supporting equally massive walls formed of large blocks of stone. Abundant evidence survives in the visible masonry to demonstrate that the building was unfinished: excavation has indicated that the timber buildings standing on the site were then burnt.

The purpose of the building is not known. One possibility is that it served as a storehouse. The extra size of the northern corners reveals that they were intended to form the piers for arches connecting the courtyard to another building. A building akin to a legionary headquarters or a civilian forum-basilica may therefore be considered, though such buildings did not normally have a range of rooms between the courtyard and the basilica. This latter function also receives some support from the dating of the **aqueduct** and **fountain** to this time, as if this was intended to be the centre of the new town. Beside the fountain, work had begun on replacing the granaries. The development was brought to a precipitate halt, perhaps by the invasion of about 180. On this basis, the last fort will have survived into the 160s or 170s, and work started on Site XI shortly after.

Following the abandonment of the grandiose new project, the south range of site XI was converted into shops, some of which continued in use into the fourth century. Buildings which have been interpreted as temples were erected across the street: only the base courses survive of these buildings.

The reign of Septimius Severus appears to have been of particular significance for Corbridge. A fragmentary inscription records the completion of one of the granaries; the fountain was rebuilt, while south of the road two military compounds were erected. These buildings, together with Site XI, form the core of the visible site.

The **granaries** exhibit evidence of different styles of work and modifications, and retain interesting features such as the unique stone mullion in one of the vents. They faced south onto the Stanegate. Successive raising of the road surface – the last sometime after 364 – caused access problems and steps, now removed, had to be provided. An officer in charge of the granaries dedicated an altar at the time of the most successful expedition to Britain, probably that of the Emperors Septimius Severus and Caracalla in 208-11.

Immediately east of the granaries is the **fountain house**, fed by an aqueduct from the north. Placed on a layer of rubble and clay with the water channel protected by capping stones, the whole was originally covered by clay and stones. The aqueduct terminated at a fountain house, the water passing through an ornamental spout into an aeration basin where the water would have been freshened before flowing into a large stone tank. From here it flowed through channels to other parts of the town, including the compounds. An ornamental pediment, in the museum, records construction by the Twentieth Legion. To each side of the fountain stood a statue, of which the bases survive.

South of the Stanegate lay **two compounds**, only partially visible. Today, this area exhibits a strange ripple effect, perhaps better interpreted as the result of differential subsidence over the buildings and roads, rather than into the ditches of an earlier fort. Each compound was surrounded by a wall which followed irregular courses to avoid existing buildings, and each was entered by an entrance leading off the *via praetoria* of the previous forts. Each compound had a small headquarters building facing the entrance. The west compound contained four double buildings which for part of their life appear to have been workshops: spear- and arrowheads, and hearths and tanks associated with iron slag were found in the northern, visible buildings. They may originally, however, have served as barracks. Only two buildings can be positively identified in the east compound, both houses of the style erected for senior army officers. Other buildings in the compound have been interpreted as barracks, stores buildings and *scholae*, that is small buildings used by guilds or clubs of soldiers.

Within the strongroom of the west compound was found an altar dedicated to the Discipline of the Emperors by the Second Legion and a fragmentary building inscription by the Sixth Legion erected during the governorship of Virius Lupus (197-200). The compounds were thus military in intent, but beyond that there is little certainty.

The compounds saw many modifications, not necessarily contemporary, and most undated. They include: the amalgamation of the two enclosures into one; rebuilding of the two officer's houses into one house, with a hypocaust installed in the north-west corner; and the construction of a potter's kiln in a room at the opposite end of the building. The workshops also saw modifications, while the adjacent headquarters building was extended on at least three occasions: a coin of the Emperor Valentinian I (364-75) was found on the uppermost floor.

The visible remains are no more than the central area of a **town** of around 11 ha (27 acres). Pre-1914 excavations coupled with aerial photography have produced the outlines of streets and buildings which lie below the surrounding fields. The town was bisected by the Stanegate, which ran east-west through the English Heritage site. To the west, it was met by Dere Street which ran up the slope from the bridge over the Tyne to turn eastward onto the Stanegate, leaving it to the east of the English Heritage site where it turned northwards. To west and east of the visible site the Stanegate was lined with strip-houses and shops. To the north lay more houses, two very large granaries, and a bath-house. Between the military compounds and the bridge lay a large house, in plan not unlike a villa, and generally interpreted as a *mansio*, an inn for travellers. The most famous find from this building is the Corbridge Lion, which was the fountain-head of a large, third-century water-basin.

The Corbridge Lion.
(865 x 950 mm)
Drawn by Miriam Daniels

Defences, in the form of traces of a rampart and ditches, are known only on the north and north-eastern sides of the town, close to the modern Corchester Lane. At the point where Dere Street crosses these, two large stone foundations 2.44 m (8 ft) square and 8.23 m (27 ft) apart were found, perhaps indicating a gateway or arch.

The later history of Corbridge is obscure. The military installations appear to have continued in use into the late fourth century, and coinage shows that life continued at least in the centre of the town into the period 388-402. At an unknown date the temples were totally demolished and their area given over to kilns, hearths and furnaces; in short, all kinds of industrial activity. The end of the site is also uncertain, although a sufficient number of Anglo-Saxon objects, including a pair of late fifth- or early sixth-century brooches, have been recovered to suggest that a pagan Saxon cemetery existed somewhere within the central area of the Roman town. Later still, the Saxon tower of Corbridge Parish Church was built of stones from the Roman site, including an arch. In 1201 King John ordered a search for treasure at Corbridge, but nothing appears to have been found.

Of the inhabitants of the town we know little. Tombstones, mostly reused in the later levels of the site, include that of Barathes, aged 68, a *vexillarius* (a *vexillum* is a flag) and native of Palmyra, who has been identified with the man of the same name who buried his wife Regina at South Shields. Soldiers are naturally represented by tombstones. Three children's tombstones commemorate Ahteha, daughter of Nobilis, aged 5, Ertolla, properly called Vellibia, aged 4 years and 60 days, and Julia Materna, aged 6, the very dear daughter of Julius Marcellinus.

Corbridge has also produced many interesting artefacts. In 1731-6 several pieces of Roman silverware were found in the river bank west of Corbridge. One is the famous lanx – a decorated silver salver – dating to the late fourth century, and now in the British Museum. Two further vessels, according to Bruce, were "speedily committed to the melting pot". In 1760 a fifth piece was found at Bywell, 6.4 km (4 miles) lower down the river. A gold betrothal ring, inscribed in Greek "Long Life to Aemilia" was found near the site: it is now in the Museum of Antiquities, Newcastle. A second gold ring, found in Site XI in 1935, is also inscribed: "The love charm of Polemius". In 1908 and 1911 two hoards of gold coins were discovered. The first consists of 48 *solidi* of the late fourth century, which includes 13 of Magnus Maximus (383-8). The second was even larger, containing 160 *aurei* from Nero to Marcus Aurelius (64-159/60). Both are now in the British Museum.

Cemeteries apparently lay both east and west of the town. To the east the line of the Stanegate is known only for a few hundred metres, as it makes for modern Corbridge: a milestone dedicated to the Emperor Victorinus (268-70) may have formerly stood here. At Trinity Terrace in 1895 was found the tombstone set up by Julius Primus to his dear wife, suggesting the existence of a cemetery beside the road. More is known of the cemetery to the west. Inhumations have been found beside the Cor Burn, beyond which a mausoleum measuring 9.75 by 10.36 m (32 by 34 ft) was excavated at Shorden Brae in 1958. Although almost completely robbed of its stonework, traces of the original central burial were found. The mausoleum had been surrounded by a precinct wall of considerable size. Fragments of two stone lions, each devouring an animal, which had once crouched upon two of the corners of this enclosure wall were also found, and are now at the site museum. A similar sculpture, known as the Corbridge Cuddy, for years stood in Corbridge market place.

To the south of the site, the massive remains of the southern abutment of the **bridge** bringing Dere Street across the Tyne were excavated in 2004: six piers are still visible in the river bed. Another four piers and the northern abutment are considered to lie to the north, now covered by the Cor Burn and present bank of the river. The piers are of well-cut stonework tied together in places with metal cramps, with cutwaters upstream.

CORBRIDGE TO NEWBROUGH

The Stanegate runs through the visible site and is soon lost as it crosses the fields to the west. It negotiated the Cor Burn by a series of right-angle bends, bringing it to the stream at the narrowest point, where remains of an abutment have been seen. In 1868 a milestone dedicated probably to the Emperor Maximinus Dia (309-13) was found here. Beyond the North Tyne, MacLauchlan traced a connection to Chesters. The Stanegate skirted the north side of the Warden Hill, continuing north of Fourstones to join the modern road where the lane runs to Frankham Farm (South View). Thereafter, it is mostly under the modern road through Newbrough, as far west as Barcombe.

NEWBROUGH

The church and churchyard of St Peter's Stonecroft overlie a Roman **fortlet** discovered in 1930. Measuring 59.44 by 57.91 m (195 by 190 ft), 0.3 ha (0.75 acres) in extent and overlooking the Newburgh burn, it was defended by a wall 1.22 m (4 ft) wide, with a 4.57 m (15 ft) wide ditch beyond. The outer facing stones of the north wall protrude beyond the north wall of the churchyard. All the pottery recovered was of fourth-century date, mostly late in that century. Traces of buildings have been found during grave-digging. 1 km (½ mile) to the east, at **Sitgate**, a rectangular enclosure of about 2.4 ha (6 acres) with rounded corners has been discovered by aerial photography, but its ditch is not broken by causeways and its Roman date must remain suspect: even if Roman, its single ditch argues against a permanent fort.

NEWBROUGH TO BARCOMBE

The Stanegate follows the modern road past **Grindon Hill**, west of which two camps have been noted on its south side. Only one is visible and that barely so. It is about 40 m (130 ft) square and covers 0.1 ha (0.3 acres).

At **Crindledykes** five complete and two fragmentary milestones were found in 1885. They record the Emperors Severus Alexander (223), Probus (276-82), Maximinus Caesar (305-9) and Constantinus as Caesar (306-7) and Augustus (307-37), and are now in Chesters Museum. The stone dedicated to Severus Alexander records the distance XIIII miles, showing that the road was measured from Corbridge 22 km (14 miles) to the east.

BARCOMBE

Immediately south of the modern junction of the Stanegate and the road leading north to Crindledykes and Housesteads is the whale-back hill of Barcombe. On the eastern shoulder of the hill, commanding wide views to the north, is an Iron Age fortification containing, in its north-west corner, a Roman tower. The tower, of timber, sat within a roughly circular enclosure measuring 19.81 m (65 ft) north-south, with a turf rampart still standing 76 cm (2 ft 6 in) high and an outer ditch with possible causeway. The site produced late-first-century pottery. Its successor, to the west of the modern road, was a stone tower erected in the second century on the western flank of Barcombe Hill, to the south-east of Vindolanda. This site can be seen from the fort as a slight hump on the skyline.

Barcombe Hill was also quarried by the Romans. Two quarries lie on the south flank of the hill. On the face of the northern quarry are a roughly carved phallic symbol, the numeral XIII and three wedge-marks, while once visible was a crude carving of a boar, symbol of the Twentieth Legion. Just to the south-west of this a former Roman quarry was reopened in 1837. There, concealed "in a crevice", was found a small bronze arm-purse, now known as the Thorngrafton Hoard. It contained 63 coins, apparently wrapped in leather. Three are of gold, the rest of silver. The gold coins (*aurei*) belong to Claudius, Nero and Vespasian (41-79); of the silver *denarii* nine are republican, the rest imperial, extending from Nero, with 17 of Trajan and 4 of Hadrian, the latest three coins dating to 119-22. The date and excellent preservation of this last group indicates that the coins were laid aside and lost early in Hadrian's reign, when stone was being quarried either for the fort or the Wall.

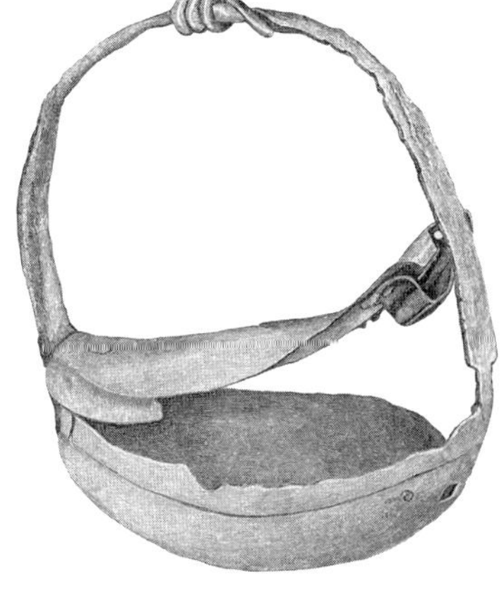

The Thorngrafton arm-purse. (115 mm across)

Vindolanda from the air looking north. Within the fort are visible the headquarters building and the commanding officer's house. To the south lies the early bath-house. The civil settlement is to the west of the fort, with the later bath-house on its north side. To its south is the reconstructed tower and stretches of Wall.

VINDOLANDA

Vindolanda was first investigated by John Warburton shortly before 1716, but the earliest work which could be characterised as archaeological excavations were by Anthony Hedley between 1818 and 1834. The modern era began with work by Eric Birley from 1930 to 1936: he placed the fort in state care in 1939. Robin Birley undertook some excavations between 1949 and 1969. In 1970 the Vindolanda Trust was established, and since then there has been a continuous series of excavations led by Robin Birley and now his son Andrew. During this period, large areas of the civil settlement have been investigated, together with parts of the fort and two external bath-houses, while replica structures have been erected and the museum regularly expanded to display the important collection of artefacts. The most significant discovery has been the writing tablets, most of which are now in the British Museum. The collection is unique in its size and the range of information which it provides. In the writing-tablets, the name of the fort is given as *Vindol.* or *Vindolande*, the locative form of *Vindolanda*. *Vindolandesses* is on an inscription from the civil settlement. The name appears to mean "white enclosure" or "white lawn". An altar found at Beltingham 3 km (2 miles) to the south-east, records the *curia Textoverdorum*, an otherwise unknown group of people, perhaps those living in this part of the Tyne valley.

The writing-tablets have provided evidence about the units based here in the late first and early second centuries. The earliest attested regiment was the First Cohort of Tungrians, who were at Vindolanda about 85 to 92. Remarkably, a strength report of the unit has been found indicating a nominal strength of 753, but of these only 296 were present at Vindolanda. 46 were serving as guards to the legate Ferox while 337 men were at *Coria* (possibly Corbridge, though an unknown place associated with the *curia Textoverdorum* has also been suggested). It is possible that the unit was in the process of being enlarged from 500 strong to 1,000 strong, its size on a diploma issued in 103. The Ninth Cohort of Batavians is attested at Vindolanda from about 97 to at least 30 April 104 and possibly until 16 July of that year: it left Britain to fight in the second Dacian War.

The Tungrians were back at Vindolanda by 105, probably staying well into the century: fragments of a diploma issued between January and March 146 and found in the fort record a veteran of the unit. This is not evidence that the unit was still based at Vindolanda, merely that a soldier recruited into the Tungrians 25 or 26 years before had retired here, presumably after serving most of his time at the fort. In the early second century, during the reign of Trajan, some legionaries and also some cavalrymen from a regiment of Vardullians were recorded at Vindolanda: the First Cohort of Vardullians is known to have later served on the northern frontier. Later in the second century a cohort of Nervians appears to have been based here, before being replaced by the Gauls, who are first attested at the site in 213. The Fourth Cohort of Gauls was recorded at Vindolanda in the third century and in the *Notitia Dignitatum*.

Altar to Jupiter and the other immortal gods and to the Genius of the Commanding Officer's house by Q. Petronius Urbicus, prefect of the Fourth Cohort of Gauls. Urbicus came from Brixia in Italy.
(1.32 m high)

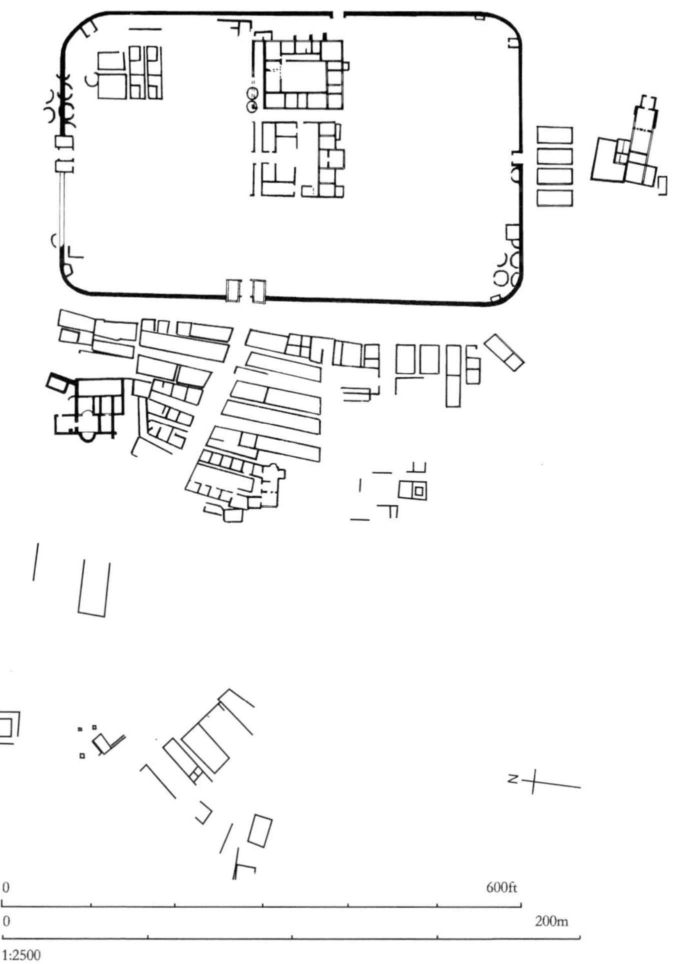

Vindolanda fort and civil settlement. Within the fort are visible the headquarters building, the commanding officer's house and parts of two third-century barrack-blocks. The late first-century bath-house lies outside the south gate. The civil settlement runs along the west wall of the fort and to each side of the road leading from the fort's west gate, with the third-century bath-house to the north.

Table 5: The forts at Vindolanda

period	date	unit	size	material of construction
I	c.85-c.92	First Cohort of Tungrians	c.1.4ha/3.5ac	timber/turf rampart
II	c.92-c.97	Ninth Cohort of Batavians	c.2.8ha/7ac	timber/turf rampart
III	c.97-104	Ninth Cohort of Batavians	-	timber/turf rampart
IV	104-c.120	First Cohort of Tungrians and detachment of Vardullians? and legionaries	<2.8ha/7ac	timber/stone fort wall
V	c.120-c.163	Third Cohort of Nervians?	1.68ha/4.15ac	timber and stone buildings
VI	c.163-c.180	-	-	stone
VIA	c.180-c.208	Second Cohort of Nervians?	-	stone
VIB	c.208-211	erection of round buildings across the whole site of the fort		
VII	c.213-	Fourth Cohort of Gauls	1.46ha/3.6ac	stone
VIII	c.300-c.400+	Fourth Cohort of Gauls	1.46ha/3.6ac	stone

The visible fort, covering 1.46 ha (3.6 acres), occupies a prominent platform. It sits on a complex sequence of earlier forts, which have been examined in several areas.

The first fort was founded about 85 and abandoned in about 92; it appears to have covered about 1.4 ha (3.5 acres). Only a section of its west ditch is known, but the pottery dumped in the fill of that ditch indicates demolition followed by rebuilding in 90-2. The new fort, about 2.8 ha (7 acres) in area, was for the Batavians. Part of the south rampart, built of turf, together with the single-portal south gate, has been located, and within a substantial building, perhaps the commanding officer's house (many writing-tablets were found here). Eight modern posts mark the site of the gate.

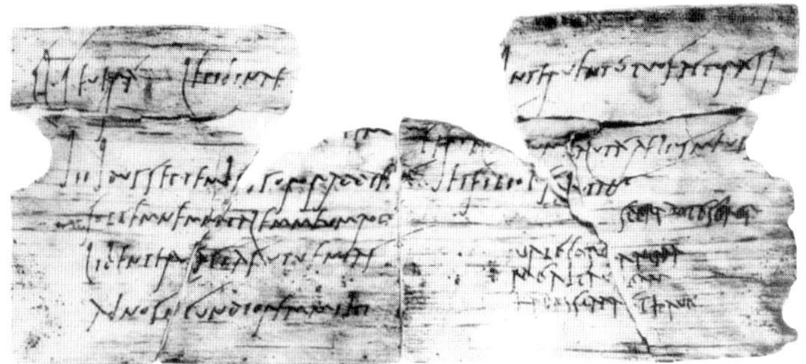

This letter from Claudia Severa to Sulpicia Lepidina inviting her to the celebration of her birthday contains a message almost certainly by Severa herself, the earliest known example of writing in Latin by a woman. (223 x 96 mm)

About 97, the fort was rebuilt; although the new buildings were on the same alignment as their predecessors, they lay 1.5- 2 m (5 - 6 ft 6 in) to the west. The main building yielded the archive of the prefect Flavius Cerialis, and was probably his own house. This is supported by the existence of shoes from at least three children, aged 2, 4 or 5 and over 7, together with more expensive shoes. Various rooms were used for the repair of tents, shoes, harnesses and metal objects, so perhaps the area excavated was the wing containing the workrooms. One room, identified as a kitchen, contained writing tablets, including a list of kitchen utensils and a recipe. In 2000, part of a possible barrack-block of this fort was located below the south wall of the third-century fort, and the regimental bath-house immediately beyond, that is just outside the south-east corner of the late-first-century fort. A writing tablet of this period records that 18 soldiers were building the bath-house. Archaeological evidence suggests that the Batavians had to leave at short notice. In comparison to the previous change of unit, they left many usable items behind as well as much litter. Many of the tablets had been consigned to a bonfire, presumably on departure of the unit, but had been saved by a timely downpour which extinguished the flames. Environmental material demonstrates that this took place in summer, but it was some months, into autumn, before a new unit arrived. Only now was the building demolished, or rather dismantled, and covered by a layer of turf and clay, 80 cm (2 ft 8 in) deep. Rebuilding did not take place immediately, but after a gap which allowed leaves to accumulate on the cleared surface. The dendrochronological date of the winter of 103/4 for the felling of the oak presumably used in the new fort is a little earlier than the date provided by the writing-tablets for the departure from the fort of the Ninth Cohort of Batavians.

The building was replaced not by one of similar character but by a structure best interpreted as a barrack-block. This fort continued in use until about 120. The purpose of the well-built timber structure which replaced its predecessors is not clear, though two rooms appear to have been used for metal-working; one contained a furnace. Within this period a stone wall, 1.2 m (4 ft) wide, was erected in front of the south rampart of the fort.

A new fort was erected at Vindolanda early in the reign of Hadrian. An inscription of Hadrian, recording building work under the governor A. Platorius Nepos, was found "in the ruins" at Vindolanda between 1830 and 1835. It ought unequivocally to indicate the date of construction of the new fort, 122 to about 126. It style, however, is so similar to the milecastle inscriptions that it has been suggested that it was brought here from such a structure when the fort was later being rebuilt or repaired. The Thorngrafton Hoard found on Barcombe Hill, also, ought to support a date at this time for rebuilding at Vindolanda for its latest coins date to 119-22, assuming that the stone was being quarried for use in the fort. The new fort was smaller than its predecessor. Its west and east walls were on the same lines as their third-century successors, the visible fort walls, but the enclosure was longer north-south. The west and east gates were investigated in the 1930s and found to be simple structures with no towers. Their location, together with the orientation of the stone headquarters building, examined in 1936, demonstrates that the fort, unusually, faced south. Fragments of timber buildings are also known.

This fort continued in occupation through the second century, though with some rebuilding about 163, presumably related to the abandonment of the Antonine Wall. In the early third century there occurred a most strange episode with the demolition of the fort and the construction of rows of small circular stone buildings across the whole site. The purpose of these is unknown: all that can be said is that they had a short life.

Their replacement was a normal fort, but the first fort whose dimensions are securely known, not least because it is the visible fort. It measures 156.8 by 93.2 m (514 by 305 feet) and covers 1.46 ha (3.6 acres). The circuit of its walls is fully exposed and beyond lay a ditch, now filled in. The fort retained the east gate of its predecessor, but otherwise new single-portal gates with towers were built to north and west, with a simpler new south gate. The headquarters building dates to this period. To the east sat the commanding officer's house, while to its west lay granaries located by trenching in the 1930s.

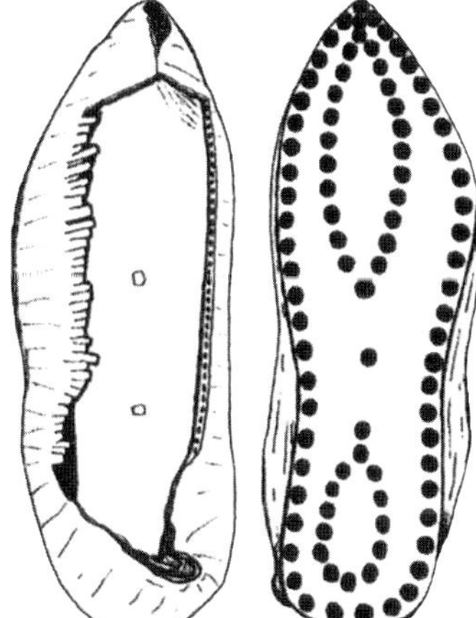

A small shoe found in the early second century fort at Vindolanda.
(234 mm long)

Excavations in 1980 in the north-east corner led both to the discovery of a barrack-block and to the revelation that there had been a delay in erecting it; it had been preceded by a building which was started and then abandoned to be replaced by a temporary structure. The double barrack-block subsequently erected is the earliest known of a new style. The building was divided into a series of seven small buildings, the centurion's quarters at the rampart end, with six separate blocks each providing the equivalent of a former normal *contubernium*, the back room being entered by a passage leading past the front room. Both latrines appear to relate to this fort. The unit based here was the Fourth Cohort of Gauls, who erected a loyalty dedication to the Emperor Caracalla in 213: the stone was found in 1933 reused in a drain in the headquarters building. Ten years later, the unit appears on an inscription recording the restoration of a gate with its towers from the foundations under the governor Claudius Xenephon. The bath-house of this fort lies beyond the north-west corner of the fort.

Towards the end of the third century the soldiers' quarters within the barrack-block were rebuilt; the officers' blocks were rebuilt about a century later. The whole of the barrack complex was subsequently demolished and replaced by a stone building, only a corner of which survived. There is some indication that the east wall of the fort was repaired early in the fifth century, not by restoration of the wall, but through the creation of an earthen bank. Of even later date is the tombstone of Brigomaglos, dating to about 500, discovered a little to the north-east of the fort about 1878, and a brooch of sixth- or seventh-century date found at the south gate.

There are **four main elements** to Vindolanda today: fort, civil settlement, replicas and museum. The main access is from the west, but it is advisable to visit the museum first which provides valuable interpretation of the site as well as displaying the remarkable discoveries made here.

The visible **fort** dates to the early third century. Its walls are complete, and stand up to 3 m (10 ft) high. The east wall shows signs of repair, in which were used tombstones. There appears to have been one ditch on all sides but the south, which was unprotected. All four gates are visible. The **east gate** is a simple structure consisting of a passage flanked by short walls. It was first erected in the early second century, but rebuilt about a hundred years later. It was originally approached by a flight of steps, removed in the early nineteenth century.

The **south gate** is of similar plan, though with responds for arches front and rear. There was a step outside the gate down to the road surface, and it would appear that the gate was not intended to be used by wheeled traffic. Three layers of cobbles were noted in the roadway, the second containing a coin of the Emperor Julian dating to 361. There is some evidence to suggest that this gate was eventually blocked.

The **north gate** dates to the fort erected in the early third century following the demolition of the round buildings. It was first examined in 1829, and again in 1930 when it was found to have been constructed of reused masonry. Each tower was entered by a door to the south. The western tower contained an oven; a scrap of late-fourth-century pottery was found in the latest flagged floor. The passage had arches towards the front and at the rear; the road surface was of gravel, replaced by flags.

The **west gate** is similar in plan to the north. A mid-fourth-century coin hoard was found within it in the nineteenth century.

Two **latrines** have been found within the fort, at the north-east and south-east corners. In both cases, the sewage debouched into the fort ditch, through two drains from the northerly building. Both latrines were constructed at the same time as the early-third-century fort, but while the northerly building continued in use into the late fourth century, its southerly companion had been demolished by the mid-fourth century. Elsewhere, buildings were erected against the inside of the fort wall. Between the south gate and the south-west angle tower, a platform was examined in 2000. Measuring 4.5 by 5.56 m (15 by 18 ft 3 in), it was revetted with stones and filled with clay and soil. It overlay a building containing a coin of 393-4. As the coin is quite worn, the platform would appear to date to after 400; it has been interpreted as a platform for artillery. Between the platform and the round base is a short length of the south wall of the fort built about 163.

Two principal buildings are displayed. The **headquarters**, excavated in the 1930s and dating to the early third century, offers some differences from the earlier arrangements in such buildings. Across its front was a verandah, later closed at the outer ends and turned into storerooms. The courtyard is smaller than usual and instead of the verandahs running round three sides, there is now a series of rooms, presumably for the storage of arms, or archives perhaps. The tribunal stood at one end of the cross-hall and is notable for the survival of two steps and the base of the ornamental front. The central of the rear five rooms still appeared to function as the regimental chapel; there was no strongroom but a pit for the money chests. To each side were rooms for the clerical staff; of particular note is the survival of one slab from the screens which closed the open ends of the rooms, and elsewhere the slots to hold the screens. In the late fourth century a hypocaust was introduced into one room, while two small latrines were added in the south-east corner. These facilities may have been for the benefit of the staff, but it has also been suggested that the area may have been given over to accommodation, and this receives some support from the use given to the floor of the ante-room to the chapel; it showed evidence of severe burning as if a fire had stood here for many years. The rooms around the courtyard now all received raised floors supported on dwarf walls, as would be appropriate for the storage of food. A well was sunk in the courtyard.

Below the building may be seen some traces of the earlier

headquarters building which faced south. Fragments of the rear rooms of the second-century building may be seen under the rooms surrounding the later courtyard. This was built in a style familiar in Africa, but not north Britain, with small stone infilling between larger piers.

The **commanding officer's house** was examined in 1997 and 1998. It was originally erected in the early third century, but reconstruction was so thorough about 300 that the original arrangements are now not clear, though the south, west and part of the north ranges could be recognised as forming part of the earlier house. In its final, fourth-century state, it was a courtyard house in the traditional style. Some of the rooms had raised floors, others were heated. *Opus signinum*, a special form of mortar, had been used to floor several rooms, while the amount of wall-plaster discovered indicates the finish inside. In spite of modern excavation, it proved difficult to assign a function to most rooms, apart from features such as a latrine and oven. Outside the east wall are three substantial buttresses, which point not just to subsidence but the existence of an upper storey, access probably being from the corridor along the east range where there is a large threshold stone, perhaps to support the staircase. In the late fourth century the east and south wings appear to have been demolished and a wooden shed erected over the north-east room. A new bath-suite was constructed over the north range, and extending further north; this was partially planned by Anthony Hedley in 1830. Excavation in 1997 led to the discovery of part of a tombstone reused as a flag in the main hall of this bath-house. It recorded the death in warfare of a centurion of a Tungrian Cohort, presumably the First, based at the fort in the late first and early second centuries.

About 400 an apsidal building was erected on the eastern side adjacent to the courtyard and partly overlying the east wing. Its base course was formed of a variety of stones, those in the apse being particularly large, probably supporting a timber superstructure. It has been suggested that this is a Christian church. While it would be expected that the apse would be at the opposite end of the building, churches with western apses are known from this time.

The **round structures** were first located in 1934 underneath the north wall of the fort. They are now known to stretch right across the fort to the south gate. They are arranged in rows and a total number of at least 300 has been estimated. They are no more than 4.6 m (15 ft) across internally, thus providing a floor space of 14.5 m^2. The doors of two of the northern rows opened onto a metalled path or street. No more than two courses of stone survive, and it may be presumed that the remaining part of each structure was of timber, covered in thatch, turf, or another organic material. The floors were of clay or brick-mortar or partially flagged, with a hearth beside the door. The few finds indicate that the buildings were in use in the early third century, at the time of the Emperor Septimius Severus, but they were unhelpful at determining the function of the buildings. Although small, these buildings are in the local vernacular tradition and are similar to those found elsewhere in Roman contexts. Various explanations have been offered for their function: that they housed prisoners-of-war; the hostages of tribes conquered by Severus; refugees from the warfare in the north; a native militia or conscript labour. Excavation in 2000 of one circular building and part of five others under the south wall of the fort revealed a layer of ash covering them all, an indication of their destruction.

Beyond the south gate lay a **bath-house** dating to the first century. A writing tablet of the 90s records 18 soldiers working on the construction of a bath-house, presumably this building. The main spine of the building contained the heated rooms. To the north, and reached first from the fort, lay the changing room (*apodyterium*). A door in its south-west corner will have led to the cold room (*frigidarium*), and thence, through a vestibule, to the warm room (*tepidarium*) and hot room (*caldarium*), at the east end of the spine; these were heated by their own furnace (*praefurnium*), over which lay a small hot bath. At the south-east corner of the changing room lay a small room of unknown purpose, and a hot dry room (*laconicum*), with its own furnace. The soldier thus had a choice of bathing, returning in each case to the cold room where there was a cold bath, to the south. Outside the main building, at the lower end of the site, lay a latrine, flushed by water from the bath-house as well as the main aqueduct. Excavation in 2000 revealed evidence for modifications to the heated rooms, including replacement of some of the pillars supporting the floor, and the repair of the floor itself. Demolition appears to have occurred in the 140s. The demolition debris included two chimney pots through which the hot air circulating under the floors and up the walls of the building would have escaped, and fragments of wall-plaster decorated with circles and wavy lines. The tiles were particularly interesting in that they bore the footprints of animals including dog, cat, pig, cattle and probably goat. Several ovens were subsequently erected over the northern area of the changing room, while iron-working took place here too. In the third or fourth century several stone buildings were erected between the fort and the bath-house site.

To the west of the fort lay the **civil settlement**. The buildings flanked the road leading out of the west gate and heading, at an angle, for the Stanegate. Archaeology often cannot determine the function of many of these buildings. It is clear, however, that they date to two main phases. Recently it has been suggested that the earlier period was the military base associated with the collection of round houses, with only the later buildings forming a civil settlement. The earlier buildings were protected by a clay rampart. They included a house with a suite of baths, appropriate for a commanding officer, but formerly interpreted as an inn. Beside it lay three long narrow buildings, two divided into many small rooms; these may have been barracks. To the north of the road were further buildings, some of which may have served the same purpose. This phase was of short duration and thereafter some of the buildings were reused, but most were replaced. Over 40 buildings of the second period, which lasted through the third century until about 270, have been planned. Most are rectangular, measuring about 12 by 4.57 m (40 by 15 ft), with low stone walls surmounted by timber. It was probably the occupants of this settlement who dedicated an altar to Vulcan, describing themselves as the *vicani Vindolandesses*, the villagers of Vindolanda; the implication of the inscription is that this was a self-governing community. The dedication to the god of metal-workers is, perhaps, not surprising as the villagers included metal-workers amongst their numbers. These people do not appear to have been very wealthy as their coinage was very worn and did not include the latest issues, while their pottery was low grade. In its last phase, some buildings were replaced in an entirely different style of construction. Substantial stones formed the lowest course and presumably acted as the bases of timber uprights, the walls being of wattle and daub.

Left: A wooden mallet found in the first century fort. (279 mm long)
Right: A hammer, complete with its wooden handle, possibly used in leatherworking, found in a workshop of the Hadrianic period. (339 mm long)

To the north of the civil settlement lay the third-century **bath-house**, which can now only be viewed from outside its perimeter. It was of a different plan from the late-first-century building, being more similar to the Hadrianic bath-houses in plan. The building was entered through a porch in the south-west corner which led into the changing room; beyond the south-east corner of this room lay the latrine. The range of rooms to the north of the changing room contained the cold room with its cold bath and the hot dry room. The most northerly range consisted of the warm room, hot room with its hot bath, and the furnace. Within the furnace room, a flight of nine steps led to the top of a platform, presumably to allow access to the boiler. The building appears to have been abandoned before the last third of the fourth century.

On the western fringes of the settlement lay a Romano-Celtic **temple**. It was demolished in the late second century and the area turned over to use as a cemetery. To its south lay a large water-tank, and further south again two small **mausolea**, probably dating to the fourth century. The principal cemetery seems to have lain along the Stanegate leading west from the fort, where many cremation urns have been found. North of the Stanegate, geophysical survey has revealed evidence for further civilian buildings and industrial activity.

To the south of the visible civil settlement, several **replicas** have been constructed. The Stone Wall is 10 Roman feet wide and nearly 6.40 m (21 ft) to the walkway and incorporates a turret. The milecastle gateway is modelled on that drawn by I. A. Richmond in 1935; it sits within a length of turf wall. Replicas of a civilian house, shop, temple, cemetery and altars have also been erected in the valley beside the museum. The **museum** contains a wealth of material, the products of 35 years of excavation: armour, shoes, wooden objects, textiles as well as the more normal glass, pottery, iron-work, small finds, inscriptions and sculpture. Several of the objects are remarkable, such as the plume from a helmet.

VINDOLANDA TO HALTWHISTLE BURN

North of the eastern entrance to Vindolanda stands a **milestone** on the north side of the Stanegate, which itself survives as a broad agger. One Roman mile (1.5 km) westwards, along the access road which sits on the Stanegate, is the stump to another milestone; it is a rare occurrence to have two milestones surviving in this way. Its shaft, now lost, bore the inscription: *bono reipublicae nato* "to him who was born for the good of the state", a compliment to the reigning emperor.

The Stanegate continues past Seatsides farm to Haltwhistle Burn under the track as far as the farm. Alongside the road several marching camps have been recorded, most no longer visible. **Seatsides Farm** sits within one camp, covering 6.7 ha (16.6 acres); the west and east gates were protected by traverses, but the south and possibly north gate also by a *clavicula*. To the north lie two more camps, one about half the size and the next about half again. To the south-east of the farm, at **Bean Burn**, are two small camps, 0.3 ha (0.7 acres) and 0.04 ha (0.09 acres); the latter presumably a practice camp. These camps can be viewed from the Northumberland National Park Visitor Centre. Two miles on, and south of the standing stones known as Mare and Foal, is one of the larger camps on the isthmus, **Milestone House**, enclosing 7 ha (17 acres). The Stanegate crosses the modern road beside the Mare and Foal and can be seen running westwards on the shoulder of the ridge.

HALTWHISTLE BURN

Where the Stanegate approaches Haltwhistle Burn, 5.6 km (3½ miles) from Vindolanda, stands a small **fortlet**, 19.80 m (65 ft) above the stream, on a bold bluff. The natural defences are good, to which deep ditches of irregular plan have been added.

The fortlet was excavated in 1908, when it was found to measure 63 by 51 m (208 by 167 ft), giving an area of about

0.3 ha (0.75 acres). It was defended by ramparts of earth with a stone facing, set not in mortar but in clay, and had gates in its east, south and west walls, the latter a postern giving on to the burn. At some stage the east gate had been blocked completely by a closing wall. Inside the fort the remains of several buildings were found, the surviving walls of clay-bonded stone, which originally most probably served to carry timber upperwork. These buildings appear to have been a barrack for a century

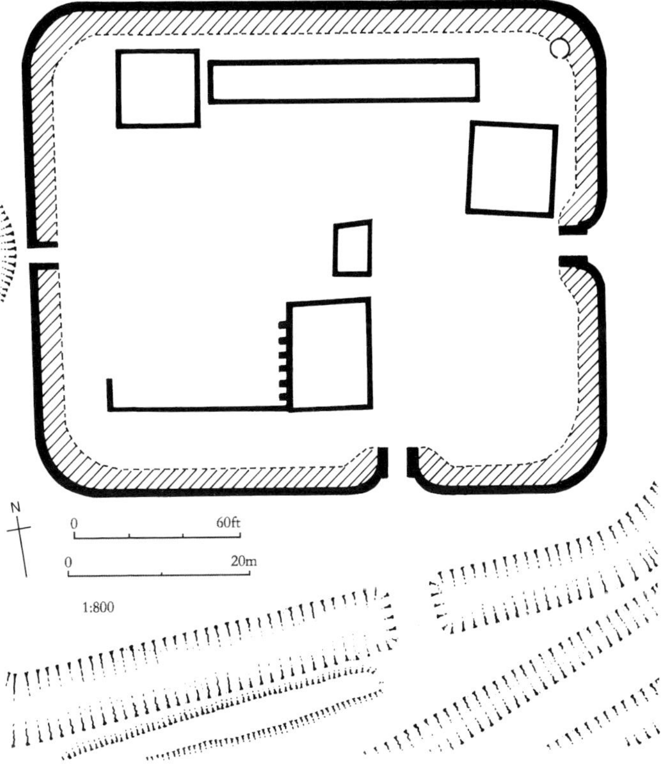

Haltwhistle Burn small fort.

with separate centurion's quarters, and possibly another centurion's or officer's quarters just inside the east gate; the two last buildings are about the same size and shape, although the former was better built. In the southern portion of the fort a roughly constructed building, about 12 by 9 m (40 by 30 ft) in size, had secondary buttresses, and an added, partly walled area on its western side. It is possible that this was a combined storehouse-granary and armoury, with perhaps an enclosed yard-area to its west. Roads lead in from the three gates to a central paved area, where the smallest building of all stood. This, like the centurion's quarters, was of better masonry than the others, and had been provided with an internal fireplace, all suggesting that it had been the administrative building, or office, of the fort.

On the strength of these buildings it appears that the garrison had been a detachment from a parent unit based elsewhere, for, although a storehouse seems to be present, there is no proper commanding officer's house nor headquarters building.

The finds alone are not conclusive in dating the lifespan of the post, but taken with other evidence they suggest a foundation during the reign of the Emperor Trajan (98-117). The fortlet had clearly been occupied for some time, for the east gate had been walled up and other signs of long-term wear were noted by the excavators. Abandonment had been accompanied by careful and thorough demolition, and the slighted west rampart was sealed by the refuse of an adjacent quarry. Clayton was shown the letters *Leg VI V* on a rock-face of this quarry in 1844, a record of the Sixth Legion cutting stone, presumably for the Wall. The demolition of the fortlet has been linked to the building of the Wall when some sites on the Stanegate were abandoned.

The **Stanegate** swings round the fortlet to the south, descends the burn on a well-graded embankment, then climbs the opposite bank in a deep cutting, to run west as a line visible across the fields.

Near the fortlet lie three **temporary camps**. That immediately to the north is situated on the highest ground; it enclosed 1 ha (2.5 acres). North again is a tiny camp, barely visible, but to the north-east is a well-preserved camp, originally covering 0.7 ha (1.7 acres), but reduced in size to 0.3 ha (0.8 acres) by the construction of a rampart and ditch; three entrances are visible.

HALTWHISTLE BURN TO THROP

After crossing Haltwhistle Burn the Stanegate again takes the line of the ridge across Haltwhistle Common, continuing all the way on the north side of the modern road. West of the burn and just short of the junction of the Stanegate with the branch road to Great Chesters, lies the largest camp on the Wall, **Markham Cottage**. It encloses 16.8 ha (41.5 acres). Its size suggests that it was either constructed for troops on the march or as a labour camp for the Wall builders. In the north-east corner sits a smaller camp, 1.4 ha (3.4 acres) in size. Beyond are a further four camps: **Lees Hall**, 1.7 ha (4.2 acres), lies south of the modern road; two at **Sunny Rigg**, 0.6 ha (1.5 acre) and the other a little smaller, are situated between the road and the Stanegate; while, straddling the Stanegate, a large camp of 8.7 ha (21.5 acres) sits on the highest point of **Fell End**. Excavation at Sunny Rigg in 1981 revealed that the ditch had never been cut.

At Fell End the road is confused by later lines, and traces of quarrying and mining are visible all around. Near the camp a milestone of the Emperor Aurelian (273-5) was found in 1932, very like that of Probus (276-82) from Crindledykes (see page 428). On Fell End the road turns slightly north to run directly to Carvoran fort, from where this last length of its course can be seen as a particularly clear line as it descends the hillside. Just to the east of the fort the road was lined by a cemetery on its northern side. (For Carvoran see pages 280-2).

The distance from Haltwhistle Burn to Carvoran is just under 5.6 km (3½ miles). Carvoran lies at the junction of the

Stanegate and the Maiden Way, and seems not to be part of the normal spacing of forts along the Stanegate road. Beyond Carvoran the road has to negotiate the steep valley of the Tipalt burn, making dog-leg turns on each side. Towards the west end of the field beyond the golf course the agger of the Stanegate is visible.

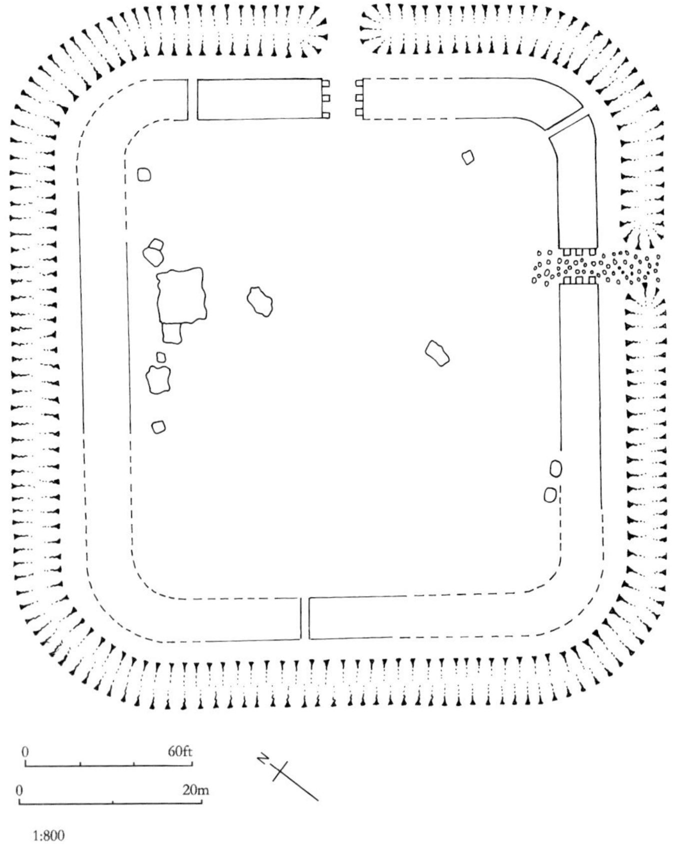

Throp small fort.

On the ridge between the Gilsland road and Throp lie three **camps**. **Glenwhelt Leazes**, end on to the Stanegate and enclosing 1.2 ha (3 acres), is unusual in each gate having an external traverse as well as an internal *clavicula*. The gates of **Chapel Rigg**, 0.6 ha (1.5 acres), are similarly protected. **Crooks**, a little larger, is more normal in only having traverses.

THROP

On top of the ridge immediately to the west of MC 48 (Poltross Burn) sits a **fortlet**, examined in 1910. About 60 m (200 ft) square, it covers 0.36 ha (0.9 acres) and was defended by a rampart of turf laid on a stone foundation 4.88 m (16 ft) wide. Its two gateways, situated in the north-eastern and south-east sides, were of timber, and, it may be presumed, so were the internal buildings. Of these, only rough patches of flagging and a series of hearths behind the north-west rampart had survived ploughing. An oven was found at the back of the south-eastern rampart. Pottery indicated a similar date of occupation to Haltwhistle Burn in the early second century, though there was also activity here in the fourth century.

THROP TO NETHER DENTON

From Throp the Stanegate runs directly to Nether Denton, almost 4 km (2½ miles) away, taking the shortest and most direct route. At first the road survives as a terrace, but, after passing the northern edge of Throp farm, it falls in below the modern Gilsland-Low Row road just east of Upper Denton, and, after crossing the railway line, continues to Nether Denton. At **Mains Rigg**, just south of the railway crossing, a stone tower was identified in 1928 and partly excavated in 1971. It is 6.40 m (21 ft) square, with walls 90 cm (3 ft) wide with offsets. No door was found on the ground floor; presumably access was by a ladder leading to an upper entrance. The tower was surrounded by a ditch, also square in plan, about 3 m (10 ft) wide, with an undug causeway at the south-east corner. The

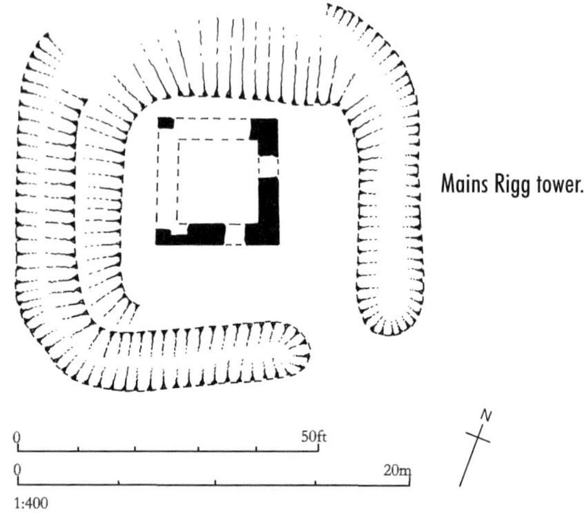

Mains Rigg tower.

purpose of the tower was presumably to aid communication between Throp and Nether Denton, which are not intervisible. The earthwork survives well, with the base of the tower also visible.

NETHER DENTON

The **fort** sits on a narrow ridge, now occupied by the church and rectory, overlooking a steep descent to the Irthing on the north. Outside the door of the church is a reused Roman altar and, across the path, the grave of the archaeologist F. G. Simpson, who was responsible for so much of our knowledge about Hadrian's Wall.

In 1868, when the rectory was being built, brooches and other metal objects, 89 coins ranging from Republican issues to the Emperor Trajan (98-117), and late-first-to early-second-century pottery in abundance were found, together with structural remains including clay and cobble foundations and stone flagging, and "traces of fire-places" with much blackening.

In 1933 excavation produced "thickly occupied ground" with many tiles south of the church. A turf rampart was located, 9 m (30 ft) thick at base and still standing 1.50 m (5 ft) high; today it survives as a distinct bump in the field wall. Beyond, mortised timbers rested on what appeared to be ditch fill, together with pre-Hadrianic pottery. The rampart ran east-west and was traced for 55 m (60 yards) to what appeared to be the south-west corner. This fort covered no more than 1.21 ha (3 acres).

Aerial photography has subsequently considerably extended our knowledge. Two sets of defences lie to the south and west of the known fort. Running south from the south-west corner of the fort is a pair of ditches which could belong to an earlier fort; or, alternatively, protect an annexe. The outer line, consisting of a single ditch, protected an area 3.28 ha (8.1 acres) in extent. This may be an outer defence of a type known elsewhere; it could relate to an early fort.

Walling and other traces of occupation were recorded in 1911 and 1933 south-west of the fort, where aerial photography has confirmed the location of the **civil settlement**. Two cremations were found south of the Stanegate. Pottery from this area has been dated to the second half of the second century suggesting that the civil settlement continued in occupation after the abandonment of the fort. An alternative is that the pottery indicates continuing occupation of the fort. Cremations were also found 700 m (760 yards) to the west of the fort at High Nook farm in 1861, 1909 and 1965, indicating the location of a second cemetery.

NETHER DENTON TO BOOTHBY

From Nether Denton westwards the line of the Stanegate is uncertain as it crosses the broken country, except where cut by tributary streams of the Irthing in the vicinity of Naworth. East of Naworth, Carling Gill and Pott's Cleugh are crossed by series of cuttings linked by a section where the road sits on a shelf as it curves round the hillside: the total length is about 320 m (350 yards). The sections to the east and west of Pott's Cleugh were examined in 1935 when metalling was found. Today, the road line can be followed from Carling Gill, across Pott's Cleugh almost to Turnershill Wood.

Two km (just over 1 mile) to the west, the Quarry Beck, which joins the Irthing at Lanercost Bridge, is crossed in a similar fashion with a deep cutting to the east, while it negotiates the west bank on a shelf cut into the hillside. These are good examples of the embanking and cutting by which Roman engineers negotiated deep ravines. Again, metalling was recorded here in 1935, when the remains of stakes were also noted, presumably revetting the sides of the cutting; elsewhere stones served the same purpose. West of the Quarry Beck the general course of the road was by Boothby, Great Eastby and Breconhill to Irthington.

BOOTHBY

Five km (3 miles) to the west of Nether Denton, excavation in 1933 at Castle Hill, Boothby, revealed a ditch, 5.18 m (17 ft) wide and 1.52-1.82 m (5-6 ft) deep, containing fragments of early-second-century Roman pottery, including a piece of a samian bowl. Behind the ditch were remains of a clay rampart. No further excavation has taken place, but aerial photography has identified the south-east and south-west corners of what could have been a small fortlet situated on top of a steep bank above the Irthing; the northern sides have been eroded by landslip into the valley of the River Irthing. There appears to be a break in the south-west rampart just short of the escarpment.

BOOTHBY TO BRAMPTON OLD CHURCH

From Boothby to Brampton the route of the road is not known, but just south-east of the bridge on the modern Brampton-Longtown road it has again been located, running west to the Irthing. For a short distance it is overlain by the A6071 and then by the access road to Crooked Holme Farm. A branch road led south to the fort at Brampton Old Church, climbing the bank in a cutting in a curve to enter the fort at the east gate.

BRAMPTON OLD CHURCH

Old Church **fort** is situated on a steep bluff overlooking the Irthing from the east, with a good outlook. The platform of the fort is still faintly visible, especially on the south, west and northern sides and at the north-east angle, about St Martin's Church and churchyard; some Roman stones are visible in the fabric of the church. The fort measured 125 by 121 m (410 by 396 ft), giving an area of 1.5 ha (3.7 acres), sufficient for a cohort 500 strong. Excavations in 1935 revealed that it had been defended by a single ditch of 3.96 m (13 ft), behind which lay a rampart 4.88 m (16 ft) wide, built of mixed turf and clay, laid on a cobble base. The south gate was partly excavated and found to have been of timber. Within lay two granaries, one at

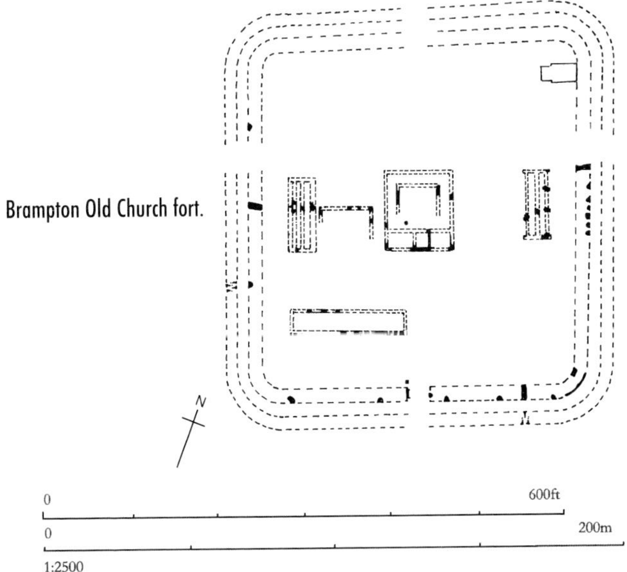

Brampton Old Church fort.

each end of the central range. Each was 7.92 m (26 ft) wide while the eastern was found to be 23 m (76 ft) long. The headquarters lay in the centre of the fort facing north and measuring 24.38 by 27.13 m (80 by 89 ft) in size. Its courtyard, cross-hall and shrine were identified. To the west lay a building which was either a small commanding officer's house or a workshop; only part of its plan was revealed. To the south, part of a barrack-block was located. All these buildings had been constructed in clay-bonded stonework, but their upper portions were, almost certainly, of timber.

Finds from the sites are few. The most spectacular is a Republican *denarius* of L. Calpurnius Piso Frugi, dated 88 BC What little pottery was recovered was said by the excavators to be "strikingly like that obtained at Haltwhistle Burn and Throp, in both fabric and type". The fort was probably erected in the early second century, with occupation continuing until forts were built on the Wall. Demolition then followed.

Little is known about any **extra-mural settlement**, but a large mass of very hard concrete lying at the bottom of the cliff, north-east of the fort, was taken in 1935 to be the remains of a substantial building, fallen from the cliff-top as the result of erosion. A road has also been traced from the north-east corner of the fort down the scarp to the river.

Almost a mile from the fort, also to the south-east, in the recreation grounds of Irthing Valley School, a series of six **tile-** and two **pottery-kilns** was excavated in 1963. In 1964 a hoard of ironwork was discovered in a well at the same site; this consisted of agricultural and artisans' tools, fragments of furniture, general fittings and structural pieces of carts and buildings. All was worn or damaged and the whole had apparently been dumped. It is now in Tullie House Museum, Carlisle. Abundant pottery from the site dates to the early second century. This accords well with the date for the fort, suggesting that the kilns were abandoned, like the fort, when its unit was transferred to the Wall.

BRAMPTON OLD CHURCH TO CARLISLE

From Old Church to Carlisle the line of the Stanegate is known as far as Linstock, although little is visible today over much of its length. After crossing the River Irthing, it runs into Irthington on the line of the modern road. A little over a quarter of a mile west it turned towards Buckjumping. Here it was cut through the bank to ease the gradient; the Roman date was confirmed by excavation in 1935. From here the Stanegate took a straight line for High Crosby. Much of this section was damaged by Carlisle airport, including a Roman temporary camp at Watchcross examined in 1935 and shown to be about 73 m (240 ft) square over the ramparts (0.6 ha/1.5 acres in size) with three gates, each defended by a traverse.

Immediately west of High Crosby, and south of the old road, another deep cutting is preserved, a scrappy copse growing in it today. This cutting is 250 m (820 ft) long and 30 m (100 ft) wide and up to 5 m (17 ft) deep. Excavations in 1934 and 1935 revealed metalling, flanked by gulleys, along the whole of the length of the cutting. On the basis of the discovery of several pieces of pottery in the road ditches, another intermediate post has been postulated, lying between the old road and the by-pass. Hereafter, the road has been traced to a point a little short of the M6 motorway, just north of Linstock.

CARLISLE (*LUGUVALIUM*)

Roman Carlisle occupied a low hill south of the River Eden, with the River Caldew defining its south-western and western sides. The town's name is given as *Lugu(v)a[l]io* on a stylus tablet and, with slight variations in spelling, in the *Antonine Itinerary*, *Notitia Dignitatum* and *Ravenna Cosmography*, which is thought to mean "strong through Lugus", or something similar, Lugus being the name of a Celtic God identified with Mercury.

Modern excavation began in the 1970s and has revolutionised our knowledge of Roman Carlisle. Unfortunately

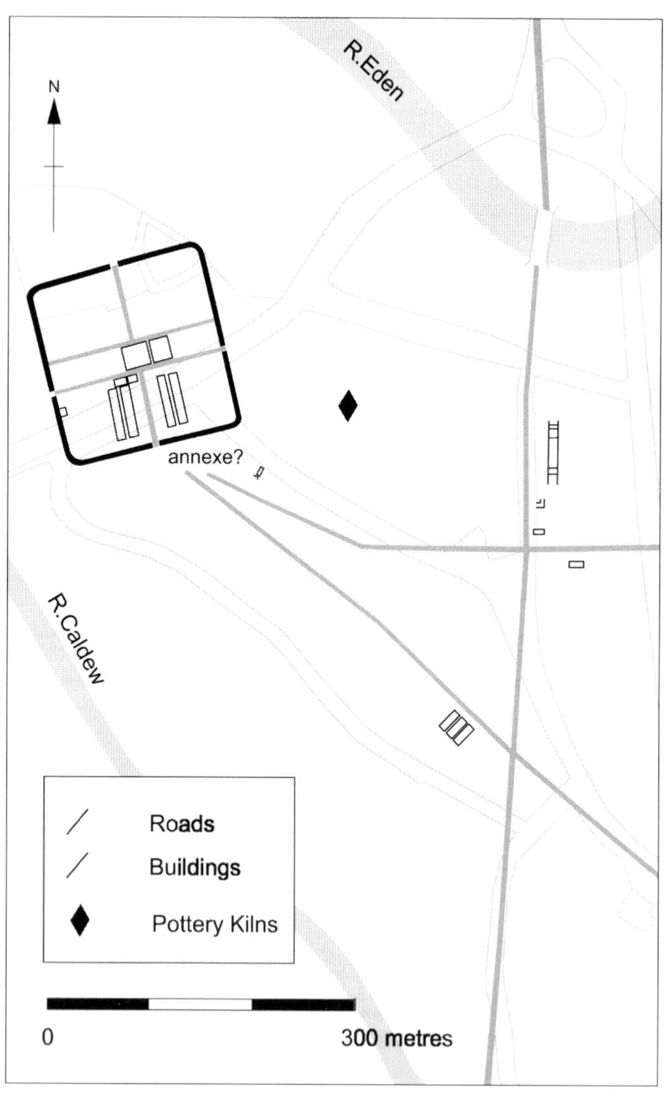

Carlisle in the late first century.

none of these discoveries is visible today. We now know the location, approximate size and history of the fort and the location of civilian buildings to the south and east of the fort. Waterlogged conditions led to the exceptional preservation of much woodwork and the discovery of several writing-tablets.

The *ala Gallorum Sebosiana*, the Sebosian Cavalry Regiment of Gauls, has been recorded on a writing-tablet and was probably at the fort in the late first century. One document records the issuing of wheat and barley to 16 decurions, the appropriate number for a cavalry regiment: this was presumably the *ala Sebosiana*. The names of the decurions suggest it had formerly served in the Rhineland, for which there is independent evidence. A further document refers to lances, again probably in connection with this regiment. There is also a reference to a trooper of the *ala Sebosiana*, *singularis* of Agricola. This soldier was a member of the governor's bodyguard and the governor can be no other than Gnaeus Julius Agricola, governor from 77 to 83. The Twentieth Legion is mentioned on one tablet dating to 83 and some of its men may have been present; this is the year that the Battle of Mons Graupius was fought.

An inscription of the *ala Petriana* found in Carlisle records only one torque, an ornamental necklace awarded for valour. As it later acquired a second, the unit may have been based here in the early second century, after it was increased in size under Trajan (98-117), but before it moved to Stanwix (see pages 341-5). The Ninth and Twentieth Legions, and probably also the Second, manufactured tiles at kilns at Scalesceugh 8 km (5 miles) to the south of Carlisle in the late first or early second centuries, but this does not necessarily imply that soldiers of these legions were based here. However, a *centurio regionarius* recorded at Carlisle about 105 was probably a legionary officer in charge of the surrounding territory.

An unusual dedication to Hercules, and probably dating to 180-92, by Publius Sextanius, a native of Xanten in the

Rhineland, prefect of the *ala Augusta ob virtutem appellata*, the Cavalry Regiment named Augusta for valour, recorded the slaughter of a band of barbarians. As the unit was attested at Old Carlisle, 16 km (10 miles) to the south-west, from the 180s onward, the regiment may not have been stationed at Carlisle. One recent discovery is an altar dedicated by M. Aurelius Syrio, tribune of the Twentieth Legion, between 213 and 222.

Under Tullie House Museum and the southern part of the castle lay a fort; it sat on the bluff overlooking the confluence of the rivers Eden and Caldew. Dendrochronology has demonstrated that the timbers for this fort were felled in the winter of 72/3. This confirms the similar date assigned to the earliest samian pottery from the site and indicates that the first fort was erected here by the governor Petillius Cerialis during his campaign against the Brigantes. The south and west ramparts and the gates have been located, allowing the fort to be estimated as 180 m (600 ft) square, covering about 3.25 ha (8 acres). Its rampart was of turf interleaved with layers of split logs; beyond lay two ditches. The south gate was double-portal, but one of the timber sills showed no signs of wear. Within, the buildings were of timber. They were constructed of oak with alder used for the wattle and daub walls. Not all appear to have been erected at once for timbers have been recovered dating to most of the 12 years that the fort was occupied. To date, the corners of the headquarters and the commanding officer's house and parts of several barrack-blocks have been discovered; between the intervallum road and the rampart lay small buildings. The barrack-blocks measured 48 by 8.5 m (158 by 28 ft). Insect remains indicate that weedy vegetation grew between these barrack-blocks. Elsewhere, different species of grain weevils were found. Unusually, a row of small buildings ran along the southern side of the *via principalis*; one was probably a workshop. Finds from this fort suggest that part of the regiment was cavalry. Some of the pottery used by these soldiers was made in kilns situated on modern Fisher

Street. An *amphora* from Cadiz, found outside the commander's house, bore a cursive text in black ink recording that its contexts were "Old Tangiers tunny-fish relish of excellent, top quality".

Plentiful evidence for the presence of cavalry comes from the next fort on the site, occupied by the *ala Gallorum Sebosiana*. One important find was much of a saddle (offcuts suggest the manufacture of shoes elsewhere in the fort). Timbers used in the construction of the fort have been dated to the winter of 83/4. The new barrack-blocks measured 48 by 9.5 m (158 by 31 ft), with the decurions' quarters to the south by the rampart. The *contubernia* measured about 8.4 by 3.3 m (26 ft 6 in by 11 ft) internally, being subdivided into two rooms 4.2 by 3.3 m and 3.8 by 3.3 m (13 ft 10 in by 11 ft and 12 ft 6 in by 11 ft). This may be part of a cavalry barrack as a drain was found in one room, while the other had a timber floor. A fresh coin of 96-8 linked to the construction of one barrack-block suggests that not all the buildings in the fort were erected at the same time. Dendrochronological dates suggest that the south gate was modified in or shortly after 94. This fort was deliberately dismantled about 105. Its replacement, also in timber, is less well known. Its rampart probably lay on the line of its predecessors, and the internal buildings were of timber; they included at least three workshops. The individual barrack-rooms were slightly smaller than in the previous fort. They may have been occupied by the *ala Petriana*. This fort was demolished about 140. Again there appears to have been a period of abandonment followed by some form of occupation which is difficult to interpret.

The new fort, apparently constructed in the early third century, was of stone, but probably retained the area of its predecessors. Its west wall, 1.1 m (3 ft 4 in) wide, lay just inside the site of former turf rampart, while that to the south lay a little outside its predecessor. Fragments of several buildings have been found, including the headquarters, a granary –

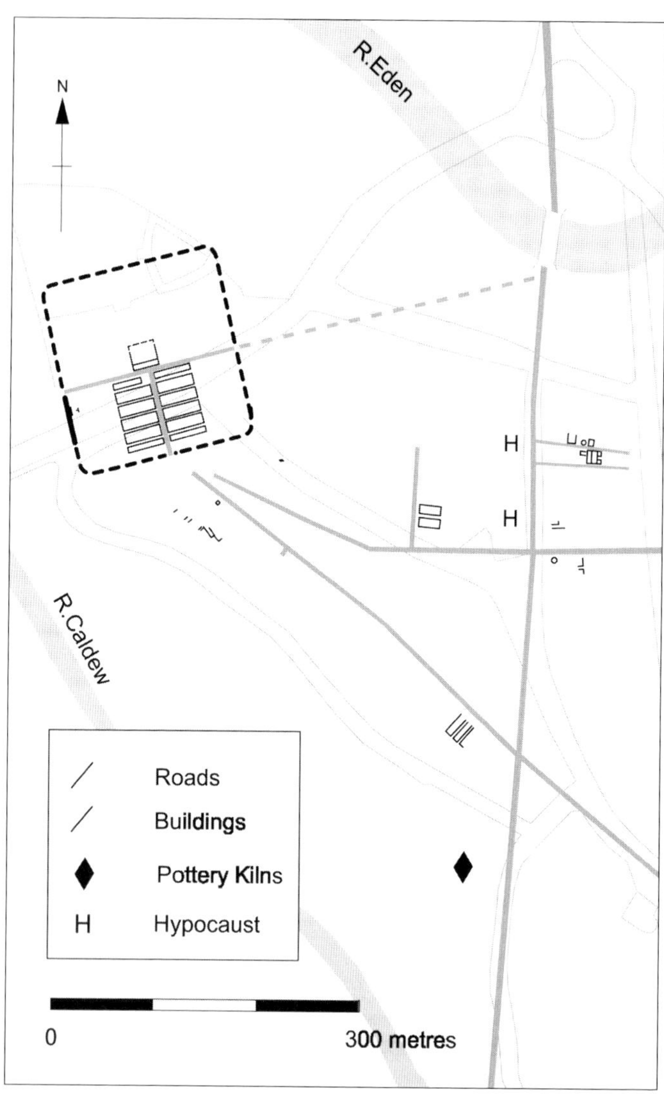

Carlisle in the second century.

unusually in the forward part of the fort – and two barrack-blocks, about 35 by 10 m (115 by 33 ft), divided into eight *contubernia*, and now running east-west. A building stone found in the headquarters records building by the Sixth Legion. Tiles of the Second, Ninth and Twentieth Legions were used in the third-century fort. As those of the Ninth must have been about 60 years old, they were presumably being reused, and the same may apply to the tiles of the other legions. It might be expected that the altar dedicated by the commander of the Twentieth Legion would indicate the presence of some soldiers from that unit. Many alterations were made to the fort during its long life. These included the insertion of a heated room in the headquarters and the placing of a possible latrine outside it, pointing to adaptation of this part of the building for residential use. The fort appears to have continued in use until the end of Roman Britain. The Roman buildings in the southern area of the fort were covered by a layer of dark soil with little evidence for occupation before the arrival of the Normans in the eleventh century.

Immediately south of the fort lay an area interpreted as an **annexe**. This was occupied from the 70s into the first half of the second century. Within, there was industrial activity – the repair and maintenance of military equipment, glass and pottery production – and possibly the corralling of animals. Subsequently, a large stone building was erected on part of the site; this has tentatively been interpreted as a *mansio*, an inn for official travellers. The stone tank visible in the garden of Tullie House and excavated in 1950 lies immediately to the east of this building.

The fort lay to the west of the main north-south **road**. From its south gate one road led eastwards and another in a south-easterly direction; an aqueduct may have entered the town from this direction as this is one interpretation of a clay bank beside the road. These roads helped to provide a framework to the **town** which grew up outside the fort. Timber buildings dating from the first century lined the road leading south-east from the fort and annexe and have been recorded at Blackfriars Street. The earliest structures were open-ended, facing on to the street, and they were replaced in the late 80s and 90s by simple rectangular buildings containing several rooms with clay floors. A break in occupation in the early Hadrianic period was followed by re-use continuing into the third century. Beyond the Citadel, Botchergate lies on the line of the Roman road south. In the early second century, the civil town expanded in this direction, buildings spreading over the earlier cemetery, and a preceding V-shaped ditch and bank. A lead-smelting furnace of this period was accurately dated to 135. Occupation continued into the late third century, and, after a period of abandonment indicated by a dark soil horizon, the area was again used as a cemetery; one of the city's rubbish tips also lay here.

East of the fort, at the Lanes, hedged and ditched enclosures alongside the north-south and east-west roads contained timber buildings; one was used for the manufacture of wooden implements. To the north, lay a rectilinear ditched enclosure, replaced in the first half of the second century by a large rectangular timber building plastered on the inside. It probably served an official purpose, but had a short life, before being demolished. The site was then occupied by several long timber buildings; their size, at least 42 m (138 ft) long, suggested a military function. These in turn were replaced by another large building probably in the middle of the second century, which continued in use with many changes for over two centuries. An adjacent hypocausted building yielded a gold coin of the Emperor Valentinian II (375-92). Further north, under the Civic Centre car-park, a clay layer was found to have been laid down on the flood plain in the third century as the base for buildings.

Inscriptions indicate the existence of a *mithraeum* amongst other temples, while antiquarians recorded the discovery of several hypocausts at various locations in the city. In 1990 such a hypocaust was excavated on the site of the present Market and was revealed to be part of a substantial bath-house.

Inscriptions from Brougham, Old Penrith and Penrith, to the south of Carlisle, refer to a *civitas Carvetiorum*. This was the local government body of the tribe known as the Carvetii. The location of this people is otherwise unknown but presumably lay in the Eden valley. The city of the tribe is likely to have been Carlisle, and this is supported by the measurement from Carlisle of the distance on a milestone erected at Middleton near Kirkby Lonsdale, 85 km (53 miles). The date of the Penrith inscription demonstrates that Carlisle had acquired this status by the reign of Severus Alexander (222-35).

It has been estimated that the city covered at least 33 ha (80 acres). St Cuthbert visited Carlisle in 685 when he was shown the city walls and "a marvellously constructed fountain of Roman workmanship". Today, none of these walls has been rediscovered, with the exception of one potential candidate observed in a trench behind the Wesleyan Chapel in 1923.

Cemeteries are known to the west, east and south of Carlisle. Tombstones provide evidence about the inhabitants of the city, now supplemented by the names of the soldiers appearing on writing-tablets. The finest of the several tombstones known is, however, uninscribed. It shows a seated woman holding a fan in her right hand, while caressing her young child, who plays with a dove in her lap. Above are a sphinx and two lions,

The tombstone of a lady with a fan found at Murrell Hill, Carlisle. (1.285 m high)

Drawn by Miriam Daniels

all symbols of death. This was found at Murrell Hill to the west of the city. A second cemetery lay slightly closer to the urban area. To the east of Carlisle, the tombstone of Vacia aged 3 and two coffins were found on Lowther Street in the nineteenth century; they are somewhat north of the road running east from the city. Further east, at Botcherby, on the line of the road, further coffins were recorded in the late nineteenth century.

Most information is known about the cemetery to the south, along Botchergate. About 100 burials, both cremations and inhumations, have been excavated since the nineteenth century, from English Street to the River Petteril. The cemetery appears to have been in use from the late first into the fifth century. Cremations were placed in pots and glass vessels, while lead, stone and wooden coffins were used and cists made of flagstones. At the north end of the cemetery, the tombstone of Aurelia Senecita, aged at least 20, was found near Blackfriars Street in 1828. The following year, at the southern end, the tombstone of Aurelia Aureliana, was found fallen face down on top of her oak coffin, 1.83 m (6 ft) long. Close by, the tombstone to Flavius Antigonus Papias, a native of Greece who lived 60 years, recovered in 1892, was erected over his coffin 2.44 m (8 ft) long. A stone lion devouring a ram (a well-

The tombstone of Aurelia Aureliana found a Gallow Hill, south of Carlisle. (1.623 m high)

known funerary motif) was also found. It has been suggested that these are the products of a local school of craftsmen.

At the point where the road south crossed the Petteril comes a milestone which probably marked the first mile south from Carlisle. Its primary dedication is a unique record of M. Aurelius Mausaeus Carausius, who formed a breakaway empire consisting of Britain and part of northern Gaul from 287 to 293. He was then assassinated by his finance minister, Allectus, who himself fell to Constantius Chlorus, Caesar of the West, in 296. The milestone has been rededicated twice, once to Constantine I as Caesar (306-7), the other text having been erased.

Tullie House Museum, opposite the Castle, is the main museum for the west end of the Wall, and the outpost forts of Bewcastle and Netherby. Its displays include inscriptions – building stones, altars and tombstones – sculpture, including stone heads, and a wide range of artefacts. In the garden of the museum lies a native shrine, while a section of road is marked out.

CARLISLE TO KIRKBRIDE

Carlisle lay at the western end of the Stanegate. Other sites pre-dating Hadrian's Wall are, however, known to the west at Burgh-by-Sands (see pages 350-4) and Kirkbride. Two roads have been recorded between Carlisle and Kirkbride. One, leading south-west from the fort at Drumburgh, is presumably a later addition. It is best known towards its destination, Kirkbride, where it lay a little north of the track of the disused railway line and is known from the Wampool crossing as far as the access road to Walker House. Further south, and running roughly east-west, a road has been located at Fingland Rigg. Parallel and to its north lay a ditch fronted by a palisade; a second palisade has been tentatively identified immediately to the south of the ditch. These features have been interpreted as relating to a pre-Hadrianic frontier control system.

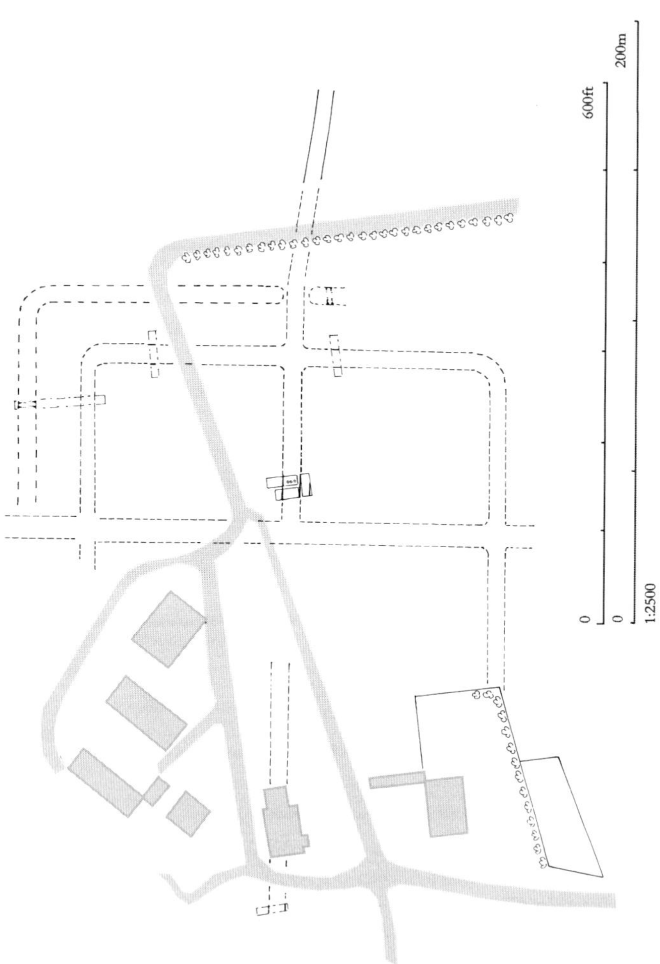

Kirkbride fort.

KIRKBRIDE

Almost due south of Bowness lay a fort at Kirkbride occupying a low ridge overlooking the River Wampool. The church of St. Bride stands on the west rampart while Bank House Farm occupies the north-west quarter. Excavations in 1976 located the north and east ramparts, near the north-eastern corner, where the ditches and some trace of the rampart survived. Indications suggest a size of a little over 2.02 ha (5 acres) for the fort. Internally, structural remains discovered consist mainly of timber construction trenches, with one instance of clay and cobble, and road surfaces, together with furnaces, which may have been used to work lead after the dismantling of the fort buildings.

An altar to Belatucadrus was discovered here in the nineteenth century, and also samian pottery sherds bearing graffiti. Pottery from the recent excavations dates to theperiod 80-120/5, suggesting a fort contemporary with the late-first- to early-second-century Stanegate sites further east. Later occupation may be indicated by the discovery of a coin of the Emperor Tetricus I (270-4).

Altar to the local god Belatocadrus by Peisius found at Kirkbride.
(290 mm high)

Chesters from the air looking west. All four main gates are visible together with the east minor gate and several towers along the south wall. The headquarters building sits in the centre, with the commanding officer's house to this side. Parts of three barrack-blocks are visible in the bottom right corner.
The regimental clerks worked in the rear rooms of the headquarters building.
The man below, who carries a tablet case, may have been such a clerk. His tombstone was found at Castlesteads.

BIBLIOGRAPHY

The purpose of this bibliography is to give references to the basic accounts of excavations or discoveries on the line of the Wall. It is not intended to be an exhaustive list of all literature upon each site. Where a modern excavation report has taken full account of earlier work on the site or in some manner totally supersedes it, only the most recent report has been quoted: references to antiquarian sources may be found in E. Birley, *Research on Hadrian's Wall* (Kendal 1961). Twentieth-century field work on the Wall is usually published in *Archaeologia Aeliana* by the Society of Antiquaries of Newcastle upon Tyne, the Cumberland and Westmorland Antiquarian and Archaeological Society's *Transactions*, the journal *Britannia*, or in separate monographs. Inscriptions are recorded in *The Roman Inscriptions of Britain*, volumes 1 and 2 (Oxford 1965-95): generally only those on stone published after 1956, the closure date for *RIB* I, are listed. Sculpture is published in the *Corpus signorum imperii Romani*, volume 1, fascicule 1 (Oxford 1977) and 6 (New York 1988). *The Literary Sources for Roman Britain* (London 1985) by J. C. Mann and R. G. Penman offers an accessible collection of material relating to the history of Roman Britain and their translations have been used in this book. A. L. F. Rivet and C. Smith, *The Place-Names of Roman Britain* (London 1979) offers comment on the meaning and derivation of fort place-names, which is accepted unless otherwise stated.

ABBREVIATIONS

AA$^{1-5}$	Archaeologia Aeliana, series 1-5
B1- 3	J. C. Bruce, *The Roman Wall*, ed. 1 (Newcastle upon Tyne 1851); 2 (Newcastle upon Tyne 1853); 3 (Newcastle upon Tyne 1867), the first page number is for the standard size volume, the second (in brackets) for the larger, folio volume
Bidwell	P. T. Bidwell, *Hadrian's Wall 1989-1999* (Kendal 1999)

Brand J. Brand, *History of Newcastle* (Newcastle 1789)

Bridges P. T. Bidwell & N. Holbrook, *Hadrian's Wall Bridges* (London 1989)

Britannia *Britannia* (1970 onwards)

Camps Humphrey Welfare and Vivien Swan, *Roman camps in England, the field archaeology* (London 1995)

CC R. L. Bellhouse, *Roman sites on the Cumberland Coast, A new schedule of coastal sites*, CWAAS Research Series, volume III (Kendal 1989)

CSIR *Corpus signorum imperii Romani, Corpus of Sculpture of the Roman World*, Volume I, fascicule 1 (London 1977) by E. J. Phillips; fascicule 6 (New York 1988) by J. C. Coulston and E. J. Phillips

CW$^{1-3}$ *Transactions of the Cumberland and Westmorland Archaeological and Antiquarian Society*, series 1-3

Daniels C. M. Daniels (compiler), *The Eleventh Pilgrimage of Hadrian's Wall, 26 August-1 September 1989* (Kendal 1989)

DUJ *Durham University Journal*

H J. Horsley, *Britannia Romana* (London 1732)

Hodgson J. Hodgson, *History of Northumberland* (Newcastle upon Tyne 1740)

JRS *Journal of Roman Studies*

M H. MacLauchlan, *Memoir written during a Survey of the Roman Wall* (London 1858)

MW H. MacLauchlan, *Memoir written during a Survey of the Watling Street* (London 1852)

NCH *Northumberland County History*

OS 1, 2 Ordnance Survey, *Map of Hadrian's Wall*, ed. 1 (1964), ed. 2 (1972)

PSAN$^{1-5}$ *Proceedings of the Society of Antiquaries of Newcastle upon Tyne*, series 1-5

R W. Roy, *The Military Antiquities of the Romans in North Britain* (London 1793)

RFS 1989	V. A. Maxfield and M. J. Dobson (eds), *Roman Frontier Studies 1989* (Exeter 1991)
RFS 1997	W. Groenman-van Waateringe *et al*. *Roman Frontier Studies* 1995. *Proceedings of the XVI International Congress of Roman Frontier Studies* (Oxford 1997)
RHW	E. Birley, *Research on Hadrian's Wall* (Kendal 1961)
RIB	R. G. Collingwood & R. P. Wright, *The Roman Inscriptions of Britain*, Vol. I (Oxford 1965); re-issued in 1995 with "Addenda and corrigenda" by R. S. O. Tomlin
SSAHS	*South Shields Architectural & Historical Society Papers*
Stukeley	W. Stukeley, *Itinerarium Curiosum* 2 (*Iter Boreale*) (London 1776)
Wilson & Caruana	R. J. A. Wilson and I. D. Caruana (eds), *Romans on the Solway, essays in honour of Richard Bellhouse* (Maryport 2004)
WMW	F. G. Simpson, *Watermills and Military Works on Hadrian's Wall,* ed. G. Simpson (Kendal 1976)
ZPE	*Zeitschrift für Papyrologie und Epigraphik*

ANCIENT GEOGRAPHICAL SOURCES

J. D. Cowan and I. A. Richmond, "The Rudge Cup", *AA*^{4} 12 (1935) 310-42

O. Cuntz, *Itinerarium Antonini; Itineraria Romana*, vol. I (Leipzig, 1929)

J. Heurgon, "The Amiens skillet", *JRS* 41 (1951) 22-4

P. Holder, "Roman place-names on the Cumbrian coast", Wilson and Caruana 52-65

E. Künzl, "Grossformatige Emailobjekte der römischen Kaiserzeit", in S. T. A. M. Mols *et. al*. (eds), *Acta of the 12th International Congress on Ancient Bronzes (Nijmegen 1992)*, *Provincial Museum G. M. Kam* (Amersfoort-Nijmegen, 1995) 39-49

J. C. Mann, Birdoswald to Ravenglass", *Britannia* 20 (1989) 75-9

M. Pitts and S. Worrell, "Dish fit for the gods", *British Archaeology* 73 (November 2003) 22-7 (the Staffordshire Moorlands bowl = *Britannia* 35 (2004) 344-5, no. 24)

I. A. Richmond and O. G. S. Crawford, "The British section of the Ravenna Cosmography", *Archaeologia* 93 (1949) 1-50

A. L. F. Rivet, "The British Section of the Antonine Itinerary", *Britannia* 1 (1970) 34-68; with Appendix II by K. Jackson on the place-names, 68-82

A. L. F. Rivet and C. Smith, *The Place-Names of Roman Britain* (London 1979)

O. Seeck, *Notitia Dignitatum* (Berlin 1876)

MODERN WORKS

L. Allason-Jones, "Small finds from Turrets on Hadrian's Wall", in J. C. Coulston (ed), *Military equipment and the identity of Roman soldiers, Proceedings of the Fourth Roman Military Equipment Conference* (Oxford 1988) 197-233

J. Bennett, "The Roman Frontier from Wallsend to Rudchester Burn Reviewed", *AA*[5] 26 (1998) 17-37

P. Bidwell, "The systems of obstacles on Hadrian's Wall: their extent, date and purpose", *Arbeia* J 8 (2005) 53-76

P. T. Bidwell and N. Holbrook, *Hadrian's Wall Bridges* (London 1989)

A. R. Birley, *Hadrian, The Restless Emperor* (London 1997)

E. Birley, *Research on Hadrian's Wall* (Kendal 1961)

E. Birley, "The deities of Roman Britain", in H Temporini and W Haase (eds), *Aufstieg und Niedergang der Römischen Welt* II, 18, 1 (Berlin and New York, 1986), 3-112

D. J. Breeze, "Warfare in Britain and the Building of Hadrian's Wall", *AA*[5] 32 (2003) 13-6

D. J. Breeze and B. Dobson, *Hadrian's Wall* (4th edition London 2000)

D. J. Breeze and P. R. Hill, "Hadrian's Wall began here", *AA*[5] 29 (2001) 1-2

P. J. Casey, "The end of garrisons on Hadrian's Wall: an historico-environmental model", *University of London Institute of Archaeology Bulletin* 29 (1992) 69-80

Dorothy Charlesworth, "The turrets on Hadrian's Wall", in M. R. Apted, R. Gilliard-Beer and A. D. Saunders (eds), *Ancient Monuments and their interpretation* (London 1977) 13-26

R. G. Collingwood, "Hadrian's Wall; a history of the problem", *JRS* 11 (1921) 37-66

R. G. Collingwood, "The purpose of the Roman Wall", *Vasculum* 8 (1921) 4-9

J. G. Crow, "The function of Hadrian's Wall and comparative evidence of Late Roman Long Walls", *Studien zur Militärgrenzen Roms* III (Stuttgart 1986) 724-9

J. G. Crow, "Construction and reconstruction in the central sector of Hadrian's Wall", *RFS 1989*, 44-7

J. G. Crow, "A review of current research on the turrets and curtain of Hadrian's Wall", *Britannia* 22 (1991) 51-63

J. G. Crow, "The northern frontier of Britain from Trajan to Antoninus Pius: Roman builders and native Britons", in M. Todd (ed), *A Companion to Roman Britain* (Oxford 2003)

B. Dobson, "The function of Hadrian's Wall", *AA*[5] 14 (1986) 5-30

G. H. Donaldson, "Thoughts on a military appreciation of the design of Hadrian's Wall", *AA*[5] 16 (1988) 125-37

L. Dumayne, "The effect of the Roman occupation on the environment of Hadrian's Wall: a pollen diagram from Fozy Moss, Northumbria", *Britannia* 25 (1994) 217-24

L. Dumayne-Peatty, "Forest clearance in northern Britain during the Romano-British times: re-addressing the palynological evidence", *Britannia* 29 (1998) 315-22

B. J. N. Edwards, "Red Rock Fault: lime and Hadrian's Wall", *CW*[3] 3 (2003) 226-8

J. P. Gillam, "The frontier after Hadrian – a history of the problem", *AA*[5] 2 (1974) 1-15.

W. S. Hanson, "Forest clearance and the Roman army", *Britannia* 27 (1996) 354-8

B. Heywood, "The Vallum – its problems restated", in M. G. Jarrett and B. Dobson (eds), *Britain and Rome* (Kendal 1966) 85-94

P. R. Hill, "The Stone Wall Turrets of Hadrian's Wall", *AA*[5] 25 (1997) 27-49

P. R. Hill, *The construction of Hadrian's Wall*, BAR British Series 375 (Oxford 2004)

P. R. Hill and B. Dobson, "The design of Hadrian's Wall and its implications", *AA*[5] 20 (1992) 27-52

N. Hodgson, "Were there two Antonine occupations of Scotland?", *Britannia* 26 (1995) 29-49

N. Hodgson and P. T. Bidwell, "Auxiliary barracks in a new light: recent discoveries on Hadrian's Wall", *Britannia* 35 (2004) 121-57

J. Hooley and D. J. Breeze, "The building of Hadrian's Wall: a reconsideration", *AA*[4] 46 (1968) 97-114

T. R. Hornshaw, "The Wall of Severus?", *AA*[5] 26 (2000) 27-36

R. Hunneysett, "The milecastles of Hadrian's Wall: an alternative identification", *AA*[5] 8 (1980) 95-107

G. D. B. Jones and D. J. Woolliscroft, *Hadrian's Wall from the air* (London 2001)

R. Kendal, "Transport logistics associated with the building of Hadrian's Wall", *Britannia* 27 (1998) 129-52

W. Lawson,"The Construction of the Military Road in Northumberland 1751-1757", *AA*[5] 1 (1973) 177-93

J. C. Mann, "The function of Hadrian's Wall", *AA*[5] 18 (1990) 51-4

V. A. Maxfield, "Mural Controversies" in B. Orme (ed) *Problems and Case Studies in Archaeological Dating* (Exeter 1982) 57-81

V. A. Maxfield, "Hadrian's Wall in its imperial setting", *AA*[5] 18 (1990) 1-27

E. Pickett, *et al.*, *Ancient Frontiers, Exploring the geology and landscape of the Hadrian's Wall area* (British Geological Survey 2006)

J. Poulter, "The direction of planning of the eastern sector of Hadrian's Wall and the Vallum, from the River North Tyne to Benwell, west of Newcastle upon Tyne", *Arbeia J* 8 (2005) 87-100

P. Salway, *The Frontier People of Roman Britain* (Cambridge 1965)

D. D. A. Shotter, *The Roman Frontier in Britain* (Preston 1996)

F. G. Simpson and R. C. Shaw, "The purpose and date of the Vallum and its crossings", *CW*² 22 (1922) 353-433

C. E. Stevens, *The Building of Hadrian's Wall*, *CW* Extra Series 20 (Kendal 1966)

B. Swinbank, *The Vallum reconsidered*, unpublished University of Durham PhD thesis (1954)

M. Symonds, "The construction order of the Milecastles on Hadrian's Wall", *AA*⁵ 34 (2005) 67-81

D. J. A. Taylor, *Forts on Hadrian's Wall, a comparative analysis of the form and construction of some buildings* (BAR British Series 305, Oxford 2000)

H. Welfare, "Causeways, at Milecastles, across the Ditch of Hadrian's Wall", *AA*⁵ 28 (2000) 13-25

H. Welfare, "Variation in the form of the Ditch, and of its equivalents, on Hadrian's Wall", *AA*⁵ 33 (2004) 9-23

A. M. Whitworth, "Recording the Roman Wall", *AA*⁵ 22 (1994) 67-77

J. J. Wilkes, "Early fourth-century rebuilding in Hadrian's Wall forts", in M. G. Jarrett and B. Dobson (eds.), *Britain and Rome* (Kendal 1966) 114-38

R. Woodside and J. Crow, *Hadrian's Wall, an historic landscape* (The National Trust 1999)

D. J. Woolliscroft, "Signalling and the design of Hadrian's Wall", *AA*⁵ 17 (1989) 5-19

D. J. Woolliscroft, "More thoughts on the Vallum", *CW*² 99 (1999) 53-65

INDIVIDUAL SITES

South Shields

Guide-book: P. T. Bidwell, *The Roman Fort of Arbeia at South Shields* (Tyne and Wear Museums 1993)

General accounts: *RHW* 152; Bidwell 73-82

Name: *Britannia* 17 (1986) 332-3; *Durham Archaeol J* 16 (2001) 21-5; *AA*⁵ 30 (2002) 173-4; *AA*⁵ 33 (2004) 60-4

Excavations: *Trans Nat Hist Soc Northumberland & Durham* 7 (1878) 126-67; *AA*^{2} 10 (1885) 223-318; *PSAN*^{2} 9 (1900) 215; *AA*^{4} 11 (1934) 83-102; *SSAHS* I, 7 (1959) 8-25; *SSAHS* I, 8 (1960) 6-10; *SSAHS* I, 9 (1961) 7-15; *SSAHS* II, 1 (1964) 7-12, 15-18; *JRS* 57 (1967) 177, 179; *AA*^{5} 4 (1976) 184-6; J. N. Dore and J. P. Gillam *The Roman Fort at South Shields* (Newcastle 1979); P. T. Bidwell and S. Speak, *Excavations at South Shields Roman Fort, Volume I* (Newcastle upon Tyne 1994); *Arbeia J* 4 (1995) 61-4; *Arbeia J* 5 (1996) 1-18; *Arbeia J* 6 (1996) 59-61; N. Hodgson, "A late Roman courtyard house at South Shields and its parallels", P. Johnson and I Haynes (eds), *Architecture in Roman Britain* (CBA 1996) 135-51; *Arbeia J* 6-7 (1997-98) 25-36, *Britannia* 30 (1999) 340; *Britannia* 31 (2000) 385-9; *Britannia* 32 (2001) 322-6; *Britannia* 33 (2002) 290-1; *Britannia* 34 (2003) 306-10; *Britannia* 35 (2004) 271-2; *Britannia* 36 (2005) 402-3; *Arbeia J* 8 (2005) 77-86

West gate: P. Bidwell, R. Miket and W. Ford (eds), *Portae cum turribus. Studies of Roman fort gates* (Oxford 1988)

Civil settlement: *Brittannia* 34 (2003) 306-10

Artefacts: *AA*^{2} 9 (1932) 91-2; *AA*^{4} 13 (1936) 139-51; *AA*^{4} 26 (1948) 89-97; *AA*^{4} 49 (1971) 135; *AA*^{5} 4 (1976) 186-9; L. Allason-Jones and R. Miket, *The catalogue of small finds from the South Shields Roman fort* (Newcastle upon Tyne 1984); *Arbeia J* 4 (1995) 45-53; *Arbeia J* 5 (1996) 19-47; *Arbeia J* 6-7 (1997-98) 55-64, 68-73

Ship wreck: *Arbeia J* 6-7 (1997-98) 1-23; *Arbeia J* 8 (2005) 132-3

Tombstones and Cemetery: *AA*^{4} 37 (1959) 203-10; *Arbeia J* 2 (1993) 55-9; *AA*^{5} 22 (1994) 43-66; *AA*^{5} 23 (1995) 312-4; *Arbeia J* 4 (1995) 64-6; *Britannia* 35 (2004) 272; *Arbeia J* 8 (2005) 101-118; *Britannia* 36 (2005) 403

Iron Age farm: *Archaeol. J* 158 (2001) 62-160

South Shields to Wallsend

Jarrow: *RHW* 157-9; *Britannia* 6 (1975) 234

Hadrianic war-memorial: *RIB* 1051

HADRIAN'S WALL - THE STONE WALL

Wallsend

Guide-book: W. B. Griffiths, *Segedunum Roman Fort, Baths and Museum* (Tyne and Wear Museums 2000)

General account: *RHW* 159-61

Excavations: *PSAN*[3] 2 (1906) 278-9; *PSAN*[3] 5 (1912) 209-14; *NCH* 13 485-93; *Britannia* 7 (1976) 306; N. Hodgson, *Excavations at Wallsend Roman Fort* (Newcastle 2003)

Wall to river: *Arbeia J* 4 (1995) 55-9

Civil settlement: *NCH* 13 495; *Arbeia J* 2 (1993) 25-36; *Arbeia J* 3 (1994) 13-32; *AA*[5] 26 (1998) 32; *Britannia* 33 (2002) 291-3; *Britannia* 34 (2003) 310

Site north of fort and Wall: *Arbeia J* 2 (1993) 25-36; *Arbeia J* 3 (1994) 58-9

Artefacts: *AA*[5] 11 (1983) 309-13; *Britannia* 15 (1984) 231-2

Wallsend to Newcastle

General accounts: *NCH* 13 493-501; *AA*[4] 38 (1960) 40-9; *Britannia* 5 (1974) 410; *AA*[5] 3 (1975) 105-15; *AA*[5] 13 (1985) 213-4; *AA*[5] 26 (1998) 17-37; *AA*[5] 29 (2001) 3-18; *AA*[5] 32 (2003) 17-24

Wall to west of Wallsend: *Arbeia J* 1 (1992) 58-62; *AA*[5] 17 (1989) 21-8; *Britannia* 31 (2000) 389; *Britannia* 32 (2001) 326

T 0a: *AA*[4] 38 (1960) 46-7

T 0b: *AA*[4] 38 (1960) 46-7; *AA*[5] 3 (1975)105-15; *AA*[5] 13 (1985) 213-4; *AA*[5] 29 (2001) 3-4

Wall: *AA*[5] 26 (1998) 23-6

Military Way: *AA*[4] 43 (1965) 77-86

MC 1: *AA*[4] 38 (1960) 41-6; *AA*[5] 3 (1975) 105-15; *AA*[5] 29 (2001) 4-5

MC 2: *AA*[4] 38 (1960) 41-6; *AA*[5] 3 (1975) 105-15; *AA*[5] 29 (2001) 4-6; *Britannia* 36 (2005) 403

T 2b: *AA*[5] 29 (2001) 6

MC 3: Stukeley 66; *NCH* 13 495; *AA*[4] 38 (1960) 41-6; *AA*[5] 26 (1998) 26; *AA*[5] 29 (2001) 5-7; *AA*[5] 32 (2003) 22-3

Wall: *AA*[5] 26 (1998) 21-3; *Arbeia J* 8 (2005) 5-28; *Britannia* 36 (2005) 403

Newcastle upon Tyne

General accounts: *NCH* 13 501-14; *RHW* 161-3; *WMW* 169-92

Fort: *AA*^{5} 31 (2002)

Bridge: *AA*^{5} 4 (1976) 171-6; *Bridges* 99-103; *AA*^{5} 19 (1991) 17-24

Inscription of Julia Domna: *AA*^{5} 8 (1980) 65-73

Burials: *AA*^{1} 3 (1844) 148-9; *AA*^{2} 25 (1904) 147-9

Newcastle to Benwell

General accounts: *NCH* 13 515-21; *WMW* 175-81

Wall and ditch: *AA*^{4} 11 (1934); *JRS* 43 (1953); *WMW* 176-8; *Britannia* 36 (2005) 404

MC 4: *Britannia* 19 (1988) 154-62; *AA*^{5} 29 (2001) 8-9

Westgate Road: *AA*^{5} 26 (1998) 26-7; *Arbeia J* 6-7 (1997-98) 49-54

Vallum: *AA*^{5} 26 (1998) 32-4; *Britannia* 35 (2004) 272

MC 5: *NCH* 13 516

MC 6: *NCH* 13 516

Benwell

General accounts: *NCH* 13 521-527; *RHW* 163-5; *Durham Archaeol. J* 13 (1997) 61-4

Excavation reports: *AA*^{4} 4 (1927) 135-192; *AA*^{4} 5 (1928) 46-74; *AA*^{4} 7 (1930) 126-30; *DUJ* (March 1939) 161-2; *AA*^{4} 19 (1942) 1-43; *AA*^{4} 25 (1948) 53-62; *AA*^{4} 38 (1960) 233-5; *AA*^{5} 19 (1991) 41-5

Praetentura: *AA*^{2} 3 (1859) 47

Baths: Brand i 607

Vallum and causeway: *AA*^{2} 6 (1865) 220-1; *AA*^{4} 11 (1934) 176-84; *AA*^{4} 33 (1955) 142-62

Temple of Antenociticus: *AA*^{2} 6 (1865) 153-5, 169-71; *AA*^{4} 19 (1941) 37-9; *AA*^{5} 32 (2003) 25-30

Mansio: *AA*^{4} 5 (1928) 52-8

Burial: *PSAN*^{4} 7 (1935) 50-4

Anglo-Saxon brooches: *AA*^{4} 13 (1936) 117-21; *AA*^{4} 35 (1957) 282-3

Benwell to Rudchester

Denton: *NCH* 13 527-40; *AA*^{5} 29 (2001) 8-14

Military Way: *Britannia* 35 (2004) 272

T 6b: Brand i 606 and pl. 1

Wall: *Britannia* 34 (2003) 310

MC 7: *AA*^{4} 26 (1939) 18, 38; *PSAN*^{4} 3 (1928) 278; *NCH* 13 528

Wall: *AA*^{4} 4 (1927) 109-12

T 7b: *AA*^{4} 7 (1930) 145-52 & pls 37-41, 50-1

Wall and Vallum: *AA*^{5} 24 (1996) 1-56; *AA*^{5} 25 (1997) 151-2

Vallum inscriptions: *RIB* 1361-5, 1367; *AA*^{4} 14 (1937) 227-42

MC 8, T 8a and T 8b: *NCH* 13 531

Wall, Vallum and Military Way: *AA*^{4} 40 (1962) 135-42; *Britannia* 35 (2004) 272

MC 9: *AA*^{4} 7 (1930) 152-64 & pls 42-53; *NCH* 13 531; *WMW* 124; *Britannia* 32 (2001) 326

T 9a and b: *NCH* 13 533

MC 10: *AA*^{2} 6 (1865) 221-4; *NCH* 13 533; *Britannia* 31 (2000) 389

Vallum: *Britannia* 32 (2001) 326-8

T 10a and b: *NCH* 13 533; *AA*^{5} 11 (1983) 27-60

Vallum: *AA*^{5} 11 (1983) 40-3

MC 11: H 139; B3 124 (97); *AA*^{5} 26 (1998) 29; *Britannia* 34 (2003) 311; *Britannia* 36 (2005) 404

Throckley hoard: *AA*^{4} 8 (1931) 12-48

T 11a and b: *NCH* 13 534

Wall and pits: *AA*^{4} 4 (1927) 113-21; *Arbeia J* 8 (2005) 29-52

Ditch and Vallum: *AA*^{4} 36 (1958) 55-60; *AA*^{4} 40 (1962) 142-3; *AA*^{5} 26 (1998) 33

MC 12: *AA*^{4} 4 (1927) 121; *AA*^{5} 26 (1998) 30

Ts 12a and b: *AA*^{4} 8 (1931) 322-7

Wall: *Britannia* 7 (1976) 308-9

MC 13: *AA*^{4} 8 (1931) 319-22

T 13a: *AA*^{4} 8 (1931) 322-7

Wall and culvert: *Britannia* 7 (1976) 308

Rudchester

General account: *RHW* 165-9

Survey: *AA*^{5} 19 (1991) 25-31

Name: *AA*^{5} 30 (2002) 49-51

Excavations: *PSAN*^{2} 10 (1901) 81-2; *CW*^{2} 2 (1902) 391-2; *AA*^{4} 1 (1925) 93-120; *AA*^{5} 1 (1973) 81-6; *Britannia* 25 (1994) 264

Vallum: *CW*^{1} 15 (1898) 178-9; *Archaeometry* 32 (1990) 71-82; *Britannia* 32 (2001) 328

Coin hoard: *AA*^{3} 8 (1912) 219-20

Mithraeum: *AA*^{4} 32 (1954) 176-219

Rudchester to Halton Chesters

Wall with moulded plinth: *AA*^{4} 1 (1924) 103

MC 14: *JRS* 37 (1947) 168; *Britannia* 32 (2001) 328

T 14a: H map

MCs 15 and 16: *NCH* 12 21

MC 17: *AA*^{4} 9 (1932) 256-7 & pl. 44; *Britannia* 31 (2000) 390

Change of construction from type A to B: *AA*^{4} 9 (1932) 258 & pl. 43

Ts 17a and b: *AA*^{4} 9 (1932) 257, 259 & pl. 45

MC 18: *NCH* 12 21; *AA*^{4} 9 (1932) 257-8 & pl. 46

Ditch: *Britannia* 32 (2001) 328

T 18a: *AA*^{4} 9 (1932) 198-204, 258-9 & pl. 47

Vallum: *AA*^{5} 11 (1983) 61-78

T 18b: *AA*^{4} 9 (1932) 258 & pl. 47; *AA*^{4} 43 (1965) 88-107, 193-8

MC 19: *AA*^{4} 9 (1932) 205-15, 258; *AA*^{4} 10 (1933) 98; *AA*^{4} 13 (1936) 259; *Britannia* 31 (2000) 390

T 19a: *AA*^{4} 10 (1933) 98

T 19b: *AA*^{4} 10 (1933) 99; *AA*^{5} 3 (1975) 222

MC 20: *AA*^{4} 13 (1936) 259-62; *Britannia* 24 (1993) 284

Wall and Military Way: *Britannia* 32 (2001) 328; *Britannia* 33 (2002) 294

T 20a and b: *PSAN*^{4} 7 (1935) 134

Vallum: *CW*^{2} 13 (1913) 389; *JRS* 43 (1953) 110

MC 21: *AA*^{4} 13 (1936) 259; *JRS* 43 (53) 110

T 21a: *PSAN*^{4} 7 (1935) 134

T 21b: *AA*^{4} 13 (1936) 317

Halton Chesters

General accounts: *NCH* 10 468-73; *RHW* 170-2

Excavation reports: *CW*^{1} 15 (1898) 177-8; *AA*^{4} 14 (1937) 151-171; *AA*^{4} 37 (1959) 177-90; *AA*^{4} 38 (1960) 153-60; *JRS* 51 (1961) 164; *JRS* 52 (1962) 164-5

Surveys: *AA*^{5} 18 (1990) 55-62; *AA*^{5} 28 (2000) 37-46

Baths: Hodgson, II iii 316

Vallum: *CW*^{1} 15 (1898) 177; *NCH* 10 468; *WMW* 159-68

Military Way: *CW*^{1} 15 (1898) 178

Jewellery: *Antiquaries J* 2 (1922) 99-100

Tombstone: *AA*^{5} 3 (1975) 212-4

Halton Chesters to Chesters

MC 22: *AA*^{4} 8 (1931) 317-9

Portgate: *PSAN*^{3} 2 (1906) 283; *AA*^{4} 45 (1967) 208

Ts 22a and b: *AA*^{4} 8 (1931) 317

Building stone: *Arbeia J* 6-7 (1997-98) 65-7

MC 23: *AA*^{4} 8 (1931) 317; *JRS* 43 (1953) 110

T 24a – T 25a: *AA*^{4} 8 (1931) 317

T 25a: *AA*^{4} 43 (1965) 120-1

T 25b: *AA*^{4} 43 (1965) 108-27, 193-8

Quarry wedges: *AA*^{4} 36 (1958) 313-4

T 26a: *AA*^{4} 43 (1965) 128-50, 193-9

Wall: *Britannia* 7 (1976) 309; *Britannia* 33 (2002) 294-5

T 26b: *AA*^{2} 8 (1880) 134; *AA*^{2} 9 (1881) 22; *JRS* 40 (1950) 43

MC 27: *AA*^{4} 31 (1953) 165-174

Chesters bridge: *AA*^{2} 5 (1874) 142; *AA*^{2} 6 (1865) 80-6; *AA*^{2}16 (1885) 328; *PSAN*^{2} 2 (1886) 178-81; *WMW* 44-9; *Bridges*; *Arbeia J* 1 (1992) 40-5; *AA*^{5} 23 (1995) 47-50; *Britannia* 22 (1991) 234; *Britannia* 23 (1992) 269

Chesters

Guide-book: J. S. Johnson, *Chesters Roman Fort* (English Heritage 1990)

General account: *RHW* 172-5

Name: RFS 1995, 339-41; *AA*[5] 33 (2004) 62

Geophysical surveys: *Britannia* 35 (2004) 273-4

T 27a: *PSAN*[3] 10 (1922) 274-5; *JRS* 36 (1946) 134; *AA*[5] 10 (1983) 199-200

Excavations: *AA*[1] 3 (1844) 142-7; *AA*[2] 1 (1857) 69-85; *AA*[2] 7 (1876) 171-6; *AA*[2] 8 (1880) 211-21; *Archaeologia* 46 (1881) 1-8; *AA*[2] 10 (1885) 133-7; *AA*[2] 13 (1889) 374-8; *AA*[2] 23 (1902) 9-21; *PSAN*[3] 4 (1909) 134-43; *CW*[2] 22 (1922) 461-2; *PSAN*[3] 10 (1923) 216-8; *PSAN*[4] 1 (1924) 319-23; *DUJ* (March 1939) 160-1; *AA*[4] 39 (1961) 321-6

Baths: *AA*[2] 12 (1886-7) 124-9; *AA*[4] 8 (1931) 219-304; *AA*[5] 30 (2002) 180-5; *AA*[5] 32 (2003) 192-3

Civil settlement: *AA*[4] 36 (1958) 228

Relation of fort to Wall and Vallum: *PSAN*[2] 9 (1900) 307; *PSAN*[3] 2 (1906) 284; *CW*[2] 1 (1901) 84-9; *AA*[2] 23 (1902) 9-21; *CW*[2] 4 (1904) 238-44; *PSAN*[3] 10 (1922) 216-8; *CW*[2] 22 (1922) 461-2; *AA*[4] 36 (1958) 230

Museum: E. A. Budge, *An Account of the Roman antiquities preserved in the museum at Chesters, Northumberland* (London 1907); *AA*[5] 7 (1979) 114-26

Chollerton Church: *PSAN*[3] 3 (1908) 322; *PSAN*[3] 10 (1922) 105; *NCH* 4 263-4

Chesters to Carrawburgh

MC 28: H 144; M 32; B3 165 (131)

MC 29: *AA*[4] 38 (1960) 50-2

Walwick Fell camp: *Camps* 132-3

T 29a: *AA*[2] 7 (1876) 256-60; *AA*[5] 1 (1973) 97-8

Ditch and Vallum: Bidwell 120-2

T 29b: *AA*[3] 9 (1913) 56-67

Military Way: *AA*[3] 9 (1913) 64-5

Wall ditch on Limestone Bank: *AA*[3] 9 (1913) 63

MC 30: *JRS* 42 (1952) 89; *AA*^{4} 38 (1960) 52

Vallum and Military Way: *CW*^{2} 22 (1922) 417-8; *JRS* 43 (1953) 110

Ts 30a and b: *AA*^{3} 9 (1913) 54-6

MC 31: M 35; B3 168 (133); *AA*^{3} 9 (1913) 54; *AA*^{4} 45 (1967) 1-16

Limestone Corner camp: *AA*^{3} 9 (1913) 70-4; *Camps* 111-3

Carrawburgh

General account: *RHW* 175-8

Excavations: *PSAN*^{2} 10 (1902) 161-4; *AA*^{4} 50 (1972) 81-144

Relation of fort to Vallum: *PSAN*^{2} 7 (1896) 283-6; *CW*^{1} 14 (1897) 416-20; *CW*^{1} 15 (1898) 175-7; *DUJ* 29 (1934) 93-9

Baths: Bruce, *The Wall of Hadrian, two lectures* (Newcastle upon Tyne 1874) 17; *AA*^{2} 24 (1903) 19-20

Civil settlement: *AA*^{4} 36 (1958) 244 p1. 25, 1; *AA*^{4} 45 (1967) 1-16

Coventina's Well: *AA*^{2} 8 (1880) 1-49, 20-42; L. Allason-Jones and B. McKay, *Coventina's Well* (Gloucester 1985)

Mithraeum: *AA*^{4} 29 (1951) 1-92

Shrine of the Nymphs: *AA*^{4} 40 (1962) 59-81

Carrawburgh to Housesteads

Vallum: *Britannia* 32 (2001) 328

T 31b: OS

MC 32: *Britannia* 3 (1972) 308

Brown Dikes camp: *Camps* 79-80

MC 33: *AA*^{4} 13 (1936) 262-3

Vallum near 33: M 90

T 33b: *AA4* 50 (1972) 145-78; *Britannia* 2 (1971) 291 no. 10

Coesike and Grindon camps: *Camps* 90-1, 106

MC 34: *JRS* 38 (1948) 84

T 34a: *AA*^{5} 1 (1973) 99-109

Wall and cists burial: *AA*^{5} 25 (1997) 61-9; *Britannia* 31 (2000) 390

MC 35: *AA*^{5} 12 (1984) 33-147; *AA*^{5} 14 (1986) 182

T 35a: *AA*[4] 43 (1965) 151-61, 200

T 35b: *JRS* 38 (1948) 84

Queen's Crag: *JRS* 52 (1962) 194 no. 10

MC 36: *JRS* 37 (1947) 168; *WMW* 70

T 36a: *PSAN*[3] 5 (1911) 66; *JRS* 37 (1947) 168

Wall: *Britannia* 7 (1976) 309

Knag Burn Gateway: *PSAN*[1] 1 (1855) 56-7; M 92-4; *AA*[4] 14 (1937) 172-84; *Britannia* 7 (1976) 309; *Britannia* 20 (1989) 273

Housesteads

Guide-book: *Housesteads Roman Fort* (English Heritage 1989)

Modern survey: J. Crow, *Housesteads* (London 2004)

General account: *RHW* 178-184

Geophysical survey: *AA*[5] 33 (2004) 51-60

T 36b: *PSAN*[4] 10 (1945-6) 274-5; *JRS* 36 (1946) 134

Excavation reports: Hodgson 85-95; *AA*[1] 1 (1822) 267; *PSAN*[1] 1 (1857) 256-7; *PSAN*[2] 2 (1886) 204-6; *AA*[2] 25 (1904) 193-300; *PSAN*[3] 4 (1911) 96; *AA*[4] 6 (1929) 169-72; *AA*[4] 14 (1937) 179, 183; *AA*[4] 38 (1960) 61-71; *AA*[4] 39 (1961) 279-99; *AA*[4] 40 (1962) 83-96; *AA*[4] 41 (1963) 37-44; *AA*[4] 49 (1971) 95-99; *Britannia* 6 (1975) 232; *Britannia* 7 (1976) 309; *AA*[5] 3 (1975) 17-42; *AA*[5] 4 (1976) 17-30; *AA*[5] 16 (1988) 61-124; *WMW* 125-52; *AA*[5] 17 (1989) 1-4

Civil settlement: *AA*[4] 9 (1932) 222-37; *AA*[4] 10 (1933) 82-96; *AA*[4] 11 (1934) 185-205; *AA*[4] 12 (1935) 204-58; *AA*[4] 39 (1961) 301-19; *AA*[4] 40 (1962) 117-33

Baths: *AA*[1] 1 (1816) 263-320

Temples: Hodgson 191-4; *AA*[1] 1 (1822) 263-320; *AA*[2] 25 (1904) 255-63; *AA*[4] 40 (1962) 119-24

Limekiln: *PSAN*[3] 4 (1909) 96; *WMW* 152-7

Artefacts: *AA*[1] 4 (1855) 274; *AA*[4] 47 (1969) 39-42; *AA*[5] 7 (1979) 127-43; *AA*[5] 13 (1985) 1-5; *Britannia* 14 (1983) 269-70

Vallum: *CW*[1] 15 (1899) 356-8; *AA*[4] 9 (1932) 225-6; *AA*[4] 11 (1934) 186-9

Housesteads to Great Chesters

Guide-book: P. Orde, *Hadrian's Wall from Housesteads to Steel Rigg* (The National Trust 1985)

MC 37: *AA*^{1} 4 (1855) 256-60; *AA*^{4} 11 (1934) 103-20; *WMW* 119-24; *Britannia* 20 (1989) 273-4

Wall: *Britannia* 20 (1989) 274

Ts 37a and b: *PSAN*^{3} 5 (1911) 66; *WMW* 108

Greenlee Lough Camp: *Camps* 104-5; *Britannia* 15 (1984) 278-80

MC 38: *AA*^{4} 13 (1936) 263-9

Native village, Milking Gap: *AA*^{4} 15 (1938) 303-50

Vallum west of Housesteads: *CW*^{1} 15 (1898) 356

Ts 38a and b: *PSAN*^{3} 5 (1911) 66; *WMW* 108

Wall: *Britannia* 15 (1984) 280; *Britannia* 17 (1986) 378; *Britannia* 22 (1991) 54-5

MC 39: *PSAN*^{1} 1 (1855) 48; *AA*^{4} 13 (1936) 268; *WMW* 81-6; *Britannia* 14 (1983) 290-1; *Britannia* 17 (1986) 379-81; *Britannia* 18 (1987) 316; *Britannia* 19 (1988) 434

T 39a: *PSAN*^{3} 5 (1911) 66; *WMW* 98-107

Peel Gap tower: *Britannia* 18 (1987) 316-8; *Britannia* 19 (1988) 434-6; *Britannia* 22 (1991) 53-5

T 39b: *PSAN*^{3} 5 (1911) 66; *WMW* 110-13

Wall at Steelrigg: *CW*^{2} 13 (1913) 307-8; *AA*^{4} 8 (1931) 316; *WMW* 76, 109-10, 114-6

MC 40: *CW*^{2} 13 (1913) 318; *WMW* 86-98

Ts 40a and b, MC 41: *JRS* 37 (1947) 168

Ts 41a and b: *AA*^{4} 46 (1968) 69; *WMW* 108

MC 42: *AA*^{1} 4 (1855) 54-9, 54; *AA*^{4} 13 (1936) 269-70; *AA*^{4} 17 (1940) 116

Vallum and Military Way: *CW*^{2} 13 (1913) 390; *JRS* 30 (1940) 163-5; *WMW* 116-9

Watermill: *PSAN*^{3} 4 (1911) 167; *WMW* 26-43

Ts 42a and b: *WMW* 80

Cawfields and Markham camps: *Camps* 82-3, 85, 113-5

Great Chesters

General accounts: *RHW* 188-92

MC 43: *JRS* 30 (1940) 161-4

Excavations: *AA*^{2} 24 (1903) 19-64; *AA*^{4} 2 (1926) 197-202

Aqueduct: M 45; B2 225; *JRS* 34 (1944) 80-1; *Britannia* 21 (1990) 285-9

Artefacts: *Archaeologia* 55 (1896) 179-94; *PSAN*^{4} 2 (1925) 22-3; *AA*^{4} 50 (1972) 282-7; *AA*^{5} 1 (1973) 225-34; *AA*^{5} 10 (1982) 200-5; *Britannia* 13 (1982) 310-5; *AA*^{5} 24 (1996) 187-214; *AA*^{5} 25 (1997) 153-7

Vallum crossing: *JRS* 42 (1952) 89; *AA*^{5} 10 (1982) 200-5

Great Chesters to Carvoran

Vallum at Cockmount: *CW*^{2} 22 (1922) 409-11; *JRS* 30 (1940) 163-5

Ts 43a and b: *WMW* 77

MC 44: M 47; B3 239 (188)

T 44a: *WMW* 77

T 44b: *AA*^{2} 24 (1903) 13-18; *AA*^{3} 9 (1913) 56, 69

MC 45: M 47; B3 240 (189)

T 45a: *AA*^{2} 9 (1883) 49-52; *AA*^{2} 10 (1885) 57-8; *AA*^{3} 9 (1913) 68; *CW*^{2} 13 (1913) 302; *AA*^{4} 43 (1965) 162-9, 200

T 45b: *AA*^{2} 9 (1883), 234; *AA*^{2} 10 (1885) 57; *AA*^{3} 9 (1913) 69

Carvoran

Modern survey: R. Birley, *The Fort at the Rock, Magna and Carvoran on Hadrian's Wall* (Carvoran 1998)

General account: *RHW* 144, 192

Geophysical survey: *Britannia* 31 (2000) 391; *Britannia* 32 (2001) 330-2

Inscriptions recording building of fort wall: *PSAN*^{4} 9 (1941) 250-7

Excavations: *Britannia* 4 (1973) 275; *Britannia* 17 (1986) 381; A. Birley, *Excavations at Carvoran (Magna) Oct/Nov 2002; Britannia* 34 (2003) 311

Baths: *Archaeologia* 24 (1832) 352

Artefacts: *AA*[4] 26 (1948) 142; *AA*[5] 7 (1979) 241-2; *AA*[5] 12 (1984) 149-56; *AA*[5] 12 (1984) 242-4

The Carvoran *modius*: *AA*[3] 13 (1916) 85-102; *AA*[5] 12 (1984) 242-3

Vallum: *JRS* 42 (1952) 89; *AA*[4] 31 (1953) 82-94

Carvoran to Birdoswald

MC 46: *PSAN*[3] 4 (1911) 167; *JRS* 37 (1947) 168

Wall and ditch: *AA*[4] 37 (1959) 211-3

MC 47: *AA*[4] 13 (1936) 270-2

Ts 47a and b: *WMW* 77

Wall: B3 251-2 (198); *Britannia* 31 (2000) 391

Vallum: *CW*[1] 9 (1887) 162-4; *CW*[1] 15 (1898) 179

MC 48: *CW*[1] 9 (1887) 162-6; *CW*[2] 11 (1911) 390-461; *CW*[2] 29 (1929) 314; *CW*[2] 67 (1967) 233-4; *WMW* 56-9

Gilsland Wall, Ditch, Vallum and Military Way: *CW*[1] 13 (1895) 467-9; *CW*[1] 14 (1897) 397-9, 401-3, 404-5; *CW*[1] 15 (1898) 185-6; *CW*[2] 13 (1913) 390-4; *CW*[2] 28 (1928) 385

T 48a: *CW*[2] 26 (1926) 437-50; *WMW* 64

T 48b: *CW*[2] 26 (1926) 429-37, 444-50; *CW*[2] 27 (1927) 236; *CW*[2] 97 (1997) 57-61

Willowford camp: *Camps* 51-2

Bridge over the Irthing at Willowford: *CW*[2] 26 (1926) 450-505; *WMW* 59-64; *Bridges*

HADRIAN'S WALL - THE TURF WALL

General accounts: *CW*[2] 34 (1934) 132-7; *JRS* 25 (1935) 1-18; *Britannia* 15 (1984) 242-4; *Britannia* 21 (1990) 289-92

MC 49: *CW*[1] 15 (1898) 352-3; *CW*[2] 56 (1956) 18-27

Vallum: *CW*[1] 14 (1897) 397-9, 415-6; *CW*[1] 15 (1898) 209-10; *CW*[1] 15 (1899) 351-4, 373-6; *CW*[2] 56 (1956) 24-6

Turf Wall hence to Birdoswald: *CW*[1] 15 (1898) 183-4; *CW*[1] 15 (1899) 347-51, 365-73

Centurial stones: *JRS* 48 (1958) 152 no. 10; *JRS* 49 (1959) 136 no.5; *JRS* 50 (1960) 237, no.12

Birdoswald

Guide-book: *Birdoswald Roman Fort* (English Heritage 1995)

Modern survey: T. Wilmott, *Birdoswald Roman Fort* (London 2001)

General accounts: *RHW* 143, 196-203; Bidwell 145-62

Geophysical Survey: *Britannia* 30 (1999) 91-110; *Britannia* 35 (2004) 159-78

Excavations: *AA*[1] 4 (1855) 63-75, 141-9; *AA*[2] 4 (1860) 249; *CW*[1] 15 (1898) 180-4; *CW*[2] 28 (1928) 377-88; *CW*[2] 29 (1929) 303-15; *CW*[2] 30 (1930) 169-205; *CW*[2] 31 (1931) 122,134; *CW*[2] 32 (1932) 141-5; *CW*[2] 33 (1933) 246-62; *CW*[2] 34 (1934) 120-30; *CW*[2] 50 (1950) 63-9; *JRS* 43 (1953) 116; T. Wilmott, *Birdoswald: excavations of a Roman fort on Hadrian's Wall* (London 1997)

T 49a TW: *PSAN*[4] 10 (1945-6) 274; *JRS* 36 (1946) 134

Artefacts: *Archaeologia* 55 (1896) 199-202; *CW*[2] 54 (1954) 56-60, 61-65; *AA*[5] 9 (1981) 348-51

Wall and Vallum: *CW*[1] 14 (1897) 415-6; *CW*[1] 15 (1898) 174-5, 197-200, 201-10; *CW*[1] 15 (1899) 347-354, 365-76; *CW*[2] 33 (1933) 247; *CW*[2] 50 (1950) 54-62

Inscriptions of Severus and Diocletian: *RIB* 1909 and 1912; *Britannia* 21 (1990) 207-214; *AA*[5] 19 (1991) 133-4

Cemetery: *CW*[2] 93 (1993) 79-85

Robin Hood's Butt and Barron's Pike: *CW*[2] 1 (1901) 82; *CW*[2] 33 (1933) 241; *CW*[2] 38 (1938) 198; *Britannia* 20 (1989) 275; *CW*[2] 90 (1990) 280

Birdoswald to Castlesteads

Wall west of Birdoswald: *CW*[2] 13 (1913) 301-62

Vallum between Birdoswald and MC 50 TW: *CW*[2] 36 (1936) 171-7

Turf Wall, discovery of: *CW*[1] 14 (1897) 185-191, 399-401; *CW*[2] 28 (1928) 380-4

T 49b TW: *CW*[2] 35 (1935) 234-6

MC 50 TW: *CW*[2] 35 (1935) 220-32

Vallum at MC 50: *CW*[2] 36 (1936) 158-70; *CW*[2] 37 (1937) 166-171, 173-77; *JRS* 42 (1952) 89

Military Way: *CW*[1] 14 (1896) 189-90

T 50a TW: *CW*^{2} 35 (1935) 234-5

T 50b TW: *CW*^{2}29 (1929) 306; *CW*^{2} 35 (1935) 232-5

Wall and Vallum: *Britannia* 31 (2000) 391-2

T 49b: *PSAN*^{1} 1 (1857) 236; *CW*^{2} 13 (1913) 303-6, 346-50

MC 50: M 56; *CW*^{2} 13 (1913) 312-59

T 50a: *CW*^{2} 13 (1913) 307-9, 350-1

T 50b: *CW*^{2} 13 (1913) 309-12, 351-6

Wall and Vallum: *CW*^{1} 14 (1896) 187-9; *CW*^{2} 14 (1897) 397

MC 51: *CW*^{2} 28 (1928) 384; *CW*^{2} 35 (1935) 251, 254-5

Vallum at MC 51: *CW*^{1} 14 (1897) 399-401; *CW*^{2} 37 (1937) 158-70, 176

Coombe Crag quarry and forgery: *CW*^{2} 30 (1930) 120-2

T 51a: *CW*^{2} 28 (1928) 382-3; *CW*^{2} 73 (1973) 67-78

T 51b: *CW*^{2} 28 (1928) 382; *AA*^{4} 43 (1965) 170-92

Appletree: *CW*^{2} 92 (1992) 49-55; *Britannia* 7 (1976) 309-10

MC 52: *CW*^{2} 34 (1934) 147; *CW*^{2} 35 (1935) 247-56

Pike Hill tower: *CW*^{1} 1 (1874) 214-5; *CW*^{2} 32 (1932) 145-7; *CW*^{2} 33 (1933) 271; *RHW* 140

T 52a: *CW*^{2} 28 (1928) 382; *CW*^{2} 34 (1934) 148-52; *CW*^{2} 78 (1978) 37-45

MC 53: *CW*^{2} 33 (1933) 267

Hare Hill: *Britannia* 36 (2005) 408

Vallum: *CW*^{1} 13 (1895) 465; *CW*^{2} 4 (1904) 245-6

T 53a: *PSAN*^{1} 1 (1857) 237; *CW*^{2} 33 (1933) 262

T 53b: *CW*^{2} 33 (1933) 270

MC 54: *CW*^{2} 34 (1934) 144-7; *CW*^{2} 35 (1935) 236-44; *AA*^{5} 12 (1984) 228-37

Clay Wall: *CW*^{2} 35 (1935) 244-7

T 54a: *CW*^{2} 34 (1934) 130, 138-44; *CW*^{2} 85 (1985) 71-6

T 54b: *CW*^{2} 34 (1934) 131

MC 55: *CW*^{2} 1 (1901) 81-2

T 55a: *CW*^{2} 34 (1934) 131

Wall T 55b – T 56a: *CW*^{2} 2 (1902) 391; *CW*^{2} 3 (1903) 346-7

MC 56: *CW*^{2} 1 (1901) 82; *CW*^{2} 2 (1902) 390-1; *CW*^{2} 3 (1903) 346; *CW*^{2} 34 (1934) 131-2

T 56a: *CW*^{2} 34 (1934) 131

T 56b: *CW*^{2} 34 (1934) 132

Vallum T 54b – Castlesteads: *CW*^{2} 1 (1901) 75-81; *CW*^{2} 2 (1902) 384-90;

Quarry inscriptions: *ZPE* 22 (1976) 179-83

Castlesteads

General accounts: *CW*^{1} 1 (1874) 204-6; *CW*^{2} 22 (1922) 198; *RHW* 203-5

Geophysical survey: *Britannia* 32 (2001) 333-5

Excavation report: *CW*^{2} 34 (1934) 159-65

Altars: *CW*^{2} 75 (1975) 91; *CW*^{2} 85 (1985) 77-80; *Chiron* 6 (1976) 267-88; *Britannia* 35 (2004) 244-8

Vallum: *CW*^{1} 15 (1899) 354-5; *CW*^{2} 3 (1903) 339-48

Castlesteads to Stanwix

MC 57: M 61; B3 276 (218), 285 (225)

T 57a: *CW*^{2} 34 (1934) 132

MC 58: M 70; B3 286 (226)

Wall: *Archaeologia* 11 (1794) 64

Vallum Castlesteads – T 58b: *CW*^{2} 3 (1903) 339-46; *CW*^{2} 4 (1904) 246-7

T 58b: *PSAN*^{2} 7 (1896) 221; *CW*^{1} 13 (1895) 465

Vallum: *CW*^{1} 13 (1895) 465-6

MC 59: *PSAN*^{2} 7 (1895) 221; *CW*^{1} 13 (1895) 465

Vallum at Bleatarn: *CW*^{1} 13 (1895) 462-5; *CW*^{1} 14 (1897) 191-5, 393-6

Bleatarn Quarry: *CW*^{1} 13 (1895) 463-4; *CW*^{1} 14 (1896) 191-3; *CW*^{1}14 (1897) 405-7

Vallum at White Moss: *CW*^{1} 13 (1896) 460-2; *CW*^{1} 14 (1897) 392-3

MC 61: M 72; *CW*^{1} 13 (1896) 462; *PSAN*^{2} 7 (1896) 220

Moss Side camps: *Camps* 41-2

Wall and Vallum: *Britannia* 12 (1981) 323-4; *Britannia* 13 (1982) 343

MC 62: M 72; *Britannia* 31 (2000) 392

Wall and Vallum: *Britannia* 7 (1976) 310

MC 63: M 73; *Britannia* 32 (2001) 333

Wall and Vallum: *CW*^{1} 13 (1895) 453-60; *CW*^{1} 14 (1897) 390-2

Military Way: *CW*^{1} 14 (1897) 403-4

MC 64: *CW*^{2} 80 (1980) 17-22; *CW*^{2} 84 (1984) 260

MC 65: *PSAN*^{4} 4 (1929) 186; *Britannia* 9 (1978) 19-57; *Britannia* 28 (1997) 415

Stanwix

General accounts: *CW*^{1} 9 (1888) 174-6; *CW*^{2} 31 (1931) 69-80; *CW*^{2} 32 (1932) 147-9; *RHW* 205-8; Bidwell 162-8

Geophysical survey: *CW*^{2} 100 (2000) 279-81

Excavations: *CW*^{2} 32 (1932) 147-9; *CW*^{2} 33 (1933) 275-6; *CW*^{2} 35 (1935) 256-7; *CW*^{2} 41 (1941) 210-13; *CW*^{2} 85 (1985) 53-69; *Britannia* 16 (1985) 271; *Britannia* 25 (1994) 263-4; *Britannia* 29 (1998) 382-3; *Britannia* 30 (1999) 334; *Britannia* 31 (2000) 390

Cemetery: *CW*^{2} 52 (1952) 154-5

Vallum: *CW*^{2} 33 (1933) 275; *CW*^{2} 34 (1934) 155-7; *CW*^{2} 35 (1935) 256-8; *Britannia* 30 (1999) 334

Stanwix to Burgh-by-Sands

MCs 66-70: *PSAN*^{4} 4 (1929) 186

Bridges: *CW*^{2} 52 (1952) 148-153; *CW*^{2} 87 (1987) 43-51; *Bridges* 107-110

Wall in Carlisle: *CW*^{1} 9 (1888) 167-74; *CW*^{2} 32 (1932) 149-51

MC 69: *Britannia* 32 (2001) 336

Grinsdale Roman camps: M 79; *AA*^{3} 5 (1907) 262; *Camps* 31-2, 42-3

Doudle Beck: M 79

MC 70: *Britannia* 32 (2001) 336

Wall at Beaumont: *JRS* 18 (1928) 196

Beaumont camp: *Camps* 31

MC 71: *CW*^{2} 61 (1961) 39-40; *Britannia* 32 (2001) 336

Wall at the Manor-house: *CW*^{2} 54 (1954) 109-10

Speergarth Holes, timber foundation of Wall: *AA*^{2} 12 (1887) 171; *CW*^{1} 9 (1888) 177

Wall east of Burgh: *CW*^{2} 23 (1923) 8

Burgh-by-Sands

General accounts: *CW*^{1} 1 (1874) 151-2; *RHW* 208-9

Excavations: *CW*^{2} 4 (1904) 247-8; *CW*^{2} 23 (1923) 1-12; *Britannia* 8 (1977) 376; *Britannia* 12 (1981) 325; *Britannia* 25 (1994) 263; *Britannia* 30 (1999) 333; *Britannia* 31 (2000) 392

Civil settlement: *CW*^{3} 5 (2005) 31-63

Artefacts: *Britannia* 10 (1979) 179-82

T 71b: *CW*^{2} 61 (1961) 38

Vallum: *JRS* 29 (1939) 202

Solway fords: *CW*^{2} 39 (1939) 152

Burgh-by-Sands to Drumburgh

MC 72: *CW*^{2} 61 (1961) 35-8; *CW*^{2} 94 (1994) 35-54

T 72a: *CW*^{2} 61 (1961) 34; *CW*^{2} 94 (1994) 35-54

T 72b: *CW*^{2} 52 (1952) 15

Stone and Turf Walls, Watch Hill: *CW*^{2} 35 (1935) 213-20

MC 73: *CW*^{2} 52 (1952) 15-6; *CW*^{2} 61 (1961) 34; *CW*^{3} 4 (2004) 55-70

The Wall and Burgh Marsh: *CW*^{2} 52 (1952) 16

MC 76: *CW*^{2} 52 (1952) 14; *CW*^{2} 61 (1961) 31

Wall east of Drumburgh: *CW*^{1} 16 (1899) 92; *CW*^{1} 62 (1962) 60

Drumburgh

General account: *RHW* 209-11

Name: *Britannia* 35 (2004) 344-5, no. 24

Excavations: *CW*^{1} 1 (1874) 209-12; *CW*^{1} 16 (1900) 80-98; *CW*^{2} 52 (1952) 9-14

Road to Kirkbride: *CW*^{2} 52 (1952) 41-5

Drumburgh to Bowness-on-Solway

T 76a: *CW*^{2} 52 (1952) 14

Vallum from Glasson to Bowness: *DUJ* 29 (1934) 29; *CW*^{2} 35 (1935) 214; *Britannia* 31 (2000) 392

Wall at Glasson: *Britannia* 5 (1974) 412; *Britannia* 23 (1992) 236-8

Sunken forest of the Solway: *AA*^{1} 2 (1832) 116-8

MC 78: *CW*^{2} 35 (1935) 217

T 78a: *CW*^{2} 52 (1952) 14

Wall T 78b – MC 79: *CW*^{2} 31 (1931) 144; *CW*^{2} 52 (1952) 22

MC 79: *CW*^{2} 52 (1952) 17-40; *Britannia* 31 (2000) 392

Vallum: *JRS* 29 (1939) 202

T 79b: *CW*^{2} 35 (1935) 217

Brackenrigg and Knockcross camps: *Camps* 32-3, 40

Bowness-on-Solway

Modern surveys: *CW*^{2} 88 (1988) 33-53; Daniels 18-20; *RFS 1989*, 6-8

General accounts: *CW*^{1} 1 (1874) 212-4; *RHW* 211-14

Excavations: *CW*^{2} 31 (1931) 140-5; *CW*^{2} 75 (1975) 29-57; T. W. Potter, *Romans in North-West England* (Kendal 1979) 321-49; *Britannia* 32 (2001) 336

Civil settlement: *CW*^{2} 39 (1939) 327-9; *CW*^{2} 60 (1960) 13-9; *Britannia* 31 (2000) 392

Artefacts: *CW*^{2} 80 (1980) 159; *CW*^{2} 87 (1987) 256; *CW*^{3} 4 (2004) 250-2

CUMBRIAN COAST GENERAL

Modern surveys: R. L. Bellhouse, *Roman Sites on the Cumberland Coast* (Kendal 1989); R. L. Bellhouse, *Joseph Robinson of Maryport, archaeologist extraordinary* (Otley, nd, c. 1992); *CW*^{2} 94 (1994) 55-64; Wilson & Caruana

General accounts: *CW*^{1} 5 (1881) 124-31; *CW*^{2} 29 (1929) 138-65; *CW*^{2} 47 (1947) 78-127; *RHW* 126-31; *CW*^{2} 69 (1969) 65-101; *CW*^{2} 70 (1970) 40-7; *CW*^{2} 80 (1980) 11-3; *Britannia* 13 (1982) 283-97; *Britannia* 21 (1990) 401-6

Bowness to Beckfoot

End of the Wall: *CW*^{2} 4 (1904) 8; *CW*^{2} 11 (1911) 352-3 (Bainbrigg 1601)

Running ditches: *Britannia* 7 (1976) 236-43; *Arch. J* 132 (1975) 20-3; *Britannia* 12 (1981) 135-42; Wilson & Caruana 186-94

Ts 0a-lb: *CW*^{2} 69 (1969) 65-79

MF 1: *Britannia* 8 (1977) 149-83

MF 2: *CW*^{2} 69 (1969) 69

T 2b: *CW*^{2} 29 (1929) 150; *CW*^{2} 47 (1947) 82; Wilson & Caruana 174-85

MF 3: *CW*^{1} 5 (1881) 124-31; *CW*^{2} 42 (1942) 6; *CW*^{2} 47 (1947) 82; *CW*^{2} 62 (1961) 61

T 3a and b: *CW*^{1} 5 (1881) 128-30; *CW*^{2} 29 (1929) 146-8

MF 4: *CW*^{2} 47 (1947) 82; *CW*^{2} 54 (1954) 54-5; *CW*^{2} 62 (1962) 67-72

T 4a: *CW*^{2} 47 (1947) 82

T 4b: *CW*^{2} 47 (1947) 82; *Britannia* 13 (1982) 292-4

MF 5: *CW*^{2} 47 (1947) 78-127

Moricambe in Roman times: *CW*^{2} 62 (1962) 54-70

MF 9: *CC* 36-8

Road: *Britannia* 13 (1982) 292

MF 10: *CW*^{2} 91 (1991) 267-8

MF 12: *CW*^{2} 66 (1966) 38-40; *CW*^{2} 69 (1969) 60-4; *CW*^{2} 81 (1981) 11; *CC* 47

T 12a: *CW*^{2} 64 (1964) 38-9; *CW*^{2} 69 (1969) 55-60

T 12b: *CW*^{2} 57 (1957) 22-6

MF 13: *CW*^{2} 66 (1966) 41

T 13a: *CW*^{2} 54 (1954) 40

T 13b: *CW*^{1} 5 (1881) 258-60; *CW*^{2} 66 (1966) 40-2

Area 14-14a: *CW*^{2} 21 (1921) 270

Beckfoot

General accounts: *CW*^{1} 4 (1880) 318-20; *CW*^{1} 5 (1881) 136-48; *CW*^{2} 36 (1936) 76-84; *CW*^{2} 58 (1958) 58; *JRS* 41 (1951) p1. IV. 2; *RHW* 214-6

Civil settlement: *Arch. J* 132 (1975) 29

Cemetery: *CW*^{2} 49 (1949) 32-7; *CW*^{2} 55 (1955) 51; *CW*^{2} 58 (1958) 57-62; *CW*^{2} 62 (1962) 68; Wilson & Caruana 134-73

Tombstone fragment: *CW*^{2} 58 (1958) 182

Beckfoot to Maryport

MF 15: *CW*^{2} 57 (1957) 21; *CW*^{2} 62 (1962) 71-2; *CW*^{2} 81 (1981) 11; *CC* 47-8; *CW*^{2} 95 (1995) 276-8

T 15a: *CW*^{2} 54 (1954) 36-40; *CW*^{2} 57 (1957) 18-21; *CW*^{2} 62 (1962) 71-2

MF 16: B3 365 (289); *CW*^{2} 70 (1970) 19-21, 32, 34-35; *CW*^{2} 73 (1973) 350-2, 360-1

T 16a: *CW*^{2} 38 (1938) 157-9; *CW*^{2} 54 (1954) 32-3; *CW*^{2} 56 (1956) 62-6

T 16b: *CW*^{2} 54 (1954) 42-7; *CW*^{2} 70 (1970) 21-3; *RIB* II 2493.7

MF 17: *CW*^{2} 86 (1986) 41-7; *CC* 41, 48

T 19a-b: *CC* 48

MF 20: *CW*^{2} 70 (1970) 23-34; *CW*^{2} 81 (1981) 7-13

T 20b: *CW*^{2} 63 (1963) 142

MF 21: *CW*^{2} 98 (1998) 61-106

T 21a: *CW*^{2} 63 (1963) 140

T 21b: *CW*^{2} 63 (1963) 142-3; *CW*^{2} 66 (1966) 37

MF 22: *CW*^{2} 63 (1963) 143-7; *CW*^{2} 70 (1970) 10-9; *CW*^{2} 81 (1981) 11; *CC* 48

T 22a: *CW*^{2} 63 (1963) 141; *CC* 48

T22b: *Britannia* 31 (2000) 435, no. 4

MF 23: *CC* 48-9

T 23a: *CC* 48

Maryport

Guide-book: *The Senhouse Roman Museum Maryport* (n.d.)

Modern survey: R. J. A. Wilson, *Roman Maryport and its setting* (Kendal 1998)

Geophysical survey: Wilson & Caruana 102-33

General accounts: *CW*[2] 22 (1922) 462-3; *CW*[2] 23 (1923) 142-53; *CW*[2] 36 (1936) 85-99; *CW*[2] 58 (1958) 63-7; *CW*[2] 223 (1922) 462-3; *Archaeologia* 2 (1773) 54-6; *Archaeologia* 10 (1792) 139-42; *RHW* 216-23; M. G. Jarrett, *Maryport, Cumbria: A Roman Fort and its Garrison* (Kendal 1976); *CW*[2] 87 (1987) 61-6

Excavations: *CW*[1] 5 (1881) 237-57; *JRS* 57 (1967) 177, 204 no. 14

Civil settlement: *CW*[1] 5 (1881) 237-57; *CW*[2] 23 (1923) 151; *CW*[2] 36 (1936) 85

Altars: *CW*[2] 39 (1939) 19; *CW*[2] 54 (1954) 268; *Britannia* 31 (2000) 23-8

Parade ground: *CW*[2] 23 (1923) 148

Site by river: *CW*[2] 26 (1926) 415

Harbour: *CW*[2] 96 (1996) 233-5

Artefacts: *CW*[2] 15 (1915) 135-72; *CW*[2] 16 (1916) 284; *CW*[2] 26 (1926) 419; *CW*[2] 86 (1986) 49-70; *CW*[2] 88 (1988) 29-31

South of Maryport

Positions of milefortlets and towers: *CW*[2] 70 (1970) 40-7

T 25a: *CW*[2] 84 (1984) 41-59; *CW*[2] 91 (1991) 266-7

T 25b: *CW*[1] 5 (1881) 124-5; *CW*[2] 29 (1929) 144

Tottergill: *CW*[2] 48 (1948) 217-8

Burrow Walls

General accounts: *CW*[2] 29 (1929) 157-9; *CW*[2] 66 (1966) 42-5; *RHW* 223-4

Excavations: *CW*[2] 55 (1955) 30-45

Moresby

General accounts: *AA*[2] 5 (1870) 138; *CW*[2] 48 (1948) 42-72; *CW*[2] 49 (1949) 218-9; *RHW* 224-6

Excavation: *CW*[2] 51 (1951) 176-7; *CW*[2] 87 (1987) 256-8

South of Moresby

Braystones finds: *CW*[2] 48 (1948) 218

Ravenglass

T. W. Potter, *Romans in North-West England* (Kendal 1979) 1-138; Wilson & Caruana 95-101

THE STANEGATE

General: *RFS 1989*, 98-107; *AA*^{5} 26 (1998) 49-58; *Britannia* 31 (2000) 11-22

Washingwells

Britannia 2 (1971) 250; *Arbeia J* 3 (1994) 33-45

Corbridge

Guide-book: J. N. Dore, *Corbridge Roman Site* (English Heritage 1989)

General accounts: *NCH* 10 474-522; *DUJ* 34 (1942) 144-53; *AA*^{4} 37 (1959) 1-31; *RHW* 149-50

Name: A. K. Bowman and J. D. Thomas, *The Vindolanda Writing Tablets* Vol. II (London 1994) 90-8; *Durham Archaeol. J.* 16 (2001) 21-5; *AA*^{5} 30 (2002) 174; *AA*^{5} 33 (2004) 61-4

Excavations: *AA*^{2} 6 (1865) 18-19, *AA*^{3} 3 (1907) 161-86; *AA*^{3} 4 (1908) 205-303; *AA*^{3} 5 (1909) 305-424; *AA*^{3} 6 (1910) 205-72; *AA*^{3} 7 (1911) 193-267; *AA*^{3} 8 (1912) 137-263; *AA*^{3} 9 (1913) 230-801; *AA*^{3} 11 (1914) 279-310; *AA*^{3} 12 (1915) 226-86; *AA*^{4} 15 (1938) 243-94; *AA*^{4} 17 (1940) 85-115; *AA*^{4} 21 (1944) 127; *AA*^{4} 28 (1950) 152-201; *AA*^{4} 30 (1952) 239-66; *AA*^{4} 31 (1953) 205-53; *AA*^{4} 37 (1959) 59-84; *AA*^{4} 38 (1960) 218-52; *AA*^{4} 49 (1971) 1-28; *AA*^{5} 7 (1979) 99-113; M. C. Bishop and J. N. Dore, *Corbridge, Excavations of the Roman fort and town*, 1947-80 (London 1988); M. C. Bishop, *Corstopitum An Edwardian Excavation* (London 1994); *AA*^{5} 23 (1995) 17-45; *AA*^{5} 26 (1998) 39-47

Artefacts: *JRS* 2 (1912) 1-20; *JRS* 5 (1915) 173-90; *AA*^{4} 13 (1936) 310-9; *JRS* 31 (1941) 100-27; *NCH* 10 515; *AA*^{4} 26 (1948) 139; *AA*^{4} 26 (1948) 172-204; *AA*^{4} 27 (1949) 60-121; *AA*^{4} 33 (1955) 116-33; *AA*^{4} 50 (1969) 205; *AA*^{4} 46 (1968) 127-62; *AA*^{4} 50 (1972) 205, 217; *AA*^{5} 8 (1980) 161-3; *AA*^{5} 23 (1995) 311-2

Hoard of armour: L. Allason-Jones and M. C. Bishop, *Excavations at Roman Corbridge: The Hoard* (London 1988)

Town: *AA*^{4} 11 (1934) 158-75; *AA*^{4} 14 (1937) 95-102; *AA*^{4} 36 (1958) 227

Religion and sculpture: *AA*^{4} 21 (1943) 127-224; *Britannia* 36 (2005) 404-6

Bridge over Tyne: *NCH* 10 457; *AA*^{4} 45 (1967) 17-26; *Arbeia J* 4 (1995) 67-70

Stanegate west of Corbridge: *AA*^{4} 19 (1941) 194-209; *NCH* 10 461

Shorden Brae Mausoleum: *AA*^{4} 39 (1961) 37-61

Red House baths and site: *AA*^{4} 37 (1959) 85-176; *AA*^{5} 7 (1979) 1-98; *Britannia* 6 (1975) 230

Newbrough

General account: *RHW* 147-9

Excavations: *PSAN*^{4} 4 (1930) 163-5

Possible camp: *Britannia* 21 (1990) 316, 319

Stanegate

From Tyne to Vindolanda: *AA*^{2} 9 (1884) 217; *AA*^{2} 11 (1886) 130-6; *AA*^{4} 13 (1936) 201-6; *AA*^{4} 14 (1937) 185-93; *AA*^{4} 16 (1939) 140-7; *AA*^{4} 36 (1958) 316

Barcombe

M 41-2; *RHW* 147; *AA*^{4} 44 (1966) 71-7; *AA*^{4} 47 (1969) 183-5; *AA*^{5} 1 (1973) 117-8; *AA*^{5} 20 (1992) 57-62; *AA*^{5} 32 (2002) 130-5

Thorngrafton hoard: *AA*^{2} 3 (1859) 269-76; *Numismatic Chronicle* 7 ser. 3 (1963) 61-6

Vindolanda

Guide-book: R. Birley, *Vindolanda* (Carvoran 2002)

Modern surveys: R. Birley, *Vindolanda, a Roman frontier post on Hadrian's Wall* (London 1977); R. Birley, *The Making of Modern Vindolanda with the life and work of Anthony Hedley 1777-1835* (Carvoran 1995); R. Birley, *Chesterholm 1830-2000* (Carvoran 2000); A. R. Birley, *Garrison Life at Vindolanda, A Band of Brothers* (London 2002)

General account: *RHW* 146-7

Geophysical survey: J. A. Biggins and J. Robinson, *Vindolanda Roman Fort, Northumberland* (TimeScape 2000)

Excavations: *AA*^{4} 8 (1931) 182-212; *AA*^{4} 9 (1932) 216-21; *AA*^{4} 13 (1936) 218-57; *AA*^{4} 15 (1938) 222-37; *AA*^{4} 40 (1962) 97-103;

AA[4] 48 (1970) 97-155; R. Birley, *The 1976 Excavations at Vindolanda, Interim Report* ((Bardon Mill 1977); P. T. Bidwell, *The Roman Fort of Vindolanda* (London 1985); R. Birley, *The Early Wooden Forts*, Vindolanda Research Reports (n.s.) 1 (Bardon Mill 1994); R. Birley, J. Blake and A. Birley, *Vindolanda 1997 Excavations, Praetorium Site, Interim Report* (Carvoran 1998); A. Birley, *Vindolanda's Military Bath Houses, The excavations of 1970 and 2000* (Bardon Mill 2001); J. Blake, *The South Western Corner of Stone Fort Two* (Bardon Mill 2001); A. Birley, *Excavations of 2001-2002* (Bardon Mill 2003); A. Birley and J. Blake, *Vindolanda Excavations 2003-2004* (Bardon Mill 2005)

Finds: *AA*[5] 1 (1973) 111-27; G. W. I. Hodgson, *The animal remains from excavations at Vindolanda 1970-1977* (Bardon Mill 1977); J. P. Wild, *The textiles from Vindolanda 1973-1975*, (Bardon Mill 1977); L. Hird, *The pre-Hadrianic pottery* (Bardon Mill 1977); *Britannia* 13 (1982) 245-51; P. P. P. Funari, "Dressel 20 amphora inscriptions found at Vindolanda…", *RFS 1989*; E. Birley, R. Birley and A. Birley, *The Early Wooden Forts: Reports on the auxiliaries, the writing tablets, inscriptions, brands and grafitti*, Vindolanda Research Report (n.s.) 2 (Bardon Mill 1993); C. Van Driel-Murray, J. P. Wild, M. Seaward and J. Hallam, *The Early Wooden Forts: Preliminary reports on the leather, textiles, environmental evidence and dendrochonology,* Vindolanda Research Reports (n. s.) 3 (Bardon Mill 1993); R. Birley, *The Small Finds: The Weapons*, Vindolanda Research Report (n. s.) 4, Fasc. 1 (Bardon Mill 1996); *Security: the keys and locks*, Vindolanda Research Reports (n. s.) 4, Fasc.2 (Bardon Mill 1997); *The Holocene* 7.2 (1997) 175-86; J. Blake, *The Tools* Vindolanda Research Reports (n. s.) 4, Fasc. 3 (Greenhead 1999); R. Birley, *Writing Materials*, Vindolanda Research Report (n. s.) 4, Fasc. 4 (Greenhead 1999); *Britannia* 32 (2001) 185-97; H. Birley, *The Vindolanda Spoons*, (Greenhead 2003)

Writing Tablets: A. K. Bowman and J. D. Thomas, *The Vindolanda Writing Tablets* Vol. II (London 1994); vol. III (London 2003); *ZPE* 100 (1994) 431-46

Tombstone: *Britannia* 29 (1998) 299-306

Brigomaglos: *AA*[5] 9 10 (1982) 61-5

Textoverdi: *AA*[4] 11 (1934) 138-45

Vindolanda to Haltwhistle Burn

Stanegate: *JRS* 29 (1939) 202

Seatsides, Twice Brewed and Milestone House camps: *Camps* 74-5; 116-8; 120-3; 131-2

Haltwhistle Burn

General account: *RHW* 145-6

Excavation: *AA*[3] 5 (1909) 213-85

Camps: *PSAN*[3] 7 (1915) 125-6; *AA*[3] 5 (1909) 259-63; *Camps* 107-11

Haltwhistle Burn to Throp

Stanegate west of fortlet: H 150; M 46

Fell End, Lees Hall and Sunny Rigg, Glenwhelt Leazes, Chapel Rigg and Crooks camps: *Camps* 83-4, 92, 100-4; 110-1, 127-9; *Britannia* 13 (1982) 343

Stanegate from Tipalt to Poltross Burn: *CW*[1] 9 (1888) 163-6

Throp

CW[2] 13 (1913) 363-81; *RHW* 143-4

Throp to Nether Denton

Stanegate W of Throp: *CW*[2] 13 (1913) 381-9; *Britannia* 7 (1977) 310

Mains Rigg signal tower: *CW*[2] 29 (1929) 314-5; *RHW* 143; *Britannia* 3 (1972) 308

Nether Denton

CW[1] 1 (1874) 88-93; *CW*[2] 13 (1913) 385-6; *CW*[2] 34 (1934) 152-4; *RHW* 141-2

High Nook cemetery: *CW*[2] 74 (1974) 14-7

Nether Denton to Boothby

Stanegate: *CW*[2]13 (1913) 386-7; *CW*[2] 36 (1936) 188-91

Boothby

General account: *RHW* 140

Excavations: *CW*^{2} 34 (1934) 154-5

Brampton

General account: *RHW* 138-40

Excavations: *CW*^{2} 36 (1936) 172-88; *CW*^{2} 98 (1998) 298-9

Tile and pottery kilns: *CW*^{2} 65 (1965) 133-68; *CW*^{2} 71 (1971) 41-4

Brampton to Carlisle

Stanegate at Buckjumping: M 70; *CW*^{2} 36 (1936) 184-6

Watchcross camp: H 108, 154; M 72; B3 288 (227); *CW*^{2} 36 (1936) 170; *Camps* 51

Stanegate at High Crosby: *CW*^{2} 36 (1936) 183-4; *RHW* 137

Hawkhirst site: *CW*^{1} 15 (1898) 358-60; *CW*^{2} 36 (1936) 179; *RHW* 139

Carlisle

Modern survey: *Arch. J* 135 (1978) 115-37; M. McCarthy, *Carlisle* (London 2002)

General accounts: *CW*^{2} 17 (1917) 235; *CW*^{2} 24 (1924) 95; *CW*^{2} 52 (1952) 155; *RHW* 136; Bidwell 168-77

Excavations: *CW*^{1} 12 (1893) 344-64; *CW*^{2} 55 (1955) 59, *CW*^{2} 64 (1964) 14; *Britannia* 5 (1974) 410; *CW*^{2} 88 (1988) 87-96; *Britannia* 13 (1982) 79-89; *Britannia* 23 (1992) 45-109; *Britannia* 27 (1996) 345-53; M. R. McCarthy, *A Roman, Anglian and Medieval Site at Blackfriars Street, Carlisle, Excavations 1981-2* (Kendal 1990); M. R. McCarthy, *Roman waterlogged remains at Castle Street, Carlisle: Excavations 1981-2* (Kendal 1991); interim reports in most issues of *Britannia*

Walls: Bede, *Vita S. Cuthberti*, 27; *CW*^{2} 74 (1974) 211

Artefacts: *CW*^{1} 7 (1883) 114-7; *CW*^{2} 86 (1986) 258-9; *Britannia* 7 (1976) 101-8; *Britannia* 14 (1983) 267-9; *CW*^{2} 89 (1989) 77-91; *Britannia* 18 (1986) 274-6; *Britannia* 23 (1992) 141-58; *The Holocene* 7 (1997) 243-5; *The Holocene* 7 (1997) 245-6

Writing tablets: *Tab. Luguval: Britannia* 29 (1998) 31-84

Carvetii inscriptions: RIB 93; JRS 55 (1965) 224, no. 11; *CW*^{3} 5 (2005) 65-77

Bridge: *CW*^{2} 52 (1952) 148-56; *Bridges CW*^{2} 87 (1987) 43-51

Cemeteries: *CW*^{1} 4 (1880) 325-8; *CW*^{2} 74 (1974) 8-13

Scalesceugh: *CW*^{2} 73 (1973) 79-89

Burgh-by-Sands

General account: Daniels 22-4

Excavations: *Britannia* 10 (1979) 281-3; *Britannia* 16 (1985) 271-2

Kirkbride

General accounts: *CW*^{2} 63 (1963) 126-39; *Britannia* 3 (1972) 308; *CW*^{2} 75 (1975) 58-90; *CW*^{2} 82 (1982) 35-50

OUTPOST FORTS

General accounts: *NCH* 15 63-129; *RHW* 227-44; *AA*^{5} 20 (1992) 53-55; *CW*^{2} 88 (1988) 23-8; *AA*^{5} 20 (1992) 53-5; *Britannia* 29 (1998) 356-9

Bewcastle: *CW*^{2} 90 (1990) 139-46; P. S. Austen, *Bewcastle and Old Penrith, A Roman Outpost Fort and a Frontier Vicus* (Kendal 1991); J. P. Gillam, I. M. Jobey and D. Welsby, *The Roman Bath-House at Bewcastle, Cumbria* (Kendal 1993)

Birrens: A Robertson, *Birrens (Blatobulgium)* (Glasgow 1975)

Risingham: *AA*^{4} 13 (1936) 170-98

High Rochester: *AA*^{2} 1 (1857) 69-85; *AA*^{4} 13 (1936) 170-98; *AA*^{5} 8 (1980) 75-87; *AA*^{5} 12 (1984) 1-31; *AA*^{5} 33 (2004) 35-50

INDEX

Note: milecastles, milefortlets, turrets and towers are not indexed by number, only by name, nor are they indexed generically in chapter 3. Only general subjects are indexed under Hadrian's Wall. The main reference for each fort is in **bold**.

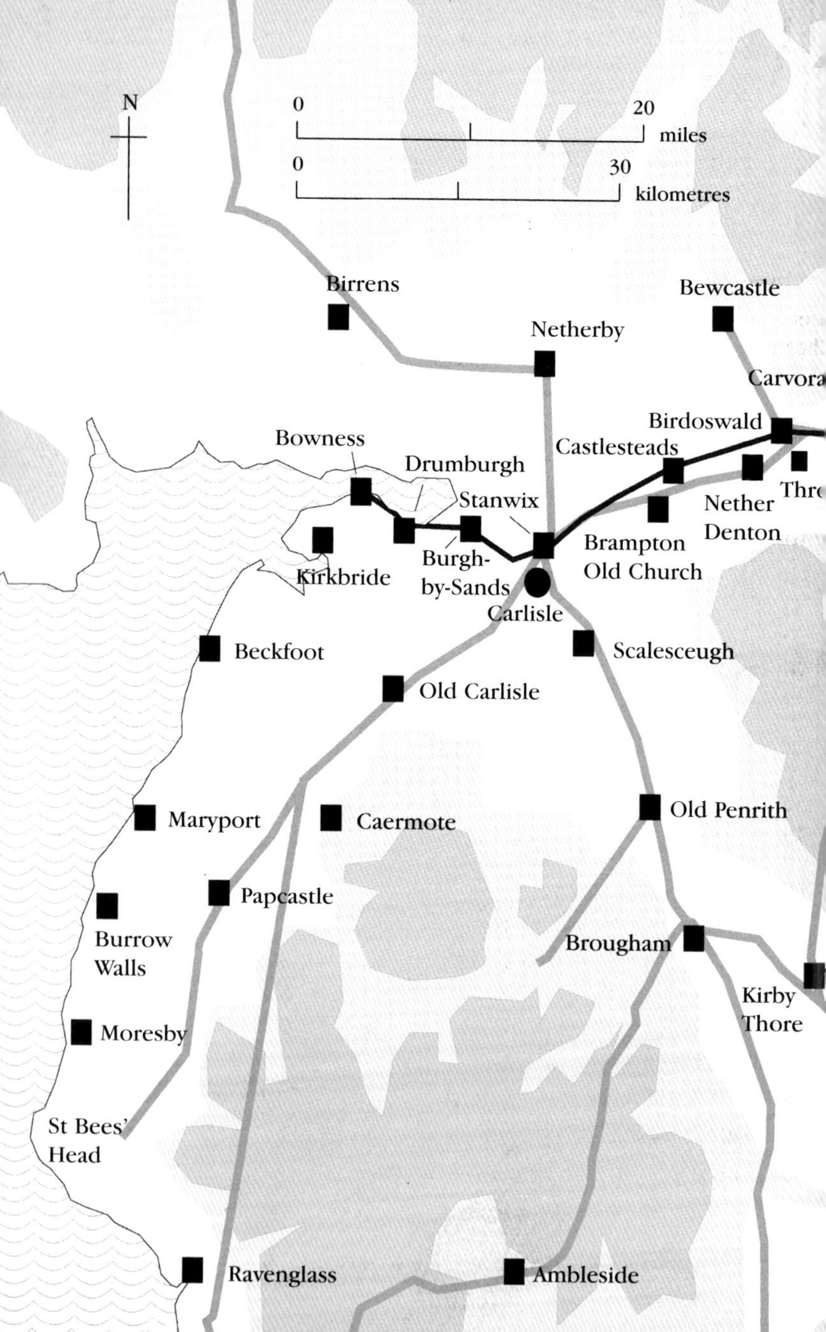

N
0
20
miles
0
30
kilometres
Birrens
Bewcastle
Netherby
Carvora
Birdoswald
Bowness
Castlesteads
Drumburgh
Stanwix
Thr
Nether
Denton
Brampton
Old Church
Burgh-
by-Sands
Kirkbride
Carlisle
Beckfoot
Scalesceugh
Old Carlisle
Maryport
Caermote
Old Penrith
Papcastle
Burrow
Walls
Brougham
Kirby
Thore
Moresby
St Bees'
Head
Ravenglass
Ambleside